T0351796

Economic Aspects of Obesity

**A National Bureau of
Economic Research
Conference Report**

Economic Aspects
of Obesity

Edited by **Michael Grossman and Naci Mocan**

The University of Chicago Press

Chicago and London

MICHAEL GROSSMAN is Distinguished Professor of Economics at the Graduate Center of the City University of New York, and the program director for health economics at the National Bureau of Economic Research.
NACI MOCAN holds the Ourso Distinguished Chair of Economics at Louisiana State University, and is a research associate of the National Bureau of Economic Research.

The University of Chicago Press, Chicago 60637
The University of Chicago Press, Ltd., London
© 2011 by the National Bureau of Economic Research
All rights reserved. Published 2011.
Printed in the United States of America

20 19 18 17 16 15 14 13 12 11   1 2 3 4 5
ISBN-13: 978-0-226-31009-1 (cloth)
ISBN-10: 0-226-31009-4 (cloth)

Library of Congress Cataloging-in-Publication Data

Economic aspects of obesity / edited by Michael Grossman and Naci
    Mocan.
        p. cm. — (National Bureau of Economic Research conference
    report)
    Includes bibliographical references and index.
    ISBN-13: 978-0-226-31009-1 (alk. paper)
    ISBN-10: 0-226-31009-4 (alk. paper)
    1. Obesity—Economic aspects—Congresses. I. Grossman,
    Michael, 1942– II. Mocan, H. Naci. III. Series: National Bureau of
    Economic Research conference report.
    RA645.O23E26 2011
    362.196'398—dc22

                                                        2010047674

Relation of the Directors to the
Work and Publications of the
National Bureau of Economic Research

1. The object of the NBER is to ascertain and present to the economics profession, and to the public more generally, important economic facts and their interpretation in a scientific manner without policy recommendations. The Board of Directors is charged with the responsibility of ensuring that the work of the NBER is carried on in strict conformity with this object.

2. The President shall establish an internal review process to ensure that book manuscripts proposed for publication DO NOT contain policy recommendations. This shall apply both to the proceedings of conferences and to manuscripts by a single author or by one or more co-authors but shall not apply to authors of comments at NBER conferences who are not NBER affiliates.

3. No book manuscript reporting research shall be published by the NBER until the President has sent to each member of the Board a notice that a manuscript is recommended for publication and that in the President's opinion it is suitable for publication in accordance with the above principles of the NBER. Such notification will include a table of contents and an abstract or summary of the manuscript's content, a list of contributors if applicable, and a response form for use by Directors who desire a copy of the manuscript for review. Each manuscript shall contain a summary drawing attention to the nature and treatment of the problem studied and the main conclusions reached.

4. No volume shall be published until forty-five days have elapsed from the above notification of intention to publish it. During this period a copy shall be sent to any Director requesting it, and if any Director objects to publication on the grounds that the manuscript contains policy recommendations, the objection will be presented to the author(s) or editor(s). In case of dispute, all members of the Board shall be notified, and the President shall appoint an ad hoc committee of the Board to decide the matter; thirty days additional shall be granted for this purpose.

5. The President shall present annually to the Board a report describing the internal manuscript review process, any objections made by Directors before publication or by anyone after publication, any disputes about such matters, and how they were handled.

6. Publications of the NBER issued for informational purposes concerning the work of the Bureau, or issued to inform the public of the activities at the Bureau, including but not limited to the NBER Digest and Reporter, shall be consistent with the object stated in paragraph 1. They shall contain a specific disclaimer noting that they have not passed through the review procedures required in this resolution. The Executive Committee of the Board is charged with the review of all such publications from time to time.

7. NBER working papers and manuscripts distributed on the Bureau's web site are not deemed to be publications for the purpose of this resolution, but they shall be consistent with the object stated in paragraph 1. Working papers shall contain a specific disclaimer noting that they have not passed through the review procedures required in this resolution. The NBER's web site shall contain a similar disclaimer. The President shall establish an internal review process to ensure that the working papers and the web site do not contain policy recommendations, and shall report annually to the Board on this process and any concerns raised in connection with it.

8. Unless otherwise determined by the Board or exempted by the terms of paragraphs 6 and 7, a copy of this resolution shall be printed in each NBER publication as described in paragraph 2 above.

Mike Grossman dedicates this book to his wife, Ilene, who continues to induce him to "choose" a long life, and to his daughters, Sandy and Barri, his sons-in-law, Steve and Dave, and his grandchildren, Zack, Ben, and Alise. Together with Ilene, they make his life terrific.

Naci Mocan dedicates this book to his wife, Madeline, for her support in his efforts to stay fit, and to his daughter, Leyla, for her sense of humor and for continuously reminding him not to take himself too seriously.

Contents

Acknowledgments

The chapters in this volume were presented at a National Bureau of Economic Research (NBER) Conference held at Louisiana State University in Baton Rouge on November 10 and 11, 2008. We are grateful to Martin Feldstein, former president of the NBER, for encouraging the NBER Health Economics Program to hold a conference on economic aspects of obesity and for his assistance in helping us to fund the conference. We also are grateful to James Poterba, current president of the NBER, for his assistance in publishing the volume.

Major funding for the conference and the publication of the volume were provided by grant number 62026 from the Robert Wood Johnson Foundation to the NBER. We owe a large debt of gratitude to the foundation. We want to thank Tracy Orleans, a distinguished fellow and senior scientist at RWJF, and especially Laura Leviton, a special advisor for evaluation at the foundation, for guiding the proposal through the funding process. Laura provided outstanding advice, persevered through a constant stream of e-mail messages, and always responded to them in a prompt manner. In addition, she made penetrating comments on preliminary versions of the chapters presented at a preconference held at the NBER Cambridge, Massachusetts, office on April 25, 2008.

Meals and lodging for the Baton Rouge conference were funded by a grant from the Blue Cross and Blue Shield Foundation of Louisiana to Louisiana State University. We are grateful to the foundation for its generosity and to Christy Oliver Reeves, its executive director, for her support. We would also like to thank Robert Newman, chairman of the economics department of LSU, for his efforts in making it possible to hold the conference at LSU. We are indebted to Mary Jo Neathery, an administrative assistant in the department, and Sarah Marx, Duha Altindag, and Colin Cannonier, all of whom are Ph.D. candidates in economics at LSU, for working tirelessly during the conference.

Each of the twelve chapters presented at the conference and contained in this volume benefited from the comments of a discussant. We would like to acknowledge and thank those discussants. Listed in the order in which the chapters they commented on appear, they are:

Kristin F. Butcher, Wellesley College and NBER
Alan C. Monheit, University of Medicine and Dentistry of New Jersey and NBER
Michael Anderson, University of California at Berkeley
Dhaval Dave, Bentley College and NBER
Tinna Laufey Ásgeirsdóttir, University of Iceland
Susan L. Averett, Lafayette College
Barbara Schone, Agency for Healthcare Research and Quality, U.S. Department of Health and Human Services
Kerry Anne McGeary, Ball State University and NBER
James Sallis, San Diego State University
Jeffrey DeSimone, University of Texas at Arlington and NBER
Roy Wada, University of Illinois at Chicago
Sara Markowitz, Emory University and NBER

The entire manuscript was read by two anonymous reviewers: one named by the NBER and one named by the University of Chicago Press. We are indebted to them for their many helpful comments. Finally, we wish to thank Helena Fitz-Patrick, coordinator of book publishing at the NBER, and David J. Pervin, senior editor at the University of Chicago Press, for editorial assistance.

Introduction

Michael Grossman and Naci Mocan

During the past three decades, the United States and most of the rest of the developed world have witnessed a rapid rise in obesity. This trend has stimulated a considerable amount of research by economists dealing with its causes and consequences and with policies to combat it. This volume contains the most recent research that addresses these issues.

The increase in obesity has extremely serious public health consequences because the condition is an important risk factor for premature death and for health problems including diabetes, coronary heart disease, hypertension, and asthma. Obesity puts stress on the health care system and raises medical expenditures. The prevalence of obesity also has implications for productivity losses.

Obesity is measured by the body mass index (BMI), defined as weight in kilograms divided by height in meters squared (kg/m^2). According to the World Health Organization (WHO) (1997) and the National Heart, Lung, and Blood Institute (NHLBI) (1998), a BMI value of between twenty and twenty-two is ideal for adults eighteen years of age and older regardless of gender in the sense that mortality and morbidity risks are minimized in this range. Adults with a BMI greater than or equal to thirty are classified as obese. An obese child is defined as having a BMI above the ninety-fifth percentile based on age- and gender-specific growth charts for children and adolescents.

As shown by the data in table I.1, obesity rates remained steady from

Michael Grossman is Distinguished Professor of Economics at the City University of New York Graduate Center, and a research associate and director of the Health Economics Program at the National Bureau of Economic Research. Naci Mocan holds the Ourso Distinguished Chair of Economics at Louisiana State University, and is a research associate of the National Bureau of Economic Research.

Table I.1   Trends in the prevalence of obesity, by age and period

	Percentage of population[a]								
	1960–1962	1963–1965	1966–1970	1971–1974	1976–1980	1988–1994	1999–2002	2003–2006	2007–2008
Ages 2–5	n.a.[b]	n.a.	n.a.	n.a.	5	7.2	10.3	12.4	10.4
Ages 6–11	n.a.	4.2	n.a.	4	6.5	11.3	15.8	17	19.6
Ages 12–19[c]	n.a.	n.a.	4.6	6.1	5	10.5	16	17.6	18.1
Ages 20–74[d]	13.3	n.a.	n.a.	14.6	15.1	23.3	31.1	34.1	33.8

Sources: National Center for Health Statistics (2009), Tables 75 and 76; Centers for Disease Control and Prevention (2009b); Flegal et al. (2010); and Ogden et al. (2010).

[a]For children, obesity is defined as body mass index (BMI) at or above the sex- and age-specific ninety-fifth percentile. BMI cutoff points based on Centers for Disease Control and Prevention (2009a) growth charts. For adults, obesity is defined by BMI greater than or equal to 30.
[b]Not available.
[c]Ages 12–17 in 1966–1970.
[d]Age-adjusted. Ages 20 and over in 2007–2008.

approximately 1960 until about 1980. Since then they have spiraled almost out of control. Between 1980 and 2000, the percentage of obese adults grew from 15 percent to 31 percent, and the percentage of overweight children ages six through nineteen rose from approximately 6 percent to 16 percent.[1] Hence, the number of obese adults doubled, and the number of obese children almost tripled in a period of two decades.

Some estimates suggest that the increasing prevalence of obesity accounts for approximately 300,000 deaths every year, next only to the preventable mortality associated with cigarette smoking (McGinnis and Foege 1993; Allison et al. 1999). In a more recent study, Flegal and colleagues (2005) report a smaller but still substantial figure of approximately 112,000 excess deaths in the year 2000. This still exceeds the third and fourth leading causes—alcohol abuse and illegal drug use. Aggregate medical spending for the United States that is attributed to obesity accounted for approximately 10 percent of total annual medical expenditures in recent years (Rashad and Grossman 2004). Obesity costs more in annual medical care expenditures than cigarette smoking—around $147 billion in 2008 (Finkelstein et al. 2009)—because of the long and costly treatments for its complications. A large percentage of these costs are borne by Medicare, Medicaid, private health insurance companies, and ultimately by the population at large rather than by the obese. To make matters worse, Americans spend $33 billion annually on weight reduction products (Rashad and Grossman 2004). There are often serious health risks associated with some of these products, which

---

1. These figures are simple averages of the percentages for children ages six to eleven and ages twelve to nineteen.

can further increase the costs of obesity. These factors underscore why one of the targets of the *Healthy People 2010* initiative of the U.S. Department of Health and Human Services (2000) is to reduce the adult obesity rate to 15 percent and the childhood obesity rate to 5 percent by 2010. The data in table I.1 clearly indicate that these goals will not be met.

Obesity is a complex public health problem, which is related to both individual characteristics that are genetic or acquired and to the individual's economic environment. Medical research has identified a number of potential determinants of obesity including genetic disposition. The stability, however, of obesity until about 1980, and the continuous and dramatic increase since that year suggest that genetics may not play a very prominent role in the upswing, as genetic change typically does not take place quickly.

Obesity is related to socioeconomic status, and over the last decade economists have begun to investigate the impact of economic factors and incentives on individuals' behaviors that can influence their body weight and that of their children. Hence, economic analysis is a potentially useful tool to understand the causes and consequences of obesity. As demonstrated by the chapters in this volume, economists can play a role in examining these determinants and consequences, although the factors at work are multifaceted, and the policy prescriptions are by no means straightforward.

The volume consists of twelve chapters: four on the determinants of adult obesity, three on the determinants of childhood obesity, two on the determinants of the proximate causes of obesity, and three on the consequences of obesity. Any model of obesity must explain at least some of the determinants of calories consumed and calories expended—the proximate causes of this outcome. This can be accomplished either by examining their direct impacts on obesity or their impacts on caloric intakes via food consumption, and on caloric outtakes via physical activity.

The first seven chapters take the former approach. They treat the probability of being obese and related weight outcomes as dependent variables. Key determinants in these studies are year- and area-specific food prices, food outlets, gymnasiums and other recreational facilities, participation in weight-loss programs, health insurance, and minimum wages. Some of these variables have subtle effects on weight outcomes. For example, economic theory predicts that body weight decisions should be responsive to the incidence of the medical care costs of obesity. If the obese do not pay for their higher medical expenditures through differential payments for health care and health insurance, the presence of insurance can lead to weight gains. Another example is that minimum wage labor is a major cost in food consumed away from home, especially at fast-food restaurants. Hence, declines in the real minimum wage over time have contributed to reductions in the real price of food consumed away from home, and are expected to lead to increases in obesity.

The next two chapters shift the emphasis to the determinants of physical activity and food consumption. The study of physical activity focuses on the roles of recreational facilities, transportation costs, and other prices. The study of total food consumption and food consumption patterns emphasizes the effects of policy changes in the food stamp and welfare programs that had causal impacts on food stamp caseloads. As in the obesity studies, some of the factors at work in these two studies are subtle. The food stamp program may have unintended consequences if it frees resources to spend on food that is dense in calories. Increases in cigarette and alcohol taxes may encourage exercise if this activity is a substitute for cigarette smoking or alcohol consumption.

Obesity surely poses health risks, but it may have other negative consequences. The three chapters on the consequences of obesity look for effects on educational and labor market outcomes. They are motivated by the possibility that the obese may be less productive in school and in the workplace and may confront discrimination in both settings. In addition, there may be indirect effects of obesity on these outcomes that operate through low self-esteem.

In the first chapter in this volume, David O. Meltzer and Zhuo Chen focus on one of the potential subtle determinants of body weight mentioned above: the real minimum wage rate. Because the real minimum wage in the United States has declined by 50 percent since 1968 and because minimum wage labor is a major contributor to the cost of food away from home, they hypothesize that changes in the minimum wage should be associated with changes in body weight. They use data from the Behavioral Risk Factor Surveillance System (BRFSS) from 1984–2006 to test whether variation in the real minimum wage is associated with changes in body mass index. They also examine whether this association varies by gender, education, and income and use quantile regression models to test whether the association varied over the BMI distribution. Finally, they estimate the fraction of the increase in BMI since 1970 attributable to minimum wage declines.

Meltzer and Chen find that a $1 decrease in the real minimum wage is associated with a 0.06 increase in BMI. This relationship is significant across gender and income groups and largest among the highest percentiles of the BMI distribution. Real minimum wage decreases can explain 10 percent of the increase in BMI since 1970. They conclude that the declining real minimum wage rate has contributed to the increasing rate of obesity in the United States.

The standard household production models of consumer behavior generate a demand function for caloric intakes (Chou, Grossman, and Saffer 2004). If adults are fully aware of the consequences of obesity and make deliberate decisions of calorie consumption given prices and income, then they may have internalized the costs associated with being overweight. One important justification of public policy formulated around various interventions is that being obese generates negative externalities. Put differently, some of the costs generated by obese individuals are shouldered by others. For example, if an increase in the obesity rate in the population raises health insurance premiums for everybody because premiums are not adjusted for the risk of obesity-related illness, then nonobese individuals face higher health insurance premiums imposed upon them by obese individuals. Furthermore, and more important from a social welfare point of view, obesity may generate moral hazard in insurance coverage. That is, pooled health insurance may cause people to gain weight because weight gain is not associated with higher insurance premiums.

In the second chapter in this volume Jay Bhattacharya, M. Kate Bundorf, Noemi Pace, and Neeraj Sood use data from the Rand Health Insurance Experiment conducted in the 1970s and early 1980s to investigate the extent to which the generosity of health insurance coverage impacts body weight among approximately 2,400 nonelderly families. The authors do not find evidence that insurance plans with higher cost-sharing induce a change in the BMI. On the other hand, when they analyze the decision at the extensive margin, they find that body weight in fact responds to insurance coverage. For this analysis they employ the National Longitudinal Survey of Youth (NLSY), covering the years of 1989–2004. They investigate the impact of the existence of private or public health insurance coverage on body weight, accounting for unobservable attributes of the individual that impact both the choice of health insurance and the health outcomes, such as body weight. Bhattacharya, Bundorf, Pace, and Sood report that being insured leads to a greater body mass index and a higher probability of being obese.

Although there is evidence in the economics literature on the impact of food prices on body weight in the short-run (Chou, Grossman, and Saffer 2004; Auld and Powell 2009), evidence on the long-run consequences of food prices is scant. In the third chapter in this volume, Dana Goldman, Darius Lakdawalla, and Yuhui Zheng use data from the Health and Retirement Study to investigate this issue. Individuals in this longitudinal data set were over the age of fifty when they were first interviewed in 1992. The authors use a sample of more than 3,000 individuals who were observed in four waves between 1992 and 2004, and allow current body weight to be related to past body weight. Empirically, they find the two variables to be positively related. They also find very modest short-term effects of the price of calories on body weight. The long-term effect, which allows for the reduction in BMI this year due to a price hike to reduce body mass index in future years, is much bigger but accrues slowly over time. Within ten years, a 10 percent permanent increase in the price of a calorie is associated with a BMI reduction of between 2 and 3 percent. Within forty to fifty years, the reduction amounts to approximately 5 percent. This reduction is modest from a clinical perspective, but is nontrivial when applied to the population at large in light of the total growth in mean BMI over the last several decades.

The assumption that consumers have rational expectations about the frequency of their future consumption behavior has been shown to be violated in some settings. For example, DellaVigna and Malmendier (2006) analyze data from health club memberships and demonstrate that consumers' behavior regarding membership and attendance at health clubs is not consistent with standard models of preferences, but can better be explained by overconfidence about future self-control. Along these lines, O'Donoghue and Rabin (1999, 2001) underline time-inconsistent and present-biased preferences and demonstrate the emergence of procrastination when choices involve immediate costs and delayed rewards. Consideration of such preferences is important in the case of obesity because attempts to lose weight typically involve immediate reduction in utility (a reduction of food consumption and an increase in physical effort to exercise), but a delayed benefit (weight loss and health benefits that are achieved after periods of effort). Thus, additional external incentives may be helpful in motivating overweight individuals to alter their behavior.

One such incentive, analyzed by John Cawley and Joshua A. Price in the fourth chapter in this volume, is financial rewards for weight loss. The authors employ data from a firm that coordinates a program of financial incentives for weight loss in various work sites. Using data on 2,407 employees in seventeen work sites who participated in a year-long program, Cawley and Price study attrition and weight loss in three types of programs: one that offers no financial rewards for weight loss, one that offers quarterly payments based on the percentage of loss from baseline weight, and a third that takes bonds that are refunded only if the employee achieves a specified weight loss goal and a quarterly lottery drawing gives away prizes to those who have lost some weight. The authors document higher attrition rates than found by previous studies. Financial rewards are associated with modest weight reductions. After one year, participants in the program that required posting a bond lost 1.9 pounds more than those in the control group that faced no financial incentives. The weight loss of those who were on the quarterly payment program was no different than those in the control group.

Chou, Grossman, and Saffer (2004) report that the growth of fast-food restaurants and the declines in the prices of food consumed in these restaurants, and in a broad measure of the price of food consumed at home, explain a significant portion of the growth in adult obesity. In the fifth chapter in this volume, Lisa M. Powell and Frank J. Chaloupka investigate the impacts of more narrowly defined food prices and several different types of food outlets on childhood obesity. They employ data drawn from the Child Development Supplement of the Panel Study of Income Dynamics, merged with food price data and food outlet density data at the zip code level. They measure food prices by a fruit and vegetable price index (the price of "healthy" food) and a fast-food price index (the price of "unhealthy" food). In addition, they distinguish among the effects of three food outlet density measures: the number of supermarkets per 10,000 residents per ten square miles, the density of grocery stores measured the same way, and the density of convenience stores. This distinction is important because fresh fruits and vegetables are more readily available at supermarkets and grocery stores than at convenience stores. Their use of the zip code, as opposed to a larger geographic area, to merge prices and outlets, minimizes the amount of measurement error in these variables.

The authors report that some of the variables just mentioned explain part of the BMI gap between high-socioeconomic status (SES) children and low-SES children. Specifically, higher fruit and vegetable prices are related to higher BMI among low-SES children, but the relationship is not significant for high-SES children. Similarly, increased supermarket availability has a negative impact on the BMI of low-SES children and increased presence of convenience stores is associated with higher BMI for the same group, while these two types of stores have no impact on the body weight of high–SES children.

In the sixth chapter in this volume, Bisakha Sen, Stephen Mennemeyer, and Lisa C. Gary investigate the link between aspects of the local neighborhood other than food prices and food outlet density and BMI of children. The authors use the Children of the NLSY79 (CoNLSY) data, where children in the data are those who were born to the female respondents of the NLSY79 survey. By design, the CoNLSY includes only those children who are fifteen years of age or younger. Their particular concern is with the impact of maternal perception of overall quality of the neighborhood. This is given by the response to a question as to whether the mother rates her neighborhood as an excellent, very good, good, fair, or poor place to raise her children.

The authors find that neighborhood quality is not associated with the BMI of the child, but one particular attribute—the perceived level of police protection—is related to this outcome. In particular, for black and Hispanic children, BMI percentiles are lower when mothers report a higher perceived level of police protection. They note that it is difficult to identify the channels through which the perception of the extent of police protection is influenced. For example, although crime rates in the country of residence might be theoretically related to the perception of police protection, crime rates are impacted by police presence, and such endogeneity makes it difficult to identify the impact of local crime on perception of police protection. On a positive note, they propose that a potential causal pathway between perceived inadequacy of police protection in the neighborhood and BMI may go through sedentary behavior. For example, if mothers are concerned about the safety of their children, they may choose to allocate less of their children's time to outdoor physical activities and more time towards indoor sedentary activities, such as TV watching at home. Sen, Mennemeyer, and

Gary find that, when mothers report inadequate police protection in their neighborhood, their children spend twenty minutes more per day watching TV.

The seventh chapter in this volume by Robert Sandy, Gilbert Liu, John Ottensmann, Rusty Tchernis, Jeffrey Wilson, and O. T. Ford also analyzes the impact of the environment in which they live on children's BMI. Specifically, the authors consider a large set of environmental factors including fast-food restaurants, supermarkets, parks, trails, violent crimes, and thirteen types of recreational amenities derived from the interpretation of annual aerial photographs. They obtain height and weight information as well as data on personal characteristics of children between the ages of three and eighteen using data from a pediatric clinic in Indianapolis. A unique aspect of their study is that they know the exact address of each child. Hence, they can measure environmental variables at very small radiuses ranging from one tenth of a mile to one mile from the child's residence.

The authors emphasize the results of the estimation of an individual fixed effects model obtained from successive visits to the clinic between 1996 and 2006 by children who stayed at the same address. This allows them to analyze the impacts of changes in environmental factors on changes in BMI while controlling for time-invariant unmeasured characteristics of neighborhoods. For example, if new recreational facilities are built in neighborhoods in which parents have strong preferences for healthy children and these facilities, the cross-sectional relationship between BMI and the facilities will be overstated in absolute value.

The relationship between some of the environmental factors and children's BMI is unclear in fixed effects specifications, and the results display some sensitivity to how access to amenities is defined. For example, if fast-food restaurants are measured within a quarter of a mile or half a mile from the child's home, the impact on BMI is negative, whereas the impact is positive if one considers the fast-food restaurants within a mile radius. This is partly due to the large number of environmental factors considered, and partly due to the fixed effects specification. Both aspects of the design are desirable, but both can result in a reduction in statistical power due to intercorrelations among regressors and reductions in their variation. The recreational amenities that appear to lower children's BMI are fitness areas, kickball diamonds, and volleyball courts. The authors estimate that locating these amenities near their homes could reduce the weight of overweight eight-year-old boys by three to six pounds.

Neeraj Kaushal and Qin Gao treat patterns of food consumption, key proximate determinants of caloric intakes and body weight, as outcomes in the eighth chapter in this volume. Obesity is more prevalent among low income families, and they analyze the extent to which food consumption patterns of low income families respond to the changes in the food stamp program. They use data from the 1994 to 2004 Consumer Expenditure Survey and focus on families with children and where mothers had at most a high school education. They form a treatment group consisting of families headed by single mothers, and a control group consisting of families with two parents. They assume that the former group is much more likely to receive food stamps than the latter. Their analyses show that per capita food expenditures of low-educated single-parent families are not related to food stamp caseloads (number of recipients) in the corresponding state. That is, expansions in the food stamp program do not appear to have any impact on food expenditures as well as on most food items for low-income families. Kaushal and Gao also find that the welfare reform in the 1990s lowered the food stamp caseload, and that the introduction of simplified reporting procedures and electronic benefit transfer cards were associated with an increase in caseloads. There is no evidence, however, that these changes had any effect on spending on food for low-income families.

The previous conclusions are subject to several qualifications. First, the authors cannot identify food stamp recipients with certainty. That is, some of the families in the treatment group may not benefit from this program, and some of the families in the control group may benefit from it. Second, they lack data on food stamp benefits. It is possible that increases in caseloads were accompanied by reductions in real benefits.

In the ninth chapter in this volume, Melayne M. McInnes and Judy A. Shinogle focus on an obvious mechanism to increase caloric outtake: namely, physical exercise. They analyze the determinants of self-reports of this measure for adults in the 2001, 2003, and 2005 Behavioral Risk Factor Surveillance System (BRFSS). Their emphasis is on the effects of household income, education, and broadly defined correlates of the price of exercise such as the availability of parks and gyms in the county of residence, local transportation costs, and the value of time allocated to exercise. In addition, they consider the impacts of the prices of goods that may be substitutes for exercise. For example, excise tax hikes on cigarettes and alcohol will promote exercise if "sin goods" and exercise are substitutes.

The authors find that income and education have strong and consistently positive effects on physical activity. The latter finding underscores the protective effect of education on health that operates through channels other than income (Grossman 2006). Employed people have lower propensities to exercise than others, which reflect the importance of the opportunity cost of exercising. Physical exercise is more likely when there are more parks and gyms per capita in a county and also is more likely when transportation costs, proxied by the price of gasoline, are lower. One surprising finding is that sin taxes have negative effects on vigorous exercise or moderate-to-vigorous exercise.

The results just summarized control for state and year, but not county, fixed effects. It is possible that individuals with preferences for physical fitness choose to live in localities with better access to these facilities. The authors argue that, if the taste for physical fitness is correlated with the taste for wellness, then the information on whether or not the individual has a flu shot can be used as a control for the taste for exercise. Inclusion of an indicator for a flu shot does not change the results. Nevertheless, it should be kept in mind that the sample period is short, which limits the extent of within area variation over time.

The last three chapters in this volume focus on the consequences of obesity in domains other than health outcomes. Robert Kaestner, Michael Grossman, and Benjamin Yarnoff analyze the impact of obesity on educational attainment. Obesity can affect education through a number of channels. Potential peer and teacher discrimination related to weight may adversely affect educational achievement. Obesity can impact education through its impact on poor health and through a potential association with cognitive difficulties. Kaestner, Grossman, and Yarnoff use data from the National Longitudinal Survey of Youth 1997, drawn from the survey years 1997 to 2002, and focus on individuals between the ages of fourteen and eighteen. They measure educational attainment by highest grade attended, highest grade completed, and whether the student had dropped out of school. The results indicate that there is no systematic relationship between weight and educational attainment. It is possible that the small and statistically insignificant estimates are due to data issues: measurement error in height and weight is possible as these are self-reported in the NLSY; there is lack of variation in the dependent variable since only 5-to-10 percent of the sample fail to progress in grade or drop out; and relatively small numbers of teens are in the upper and lower tails of the weight distribution.

Increases in weight can have negative effects on wages through channels related to discrimination and productivity. In addition, wage cuts, rather than insurance premium hikes, may be a mechanism via which the obese pay for the excess medical care costs. Finally, a negative relationship between physical attractiveness and BMI may account for part of the impact of BMI on wages. In the eleventh chapter in this volume, Christian A. Gregory and Christopher J. Ruhm use data on twenty-five to fifty-five-year-olds from the 1986, 1999, 2001, 2003 and 2005 waves of the Panel Study of Income Dynamics to study these issues. Since some of these mechanisms imply nonlinear BMI effects, they estimate semiparametric wage equations. In some specifications, they address potential endogeneity of BMI by using sibling BMI as an instrument, and by employing at least thirteen-year-lagged values of BMI to avoid reverse causality from wages to BMI.

Gregory and Ruhm estimate gender-specific wage regressions and find that women's wages peak at around the BMI level of 23, which is well below the obesity cut-off of 30. They report similar results for men in instrumental variables models or in those that employ long lags of BMI. For men, the estimated wage-BMI profile is reasonably flat, with a peak at around the overweight range of a BMI of 25. There is, however, little evidence that serious health effects occur in this range. Moreover, the results of instrumental variables (IV) models or specifications focusing on long-lags of BMI for men are more similar to those for women. The findings for females (and the IV and lag estimates for males) suggest that it is not obesity, but rather some other factor—such as physical attractiveness—that produces the observed relationship between BMI and wages.

Gregory and Ruhm also use data from the Medical Expenditure Panel Survey to estimate total health expenditures as a function of BMI. The pattern of the medical expenditure-BMI profile for women suggests that medical costs do not explain the behavior of wages for women as the medical expenditures start rising after a BMI of 30, while wages decline after a BMI of 23. For men, a monotonically increasing medical expenditure-BMI profile is detected. This finding has some potential for explaining wage behavior in specifications that employ actual BMI, but not in those that employ IV or long lags of BMI.

Recently, economists have identified the importance of noncognitive factors in wage determination. In the final chapter in this volume, Naci Mocan and Erdal Tekin point out that self-esteem is one of these factors, and that it in turn can be influenced by BMI and obesity. They use data from the National Longitudinal Study of Adolescent Health to analyze the interplay between BMI, self-esteem, and wages among young adults in the age range of twenty-one to twenty-six in 2001 to 2002. They hypothesize that, in addition to its direct impact on wages, obesity can influence wages indirectly through self-esteem.

Mocan and Tekin find that BMI has an independent effect on self-esteem for females and for black males. The authors also find that there is a wage penalty for being obese for both white and black women. In addition, self-esteem has an impact on wages in the case of whites. Taken together, the results suggest that obesity has the most significant impact on white women's wages because their wages are affected directly by obesity and indirectly through the impact of obesity on self-esteem. These results differ from those in the study by Gregory and Ruhm in part because different age groups and different measures of body weight are employed in the two studies.

What have we learned from these twelve chapters? Clearly, weight outcomes and their determinants respond to broadly defined measures of prices. Goldman, Lakdawalla, and Zheng report an inverse relationship between the price of a calorie and BMI. Meltzer and Chen show that body weight is positively related to the minimum wage and argue that it is because the price of fast-food falls when the minimum wage falls. Powell and Chaloupka's findings can be interpreted as evidence that an increase in the price of fruit and vegetables relative to the price of caloric food leads to a rise in obesity.

The negative effect of the availability of supermarkets and the positive effect of the availability of convenience stores on obesity in the Powell-Chaloupka study point to the role of transportation costs required to obtain food (the sum of direct outlays on modes of transportation and shopping time valued at its opportunity cost) in weight outcomes. Similar interpretations apply to the negative effects of recreational facilities on children's body weight uncovered by Sandy, Liu, Ottensmann, Tchernis, Wilson, and Ford, and to the positive effects of these facilities on exercise by adults uncovered by McInnes and Shinogle. The negative impact of gasoline prices on exercise and the negative differential in this activity between employed persons and others in the latter study highlight money and time prices as rationers of this activity.

Some of the estimated price effects are subtle. For example, Bhattacharya, Bundorf, Pace, and Sood find that being insured leads to higher BMI and a larger probability of being obese because weight gain is not associated with higher premiums in pooled health insurance plans. To cite another example, the negative relationship between cigarette taxes and exercise in the McInnes-Shinogle study suggests complementarity between sin goods and exercise, possibly because food consumption and exercise are substitutes. Chou, Grossman, and Saffer (2004) report that an increase in the price of cigarettes leads to higher body weight and argue that it is because cigarette smoking and food consumption are substitutes. While intuition suggests substitution between smoking and exercise, that relationship appears to be dominated by substitution between smoking and food consumption.[2]

What insights do the chapters offer with regard to the sources of the upward trend in obesity during the past three decades? Several chapters point to reductions in the real prices of unhealthy foods and increases in the prices of healthy foods in the period at issue as contributory factors. An increase in the proportion of the population covered by health insurance, perhaps with a lag, is another contributory factor. Large cigarette excise tax hikes that have accompanied the antismoking campaign may have had unintended consequences. Increases in the value of time, especially of women, due to their rising labor force participation rates, make it more costly for them to exercise. Previous studies (for example, Anderson, Butcher, and Levine 2003) have identified this trend as a partial explanation of the growth in obesity among children. Finally, reductions in population density due to urban sprawl (a low density development pattern, which changes the built environment in which individuals reside) have negative consequences for the proximate determinants of exercise that have been shown to have important impacts on this activity in several chapters in this volume.[3]

The chapters that address the education and labor market effects of excessive body weight reveal that the economic consequences of obesity are complex. Kaestner, Grossman, and Yarnoff find that overweight teens

2. Courtemanche (2009) reaches somewhat different conclusions using specifications that allow for lagged effects.
3. See Zhao and Kaestner (forthcoming) for a summary of the literature on the effects of urban sprawl on obesity and some new estimates.

have about the same levels of educational attainment as teens of normal weight. One explanation is that the overweight offset the factors associated with poor health and discrimination by allocating more time to schoolwork and less time to sports and other leisure time activities. Gregory and Ruhm report that the observed negative relationship between obesity and wages is not caused by obesity per se, but rather by a factor such as physical attractiveness or discrimination. Mocan and Tekin present suggestive evidence that this negative relationship between obesity and wages can be attributable in part to low self-esteem on the part of the obese.

The studies in this volume employ very different data and methods and do not include a unified set of determinants of obesity. Hence, they cannot be used to provide a complete accounting of the sources of the growth in weight. But they do provide a firm foundation for future research in this key area. A similar comment applies to the studies on the consequences of obesity.

What are the implications of the chapters in this volume for public policy? If obesity were purely a cosmetic problem, the pressing need for solutions to reverse it would not seem necessary. Yet, obesity has been linked to various medical conditions and poor health outcomes. Clearly, obesity carries a high personal cost. But does it carry a high enough social cost to make it a concern of public policy? The case for government intervention is weakened if consumers are fully informed, and if the obese bear all the consequences of their actions. The case is strengthened if consumers do not have full information or something that reasonably approximates it, or if third parties like Medicare, Medicaid, private health insurance companies and ultimately the nonobese end up bearing significant amounts of the costs.

In the case of children, one justification for government intervention is that society as a whole may reap substantial current and future production and consumption benefits from improvements in children's health. The case is strengthened because overweight children are extremely likely to become obese adults, and because children are less likely to have information about the consequences of their actions or to heavily discount these consequences. The case is weakened because parents may more easily and immediately affect the choices made by their children than can the government.

With these caveats in mind, we note that the chapters in this volume that report that reductions in real food prices can account for part of the increase in obesity bear on the question of whether taxes on food, especially dense and high-caloric fast-food and soda, provide an effective public policy tool for addressing obesity. But, it is possible that a tax on fast-food could actually increase caloric intakes via substitution towards nontaxed food. Moreover, Yaniv, Rosin, and Tobol (2009) develop a theoretical model in which fast-food or junk-food taxes increase obesity for health-conscious consumers who increase the time they allocate to the preparation of healthy meals at the expense of exercise.

An alternative policy might be financial rewards for weight loss. But Cawley and Price find very small average weight loss associated with work site programs with this feature in their chapter in this volume. One interpretation of this finding is that consumers are time inconsistent and have present-biased preferences. Gruber and Köszegi (2001) show that very stiff excise tax hikes or other policies to increase the cost of consuming the good in question are required in this situation. But Becker (2009) interprets the failure of weight loss programs and the upward trend in obesity as the response of rational and forward-looking consumers to past, current, and anticipated future medical innovations that have reduced and are expected to reduce the health consequences of being overweight. Bhattacharya and Packalen (2008) go one step further and point out that there is a positive externality from the upward trend in obesity because it induces medical research on, for example, heart attacks and diabetes that will benefit the nonobese as well as the obese.

Other results in the chapters in this volume carry mixed messages with regard to public policy. For example, whether the evidence that access to parks, gymnasiums, and other recreational facilities increase exercise and reduce obesity bears directly on the suggestion that such facilities should receive public subsidies, not only depends on the issues raised earlier, but also depends on the extent to which people with unobserved tastes for physical activities choose to locate in areas with better access to these facilities. Effective policy levers exist to make it easier or harder for low income groups to obtain food stamps. But these levers do not appear to change food consumption patterns in ways that promote weight gain or healthy food choices based on the evidence presented by Kaushal and Gao in their chapter in this volume. To cite a final example, the labor market benefits of policies to combat obesity may be significantly smaller than the benefits of policies that seek to improve outcomes in these settings for the obese by reducing discrimination or improving self-esteem.

Perhaps the main message of the chapters in this volume and related current research on economic aspects of obesity is that there is no free lunch, that with benefits come costs. Positive changes such as increases in technology that lowered the real price of food, reduced smoking, and increased female participation in the labor force have also carried unforeseen negative consequences. Was the antismoking campaign a mistake if it also encouraged obesity? Of course, we do not believe people should start smoking in order to become thin, substituting one type of unhealthy behavior for another. This was simply one of the unintended consequences of social change and government action. Nor do we suggest that women abandon the labor force to provide their families with home-cooked meals. Whether public policies should be pursued that offset the ignored or unanticipated consequence of previous policies that contributed to the rise in obesity will depend, in the end, on evaluations of the external costs and benefits of these policies. We hope that the chapters in this volume will contribute to this exercise.

References

Allison, D. B., K. R. Fontaine, J. E. Manson, J. Stevens, and T. B. VanItallie. 1999. Annual deaths attributable to obesity in the United States. *Journal of the American Medical Association* 282 (16): 1530–8.

Anderson, P. M., K. F. Butcher, and P. B. Levine. 2003. Maternal employment and overweight children. *Journal of Health Economics* 22 (3): 477–504.

Auld, M. C., and L. M. Powell. 2009. Economics of food energy density and adolescent body weight. *Economica* 76 (304): 719–40.

Becker, G. S. 2009. The growth in obesity. Available at: www.becker-posner-blog .com.

Bhattacharya, J., and M. Packalen. 2008. The other ex-ante moral hazard in health. NBER Working Paper no. 13863. Cambridge, MA: National Bureau of Economic Research, March.

Centers for Disease Control and Prevention. 2009a. CDC growth charts. Available at: www.cdc.gov/growthcharts.

———. (CDC). 2009b. Obesity and overweight for professionals: Childhood: Contributing factors. Available at: www.cdc.gov/obesity/childhood/prevalence.html.

Chou, S.-Y., M. Grossman, and H. Saffer. 2004. An economic analysis of adult obesity: Results from the Behavioral Risk Factor Surveillance System. *Journal of Health Economics* 23 (3): 565–87.

Courtemanche, C. 2009. Rising cigarette prices and rising obesity: Coincidence or unintended consequence? *Journal of Health Economics* 28 (4): 781–98.

DellaVigna, S., and U. Malmendier. 2006. Paying not to go to the gym. *American Economic Review* 96 (3): 694–719.

Finkelstein, E. A., J. G. Trogdon, J. W. Cohen, and W. Dietz. 2009. Annual medical spending attributable to obesity: Payer- and service-specific estimates. *Health Affairs* 28 (5): w822–w31.

Flegal, K. M., M. D. Carroll, C. L. Ogden, and L. R. Curtin. 2010. Prevalence and trends in obesity among U.S. adults, 1999–2008. *Journal of the American Medical Association* 303 (3): 235–41.

Flegal, K. M., B. I. Graubard, D. F. Williamson, and H. G. Mitchell. 2005. Excess deaths associated with underweight, overweight, and obesity. *Journal of the American Medical Association* 293 (15): 1861–67.

Grossman, M. 2006. Education and nonmarket outcomes. In *Handbook of the economics of education*, vol. 1, ed. E. Hanushek and F. Welch, 577–633. Amsterdam: North-Holland, Elsevier.

Gruber, J., and B. Köszegi. 2001. Is addiction 'rational'? Theory and evidence. *Quarterly Journal of Economics* 116 (4): 1261–303.

McGinnis, J. M., and W. H. Foege. 1993. Actual causes of death in the United States. *Journal of the American Medical Association* 270 (18): 2207–12.

National Center for Health Statistics (NCHS). 2009. *Health United States 2008.* Hyattsville, MD: National Center for Health Statistics.

National Heart, Lung, and Blood Institute, National Institutes of Health. 1998. Clinical guidelines on the identification, evaluation, and treatment of overweight and obesity in adults—The evidence report. *Obesity Research* 6 (Supplement 2): 51S–215S.

O'Donoghue, T., and M. Rabin. 1999. Doing it now or later. *American Economic Review* 89 (1): 103–24.

———. 2001. Choice and procrastination. *Quarterly Journal of Economics* 116 (1): 121–60.

Ogden, C. L., M. D. Carroll, L. R. Curtin, M. M. Lamb, and K. M. Flegal. 2010. Prevalence of high body mass index in U.S. children and adolescents, 2007–2008. *Journal of the American Medical Association* 303 (3): 242–49.

Rashad, I., and M. Grossman. 2004. The economics of obesity. *The Public Interest* 156 (Summer): 104–12.

U.S. Department of Health and Human Services. 2000. *Healthy people 2010,* 2nd ed. Washington, DC: U.S. Government Printing Office.

World Health Organization (WHO). 1997. *Obesity: Preventing and managing the global epidemic.* Geneva: World Health Organization.

Yaniv, G., O. Rosin, and Y. Tobol. 2009. Junk-food, home cooking, physical activity and obesity: The effect of the fat tax and the thin subsidy. *Journal of Public Economics* 93 (5-6): 823–30.

Zhao, Z., and R. Kaestner. Forthcoming. Effects of urban sprawl on obesity. *Journal of Health Economics.*

1

The Impact of Minimum Wage Rates on Body Weight in the United States

David O. Meltzer and Zhuo Chen

Since 1970, the rate of obesity in the United States has increased from about 14 percent to over 25 percent and has come to be recognized as a major public health concern (NIH 1998; Flegal et al. 1998, 2005; Ogden et al. 2006). Understanding the causes of obesity is important because it may suggest strategies to address the increase in obesity. Increases in body weight are the result of an excess of caloric intake relative to caloric expenditure. Changes in both caloric expenditure and caloric intake have been hypothesized to have contributed to increasing obesity in the United States. Factors that have been suggested to have decreased caloric expenditure include the development of a more sedentary lifestyle due to the decreasing role of physical labor in work and the increasingly sedentary nature of leisure activities due to the growth of television and video games. Factors affecting food consumption that have been emphasized include the greater consumption of "fast-food" away from home and the declining cost of eating a diverse set of foods at home due to the increased availability of low-cost prepared and highly

David O. Meltzer is associate professor in the Department of Medicine and associated faculty member in the Harris School of Public Policy and the Department of Economics at the University of Chicago, and a research associate of the National Bureau of Economic Research. Zhuo Chen is an economist at The Centers for Disease Control and Prevention (CDC), U.S. Department of Health and Human Services.

The authors would like to acknowledge the financial support of the Chicago Center of Excellence in Health Promotion Economics (P30 CDC000147-01, PI: Meltzer) from the Centers for Disease Control and Prevention and a Midcareer Career Development Award from the National Institute of Aging (1 K24 AG031326-01, PI: Meltzer). Dr. Meltzer would also like to acknowledge salary support from the Agency for Healthcare Research and Quality through the Hospital Medicine and Economics Center for Education and Research on Therapeutics (CERT) (U18 HS016967-01, PI: Meltzer). The work of Zhuo Chen was done when he was a postdoctoral scholar at the Chicago Center of Excellence in Health Promotion Economics, The University of Chicago.

processed foods (Cutler, Glaeser, and Shapiro 2003; Philipson and Posner 2003; Mello, Studdert, and Brenna 2006; Nestle 2006).

The consumption of fast-food has received particular attention as a cause of obesity. Chou, Grossman, and Saffer (2004) found that people who live in closer proximity to fast-food restaurants are more likely to be obese. However, this finding might not reflect a causal effect of the presence of fast-food restaurants on obesity, but instead a tendency for fast-food restaurants to locate in areas where the demand for their products will be greater. Even if this association were viewed to reflect a causal effect of fast-food restaurants on obesity, it would not explain why the number of fast-food restaurants should have increased. Recent studies present mixed evidence. Anderson and Matsa (2009) found no causal link between proximity to restaurants and obesity. Currie et al. (2009) used data from 3 million school children in California and over 1 million pregnant women in Michigan, New Jersey, and Texas to estimate the impact of fast-food restaurants on obesity. They found that a fast-food restaurant within a tenth of a mile of a school is associated with 5.2 percent increase in obesity rates among ninth grade children, and that a fast-food restaurant within a half mile of residence results in a 2.5 percent increase in the probability of gaining over 20 kilograms among pregnant women.

Because minimum wage labor makes up about one third of the cost of fast-food, and because the real minimum wage has varied nationally and across states over time due to inflation and changes in state and federal minimum wage laws that would not seem to have any independent reasons to affect obesity, variation in real minimum wages may provide a powerful mechanism to provide a test for the hypothesis that fast-food consumption may play a role in increasing obesity in the United States. While the variation in the real minimum wage across states over time is the critical element for this test of the hypothesis, the fact that the real minimum wage in 2007 constant dollars fell from a maximum of about $9.15 in 1968 to a low of about $5.80 in 2007 suggests that it is possible that the decline in real minimum wage itself may have played a role in the long-term increase in obesity over this period.[1] Although our analysis does not support a direct test of the hypothesis that a decline in the minimum wage could affect obesity by increasing the consumption of fast-food, we complement this analysis in our discussion by calibrating our findings against the results of other studies that have examined how declines in the minimum wage would translated into lower prices for food away from home (Aaronson, French, and MacDonald 2008; Aaronson 2001; MacDonald and Aaronson 2006; Lee and O'Roark 1999; Piggott 2003) and how increased consumption of food away from

1. Nominal minimum wage rates can be found in a document provided by the Employment Standard Administration, U.S. Department of Labor, "Changes in basic minimum wages in non-farm employment under state law: Selected years 1968 to 2008." Available at: http://www .dol.gov/whd/state/stateMinWageHis.htm.

home would increase obesity (Chou, Grossman, and Safer 2004). Since the results of this calibration exercise are similar in magnitude to the results of our primary analysis of the association of minimum wages and obesity, this helps provide confidence that the association we observe may reflect a causal pathway to obesity through increased consumption of fast-food. We also recognize that increases in the minimum wage may affect incomes. However, as we will discuss later, because a relatively small fraction of the population earns minimum wage and because the effects we find are larger in higher income persons, we do not think this potential income effect explains our findings.

1.1 Methods

Real minimum wages were calculated using data on nominal minimum wages and consumer price indices (CPI) from 1984 to 2006, the years for which our obesity data were available. Nominal minimum wage data by state was obtained from the Bureau of Labor Statistics.[2] We then calculated the real wage rates in 2006 dollars by dividing the nominal wage rates by the census-region-specific all items CPI.[3] Because most fast-food restaurants are part of chains that are classified as interstate commerce and are therefore subject to federal minimum wage legislation,[4] we used the higher of the federal minimum wage and the state minimum wage. Figure 1.1 reports the trends in mean nominal and real minimum wage rates across states, weighted to reflect the distribution of population in our obesity data, which is intended to be representative of the U.S. noninstitutionalized adult population. The pattern of changes in these average real minimum wages reflects a combination of federal nominal minimum wages increases in 1990 and 1996 (denoted by large squares) and multiple state increases over time, and the tendency for inflation to erode the average real minimum wage in the absence of legislated increases. Despite the two increases in the federal minimum wage and numerous increases in state minimum wages, the mean real minimum wage rate faced by respondents in our sample declined from $6.40 in 1984 to $5.82 in 2006. Although this overall change was modest, the powerful effect of the federal minimum wage caused much larger variations in average real minimum wages over shorter time periods. For example, from September 1997 when the federal minimum was raised to $5.15 an hour to the end of the period studied, the average real minimum wage fell from $6.47 to $5.82. Seventeen states had state minimum wage rates above the federal minimum wage by April 2006. Oregon, Vermont, and Washington

2. Full set of the minimum wage rates data is compiled by using various issues of *Monthly Labor Review.* Available at: http://www.bls.gov/opub/mlr/archive.htm.
3. Bureau of Labor Statistics, U.S. Department of Labor (July series, without seasonal adjustment) extracted from the BLS website. Available at: http://www.bls.gov/CPI/#data.
4. U.S. Department of Labor, Employment Standards Administration (2004).

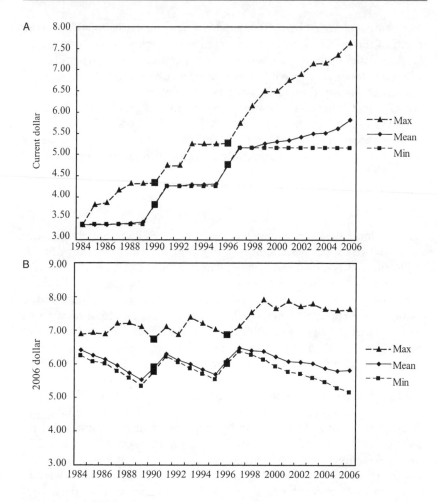

Fig. 1.1   Nominal (panel *A*) and real (panel *B*) minimum wage in the United States. Enlarged squares indicate values at 1990 and 1996, when increases in federal minimum wage occurred.

automatically adjust minimum wage rates each year using state consumer price indices.

We studied the effects of these minimum wage changes among respondents to the Behavior Risk Factor Surveillance System (BRFSS) from 1984 to 2006.[5] The BRFSS surveys health risk behaviors among noninstitutionalized American civilian adults age 18 and older and is the most commonly used source of data for national studies of obesity and physical activity in the United States (See Chou, Grossman, and Saffer 2004). Data for BRFSS

5. CDC (1984–2006).

is collected by state health departments using computer assisted telephone interviewing with coordination by the Centers for Disease Control and Prevention (CDC). When data collection for BRFSS began, only fifteen states participated. However, by 1994, all fifty states, the District of Columbia, and three territories participated.

The 1984 to 2006 BRFSS includes 3,256,947 valid interview records. We excluded pregnant women (33,385) and records with missing information on weight, height, and key confounding factors (165,410). We also excluded records with values of body mass index (BMI) (weight in kilograms divided by height in meters squared) that we considered implausible: 863 with BMI < 14 and 8,911 with BMI > 50. This left a final study sample of 3,048,378 individuals with complete information. The CDC BRFSS group provides a final sampling weight to account for the sampling design. Figure 1.2

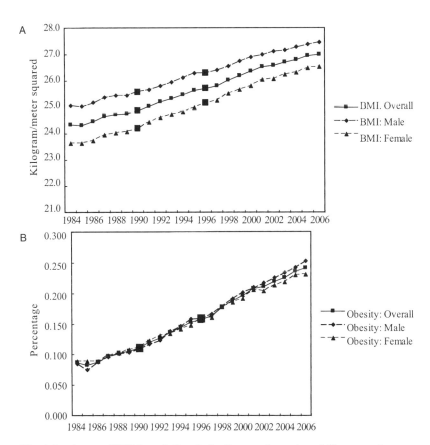

Fig. 1.2   **Average BMI (panel *A*) and obesity prevalence (panel *B*) among the BRFSS sample. Enlarged squares indicate values at 1990 and 1996, when increases in federal minimum wage occurred.**

illustrates the trend of the weighted mean of BMI and proportion of obesity individual among the BRFSS sample and subsamples by gender group.

1.2   Empirical Analysis

Multivariate linear regression models were used to study the effects of the real minimum wage on BMI. Regressions controlled for race and ethnicity, age, marital status, education, income, state fixed effects, and year effects, with coding as described in table 1.1. Categories for household income interval indicators were obtained from the original surveys. Due to changes in

Table 1.1   Summary statistics of the BRFSS sample: 1984–2006[a]

Characteristics	Overall ($N = 3,048,378$)	Male ($N = 1,274,462$)	Female ($N = 1,773,916$)
Body mass index	25.812 ± 0.005	26.401 ± 0.007	25.231 ± 0.007
Obese	0.166	0.169	0.163
Minimum wage: CPI adjusted, 2006 dollar	6.032 ± 0.001	6.033 ± 0.001	6.032 ± 0.001
Minimum wage: nominal	4.714 ± 0.001	4.72 ± 0.002	4.708 ± 0.001
Age	44.787 ± 0.019	43.432 ± 0.028	46.127 ± 0.026
White (reference)	0.765	0.764	0.766
Black	0.093	0.086	0.101
Hispanic	0.097	0.102	0.093
Others	0.044	0.048	0.040
Less than high school (reference)	0.051	0.051	0.050
Some high school	0.089	0.087	0.092
High school or GED	0.323	0.310	0.336
Some college	0.262	0.253	0.271
College or above	0.275	0.300	0.251
Married (reference)	0.090	0.077	0.101
Divorced	0.090	0.077	0.101
Widowed	0.071	0.027	0.115
Separated	0.022	0.018	0.026
Never been married	0.192	0.221	0.162
Member of an unmarried couple	0.026	0.028	0.025
Income less than $10k (reference)	0.079	0.061	0.098
Income btw $10k and $15k	0.069	0.061	0.077
Income btw $15k and $20k	0.081	0.076	0.085
Income btw $20k and $25k	0.093	0.093	0.094
Income btw $25k and $35k	0.142	0.148	0.137
Income greater than $35k	0.413	0.458	0.369
Income missing	0.122	0.104	0.141
Income greater than $50k	0.148	0.165	0.131
Income greater than $75k	0.107	0.123	0.092
Male	0.497		

[a]All mean values are weighted. Cells with plus-minus signs indicate means ±Taylor linearized standard errors.

survey design over time, the indicator for household income greater than $50,000 applies only to responses after 1984, and the indicator for income greater than $75,000 applies only from 1994 to 2006. We assign zero to these variables when they are not applicable. Because the categorical nature of these income variables makes adjustment for inflation difficult, we include interaction terms of categorical income indicators and years. In addition, we also examined specifications that did not include income and that interacted income with indicators for time period. Furthermore, because the minimum wage could have a direct effect on income, especially for low income persons (Lakdawalla and Philipson 2002), we also examined specifications that divided the sample into high and low income groups that were further divided by educational attainment. Because health status and weight may decline with advancing age and more rapidly among older persons, we estimated models without persons older than sixty. Because trends in minimum wage and obesity may vary across states, we added interaction terms to control for state-specific linear trends. We estimated all models on the full sample and on male and female samples separately. Robust or Huber-White errors are used in calculating the confidence intervals and the *p*-values to account for serial correlation and state clustering in the linear models (Bertrand, Duflo, and Mullainathan 2004).

The effects of the minimum wage on body weight might not be uniform across different parts of the body weight distribution, thus we also examined our model using quantile regressions.

Statistical analyses were performed using the survey data analysis commands of Stata software, version 9 (Stata Corporation).

1.3   Results

The summary statistics are presented in table 1.1. Over the study period, the average BMI is 25.8 for the full sample, 26.4 for men, and 25.2 for women. The percentage of obese individuals is roughly 17 percent for the full sample and for both genders. The weighted mean age is 44.8 for full sample, but the male sample is about two years younger than the female sample. This presumably reflects the greater life expectancy of women.

Table 1.2 provides the estimates of the linear regression models for BMI. The results suggest that a one-dollar increase in minimum wage is associated with a 0.06 decrease in mean BMI. The results for male and female samples separately are similar.

Quantile regression results showed that the effects vary by BMI, with the effects increasing steadily across the BMI distribution to a maximum effect of a one dollar increase in the real minimum wage on BMI of 0.13 for the ninetieth percentile. Results were again similar when men and women were analyzed separately (see figure 1.3).

Table 1.2 Effects of minimum wage rates on body weight (BMI)

Sample	Full sample Coefficient estimate (95% CI)	p-value	Male sample Coefficient estimate (95% CI)	p-value	Female sample Coefficient estimate (95% CI)	p-value
Minimum wage	−0.060 (−0.105; −0.014)	0.013	−0.055 (−0.106; −0.003)	0.044	−0.063 (−0.113; −0.014)	0.015
Male	1.307 (1.262; 1.352)	0.000				
Black	1.518 (1.405; 1.630)	0.000	0.561 (0.423; 0.699)	0.000	2.322 (2.190; 2.454)	0.000
Hispanic	0.622 (0.469; 0.775)	0.000	0.413 (0.232; 0.595)	0.000	0.859 (0.707; 1.011)	0.000
Others	−0.702 (−0.961; −0.444)	0.000	−0.900 (−1.154; −0.646)	0.000	−0.475 (−0.772; −0.178)	0.003
Some high school	−0.187 (−0.242; −0.131)	0.000	−0.087 (−0.162; −0.012)	0.027	−0.481 (−0.604; −0.358)	0.000
High school or GED	−0.526 (−0.586; −0.466)	0.000	−0.104 (−0.196; −0.012)	0.031	−1.137 (−1.244; −1.030)	0.000
Some college	−0.670 (−0.745; −0.595)	0.000	−0.155 (−0.249; −0.062)	0.002	−1.352 (−1.469; −1.235)	0.000
College or above	−1.384 (−1.504; −1.264)	0.000	−0.810 (−0.942; −0.678)	0.000	−2.176 (−2.320; −2.032)	0.000
Divorced	−0.405 (−0.450; −0.359)	0.000	−0.568 (−0.611; −0.525)	0.000	−0.413 (−0.465; −0.362)	0.000
Widowed	0.215 (0.170; 0.259)	0.000	−0.145 (−0.221; −0.068)	0.001	−0.090 (−0.147; −0.033)	0.003
Separated	−0.188 (−0.265; −0.112)	0.000	−0.666 (−0.734; −0.598)	0.000	−0.052 (−0.163; 0.060)	0.367
Never been married	−0.211 (−0.268; −0.154)	0.000	−0.605 (−0.647; −0.563)	0.000	0.087 (−0.006; 0.179)	0.073
Member of an unmarried couple	−0.271 (−0.329; −0.212)	0.000	−0.529 (−0.601; −0.457)	0.000	0.010 (−0.078; 0.099)	0.817
Constant	22.248 (21.824; 22.672)	0.000	23.604 (23.119; 24.088)	0.000	22.409 (21.883; 22.935)	0.000

Notes: The federal minimum wage is used when it is greater than the state level. Minimum wages are adjusted to 2006 dollars with the Consumer Price Index (all components). Coefficient estimates of age, year, and state fixed effects, income, and income*year interaction terms are not shown. Reference groups are: female, white, less than high school, married, and aged between 18 and 20, Alabama, year 1984, and income < $10,000 respectively. CI denotes confidence interval.

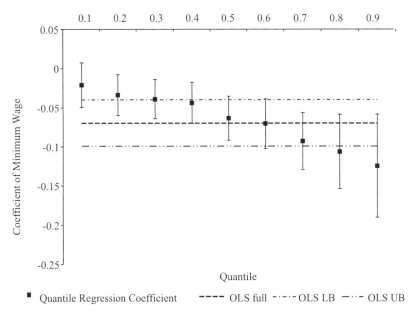

Fig. 1.3   Quantile regression effects of minimum wage on BMI

1.4   Contribution of Minimum Wage Decreases to Increasing BMI and Obesity

During the period covered by the BRFSS data, the average real minimum wage fell from a maximum of $6.40 in 1984 to $5.82 in 2006, with the federal minimum real wage falling even further, from $6.30 to $5.20. From when the federal minimum wage was last increased during our study period (1997) to the conclusion of our study period in 2006, the average real minimum wage fell from $6.50 to $5.82, and the real value of the federal minimum wage fell from $6.40 to $5.20. Multiplying these changes in the average real wage by the estimates from the linear model suggest that the $0.58 decline in the real minimum wage from 1984 to 2006 would produce a $0.58 • 0.06 = 0.035 increase in BMI. Since average BMI increased by about 2.6 from 1984 to 2006 (from about 24.4 to 27.0), this is only 1 to 2 percent of the increase in BMI over the period. If we consider the most recent period during which the real minimum wage has been continuingly decreasing, 1997 to 2006, the $0.68 decline can explain 0.68 × 0.06 = 0.04 (4 percent) of the 1.3 (25.7 to 27) increase in BMI. However, both these periods exclude the major decline in the real minimum wage that occurred from about 1970 to 1984. If the longer term $3.33 decline in the real minimum wage from its peak at $9.15 in 1968 to $5.82 in 2006 is considered, it can explain 3.33 × 0.06 = 0.2 (10 percent) of the total increase in average BMI from 25.0 to 27.0 over the period (Flegal et al. 1998; Kuczmarski et al. 1994).

Table 1.3 presents results of the sensitivity analysis. The first two specifications show that the results are robust to whether they include the controls for income. Specifications 3 and 4 show the results are stronger for persons below age sixty than for older persons. Specifications 5 to 8 show that, excluding persons older than sixty among whom income is more likely to be a misleading measure of financial resources, the effects of minimum wage on BMI are greatest among persons with at least a high school education and with incomes above $35,000. Specification 9 shows that our results are robust to the inclusion of state-specific linear trends. We include this specification test because we did not include state-specific time trends in an earlier version of this manuscript, and this was highlighted by discussants of our initial paper and by a later manuscript by Cotti and Tefft (2009) that did not find an effect of minimum wages on obesity. However, as specification 9 indicates, inclusion of this time trend did not change our results. Reasons we have considered for the difference between their findings and ours include that they (a) controlled for fast-food price, which creates potential problems of endogeneity and multicollinearity since fast-food price likely depends on minimum wage, (b) did not account for the BRFSS sampling weights, (c) used a much smaller number of observations than we used, without an apparent cause of the smaller sample size, and (d) used a correction for potential bias in self-reported BMI that was based on the relationship between self-reported and clinically measured body weight and height in the National Health and Nutritional Examination Survey (NHANES). We chose not to use this correction because we are concerned that it may not be appropriate for BRFSS because NHANES respondents knew that the measures they reported would be verified by a physical exam, but BRFSS respondents knew their reports would not be verified.

1.5   Discussion

The association we observe between changes in the real minimum wage and BMI among BRFSS respondents are consistent with our hypothesis that a decrease in real minimum wage rates can increase body weight. Although we cannot prove that this relationship is causal, several lines of evidence argue against alternative interpretations, such as that changes in body weight influence real minimum wage rates, or that a third factor influences both real minimum wage rates and body weight. The first possibility seems unlikely because there is no apparent reason why changes in obesity would cause changes in minimum wage laws or inflation. It does seem possible that some third factor could lead to both decreases in the real minimum wage and increases in BMI. One candidate might be that falling incomes within states that we somehow do not adequately control for could both cause states to allow the minimum wage to drift downward and lead to increases in obesity if declines in socioeconomic status due to falling incomes caused people to

Table 1.3   Sensitivity analyses: Coefficient estimate of real minimum wage (Dependent variable: Body mass index)

Model	No. of observations Total (Men; Women)	Full sample Coefficient estimate (95% CI)	Full sample p-value	Male sample Coefficient estimate (95% CI)	Male sample p-value	Female sample Coefficient estimate (95% CI)	Female sample p-value
(1)	3,048,378 (1,274,462; 1,773,916)	−0.060 (−0.106; −0.013)	0.013	−0.055 (−0.108; −0.002)	0.044	−0.063 (−0.114; −0.013)	0.015
(2)	3,048,378 (1,274,462; 1,773,916)	−0.059 (−0.109; −0.010)	0.019	−0.058 (−0.111; −0.005)	0.031	−0.060 (−0.115; −0.006)	0.032
(3)	2,188,122 (954,522; 1,233,600)	−0.071 (−0.126; −0.015)	0.013	−0.067 (−0.128; −0.006)	0.031	−0.070 (−0.132; −0.008)	0.028
(4)	860,256 (319,940; 540,316)	−0.023 (−0.076; 0.029)	0.372	−0.004 (−0.076; 0.067)	0.907	−0.039 (−0.090; 0.012)	0.131
(5)	484,206 (200,042; 284,164)	−0.037 (−0.134; 0.060)	0.444	0.015 (−0.127; 0.156)	0.837	−0.083 (−0.243; 0.077)	0.302
(6)	379,137 (178,824; 200,313)	−0.017 (−0.115; 0.082)	0.737	−0.050 (−0.179; 0.079)	0.442	0.026 (−0.112; 0.163)	0.711
(7)	908,468 (412,579; 495,889)	−0.086 (−0.130; −0.042)	0.000	−0.096 (−0.156; −0.036)	0.002	−0.074 (−0.156; 0.009)	0.080
(8)	416,311 (163,077; 253,234)	−0.121 (−0.202; −0.040)	0.004	−0.062 (−0.146; 0.021)	0.140	−0.178 (−0.293; −0.062)	0.003
(9)	3,048,378 (1,274,462; 1,773,916)	−0.038 (−0.074; −0.002)	0.037	−0.016 (−0.064; 0.032)	0.513	−0.059 (−0.128; 0.009)	0.087

Notes: (1) Baseline: with full set of covariates; (2) Baseline: do not control for income; (3) Excluding elderly (age ≥ 60), full set of covariates; (4) Only elderly (age ≥ 60), full set of covariates; (5) Age < 60, Income < $35,000, and education less than high school; (6) Age < 60, Income > $35,000, and education level is less than high school; (7) Age < 60, Income > $35,000, and education level is more than high school; (8) Age < 60, Income < $35,000, and education level is more than high school; (9) Baseline specification plus state specific linear trends. Coefficient estimates for age, year, and state fixed effects, race and ethnicity, marital status, education, income, and income*year interaction terms (when included) not shown. Reference groups are: female, white, less than high school, married, and aged between 18 and 20, Alabama, year 1984, white, married, less than high school, and income < $10,000.

substitute cheaper but more fattening foods for more expensive ones that are less likely to cause obesity. Arguing against this is that we control for both state fixed effects and time trends, so that changes in state minimum wage legislation or local price levels would have to be explained by changes in income over time within states. We also performed additional sensitivity analyses that included state-specific time linear time trends, and these generally confirmed our overall findings, though these specifications have had difficulties converging in some of the quantile regressions.

The hypothesis that changes in the real minimum wage could cause changes in obesity, in contrast, seems highly plausible. Here, there are at least two stories one could tell. The first is the one that we have emphasized—that decreases in the minimum wage would lower the price of fast-food and thereby increase its consumption, and thus, obesity. The second is that a decrease in the minimum wage could raise obesity by lowering incomes of people who earn minimum wage and encouraging them to eat more unhealthy food. However, this second argument is not a convincing explanation of the results we observe because the effect of the minimum wage is greater among high income persons than among low income persons, who would be most likely to earn minimum wage. In addition, low income persons consume so little food away from home, (<$250 per family of four per year), that it seems unlikely to be enough to contribute to obesity (Frazao et al. 2007). It is also interesting that even though lower income persons are more likely than higher income persons to be obese (Gibson 2003, 2004; Kim et al. 2006), obesity has increased most among higher income persons in recent years, as might be expected if changes in the price of food away from home were driving increases in obesity (Chang and Lauderdale 2005).

Further evidence supporting the hypothesis that the decline in real minimum wage has increased obesity by encouraging food away from home (FAFH) is that the effect we observe can be assessed by calibrating it against the published literature on how the price of food away from home affects the quantity of it consumed and how that, in turn, affects obesity. To do this, the effect of the minimum wage on BMI can be approximated by:

$$\Delta \, BMI / \Delta \text{ minimum wage} = \Delta \, BMI / \% \Delta \text{ calories intake}$$

$$\cdot \, \% \Delta \text{ calories intake} / \% \Delta \text{ quantity of FAFH}$$

$$\cdot \, \% \Delta \text{ quantity of FAFH} / \% \Delta \text{ price FAFH}$$

$$\cdot \, \% \Delta \text{ price FAFH} / \% \Delta \text{ minimum wage}$$

Assuming the median height of a person in the United States of 1.78 meters and average caloric intake of about 2000 calories per day, and estimates by Cutler, Glaeser, and Shapiro (2003) that the approximately 5 kg (equivalent to 1.6 unit of BMI) increase in median weight over the past two decades requires a net caloric imbalance of about 100 to 150 calories per day, the change in BMI per percent increase in caloric intake can be estimated as $(5 \div 1.78^2) \div (125/2000) = 25$. Estimates of the elasticity of FAFH with respect to price are available from a recent study on demand of food consumption, which suggested estimates of price elasticity as from -2.03 to -1.16 (Lee and O'Roark 1999; Piggott 2003). Estimating how total calories consumed increases as FAFH increases is difficult because FAFH may substitute for food at home. However, assuming it does not subsitutue for food at home places an upper bound on the increase in total calories. Aaronson, French, and MacDonald (2008) have provided fairly consistent estimates of the effect of minimum wage on food price, ranging from elasticity estimates of 0.73 percent for full service establishments, to 1.56 percent for limited service establishments, for a 10 percent change of minimum wage. An alternative study suggested that 1 percent change of food price per \$0.50 change in minimum wage rate, consistent again with about a 1 percent change (Lee and O'Roark 1999). Multiplying these $(25 \times (-1.16 \text{ to } -2.03) \times 0.01) = -0.29$ to -0.50, about five times the size of the 0.06 effect we estimate. This seems likely to reflect the extent to which our calculations fail to account for the degree to which calories for FAFH reduce calories consumed at home, but suggests that the hypothesis that increased consumption of food away from home could explain the increase in body weight we find with increases in the minimum wage, even if as little as 20 percent of the increase in calories consumed away from home represents a net increase in total caloric consumption.

Our analysis has several limitations. First, BRFSS body weight and height information was self-reported, which could lead to bias in estimates of weight and height (Cawley 2004). However, there is no obvious reason why such bias would change our findings. Another limitation is that BRFSS excludes children and youth, institutionalized populations, and households without phone service. Finally, our analysis assumes that changes in minimum wages affect obesity currently, and it may well be that there is some lag structure to effects that we have failed to account for and would be complex to implement empirically given the serial correlation of wages within states over time.

1.6   Potential Policy Implications

If the decline in minimum wages has contributed to increasing obesity in the United States, then it is tempting to consider whether increases in the minimum wage might reduce obesity in the United States, producing benefits in both better health and lower health care costs. Indeed, the federal real minimum wage has already increased by about 40 percent since 2006. Real minimum wages would have to rise by an additional 60 percent to restore them to their 1968 levels, and such increases could have adverse effects on employment, companies that depend on minimum wage labor, and the prices of other goods and services that are heavily dependent on minimum wage labor (Card and Krueger 2000; Neumark and Wascher 2000; Flinn 2006).

To put the potential policy implications of a minimum wage increase in context, it is useful to consider the expected effects of minimum wage on health outcomes, such as mortality. Precisely forecasting the effects of a minimum wage change on mortality is complex because minimum wage may change obesity differently across different groups, and those changes may have varying effects on health outcomes across those groups (Flegal et al. 2005). However, using published estimates that there is an average reduction in life expectancy of about six months with each one unit increase in BMI (Fontaine et al. 2003), the change of 0.07 over the population for each dollar increase in the minimum wage would increase life expectancy in the United States by fifteen days, producing an additional twelve million life-years of the U.S. population. To the extent that BMI would decrease most among the most obese, as suggested by our quantile regressions, and that the health benefits of BMI reduction would be greatest at the highest levels of BMI, these estimates of the mortality reductions from an increase in the real minimum wage would be conservative.

Were an increase in the minimum wage to be viewed as a health intervention, it would be useful to consider its benefits from the perspective of cost-effectiveness. As a back-of-the-envelope calculation, using common estimates that a year of life is valued at $100,000 (Braithwaite et al. 2008) and assuming that the added year of life would occur on average forty years from now (since the average age of the U.S. population is slightly above thirty-five and life expectancy at birth is slightly above seventy-five),[6] and discounting future benefits at 3 percent (Gold et al. 1996), this increase in life expectancy would be valued at about $375 billion. Reductions in morbidity with decreasing levels of obesity have also been quantified and are probably roughly on the same order of magnitude as reductions in mortality (Muennig et al. 2006). Health care costs related to obesity are smaller, probably less than $50 billion annually, so the value of these savings would be small compared to the value of health improvements (Allison, Zannolli, and Narayan 1999; Raebel et al. 2004). Dividing these benefits that would accrue across all cohorts evenly among all the cohorts suggests an annual health benefit valued at about $50 billion. The total of these societal benefits is clearly very large, but need to be interpreted in light of an estimated annual cost of a one dollar increase in minimum wage increases of about $195 billion per year assuming that there are thirteen million minimum wage workers who each work about 1,500 hours per year.[7] This suggests that an increase in the minimum wage would cost consumers on average more than they would gain in health benefits, but does not include the benefits to minimum wage workers. To the extent that these are transfer payments from consumers

6. U.S. Census Bureau (2008).
7. See, e.g., *Minimum Wage Issue Guide.* Economic Policy Institute, Washington, DC, July 2008.

paying higher costs for minimum wage earners, such benefits to minimum wage earners would completely offset the costs of a minimum wage increase. However, to the extent higher minimum wages induce unemployment or other inefficiencies in labor and product markets, a result suggested by classical microeconomic theory but still controversial empirically (Neumark and Wascher 2007), such losses would have to be viewed as arguing against increases in the minimum wage. Unfortunately, estimates of the magnitude of such welfare losses due to a higher minimum wage are not available. For this reason, and because an increase in the minimum wage might have a series of complex distributional effects on different subgroups in the population, recommendations about the desirability of a further increase in the minimum wage are beyond the scope of this chapter.

Whether or not additional minimum wage increases would be a desirable policy option, our results may have important policy implications if they focus attention on the mechanisms by which an increase in the minimum wage might affect obesity. While we have emphasized food away from home, we recognize that other explanations could be produced. For example, it is possible that prices for food at home could also be influenced by changes in the minimum wage, though this seems less likely given the smaller share for minimum wage labor in the manufacture of food at home. If we are willing to focus on the price of food away from home as a determinant of obesity, then perhaps policy changes such as better labeling, public health education, regulation of serving size, or "sin taxes" on food away from home might be worth greater attention (Garson and Engelhard 2007). Although prior studies have suggested an association between obesity and increased consumption of food away from home, the direction of causation has been unclear. Our findings on the relationship of obesity to minimum wage changes support the argument that the association of increased consumption of food away from home and obesity may reflect a causal relationship. Our results also increase the importance of experiments to test approaches to control obesity by changing the consumption of food away from home, whether through changes in prices, availability, or information about health consequences.

That our findings explain only a moderate percent of the observed change in body weight suggest that other explanations, such as decreased physical activity, may also play important roles in the increase in obesity. Peer effects have also recently received significant attention in the literature (Christakis and Fowler 2007; Chen and Meltzer 2008), though these would presumably be reflected in the total response we observe in response to a change in the minimum wage, only perhaps more broadly distributed over time. Peer effects also cannot explain why a trend towards increasing obesity may have started; it is possible that decreases in the minimum wage may have had local effects that explain only ten to twenty percent of the increase in BMI as we identify here, but larger effects across the country through peer effects that we are unable to identify using the approach we apply here. Finally, we should note that labor saving approaches to the production of fast-food have presumably also played a major role in decreasing its cost and increasing its consumption. To the extent such labor saving continues, minimum wage labor may be an increasingly less important contributor to the cost of food away from home over time regardless of wage increases. While this may decrease the potential impact of minimum wage policies on obesity, our findings highlight the possibility that policies that focus on the consumption of food away from home deserve particular attention in public health efforts to control obesity.

References

Aaronson, D. 2001. Price pass-through and the minimum wage. *Review of Economic and Statistics* 83 (1): 158–69.

Aaronson, D., E. French, and J. MacDonald. 2008. The minimum wage, restaurant prices, and labor market structure. *Journal of Human Resources* 43 (3): 688–720.

Allison, D., R. Zannolli, and K. M. Narayan. 1999. The direct health care costs of obesity in the United States. *American Journal of Public Health* 89 (8): 1194–9.

Anderson, M., and D. A. Matsa. 2009. Are restaurants really supersizing America? *American Economic Journal: Applied Economics,* forthcoming.

Bertrand, M., E. Duflo, and S. Mullainathan. 2004. How much should we trust differences-in-differences estimates? *Quarterly Journal of Economics* 119 (1): 249–75.

Braithwaite, R. S., D. O. Meltzer, J. T. King, D. Leslie, and M. S. Roberts. 2008. What does the value of modern medicine say about the $50,000 per quality-adjusted life-year decision rule? *Medical Care* 46 (4): 349–56.

Card, D., and A. B. Krueger. 2000. Minimum wages and employment: A case study of the fast-food industry in New Jersey and Pennsylvania: Reply. *American Economic Review* 90 (5): 1397–420.

Cawley, J. 2004. The impact of obesity on wages. *Journal of Human Resources* 39 (2): 451–74.

Centers for Disease Control and Prevention (CDC). 1984–2006. *Behavioral risk factor surveillance system survey data.* Atlanta, GA: U.S. Department of Health and Human Services, CDC.

Chang, V. W., and D. S. Lauderdale. 2005. Income disparities in body mass index and obesity in the United States, 1971–2002. *Archives of Internal Medicine* 165 (18): 2122–8.

Chen, Z., and D. O. Meltzer. 2008. Beefing up with the Chans: Evidence for the effects of relative income and income inequality on health from the China health and nutrition survey. *Social Science & Medicine* 66 (11): 2206–17.

Chou, S.-Y., M. Grossman, and H. Saffer. 2004. An economic analysis of adult obesity: Results from the behavioral risk factor surveillance system. *Journal of Health Economics* 23:565–87.

Christakis, N. A., and J. H. Fowler. 2007. The spread of obesity in a large social network over 32 Years. *New England Journal of Medicine* 357:370–9.

Cotti, C. D., and N. Tefft. 2009. Do changes in the minimum wage impact obesity in the U.S.? Available at: SSRN: http://ssrn.com/abstract=1479307.

Currie, J., S. DellaVigna, E. Moretti, and V. Pathania. 2009. The effect of fast food restaurants on obesity and weight gain. NBER Working Paper no. 14721. Cambridge, MA: National Bureau of Economic Research, February. *Economic Policy*

Cutler, D. M., E. L. Glaeser, and J. M. Shapiro. 2003. Why have Americans become more obese? *Journal of Economic Perspectives* 17 (3): 93–118.

Flegal, K. M., M. D. Carroll, R. J. Kuczmarski, and C. L. Johnson. 1998. Overweight and obesity in the United States: Prevalence and trends, 1960–1994. *International Journal of Obesity* 22:39–47.

Flegal, K. M., B. I. Graubard, D. F. Williamson, and M. H. Gail. 2005. Excess deaths associated with underweight, overweight, and obesity. *Journal of the American Medical Association* 293:1861–67.

Flinn, C. J. 2006. Minimum wage effects on labor market outcomes under search, matching, and endogenous contact rates. *Econometrica* 74 (4): 1013–62.

Fontaine, K. R., D. T. Redden, C. Wang, A. O. Westfall, and D. B. Allison. 2003. Years of life lost due to obesity. *Journal of the American Medical Association* 289 (2): 187–93.

Frazao, E., M. Andrews, D. Smallwood, and M. Prell. 2007. *Food spending patterns of low-income households: Will increasing purchasing power result in healthier food choices?* USDA Economic Research Service Economic Information Bulletin 29 (4), September.

Garson, A., and C. L. Engelhard. 2007. Attacking obesity: Lessons from smoking. *Journal of the American College of Cardiology* 49:1673–5.

Gibson, D. 2003. Food stamp program participation is positively related to obesity in low income women. *Journal of Nutrition* 133:2225–31.

———. 2004. Long-term food stamp program participation is differentially related to overweight in young girls and boys. *Journal of Nutrition* 134:372–9.

Gold, M. R., J. E. Siegel, L. B. Russell, and M. C. Weinstein. 1996. *Cost-effectiveness in health and medicine.* Oxford and New York: Oxford University Press.

Kim, D., S. V. Subramanian, S. L. Gortmaker, and I. Kawachi. 2006. U.S. state- and county-level social capital in relation to obesity and physical inactivity: A multilevel, multivariable analysis. *Social Science & Medicine* 63 (4): 1045–59.

Kuczmarski, R. J., K. M. Flegal, S. M. Campbell, and C. L. Johnson. 1994. Increasing prevalence of overweight among U.S. adults—The national health and nutrition surveys, 1960 to 1991. *Journal of the American Medical Association* 272 (3): 205–11.

Lakdawalla, D., and T. Philipson. 2002. The growth of obesity and technological change: A theoretical and empirical examination. NBER Working Paper no. 8946. Cambridge, MA: National Bureau of Economic Research, May.

Lee, C., and B. O'Roark. 1999. The impact of minimum wage increases on food and kindred products prices: An analysis of price pass-through. Food and Rural Economics Division, Economic Research Service, U.S. Department of Agriculture, Technical Bulletin No. 1877.

MacDonald, J. M., and D. Aaronson. 2006. How firms construct price changes: Evidence from restaurant responses to increased minimum wages. *American Journal of Agricultural Economics* 88 (2): 292–307.

Mello, M. M., D. M. Studdert, and T. A. Brenna. 2006. Obesity—The new frontier of public health law. *New England Journal of Medicine* 354 (24): 2601–9.

Muennig, P., E. Lubetkin, H. Jia, and P. Franks. 2006. Gender and the burden of disease attributable to obesity. *American Journal of Public Health* 96 (9): 1662–8.

National Institutes of Health (NIH). 1998. Clinical guidelines on the identification, evaluation and treatment of overweight and obesity in adults: The evidence report. *Obesity Research* 6:51S–209S.

Nestle, M. 2006. Food marketing and childhood obesity—A matter of policy. *New England Journal of Medicine* 354:2527–9.

Neumark, D., and W. Wascher. 2000. Minimum wages and employment: A case study of the fast-food industry in New Jersey and Pennsylvania: Comment. *American Economic Review* 90 (5): 1362–96.

———. 2007. Minimum wages and employment. IZA Discussion Paper no. 2570. Bonn, Germany: Institute for the Study of Labor.

Ogden, C. L., M. D. Carroll, L. R. Curtin, M. A. McDowell, C. J. Tabak, and K. M. Flegal. 2006. Prevalence of overweight and obesity in the United States, 1999–2004. *Journal of the American Medical Association* 295 (13): 1549–55.

Philipson, T. J., and R. A. Posner. 2003. The long-run growth in obesity as a function of technological change. *Perspectives in Biology and Medicine* 46 (3 Suppl): S87–107.

Piggott, N. E. 2003. The nested PIGLOG model: An application to U.S. food demand. *American Journal of Agricultural Economics* 85 (1): 1–15.

Raebel, M. A., D.C. Malone, D. A. C. Conner, S. Xu, J. A. Porter, and F. A. Lanty. 2004. Health services use and health care cost of obese and nonobese individuals. *Archives of Internal Medicine* 164:2135–40.

U.S. Census Bureau. 2008. Statistical abstract of the United States: Various issues. Washington, DC: GPO. Available at: http://www.census.gov/statab/www/.

U.S. Department of Labor, Employment Standards Administration. 2004. *The fair labor standards act of 1938, as Amended,* Wage and Hour Division. Washington, DC: WH Publication 1318, revised March 2004.

Does Health Insurance Make You Fat?

Jay Bhattacharya, M. Kate Bundorf, Noemi Pace, and
Neeraj Sood

2.1 Introduction

Adult obesity is a thorny problem. Several studies document rising obesity prevalence in the United States (See Mokdad et al. 1999; Mokdad et al. 2003). Economists have argued that the primary cause of increasing obesity prevalence are: (a) a falling relative price of food; (b) a technologically induced shift away from physically demanding work; and (c) a decline in time spent on food production at home (see Lakdawalla and Philipson 2002; Cutler, Glaeser, and Shapiro 2003; and Anderson, Butcher, and Levine 2003).[1] As most view these fundamental changes in the economy as desirable and would not want to undo them, developing public policy to address the root causes of rising obesity prevalence is difficult, if not entirely problematic.

Jay Bhattacharya is associate professor of medicine and a core faculty member of the Center for Health Policy/Center for Primary Care and Outcomes Research (CHP/PCOR) at Stanford University, and a research associate of the National Bureau of Economic Research. M. Kate Bundorf is assistant professor of Health Research and Policy and fellow of the Center for Health Policy/Center for Primary Care and Outcomes Research (CHP/PCOR) at Stanford University, and a faculty research fellow of the National Bureau of Economic Research. Noemi Pace is assistant professor of economics at Ca' Foscari University of Venice. Neeraj Sood is associate professor of Clinical Pharmacy and Pharmaceutical Economics and Policy at the University of Southern California School of Pharmacy, and a faculty research fellow of the National Bureau of Economic Research.

We thank Michael Grossman and the participants at the NBER Conference on the Economics of Obesity for helpful comments. Bhattacharya, Sood, and Bundorf thank the National Institute of Aging for financial support on this project.

1. There are, of course, many other noneconomic determinants of body weight, including genetic predispositions to obesity and nonrational impulses (such as myopic decision making and lack of self-control) that prevent optimal body weight control. These are unlikely explanations for the observed trends in body weight, even if they help explain baseline levels. There is certainly no evidence that we are more irrational or have different genes than our parents or grandparents.

Nevertheless, the health care and other costs associated with obesity are enormous. For example, Wolf and Colditz (1994) estimate that over $68 billion are lost annually in increased health care costs and job absenteeism as a result of obesity in the United States. The morbidity and accounting costs associated with obesity have led public health experts (such as Nestle 2003; Brownell and Horgen 2003; and Sturm 2002) to advocate vigorous public intervention, including regulation of fast-food establishments and taxes on nutritionally questionable foods.

The economic justification for these sorts of policy interventions, such as taxes on food, favored by some of these authors, rests on the idea that when one person becomes obese, many other people pay the cost. In economic jargon, there are negative externalities from body weight decisions that lead to obesity. If external costs are high, then public welfare can be improved by interventions that change the incentives adults face when making decisions about body weight. If external costs are small, then adults pay fully for their body weight decisions and public interventions aimed at decreasing body weight can play only a limited role in improving public welfare.[2]

The main mechanism by which obesity imposes external costs is through pooled health insurance. In a health insurance pool with inadequately risk-adjusted premiums, one person's increase in body weight really is everyone else's business, since obesity often leads to higher medical expenditures. In this chapter, we describe a model of this negative obesity externality associated with health insurance.[3] The main insight of this model is that measuring the obesity externality involves more than just measuring the subsidy to obese individuals induced by health insurance. The welfare loss due to the obesity externality depends upon both the size of the subsidy and upon the extent to which body weight decisions are distorted on the margin by the subsidy—that is, does coverage with pooled health insurance cause enrollees to gain weight? If the answer is no, and there is no moral hazard of this sort caused by insurance coverage, then the subsidy induced by one person's obesity would simply represent a transfer from the thinner individuals in his insurance pool to the obese person, with no net effect on social welfare.

Despite the importance of this parameter—the health insurance elasticity of body weight—to the welfare economics of obesity, there has been scant work in the economics literature on the topic.[4] The one exception is a paper by Rashad and Markowitz (2010) who find a zero elasticity of insurance coverage on body weight or obesity rates. These authors rely on the size of a firm where an individual works as an instrument for insurance coverage in their body weight regressions. We extend this work along three dimen-

---

2. Cawley (2004) provides a detailed discussion of possible market failures related to obesity.

3. See Bhattacharya and Sood (2007) for a full description of this model.

4. In a related study, Dave and Kaestner (2009) analyze the effect of insurance on smoking, drinking, and exercise in the elderly population. They find that obtaining health insurance reduces prevention and increases unhealthy behaviors among elderly men.

sions. First, we measure separate elasticities for the extensive margin (people gaining or losing insurance altogether) and the intensive margin (insurance becoming more generous). In principle, these elasticities may be different, and as we show in the concluding section of the chapter, they have different policy implications. Second, we distinguish different elasticities for public and private insurance coverage for our estimates of the elasticity along the extensive margin. Finally, we adopt econometric methods that account for the discrete nature of the insurance coverage variable.

2.2   Background

Not surprisingly, expected health care expenditures are higher for obese individuals than for normal weight individuals. A large number of studies document this fact. The vast majority of these studies use convenience samples consisting of individuals from a single employer or a single insurer (Elmer et al. 2004; Bertakis and Azari 2005; Burton et al. 1998; Raebel et al. 2004). There are also studies of obesity-related medical expenditure differences in an international setting. Both Sander and Bergemann (2003), in a German setting, and Katzmarzyk and Janssen (2004), in a Canadian setting, find higher medical expenditures for obese people.

There are a few studies that use nationally representative data. Finkelstein, Fiebelkorn, and Wang (2003) use data from the linked National Health Interview Survey (NHIS) and Medical Expenditure Panel Survey (MEPS). They estimate that annual medical expenditures are $732 higher for obese than normal weight individuals. From an accounting viewpoint, approximately half of the estimated $78.5 billion in medical care spending in 1998 attributable to excess body weight was financed through private insurance (38 percent) and patient out-of-pocket payments (14 percent). Sturm (2002), using data from the Health Care for Communities (HCC) survey, finds that obese individuals spend $395 per year more than nonobese individuals on medical care. Thorpe et al. (2004) also use MEPS data, but they are interested in how much of the $1,100 increase between 1987 and 2000 in per-capita medical expenditures is attributable to obesity. Using a regression model to calculate what per-capita medical expenditures would have been had 1987 obesity levels persisted to 2000, they conclude that about $300 of the $1,100 increase is due to the rise in obesity prevalence.

This is a large literature, which space constraints prevent us from surveying in more detail. The many studies that we do not discuss here vary considerably in generality—some examine data from a single company or from a single insurance source—though they all reach the same qualitative conclusion that obesity is associated with higher medical care costs.[5]

5. Some of the studies we reviewed, but arbitrarily do not discuss here, include Bungam et al. (2003); Musich et al. (2004); Quesenberry Jr., Caan, and Jacobson (1998); Thompson et al. (2001); and Wang et al. (2003).

2.2.1   External Costs of Obesity Associated with Health Insurance

Despite the extensive literature on medical expenditure differences, very few studies attempt to estimate the degree to which health insurance coverage leads to subsidies for the obese. Some studies have attempted to estimate how much of obesity-related medical costs are subsidized by public insurance. Finkelstein, Ruhm, and Kosa (2005), in a literature review of the causes and consequences of obesity, estimate that "the government finances roughly half the total annual medical costs attributable to obesity. As a result, the average taxpayer spends approximately $175 per year to finance obesity related medical expenditures among Medicare and Medicaid recipients" (248). To arrive at this conclusion, they rely on a study by Finkelstein, Fiebelkorn, and Wang (2004), who calculate state and federal level estimates of Medicare and Medicaid expenditures attributable to obesity. Another study, conducted by Daviglus et al. (2004), links together data from a sample of Chicago-area workers in the labor force between 1967 to 1973, to Medicare claims records from the 1990s. They estimate substantial obesity-related differences in Medicare expenditures. For example, women workers who were obese between 1967 and 1973 spent $176,947 in the 1990s on Medicare, while analogous nonobese, nonoverweight female workers spent $100,431 in undiscounted costs. Obese male workers spent $125,470, while nonobese, nonoverweight male workers spent $76,866.

However, estimating how much of obesity-related medical costs are financed by public insurance is merely an accounting exercise and not sufficient for calculating the true economic subsidy for obesity. Conceptually, calculating the size of the subsidy also requires estimating payments by obese and nonobese individuals for enrolling in health insurance in addition to the expected benefits of enrollment. Roughly speaking, obese and nonobese people alike pay for Medicare when they are under sixty-five and spend (receive benefits) when they are older.[6] Since obese people work, earn, are taxed, and die at different rates than nonobese people, looking at Medicare expenditure differences alone will paint a misleading picture of the Medicare subsidy for the obese.

Calculating the obesity subsidy induced by private insurance also requires estimating both payments for health insurance and medical expenditures. Since private insurance is typically provided in an employment setting, it is not enough to look at premiums for health insurance paid by employers and employees.[7] The key question is whether employers adjust the cash wages of obese workers with health insurance in order to account for the higher cost

---

6. For example, McClellan and Skinner (1999, 2006) and Bhattacharya and Lakdawalla (2006), in estimating Medicare progressivity, estimate lifetime profiles of tax receipts for Medicare as well as Medicare expenditures.

7. For employees enrolling in the same insurance plan, premiums do not depend upon body weight (see Keenan et al. 2001), so in that case, there are no obesity-related payment differen-

of insuring these workers. Although theory predicts that employers would have incentives to do so (Rosen 1986), in practice, it is not clear that they would be able to make these adjustments.[8] According to Gruber (2000), ". . . the problems of preference revelation in this context are daunting; it is difficult in reality to see how firms could appropriately set worker specific compensating differentials" (656).

As is the case with Medicare, however, there is very little research on obesity-related payment differences in a private insurance setting. An important exception is Bhattacharya and Bundorf (2009), who find some evidence that obese workers receive lower pay than nonobese workers primarily at firms that provide health insurance.

In related work, Keeler et al. (1989) and Manning et al. (1991), using data from the RAND Health Insurance Experiment (RAND HIE) and from the National Health Interview Survey (NHIS), report estimates of lifetime medical costs attributable to physical inactivity (rather than obesity): "At a 5 percent rate of discount, the lifetime subsidy from others to those with a sedentary life style is $1,900" (Keeler er al. 1989). Though they label this estimate the "external cost of physical inactivity," like the rest of the literature they focus on physical inactivity-related medical expenditure differences, while ignoring payment differences that occur outside experimental settings in their calculation of the subsidy

2.3   A Model of the Social Costs of Obesity

The timeline in figure 2.1 illustrates the basic setup of the model. Each consumer starts with an initial endowment of weight W_0. This endowment might be seen as reflecting the consumer's genetic propensity to be overweight or obese, and in any case it cannot be chosen by the consumer. In the first stage, consumers decide how much weight to lose, ω. Weight loss (exercising, dieting) gives consumers some disutility but has two associated benefits: (a) it increases productivity, consequently raising consumer income and (b) it improves health (more precisely, it decreases the probability of

---

ces. However, when employers offer multiple health plans, obese workers may tend to select into a different set of plans than their thinner colleagues. In that case, premiums may differ.

8. The literature on medical expenditure-associated obesity costs has a parallel and often intersecting literature on the labor market productivity costs associated with obesity (often these latter costs are called "indirect" costs of obesity). The theory of compensating wage differentials has important implications for whether these labor market costs are external; that is, whether obese individuals pay for lower productivity levels (such as through more sick days) associated with their body weight, or someone else pays. This theory suggests that obese workers will pay for lower productivity through reduced wages. The economics literature on obesity-related wage differences—for example, Register and Williams (1990), Pagan and Davila (1997), and Cawley (2000)—unanimously finds that obese workers earn lower wages than their thinner colleagues, and that these differences are equal to or greater than the wage differences that would arise from measurable productivity differences. Hence, both theory and evidence suggest that these "indirect" costs of obesity are not external.

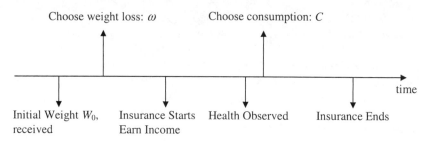

Fig. 2.1   Model timeline

receiving severe and costly health shocks).[9] Since consumers are insured, they are reimbursed for all of these additional medical care expenditures associated with health shocks. In the second stage, nature reveals a health shock with $i = 1 \ldots N$ points of support.[10] Each type of health shock entails additional medical expenses, M_i. Essentially, weight gain shifts the health shock distribution so that expected medical care expenditures increase with weight. Consumers first observe this health shock, and then decide how much to consume. The consumers' problem is to maximize expected utility by jointly choosing weight change (ω) and a consumption plan $\{C_i\}_{i=1}^{N}$ for each of the N possible health states:

$$(1) \qquad \max_{\omega, \{C_i\}_{i=1}^{N}} EU = \sum_{i=1}^{N} \pi_i (W_0 - \omega) U(C_i) - \Phi(\omega),$$

where $U(C_i)$ represents utility from consumption; $\pi_i(W_0 - \omega)$ is the probability of health state i given weight $(W_0 - \omega)$; C_i is the consumption in health state i; and, $\Phi(\omega)$ is the disutility from weight loss.

We divide our analysis now into two cases: (a) health insurance pools risk across people with heterogeneous risk (so that premiums do not change with body weight); and (b) people pay the risk-adjusted premiums for their own body weight. The primary difference between these cases manifests itself in consumer budget constraints.

2.3.1   Risk Pooling

In this case, health risk is pooled across people of different body weight. As long as the pool size is large enough, a single individual's medical expenditures will have a negligible effect on the common premium, $\bar{P}$, charged to everyone in the pool. Hence, from the point of view of each individual, premiums are taken as fixed, and the budget constraint is:

9. The model can also be interpreted as a model of weight gain, with a reinterpretation of the source of disutility from this gain (diminished body image, perhaps). The main point is that a change in weight away from the optimum choice induces disutility.

10. The results of the model are similar when health shocks are permitted to be continuous, but the solution technology is less transparent.

(2) $I(W_0 + \omega) = C_i + \overline{P} \; \forall i.$

In equation (2), $I(W_0 + \omega)$ is the income earned by an individual who weighs $W_0 + \omega$. By allowing income to depend upon weight, we are modeling the effect of health on labor market productivity. We assume that $I'(.) > 0$.

The budget constraint specifies that in each health state i, income equals expenditures on consumption and health insurance premiums. An immediate consequence of equation (2) is that consumption is identical in each health state, which makes sense since consumers are fully insured against medical expenditures.

The consumer's problem is to maximize expected utility, equation (1), subject to the budget constraint, equation (2). We solve the consumer's problem using standard discrete numerical programming methods. In the first step, taking the amount of weight as given, we calculate the optimal demand for consumption in each health state. Inputting the optimal consumption plan in the utility function gives the maximum utility attainable in each health state. In the second stage, we choose weight to maximize expected utility given optimal consumption in each health state.

Plugging the budget constraint into equation (1), we reformulate the consumers' problem in the second stage:

(3) $\max_{\omega} EU = U(I(W_0 - \omega) - \overline{P}) - \Phi(\omega).$

The first-order condition for the consumer's maximization problem is:

(4) $-I'(W_0 - \omega^*)U'(I(W_0 - \omega^*) - \overline{P}) - \Phi'(\omega^*) = 0.$

Here, ω^* is the consumer's optimal weight in the pooling case. The first term in equation (4) is the marginal gain from weight loss; it is entirely due to the marginal increase in income from increased productivity arising from weight loss (scaled by the marginal utility of consumption). In equilibrium, consumers will lose weight until the marginal gain from weight loss equals the marginal disutility from weight loss.

If the insurance market is in competitive equilibrium, then premiums will be actuarially fair. They will equal the expected medical expenses for individuals in the insurance pool:

(5) $\overline{P} = \sum_{i=1}^{N} \pi_i (W_0 - \omega^*) M_i.$

Equation (4) also shows that since consumers are fully insured against medical expenses, the only incentive for weight loss is the increase in income due to weight loss. Thus, when insurance premiums do not depend on weight, consumers do not view the reduction in medical expenditures as an additional benefit of weight loss when making decisions about body weight. Insurance induces a form of moral hazard with respect to weight loss incentives since the benefits of weight loss are not fully internalized by the consumer. As a consequence, weight loss creates a positive externality for everyone else in the insurance pool, since it lowers their health insurance premiums.[11] Because this benefit is not fully captured by the consumer losing the weight, insured people will tend to lose less weight than would be optimal. By contrast, the productivity benefits of weight loss are fully internalized as changes in productivity lead to an increase in consumer income.

2.3.2   Risk-Adjusted Insurance

We now turn to the case where health insurance premiums adjust to reflect the weight choice of consumers. In contrast to the previous case, where the premium is taken as fixed, consumers now face a risk-adjusted schedule of health insurance premiums that depends upon their own body weight. In the context of employer provided insurance, this could be achieved by wage reductions for obese employees, or simply by offering premium rebates to individuals who lose weight. In this case, the budget constraint is given by:

$$(6) \qquad I(W_0 - \omega) = C_i + P(W_0 - \omega) \; \forall i.$$

Here, $P(W_0 - \omega)$ is the health insurance premium for an individual who weighs $W_0 - \omega$. Again, if the insurance market is competitive, premiums will be actuarially fair. Hence, they will be an increasing function of weight, reflecting the increase in expected medical expenses:

$$(7) \qquad P(W_0 - \omega) = \left(\sum_{i=1}^{N} \pi_i (W_0 - \omega) M_i \right).$$

The consumers' problem in this case can be reformulated as:

$$(8) \qquad \max_{\omega} EU = U(I(W_0 - \omega) - P(W_0 - \omega)) - \Phi(\omega).$$

The first-order condition for the consumer's maximization problem is:

$$(9) \quad -[I'(W_0 - \omega^{**}) - P'(W_0 - \omega^{**})]U'(I(W_0 - \omega^{**}) - P(W_0 - \omega^{**})) \\ - \Phi'(\omega^{**}) = 0.$$

Here, ω^{**} is the consumer's optimal weight in the risk-adjusted case. Clearly, equation (9) is necessary for ω^{**} to be individually optimal, but whether it is also socially optimal depends upon what is meant by social optimality. Suppose EU is the expected utility of the representative consumer in the economy, and all individuals start with the same initial weight, W_0. In that (unrealistic) case, ω^{**} can be said to be socially optimal, since the full social costs of body weight decisions are internalized. In the appendix, we consider a more realistic case where W_0 differs across individuals in the

---

11. This argument is developed in more detail in the appendix.

population. We show that, aside from transfers that do not depend upon final weight, $W_0 - \omega^{**}$, equation (9) is a necessary condition for the social optimum.

It is instructive to compare the first order condition in equation (9) with the analogous condition in equation (4), when there was a single risk pool. Both equations have a single term reflecting the marginal costs of weight loss: $\Phi'(.)$. However, equation (9) has two terms, $I'(.)$ and $P'(.)$, reflecting the marginal benefit of weight loss accruing from an increase in productivity and a decrease in the health insurance premium. By contrast, equation (4) has only a single term reflecting the marginal productivity benefit of weight loss: $I'(.)$. Thus, when premiums reflect individual health risk, consumers have two incentives for weight loss—productivity gains and lower health insurance premiums. In this case, there is no moral hazard induced by health insurance and consumer body weight decisions.

2.3.3   Deadweight Loss From the Obesity Externality

In this section, we show that the size of the loss in social welfare from the obesity externality under-pooled premiums depends upon both the fact that expected health expenditures are higher for the obese, and also upon how responsive people would be in their weight loss decisions to a switch from pooled to risk-adjusted premiums. This calculation is important because, while there is a lot of empirical evidence that obese people are more likely to have higher medical care expenditures than nonobese people, there is no empirical evidence on whether pooled insurance causes obesity or weight gain. Whether the rise in obesity prevalence is a public health crisis, or merely a private crisis for many people, depends on the evidence on both quantities.

We start with the expression for expected utility, evaluated at the optimum under risk-adjusted insurance:

$$(10) \qquad EU(\omega^{**}) = U(I(W_0 - \omega^{**}) - P(W_0 - \omega^{**})) - \Phi(\omega^{**}).$$

We have imposed the condition that consumption does not vary with health outcome since consumers are fully insured under both cases.

Next, we consider a first-order Taylor series approximation of equation (10) around ω^*, which is optimal weight loss under pooled insurance:

$$(11) \qquad EU(\omega^{**}) \approx EU(\omega^*) + \left.\frac{\partial EU}{\partial \omega}\right|_{\omega^*} (\omega^{**} - \omega^*).$$

The deadweight loss (DWL) from the obesity externality is the change in expected utility resulting from pooling. Equation (11) suggests an approximation to this quantity:

$$(12) \qquad DWL = EU(\omega^{**}) - EU(\omega^*) \approx \left.\frac{\partial EU}{\partial \omega}\right|_{\omega^*} \Delta\omega.$$

Here, $\Delta\omega \equiv \omega^{**} - \omega^*$ is the difference between optimal weight under risk-adjusted and pooled risk cases. Since weight is socially optimal in the risk-adjusted case, $\Delta\omega$ also reflects the degree to which weight choice differs from socially optimal when pooling pertains.

Using a first-order Taylor series approximation, the dead weight loss (DWL) in expected utility terms due to the obesity externality is:

$$(13) \quad \text{DWL} \approx \{U'(I(W_0 - \omega^*) - P(W_0 - \omega^*))$$

$$\times [-I'(W_0 - \omega^*) + P'(W_0 - \omega^*)] - \Phi'(\omega^*)\}\Delta\omega.$$

Substituting the first order condition in equation (4) in equation (13) yields a simple expression for the dead weight loss from the obesity externality:

$$(14) \qquad\qquad \text{DWL} \approx U'(.)P'(W_0 - \omega^*)\Delta\omega.$$

Equation (14) shows that the deadweight loss is proportional to two crucial factors: the extent to which body weight deviates from the optimal due to pooled health insurance when individuals do not bear the full medical care costs of obesity, $\Delta\omega$, and the responsiveness of medical care expenditures to changes in weight, $P'(W_0 - \omega^*)$. The dead weight loss from the obesity externality is zero if individual weight choice does not respond to subsidies for obesity, or if medical expenditures do not change with body weight.

While several estimates of $P'(W_0 - \omega^*)$ are available from the public health and economics literatures, there is no work that quantifies $\Delta\omega$. To estimate $\Delta\omega$, ideally, we would like to know: (a) body weight under pooled insurance when the consumer is shielded from the medical care costs of obesity and (b) under risk-adjusted premiums when the individual faces the full medical care costs of obesity. To answer whether obesity creates a negative externality and lost social welfare through the health insurance mechanism, we need to know whether risk-rating insurance premiums affects body weight. Unfortunately, there are no real world data that we are aware of that would permit us to ascertain the effect of risk rating on body weight.

Instead, we aim at answering a related question—whether insurance coverage expansions along both extensive and intensive margins cause body weight to change. It is our conjecture that if insurance coverage does not influence body weight choices, it is unlikely that risk rating would influence body weight choices. Conversely, if health insurance expansion (along either intensive or extensive margins) does influence body weight, it is likely, depending on the mechanism by which risk rating is implemented, that risk rating would influence body weight. We start with an empirical consideration of the intensive margin—expansions in health insurance generosity. Next, we examine the effect of insurance status on the extensive margin; that is, whether the uninsured, who face the full medical care costs of obesity, weigh less than the insured.

2.4   The Intensive Margin: Increasing Generosity of Coverage

Using data from the RAND Health Insurance Experiment (HIE), we are able to examine the effect of health insurance on body weight when people are randomly assigned to different levels of insurance coverage (the intensive margin). In the HIE, which was conducted in six areas of the country during the late 1970s and early 1908s, approximately 2,000 nonelderly families were assigned to differing levels of insurance coverage.[12] The purpose of the HIE was to determine the effects of patient cost sharing on medical care utilization and health. The participants were assigned to different fee-for-service plans that varied along two dimensions: the coinsurance rate (the fraction of billed charges paid by patients), and the maximum dollar expenditure (the maximum amount a family would spend on covered expenditures during a twelve-month period). The coverage was comprehensive in the sense that it included nearly all types of medical care. Participants remained enrolled in their assigned plan and were followed for either three (70 percent) or five years.

The plans were characterized by four different coinsurance percentages—0 (often referred to as "free care"), 25 percent, 50 percent, and 95 percent—and three levels of maximum out-of-pocket spending—5 percent, 10 percent, and 15 percent of family income up to a maximum of $1,000. In one plan, the maximum dollar expenditure (MDE)—also known as maximum out-of-pocket expenditures—was set at $150 per individual, and $450 per family (often referred to as the "individual deductible plan").[13] In this plan, the coinsurance rate was 95 percent. In our empirical work, we categorize plans based on their coinsurance rate and control for the MDE.[14] We categorize the individual deductible plan separately due to the more complicated structure of the MDE.

In order to minimize participation bias, the investigators offered a participation incentive. The participation incentive for a given family was defined as "the maximum loss risked by changing to the experimental plan from existing coverage," and was intended to ensure that families were equally likely to participate independent of their prior health insurance status and the plan to which they were assigned.

The study collected data on demographic and socioeconomic character-

12. This description of the HIE is based on information from Newhouse and the Insurance Experiment Group, 1993.

13. The HIE also included an analysis of the effects of enrolling in an HMO on the study outcomes. Because it is difficult to measure the generosity of a health maintenance organization (HMO) relative to a fee-for-service (FFS) plan, we drop these enrollees from the analysis.

14. The coinsurance rate was constant across different types of services with one exception. In one plan, the coinsurance rate was 25 percent for all services except outpatient mental health and dental, which had a 50 percent coinsurance rate. We include this plan in the 25 percent coinsurance rate group.

Table 2.1   Study population characteristics by plan assignment

	All	Free	25%	50%	95%	Individual
N	2,461	824	492	167	442	536
BMI at entry	24.79	24.80	24.70	24.89	24.73	24.89
	(4.53)	(4.45)	(4.81)	(4.02)	(4.41)	(4.63)
BMI at exit	25.31	25.39	25.03	25.43	25.31	25.40
	(4.78)	(4.64)	(4.76)	(4.63)	(5.16)	(4.76)
BMI change	0.52	0.59	0.33	0.55	0.58	0.51
	(2.45)	(2.46)	(2.16)	(2.42)	(2.75)	(2.44)
BMI change per year	0.15	0.16	0.10	0.15	0.17	0.15
	(0.74)	(0.74)	(0.62)	(0.66)	(0.86)	(0.74)
Obese at entry	0.12	0.12	0.12	0.13	0.11	0.13
Obese at exit	0.14	0.14	0.13	0.16	0.12	0.15
Became obese	0.04	0.04	0.03	0.06	0.04	0.05

Note: Used chi-square test for categorical variables and *t*-test of mean relative to free for continuous variables. No differences are statistically significant.

istics of enrollees, as well as health status and medical care utilization, both at baseline and during the experiment. This information included enrollee height and weight, both at baseline and at exit, and we use these measures to calculate body mass index (BMI) at each point in time for each enrollee. We limit our analysis to adults (age $\geq$ 21), and drop observations with missing data for key control variables (age, education, family income, race, gender, marital status, and self-reported health status).

Table 2.1 presents data on body weight by plan type. We find no evidence of statistically significant differences by plan type in body weight, as measured by either BMI or obesity status, either at entry or at exit. In addition, we find no evidence of differences across the plans in changes in these measures. The directions of the differences between plans in changes in BMI, however, are consistent with the hypothesized effect. In other words, enrollees in the free plan experienced the largest change in BMI over the study period (0.59) and the difference in change in BMI between the free plan (0.59) and the 25 percent coinsurance plan (0.33) is statistically significant at $p \leq 0.06$.[15] The results are less consistent for the indicator of becoming obese. In this case, the differences across plans based on their level of cost-sharing are not consistent across plans.

In appendix table 1A.1, we document some differences across the plans in enrollee characteristics despite random assignment. In particular, average family income varies across the plans, and correspondingly, the participation

15. This finding is consistent with results reported by the HIE which find that, while the difference in weight/height^2 at exit between enrollees in the free plan and enrollees in the other plans was not statistically significant, the direction of the effect favored the cost sharing plans (Newhouse and Insurance Experiment Group 1993, 198).

incentive as well. In addition, enrollee assignment to plans is not balanced by site.

In table 2.2, we determine whether the estimates of the effects of plan cost-sharing are influenced by these differences by controlling for them in multivariate models. The multivariate models also allow us to control for the enrollees' maximum dollar expenditure. We estimate models with two different dependent variables: the BMI change per year (to control for differences across enrollees in their enrollment period), and an indicator of whether an individual became obese during the study period. We estimate three versions of each model. In the first, we control for plan characteristics only (the dummy variable indicating the coinsurance rate and the MDE). In the second, we add the controls for individual characteristics presented in appendix table 1A.1. In the third, we control for both individual characteristics and aspects of study design including the site and the enrollee's participation incentive. We estimate the models using least squares. The results from the model of the probability of becoming obese are similar when we estimate a maximum likelihood logit model.

Table 2.2   The effect of insurance coverage on body weight and obesity—Randomized health plan assignment

	BMI change per year			Became obese		
	(1)	(2)	(3)	(1)	(2)	(3)
25% coinsurance rate	–0.109	–0.175	–0.179	–0.005	–0.012	–0.016
	[1.48]	[2.20]*	[2.25]*	[0.23]	[0.57]	[0.71]
50% coinsurance rate	–0.062	–0.139	–0.132	0.025	0.016	0.007
	[0.64]	[1.36]	[1.26]	[0.92]	[0.56]	[0.24]
95% coinsurance rate	–0.032	–0.111	–0.114	0	–0.01	–0.015
	[0.40]	[1.28]	[1.31]	[0.00]	[0.41]	[0.61]
Individual deductible	–0.037	–0.071	–0.079	0.01	0.007	0.004
	[0.72]	[1.33]	[1.45]	[0.68]	[0.46]	[0.25]
Maximum $ expenditure	0	0	0	0	0	0
	[0.70]	[1.65]	[1.93]	[0.35]	[0.18]	[0.73]
Constant	0.161	0.442	0.39	0.051	0.168	0.197
	[6.32]**	[1.92]	[1.66]	[2.88]**	[2.59]**	[2.95]**
Includes individual controls		X	X		X	X
Includes site effects and participation incentive			X			X
Observations	2,441	2,441	2,441	2,441	2,441	2,441
R-squared	0	0.01	0.01	0	0.01	0.01

Note: Absolute value of *t* statistics in brackets. "X" means that the regression includes either individual controls and controls for site effects and the participation incentive (as the case may be).

**Significant at the 5 percent level.

*Significant at the 10 percent level.

The results from the multivariate models are substantively similar to those from the unadjusted comparisons (table 2.2). While people randomly assigned to plans with cost-sharing experienced a smaller annual change in BMI during the experiment relative to those assigned to the free plan, the effect is statistically significant only in the case of the plan with the 25 percent coinsurance rate. And in this case, the effect is quite small. A 0.175 reduction in BMI represents less than 1 percent of BMI at entry among this group. Correspondingly, we do not find consistent evidence of differences by plan type in the probability of becoming obese during the study period. The direction of the effect varies by plan and none of the estimates are statistically significant.

2.5   The Extensive Margin: Insured vs. Uninsured

While the RAND data allow us to examine the responsiveness of body weight to a change in the generosity of coverage, the fact that everyone in the experiment had health insurance coverage leaves open the possibility of an effect along the extensive margin. In other words, the responsiveness of body weight to any insurance relative to none may be greater than the responsiveness to changes in the generosity of that coverage.

2.5.1   Methods

We use instrumental variables (IV) regressions to estimate the causal effects of private and public insurance coverage on body weight as measured by BMI and obesity status. If our instruments are valid, IV methods purge the estimates of confounding due to observable and unobservable characteristics. We first estimate a linear instrumental variables model estimated via two stage least squares. These models are widely used and a powerful tools in such contexts. However, for nonlinear and limited dependent variable models in general, the linear IV model may either be inappropriate or not work well in practice. Specifically, in our case, although the outcomes of interest are either binary or linear, the endogenous regressors (dummy variables for private and public insurance) are limited dependent variables. A linear IV model would treat the endogenous regressors as if they were linear and unrelated, when, in fact, the insurance choices are mutually exclusive and exhaustive.

To address the discrete nature of our data, we next estimate a nonlinear instrumental variables model using latent factors to account for selection on unobservables. Our model respects the multinomial nature of the endogenous regressors as well as the binary or linear nature of the outcome. Specifically, we assume that the endogenous regressors have a multinomial logit form, while the outcome equations have logit and normal (linear) forms respectively. Then, latent factors are incorporated into the equations to allow for unobserved influences on insurance choice to affect outcomes, and their joint distribution specified (Deb and Trivedi 1997).

The main computational problem is that the joint distribution, which involves a multidimensional integral, does not have a closed form solution. This difficulty can be addressed using simulation-based estimation. Using normally distributed random draws for the latent variables, a simulated likelihood function for the data is defined and its parameters estimated using a Maximum Simulated Likelihood Estimator. Because of the complexity of our model and the large sample size, standard simulation methods are quite slow. Therefore, we adapt an acceleration technique that uses quasi-random draws based on Halton sequences. The formulation, estimation methods, and exposition borrows heavily from Deb and Trivedi (2006).

The model is represented by two sets of equations. In the first set of equations, the insurance choices (private, public, or uninsured) are represented by a multinomial logit model. The second equation, representing the outcome, is modeled as an ordinary least squares (OLS) (BMI as outcome) or logit (obese status as outcome) model. In this model, the choice of insurance and outcome are linked because insurance choices are regressors in the outcome module and because there are common unobservable (latent) factors.

Let Pvt and Pub be binary variables representing private and public insurance coverage. For BMI, we specify the outcome equation as follows:

$$(15) \qquad \text{BMI} = x\beta + \gamma_1\text{private} + \gamma_2\text{Public} + \lambda_1 l_{\text{pvt}} + \lambda_2 l_{\text{pub}} + \varepsilon,$$

where x is a set of exogenous covariates and β, γ_1, and γ_2 are parameters associated with the exogenous covariates and the endogenous insurance variables. The error term is partitioned into ε, an independently distributed random error, and latent factors l_{pvt} and l_{pub} which denote unobserved characteristics common to an individual's choice of insurance and the outcome of that individual. The λ_1 and λ_2 are factor loadings or parameters associated with the latent factors that capture the degree of correlation between unobserved determinants of insurance choice and outcomes. If ε is normally distributed, then

$$(16) \quad \Pr(\text{BMI} = \text{BMI}^* \mid x, \text{Pvt}, \text{Pub}, l_{\text{pvt}}, l_{\text{pub}}) =$$

$$\phi(BMI^* - (x\beta + \gamma_1\text{Pvt} + \gamma_2\text{Pub} + \lambda_1 l_{\text{pvt}} + \lambda_2 l_{\text{pub}})).$$

We estimate a separate version of this model with an indicator of obesity, which we define as BMI greater than 30, as the outcome variable. In this second version of the model, we assume a logit functional form.

$$(16') \quad \Pr(\text{obese} = 1 \mid x, z, \text{Pvt}, \text{Pub}, l_{\text{pvt}}, l_{\text{pub}}) =$$

$$(1 + \exp(x\beta + \gamma_1\text{Pvt} + \gamma_2\text{Pub} + \lambda_1 l_{\text{pvt}} + \lambda_2 l_{\text{pub}}))^{-1}$$

Following the multinomial logit framework (McFadden 1980, S15), we formulate the probability of choosing in private insurance, public insurance or remaining uninsured as:

$$\Pr(\text{Pvt} = 1 \mid z, I_{\text{pvt}}, I_{\text{public}}) = \frac{\exp(z\alpha_{\text{pvt}} + \delta_1 l_{\text{pvt}})}{1 + \exp(z\alpha_{\text{pvt}} + \delta_1 l_{\text{pvt}}) + \exp(z\alpha_{\text{pub}} + \delta_1 l_{\text{pub}})}$$

$$(17) \quad \Pr(\text{Pub} = 1 \mid z, I_{\text{pvt}}, I_{\text{public}}) = \frac{\exp(z\alpha_{\text{pub}} + \delta_1 l_{\text{pub}})}{1 + \exp(z\alpha_{\text{pvt}} + \delta_1 l_{\text{pvt}}) + \exp(z\alpha_{\text{pub}} + \delta_1 l_{\text{pub}})}$$

$$\Pr(\text{Pvt} = 0, \text{Pub} = 0 \mid z, I_{\text{pvt}}, I_{\text{public}}) = 1 - \Pr(\text{private} = 1) - \Pr(\text{public} = 1),$$

where z denotes exogenous covariates (instrumental variables) that enter only the insurance choice model, but not the main outcome model. We denote covariates in this site-choice module by z, and covariates in the outcome equation by x to highlight the fact that they contain the instrumental variables in the empirical analysis.

Because the latent factors l_{pvt} and l_{pub} enter both choice of insurance equation (17), and outcome (16 and 16′) equations, they capture the unobserved factors that induce self-selection into insurance and are also correlated with unobservable factors related to outcomes. Under these assumptions, the joint distribution of selection and outcome variables, conditional on the common latent factors, is simply the product of the functions described in equations (16), (16′), and (17).

The problem in estimation arises because the common latent factors l_{pvt} and l_{pub} are unknown. We assume that these latent factors are distributed bivariate normal with mean zero, variance one, and arbitrary covariance. Given this assumption, the latent factors can be integrated out of the joint density. For example, the joint density of observing outcome obese = 1 and Pvt = 1 is:

$$\Pr(\text{obese} = 1, Pvt = 1 \mid x, z) =$$

$$(18) \qquad \iint_{\Re^2} \frac{\exp(z\alpha_{\text{pvt}} + \delta_1 l_{\text{pvt}})}{1 + \exp(z\alpha_{\text{pvt}} + \delta_1 l_{\text{pvt}}) + \exp(z\alpha_{\text{pub}} + \delta_1 l_{\text{pub}})}$$

$$\times \frac{1}{(1 + \exp(x\beta + \gamma_1 Pvt + \gamma_2 \text{Pub} + \lambda_1 l_{\text{pvt}} + \lambda_2 l_{\text{pub}}))}$$

$$\times \phi(I_{\text{pub}}, I_{\text{pvt}}) dI_{\text{pvt}} dI_{\text{pub}},$$

where $\phi(I_{\text{pub}}, I_{\text{pvt}})$ is the bivariate normal partial density function.

Cast in this form, the unknown parameters of the model may be estimated by maximum likelihood estimators (MLE). The main computational problem is that the double integral in equation (18) does not have, in general, a closed form solution. But this difficulty can be addressed using simulation-based estimation (Gouriéroux and Monfort 1996) to numerically integrate equation (18). Because of the complexity of our model, standard simulation methods are quite slow. Therefore, we adapt an acceleration technique that uses quasi-random draws based on Halton sequences (Bhat 2001; Train 2002). We maximize the simulated likelihood using a quasi-Newton algorithm.

2.5.2   Data and Instruments

Data

The primary data source for our analysis is the National Longitudinal Survey of Youth (NLSY). The NLSY includes a nationally representative sample of 12,686 people aged fourteen to twenty-two years in 1979, who were surveyed annually until 1994, and biennially through 2004. Our study uses NLSY data from 1989 to 2004. We exclude the years prior to 1989, as well as 1991, because the survey did not collect information on health insurance status in those years. We further restrict the sample, excluding pregnant women. After these restrictions, 79,876 person-year observations (40,223 male and 39,653 female) were eligible to be included in the study sample.

Instruments

We use the two sets of instruments for insurance choice. The first set of instruments captures the distribution of firm size in every state and year. These data are obtained from the Statistics of U.S. Businesses (SUSB) available online at http://www.sba.gov/advo/research/data.html. We use these data to construct two instruments at the state-year level: (a) percentage of workers employed in firms with 100 to 499 employees, (b) percentage of workers employed in firms with 500 or more employees. These instruments would be valid under two conditions. First, they should be strong predictors of private insurance coverage. Second, they should affect weight choice only through their effect on insurance choice. In the next section, we show that the instruments are strong predictors of private insurance as large firms are more likely to cover employees. The second assumption cannot be directly tested; however, it seems unlikely that changes in firm size distribution within a state (our models have state fixed effects) would be related to weight choices, except through insurance coverage. However, one important caveat is that it is possible that obese workers might prefer to live in states with larger firms to enjoy the benefits of pooled health insurance at these firms. To the extent that this is true, our IV estimates will overestimate the effects of insurance on body weight and obesity.

The second instrument captures generosity of Medicaid coverage. There has been a significant expansion of Medicaid eligibility during this period, and there is significant variation across states in the pace at which these expansions have occurred. Prior research documents a strong association between Medicaid expansions and public insurance coverage. We use data from several years of the Current Population Survey (CPS) to construct this instrument. First, we regress a binary variable for Medicaid coverage on detailed information on demographics, family composition, income, and state × time fixed effects. The state × time fixed effects measure the generosity of Medicaid coverage in each state and year after controlling for other important determinants of Medicaid coverage. We posit that these state × time fixed effects essentially capture differences in Medicaid eligibility rules or enforcement of these rules. We use these fixed effects to create a predicted probability of Medicaid coverage for a standardized population and use these predicted probabilities as an instrument for public insurance coverage. Again, our instrument is valid if variation in our measure of Medicaid eligibility within a state is not correlated with unobserved determinants of obesity within a state. For example, our IV estimates would be biased upwards if deteriorating economic conditions increased obesity rates and also prompted states to expand Medicaid eligibility.

Finally, we also explored using state marginal income tax rates as an instrument for insurance coverage. State marginal income taxes are an attractive candidate for an instrumental variable because employer-sponsored health insurance premiums are exempt from state and federal payroll taxes. Therefore, the subsidy for employer-sponsored insurance is greater in states with higher marginal income taxes. If the demand for insurance slopes downward, then states with higher marginal income tax rates should have a higher proportion of people with employer-provided insurance. Unfortunately, this did not hold true in our sample. We found no significant relationship between state marginal income tax rates and insurance coverage.

Other Explanatory Variables

We include several other explanatory variables including race, age, gender, income, Armed Forces Qualifying Test (AFQT) scores and year fixed effects. All these variables are plausibly exogenous and important predictors of weight and insurance choices. In addition, in our preferred specifications we include state fixed effects to control for time invariant differences across states. This is important as our instruments are measured at the state level.

2.5.3   Results

Table 2.3 presents the results from the second stage of the two-stage least squares (2SLS) regressions. Appendix table 2A.2 presents the first stage results. The aim of these regressions is to estimate the causal effect of public and private insurance on BMI and obesity. The first model presents results from the regression model without state fixed effects. The results show that both private and public insurance have no statistically significant effect on BMI. The point estimates for both public and private insurance are positive, but are estimated imprecisely. This is despite the strong predictive power of the instruments in the first stage [F-stat = 139].

The next model includes state fixed effects to capture time invariant

Table 2.3 Effect of public and private insurance on BMI and obesity: 2SLS results

	BMI-no state FE		BMI-state FE		Obese-no state FE		Obese-state FE	
	Coefficient	Std. error	Coefficient	Std. error	Coefficient	Std. error	Coefficient	Std. error
Public ins.	0.7002	1.2298	-3.8172	10.7426	-0.0840	0.0931	-0.1239	0.7831
Private ins.	0.9065	0.7741	-7.7786	4.8906	0.0168	0.0570	-0.4573	0.3595
Year—1990	0.2208	0.0765	0.2926	0.1095	0.0119	0.0056	0.0151	0.0077
Year—1992	0.5856	0.0889	0.5303	0.1086	0.0330	0.0066	0.0300	0.0077
Year—1993	0.7054	0.1047	0.4364	0.3817	0.0415	0.0078	0.0188	0.0272
Year—1994	0.7935	0.1091	0.6006	0.3900	0.0485	0.0082	0.0298	0.0279
Year—1996	0.9836	0.1129	0.8122	0.2803	0.0525	0.0085	0.0378	0.0200
Year—1998	1.2102	0.1216	1.2379	0.2245	0.0708	0.0092	0.0687	0.0162
Year—2000	1.6074	0.1339	1.7121	0.1918	0.0999	0.0102	0.1041	0.0139
Year—2002	1.7830	0.1506	1.6174	0.2067	0.1029	0.0114	0.0919	0.0148
Year—2004	1.8644	0.1740	1.5763	0.2957	0.1091	0.0132	0.0889	0.0212
Age	0.3858	0.0652	0.4975	0.1064	0.0230	0.0049	0.0284	0.0077
Age square	-0.0039	0.0009	-0.0051	0.0013	-0.0002	0.0001	-0.0003	0.0001
Nonwhite	1.3416	0.0657	1.0474	0.4127	0.0789	0.0050	0.0556	0.0295
Male	0.8224	0.0857	0.4774	0.6630	-0.0151	0.0065	-0.0214	0.0484
Educ 0 to 8 yrs.	1.1532	0.2615	-1.1703	1.2250	0.0732	0.0188	-0.0633	0.0890
Educ 8 to 12 yrs.	0.4730	0.0959	-0.4040	0.5038	0.0322	0.0072	-0.0222	0.0363
Income ($000s)	-0.0007	0.0002	0.0013	0.0012	-0.0001	0.0000	0.0001	0.0001
AFQT quartile 1	1.0038	0.2004	-0.8140	1.1223	0.0666	0.0149	-0.0549	0.0801
AFQT quartile 2	0.6752	0.1019	-0.1584	0.4249	0.0397	0.0075	-0.0106	0.0309
AFQT quartile 3	0.3557	0.0658	0.0390	0.1703	0.0215	0.0050	0.0023	0.0124
Constant	14.8588	1.2164	20.5830	3.4176	-0.4152	0.0910	-0.0761	0.2477
Number of observations: 70,168								

differences across states. The point estimates from this model are implausibly large and very imprecisely estimated. The results indicate that public and private insurance coverage reduce BMI by 3.8 and 7.7 points respectively. However, despite these large point estimates, these estimates are statistically insignificant. These are classical symptoms of the weak instruments problem in a two stage least squares estimate (Staiger and Stock 1997). In this specification the instruments are weak predictors of insurance coverage [F-stat 2.9].

The last models present results from models with obese status as the outcome variable. The results are consistent with the BMI model. Public and private insurance coverage have no statistically significant effect on obesity, and the point estimates from the specification with state fixed effects are implausibly large.

Table 2.4 and appendix table 2A.3 present the results from the MLE models. These models are our preferred specification. The MLE models have several advantages in this context. First, they respect the categorical nature of the endogenous variable. Second, well-specified MLE models are more efficient than 2SLS models. Third, MLE models are less affected by weak instruments in terms of both bias and confidence intervals of the regression coefficient (Staiger and Stock 1997; Lakdawalla, Sood, and Goldman 2006).

The results from the first model show that both public and private insurance have a statistically significantly effect on BMI. The results indicate that private insurance increases BMI by 1.3 points, and public insurance increases BMI by 2.1 points. Both these effects are quite large and are precisely estimated. For example, the effects of private insurance on BMI are similar to moving from the highest AFQT quartile to the lowest AFQT quartiles or moving from less than eight years of education to more that twelve years of education. The second model includes state fixed effects. The results are virtually unchanged. The last two models use obesity as an outcome model. The results from these regressions are consistent with the BMI models—both public and private insurance increase obesity.

2.6   Conclusion

Our results indicate that extending insurance coverage to the uninsured will increase body weight. We find that both public and private insurance increase body weight, with somewhat larger effects for public insurance coverage. The effect sizes we measure of the effect of both public and private insurance coverage on body weight are large and precisely estimated. By contrast, we find no evidence that increasing the generosity of insurance coverage for the already insured leads to increases in body weight.

There are several reasons why the extensive margin of insurance matters and the intensive margin is less effective in influencing body weight choices.

Table 2.4   Effect of public and private insurance on BMI and obesity: MLE results

	BMI-no state FE		BMI-state FE		Obese-no state FE		Obese-state FE	
	Coefficient	Std. error	Coefficient	Std. error	Coefficient	Std. error	Coefficient	Std. error
Private ins.	1.269	0.093	1.309	0.094	0.847	0.245	0.987	0.311
Public ins.	2.092	0.151	2.190	0.154	0.667	0.205	0.873	0.264
Year—1990	0.214	0.076	0.217	0.076	0.125	0.053	0.130	0.056
Year—1992	0.586	0.089	0.583	0.089	0.318	0.060	0.332	0.066
Year—1993	0.667	0.092	0.655	0.092	0.366	0.064	0.376	0.072
Year—1994	0.751	0.098	0.744	0.098	0.406	0.067	0.420	0.076
Year—1996	0.957	0.108	0.956	0.108	0.443	0.075	0.462	0.086
Year—1998	1.187	0.120	1.187	0.120	0.544	0.082	0.565	0.095
Year—2000	1.593	0.133	1.594	0.133	0.718	0.095	0.752	0.116
Year—2002	1.777	0.149	1.783	0.149	0.762	0.107	0.803	0.132
Year—2004	1.849	0.170	1.851	0.170	0.806	0.118	0.848	0.144
Age	0.378	0.064	0.376	0.064	0.190	0.036	0.196	0.039
Age square	-0.004	0.001	-0.004	0.001	-0.002	0.000	-0.002	0.001
Nonwhite	1.308	0.050	1.325	0.052	0.482	0.044	0.531	0.065
Male	0.906	0.041	0.918	0.041	0.028	0.038	0.048	0.044
Educ 0 to 8 yrs.	1.199	0.156	1.166	0.155	0.598	0.106	0.638	0.131
Educ 8 to 12 yrs.	0.470	0.049	0.505	0.049	0.244	0.040	0.286	0.053
Income ($000s)	-0.001	0.000	-0.001	0.000	-0.004	0.002	-0.004	0.002
AFQT quartile 1	0.965	0.077	0.877	0.078	0.476	0.067	0.454	0.079
AFQT quartile 2	0.694	0.065	0.650	0.066	0.327	0.047	0.316	0.054
AFQT quartile 3	0.366	0.057	0.345	0.058	0.180	0.036	0.170	0.039
Constant	14.671	1.089	14.494	1.093	-7.108	0.830	-7.508	1.052
Number of observations: 70,168								

First, changes in the intensive margin of insurance likely have a smaller effect on changes in expected out-of-pocket medical expenditures due to obesity. This means that changes in the intensive margin of insurance produce weaker financial incentives to change body weight. Second, changes in the extensive margin of insurance might be more salient to consumers; consequently, such changes might affect behavior more than changes in insurance benefits. Finally, risk-averse consumers might respond more to changes in the likelihood of large losses. Changes in the intensive margin of insurance do affect the probability of catastrophic out-of-pocket expenditures, thus they might not influence body weight choices by much. One interpretation of our findings is that large changes in financial incentives (such as those encountered along the extensive margin) affect body weight outcomes, while smaller changes in financial incentives (such as those encountered along the intensive margin) do not.

While our results indicate that insurance increases obesity, other authors have come to a different conclusion using a similar approach (Rashad and Markowitz 2010). We demonstrate that the difference is likely due to the method of estimation. When we estimate the model using two-stage least squares, which does not account for the discrete nature of the endogenous indicator of health insurance, our estimates are similar in the sense that we find little evidence that body weight is elastic with respect to insurance coverage. Adopting an alternative maximum likelihood method of estimation, which handles explicitly the discrete endogenous variable and is more robust to weak instruments problem, we reach a different conclusion. Body weight is responsive to health insurance coverage in these models. The estimate is both relatively large in magnitude and precise, and does not vary across the different model specifications.

Our estimates suggest that, by insulating people from the costs of obesity-related medical care expenditures, insurance coverage expansions create moral hazard in behaviors related to body weight. These effects are larger in public insurance programs where premiums are not risk-adjusted, and smaller in private insurance markets where the obese might pay for incremental medical care costs in the form of lower wages (Bhattacharya and Bundorf 2009). By contrast, our estimates also suggest that making insurance more generous has no effect on body weight. Taken together, these findings indicate that providing incentives for healthy behaviors such as risk-rating insurance premiums in private may be effective in reducing body weight in the population (though Bhattacharya and Bundorf [2009] find that employer provided health insurance is already implicitly risk-rated for obesity). Policies that impose costs on increases in body weight among those with public coverage may also reduce body weight, though in that case equity concerns are certain to be important in the policy discussion. The policy challenge will be to design mechanisms that impose costs along the extensive margin, which given our results are likely to be effective, but not along the intensive margin, which are not.

Appendix
A Characterization of the Social Optimum

In this section, we derive necessary conditions characterizing the socially optimal level of weight loss for a society of $j = 1 \ldots J$ individuals. Each has the following expected utility, taken from equation (1):

$$(A.1) \qquad EU_j = \sum_{i=1}^{N} \pi_i (W_{0j} - \omega_j) U(C_{ij}) - \Phi(\omega_j).$$

We define total social welfare, $\mho$, as the sum of expected utilities over all individuals in the society:

$$(A.2) \qquad \mho = \sum_{j=1}^{J} \gamma_j EU_j.$$

In equation (A.2), γ_j represents the Pareto weight that individual J has in the social welfare function. In the social budget constraint, total income equals total expenditures on consumption plus total medical expenditures over all individuals. Both income and the distribution of medical expenditures depend upon body weight decisions:

$$(A.3) \qquad \sum_{j=1}^{J} \left\{ I(W_{0j} - \omega_j) - \sum_{i=1}^{N} \pi_i (W_{0j} - \omega_j)(M_i + C_{ij}) \right\} = 0.$$

Equation (A.3) builds in our assumption that expectations about the distribution of medical expenditures in the population correspond to the observed distribution of expenditures.

The social problem is to pick consumption and body weight for all individuals in every state of the world—$\{C_{ij}, \omega_j\}$ $\forall i, j$—to maximize $\mho$ subject to the social budget constraint. To this end, we construct the following Lagrangian function, where λ is the multiplier associated with the social budget constraint, (A-3):

$$(A.4) \qquad L = \sum_{j=1}^{J} \sum_{i=1}^{N} \gamma_j \pi_i (W_{0j} - \omega_j) U(C_{ij}) - \gamma_j \Phi(\omega_j)$$
$$- \lambda \sum_{j=1}^{J} \left\{ I(W_{0j} - \omega_j) - \sum_{i=1}^{N} \pi_i (W_{0j} - \omega_j)(M_i + C_{ij}) \right\}.$$

There are two sets of first order conditions:

(A.5) $\qquad \dfrac{\partial L}{\partial C_{ij}} = \gamma_j U'(C_{ij}) + \lambda = 0 \; \forall i, j,$ and

(A.6) $\qquad \dfrac{\partial L}{\partial \omega_j} = -\displaystyle\sum_{i=1}^{N} \pi_i'(W_{0j} - \omega_j)\gamma_j U(C_{ij}) - \gamma_j \Phi'(\omega_j)$

$$+ \lambda\!\left(I'(W_{0j} - \omega_j) + \sum_{i=1}^{N} \pi_i'(W_{0j} - \omega_j)(M_i + C_{ij}) \right) = 0 \; \forall j.$$

An immediate implication of equation (A.5) is that at the social optimum, each individual j in the society must set his (or her) consumption level to the same value, say C_j^*, across all the N different health states:

(A.7) $\qquad\qquad\qquad\qquad C_{ij} = C_j^* \; \forall i, j.$

Applying equation (A.7) to equation (A.6) yields the following:

(A.8) $\quad -(\gamma_j U(C_j^*) + \lambda C_j^*)\displaystyle\sum_{i=1}^{N} \pi_i'(W_{0j} - \omega_j) - \gamma_j \Phi'(\omega_j)$

$$+ \lambda\!\left(I'(W_{0j} - \omega_j) + \sum_{i=1}^{N} M_i \pi_i'(W_{0j} - \omega_j) \right) = 0 \; \forall j.$$

By definition, $\sum_{i=1}^{N} \pi_i(W_{0j} - \omega_j) = 1$, so we have $\sum_{i=1}^{N} \pi_i'(W_{0j} - \omega_j) = 0$. Furthermore, differentiating equation (7), which defines the risk-adjusted premium, $P(W_{0j} - \omega_j)$, yields the fact that:

(A.9) $\qquad\qquad P'(W_{0j} - \omega_j) = -\displaystyle\sum_{i=1}^{N} \pi_i'(W_{0j} - \omega_j)M_i \; \forall j.$

These equations and equation (A-5) permit a further simplification of equation (A-8):

(A.10) $\quad -\Phi'(\omega_j) - U'(C_j^*)(I'(W_{0j} - \omega_j) - P'(W_{0j} - \omega_j)) = 0 \; \forall j.$

Hence, the social optimum requires each individual to equate the marginal (utility) costs of weight loss with the marginal (utility) benefits from the weight loss—an increase in income and a reduction in expected medical costs.

One feasible allocation that meets equation (A.10) would set consumption for each individual equal to income, less the risk-adjusted premium given weight:

(A.11) $\qquad\qquad C_j^* = I(W_{0j} - \omega_j) - P(W_{0j} - \omega_j) \; \forall j.$

It is easy to show that this allocation would be optimal for some distribution of initial body weight, $\{W_{0j}\}$, and some set of Pareto weights, $\{\gamma_j\}$. In this allocation, there are no transfers between individuals with different initial body weights. Other optimal and feasible allocations are possible, but these would involve fixed transfers between individuals that do not

Table 2A.1   RAND enrollees demographic and health status covariates are balanced at start of experiment

	All	Free	25%	50%	95%	Individual
N	2,461	824	492	167	442	536
Age (years)	37.36	37.85	36.91	38.35	37.35	36.70
	(11.18)	(11.51)	(10.69)	(11.16)	(11.14)	(11.14)
Education (years of school completed)	12.34	12.15	12.48	12.47	12.41	12.39
	(3.03)	(3.20)	(2.91)	(3.07)	(2.87)	(3.00)
Family income (year preceding enrollment)	11,524	11,135	11,879*	12,993**	11,654	11,229
	(5,772)	(5,734)	(5,785)	(5,825)	(5,791)	(5,710)
Participation incentive offered at enrollment	461.17	175.32	702.81**	811.14**	733.22**	345.40
	(370)	(238)	(281)	(324)	(348)	(211)
Race—white	0.88	0.87	0.87	0.92	0.86	0.88
Race—black	0.11	0.12	0.11	0.07	0.13	0.11
Race—other	0.01	0.01	0.02	0.01	0.01	0.01
Married	0.80	0.81	0.81	0.83	0.77	0.79
Female	0.54	0.54	0.53	0.56	0.57	0.53
Self reported health status—excellent	0.45	0.45	0.45	0.49	0.46	0.45
Self reported health status—good	0.43	0.42	0.43	0.40	0.43	0.45
Self reported health status—fair	0.09	0.10	0.10	0.10	0.09	0.07
Self reported health status—poor	0.02	0.03	0.01	0.02	0.02	0.02
Self reported health status—missing	0.01	0.01	0.01	—	0.01	0.00

Note: Dashed cell means that there are no observations in that category (50 percent copayment) who had a missing value for self-reported health status.

**Significant at the 5 percent level.

*Significant at the 10 percent level.

Table 2A.2 First stage results for 2SLS models

	Public-no state FE		Public-state FE		Private-no state FE		Private-state FE	
	Coefficient	Std. error	Coefficient	Std. error	Coefficient	Std. error	Coefficient	Std. error
% in firms 0 to 499	0.5466	0.0981	0.2126	0.2822	2.3617	0.1736	0.8901	0.4992
% in firms 500+	-0.0248	0.0315	0.1117	0.1035	0.7434	0.0558	0.3727	0.1831
Pr. Medicaid enrollment	0.2074	0.0125	0.0650	0.0233	-0.2722	0.0221	-0.1143	0.0412
Year—1990	0.0030	0.0038	0.0034	0.0038	0.0057	0.0067	0.0058	0.0066
Year—1992	-0.0127	0.0044	-0.0037	0.0046	0.0080	0.0077	-0.0008	0.0082
Year—1993	0.0240	0.0045	0.0345	0.0048	-0.0395	0.0079	-0.0454	0.0085
Year—1994	0.0190	0.0048	0.0334	0.0054	-0.0276	0.0084	-0.0358	0.0095
Year—1996	-0.0027	0.0053	0.0168	0.0063	-0.0108	0.0094	-0.0242	0.0111
Year—1998	-0.0045	0.0057	0.0081	0.0066	-0.0024	0.0100	-0.0045	0.0116
Year—2000	-0.0117	0.0061	-0.0019	0.0075	-0.0020	0.0109	0.0026	0.0133
Year—2002	-0.0144	0.0067	-0.0004	0.0079	-0.0252	0.0118	-0.0259	0.0139
Year—2004	-0.0124	0.0075	0.0083	0.0091	-0.0401	0.0133	-0.0431	0.0161
Age	0.0024	0.0028	0.0026	0.0028	0.0115	0.0050	0.0115	0.0050
Age square	0.0000	0.0000	0.0000	0.0000	-0.0001	0.0001	-0.0001	0.0001
Nonwhite	0.0384	0.0021	0.0452	0.0022	-0.0489	0.0037	-0.0604	0.0038
Male	-0.0581	0.0018	-0.0591	0.0018	-0.0099	0.0031	-0.0093	0.0031
Educ 0 to 8 yrs.	0.0444	0.0058	0.0486	0.0058	-0.2875	0.0103	-0.2891	0.0103
Educ 8 to 12 yrs.	0.0314	0.0021	0.0330	0.0021	-0.1177	0.0037	-0.1217	0.0037
Income ($000s)	0.0000	0.0000	0.0000	0.0000	0.0000	0.0000	0.0000	0.0000
AFQT quartile 1	0.0991	0.0032	0.1016	0.0032	-0.2578	0.0057	-0.2532	0.0057
AFQT quartile 2	0.0166	0.0028	0.0166	0.0028	-0.1049	0.0049	-0.1000	0.0050
AFQT quartile 3	0.0039	0.0026	0.0040	0.0026	-0.0393	0.0046	-0.0363	0.0046
Constant	-0.2159	0.0550	-0.2087	0.0954	0.1500	0.0973	0.4747	0.1688
Number of observations: 70,168								
F-statistic	139.14		2.91		120.51		4.52	

Table 2A.3   First stage results for MLE models

	Public-no state FE		Public-state FE		Private-no state FE		Private-state FE	
	Coefficient	Std. error	Coefficient	Std. error	Coefficient	Std. error	Coefficient	Std. error
% in firms 0 to 499	30.8556	2.4072	4.3208	7.6902	19.1894	1.3751	7.3312	3.9023
% in firms 500+	4.3796	0.7933	1.6022	2.7916	5.2915	0.3981	2.9991	1.4132
Pr. Medicaid enrollment	4.4842	0.3433	2.6147	0.6278	-0.9681	0.1700	-0.5031	0.3142
Year—1990	0.3162	0.1116	0.3262	0.1127	0.0007	0.0489	0.0050	0.0492
Year—1992	-0.0120	0.1262	0.1355	0.1351	-0.1021	0.0582	-0.1165	0.0621
Year—1993	0.4193	0.1160	0.6246	0.1271	-0.2763	0.0581	-0.2648	0.0642
Year—1994	0.3185	0.1244	0.6093	0.1416	-0.2482	0.0632	-0.2332	0.0726
Year—1996	-0.0108	0.1413	0.3621	0.1672	-0.3029	0.0729	-0.3035	0.0868
Year—1998	0.0382	0.1503	0.3687	0.1769	-0.3046	0.0795	-0.2501	0.0929
Year—2000	-0.0818	0.1633	0.2923	0.2035	-0.4447	0.0911	-0.3552	0.1108
Year—2002	-0.2835	0.1747	0.1370	0.2090	-0.7410	0.1012	-0.6743	0.1184
Year—2004	-0.3777	0.1922	0.2090	0.2387	-0.9700	0.1175	-0.8876	0.1392
Age	0.0110	0.0744	0.0206	0.0756	0.0283	0.0390	0.0292	0.0393
Age square	0.0005	0.0010	0.0003	0.0011	-0.0001	0.0006	-0.0001	0.0006
Nonwhite	0.6359	0.0498	0.7414	0.0523	-0.1566	0.0274	-0.2274	0.0287
Male	-1.2173	0.0510	-1.2798	0.0518	-0.8610	0.0600	-0.8638	0.0606
Educ 0 to 8 yrs	-0.4444	0.1125	-0.3718	0.1149	-1.3949	0.0734	-1.4182	0.0736
Educ 8 to 12 yrs	0.0239	0.0614	0.0572	0.0630	-0.6009	0.0330	-0.6471	0.0330
Income ($000s)	-0.0001	0.0000	-0.0001	0.0000	0.0001	0.0000	0.0001	0.0000
AFQT quartile 1	1.2465	0.1160	1.3352	0.1183	-1.0656	0.0556	-1.0274	0.0574
AFQT quartile 2	0.8320	0.1115	0.8737	0.1136	-0.6747	0.0432	-0.6411	0.0441
AFQT quartile 3	0.6693	0.1125	0.6819	0.1140	-0.3459	0.0416	-0.3292	0.0420
Constant	-11.4118	1.4551	-6.5811	2.5957	-3.4054	0.7344	-0.8305	1.3061
Number of observations: 70,168								

depend upon final body weight (though they might depend upon initial body weight). Optimal transfers would clearly vary with $\{\gamma_j\}$, though all optimal allocations would need to obey condition (A.10).

References

Anderson, P. M., K. F. Butcher, and P. B. Levine. 2003. Maternal employment and overweight children. *Journal of Health Economics* 22 (3): 477–504.

Bertakis, K. D., and R. Azari. 2005. Obesity and the use of health care services. *Obesity Research* 13 (2): 372–9.

Bhat, C. R. 2001. Quasi-random maximum simulated likelihood estimation of the mixed multinomial logit model. *Transportation Research: Part B* 35:677-93.

Bhattacharya, J., and K. Bundorf. 2009. The incidence of the healthcare costs of obesity. *Journal of Health Economics* 28 (3): 649–58.

Bhattacharya, J., and D. Lakdawalla. 2006. Does medicare benefit the poor? *Journal of Public Economics* 90 (1-2): 277–92.

Bhattacharya, J., and N. Sood. 2007. Health insurance and the obesity externality. *Advances in Health Services Research* 17:279–318.

Brownell, K., and K. B. Horgen. 2004. *Food fight: The inside story of the food industry, America's obesity crisis, and what we can do about it.* New York: McGraw-Hill.

Bungam, T., M. Satterwhite, A. W. Jackson, and J. R. Morrow. 2003. The relationship of body mass index, medical costs, and job absenteeism. *American Journal of Health Behavior* 27 (4): 456–62.

Burton, W. N., C. Y. Chen, A. B. Schultz, and D. W. Edington. 1998. The economic costs associated with body mass index in a workplace. *Journal of Occupational and Environmental Medicine* 40 (9): 786–92.

Cawley, J. 2000. An instrumental variables approach to measuring the effect of body weight on employment disability. *Health Services Research* 35 (5 Pt 2): 1159–79.

———. 2004. An economic framework for understanding physical activity and eating behaviors. *American Journal of Preventive Medicine* 27 (3S): 117–25.

Cutler, D., E. Glaeser, and J. Shapiro. 2003. Why have Americans become more obese? *Journal of Economic Perspectives* 17 (3): 93–118.

Dave, D., and R. Kaestner. 2009. Health insurance and ex ante moral hazard: Evidence from Medicare. *International Journal of Health Care Finance and Economics* 9 (4): 367–90.

Daviglus, M. L., K. Liu, L. L. Yan, A. Pirzada, L. Manheim, W. Manning, and D. B. Garside. 2004. Relation of body mass index in young adulthood and middle age to Medicare expenditures in older Age. *Journal of the American Medical Association* 292 (22): 2243–749.

Deb, P., and P. K. Trivedi. 1997. Demand for medical care by the elderly: A finite mixture approach. *Journal of Applied Econometrics* 12 (3): 313–36.

———. 2006. Specification and simulated likelihood estimation of a non-normal treatment-outcome model with selection: Application to health care utilization. Econometrics Journal 9:307–31.

Elmer, P. J., J. B. Brown, G. A. Nichols, and G. Oster. 2004. Effects of weight gain on medical care costs. *International Journal of Obesity* 28:1365–73.

Finkelstein, E. A., I. C. Fiebelkorn, and G. Wang. 2003. National medical spending attributable to overweight and obesity: How much, and who's paying? *Health Affairs* W3-219-26.

———. 2004. State-level estimates of annual medical expenditures attributable to obesity. *Obesity Research* 12 (1): 18–24.

Finkelstein, E. A., C. J. Ruhm, and K. M. Kosa. 2005. Economic causes and consequences of obesity. *Annual Review of Public Health* 26:239–57.

Gouriéroux, C., and A. Monfort. 1996. *Simulation based econometrics methods.* New York: Oxford University Press.

Gruber, J. 2000. Health insurance and the labor market. 2000. In *Handbook of health economics,* ed. A. J. Cuyler and J. P. Newhouse, 645–700. Amsterdam: Elsevier.

Katzmarzyk, P. T., and I. Janssen. 2004. The economic costs associated with physical inactivity and obesity in Canada: An update. *Canadian Journal of Applied Physiology* 29 (1): 90–115.

Keeler, E. B., W. G. Manning, J. P. Newhouse, E. M. Sloss, and J. Wasserman. 1989. The external costs of a sedentary lifestyle. *American Journal of Public Health* 79:975–81.

Keenan, P. S., M. J. Buntin, T. G. McGuire, and J. P. Newhouse. 2001. The prevalence of formal risk adjustment in health plan purchasing. *Inquiry* 38 (Fall): 245–59.

Lakdawalla, D., and T. Philipson. 2002. The growth of obesity and technological change: A theoretical and empirical examination. NBER Working Paper no. 8946. Cambridge, MA: National Bureau of Economic Research, May.

Lakdawalla, D., N. Sood, and D. Goldman. 2006. HIV breakthroughs and risky sexual behavior. *Quarterly Journal of Economics* 121 (3): 1063–102.

Manning, W. G., E. B. Keeler, J. P. Newhouse, E. M. Sloss, and J. Wasserman. 1991. *The costs of poor health habits.* Cambridge, MA: Harvard University Press.

McClellan, M., and J. Skinner. 1999. Medicare reform: Who pays and who benefits? *Health Affairs* 18 (1): 48–62.

———. 2006. The incidence of Medicare. *Journal of Public Economics* 90 (January): 257–76.

McFadden, D. 1980. Econometric models for probabilistic choice among products. Journal of Business 53:S13–S29.

Mokdad, A. H., M. K. Serdula, W. H. Dietz, B. A. Bowman, J. S. Marks, and J. P. Koplan. 1999. The spread of the obesity epidemic in the United States, 1991–1998. *Journal of the American Medical Association* 282 (16): 1519–22.

Mokdad, A. H., E. S. Ford, B. A. Bowman, W. H. Dietz, F. Vinicor, V. S. Bales, and J. S. Markes. 2003. Prevalence of obesity, diabetes, and obesity-related health risk factors, 2001. *Journal of the American Medical Association* 289 (1): 76–9.

Musich, S., C. Lu, T. McDonald, L. J. Champagne, and D. W. Edington. 2004. Association of additional health risks on medical charges and prevalence of diabetes within body mass index categories. *American Journal of Health Promotion* 18 (3): 264–68.

Nestle, M. 2003. *Food politics: How the food industry influences nutrition and health.* Berkeley, CA: University of California Press.

Newhouse, J. P., and Insurance Experiment Group. 1993. *Free for all? Lessons from the RAND health insurance experiment.* Cambridge, MA: Harvard University Press.

Pagan, J. A., and A. Davila. 1997. Obesity, occupational attainment, and earnings. *Social Science Quarterly* 78 (3): 756–70.

Quesenberry, C. P., Jr., B. Caan, and A. Jacobson. 1998. Obesity, health services use, and health care costs among members of a health maintenance organization. *Archives of Internal Medicine* 158 (5): 466–72.

Raebel, M. A., D.C. Malone, D. A. Conner, S. Xu, J. A. Porter, and F. A. Lanty. 2004. Health services use and health care costs of obese and non-obese individuals. *Archives of Internal Medicine* 164:2135–40.

Rashad, I. K., and S. Markowitz. 2010. Incentives in obesity and insurance. *Inquiry* 46 (4): 418–32.

Register, C. A., and D. R. Williams. 1990. Wage effects of obesity among young workers. *Social Science Quarterly* 71 (1): 130–41.

Rosen, S. 1986. The theory of equalizing differences. In *Handbook of labor economics,* ed. O. Ashenfelter and D. Card, 641–92. Amsterdam: Elsevier.

Sander, B., and R. Bergemann. 2003. Economic burden of obesity and its complications in Germany. *European Journal of Health Economics* 4 (4): 248–53.

Staiger, D., and J. H. Stock. 1997. Instrumental variables regression with weak instruments. *Econometrica* 65 (3): 557 86.

Sturm, R. 2002. The effects of obesity, smoking, and drinking on medical problems and costs. *Health Affairs* 21 (2): 245–53.

Thompson, D., J. B. Brown, G. A. Nichols, P. J. Elmer, and G. Oster. 2001. Body mass index and future healthcare costs: A retrospective cohort study. *Obesity Research* 9 (3): 210–18.

Thorpe, K. E., C. S. Florence, D. H. Howard, and P. Joski. 2004. The impact of obesity on rising medical spending. *Health Affairs* Web Exclusive (W4): 480–6.

Train, K. 2002. *Discrete choice methods with simulation.* New York: Cambridge University Press.

Wang, F., A. B. Schultz, S. Musich, T. McDonald, D. Hirschland, and D. W. Edington. 2003. The relationship between National Heart, Lung, and Blood Institute weight guidelines and concurrent medical costs in a manufacturing population. *American Journal of Health Promotion* 17 (3): 183–9.

Wolf, A. M., and G. A. Colditz. 1994. The cost of obesity. *Pharmacoeconomics* 5 (Suppl 1): 34–7.

3

Food Prices and the Dynamics of Body Weight

Dana Goldman, Darius Lakdawalla, and Yuhui Zheng

3.1 Introduction

A great many policy approaches to the obesity epidemic have been proposed. A popular choice among these has been the imposition of a "fat tax" on selected foods that are deemed to promote obesity, as a result of high caloric density, low nutritional value, or high fat content (Jacobson and Brownell 2000; Nestle and Jacobson 2000). In the year 2000, for example, there were nineteen states and cities in the United States that imposed taxes on less nutritious foods like soft drinks, sweets, or snack foods (Jacobson and Brownell 2000). In the past, policymakers viewed these primarily as "sin taxes" designed to raise revenue rather than influence health. Most localities use revenues for general purposes. Others earmark them for specific purposes, like violence prevention (Washington), Medicaid (Arkansas), or medical schools (West Virginia). Such taxes were strongly opposed by the soft drink and food industries. Perhaps as a result, twelve localities have reduced or repealed such taxes in recent years.

Understanding the public economics of fat taxes requires an understand-

Dana Goldman is a professor and the Norman Topping Chair in Medicine and Public Policy at the University of Southern California and a research associate of the National Bureau of Economic Research. Darius Lakdawalla is an associate professor in the University of Southern California (USC) School of Policy, Planning, and Development (SPPD), director of research at the USC Schaeffer Center for Health Policy and Economics, and a research associate of the National Bureau of Economic Research. Yuhui Zheng is a postdoctoral research fellow at the National Bureau of Economic Research.

We are grateful to participants at the November 2008 Economics of Obesity Conference, as well as Michael Anderson, Michael Grossman, and Bob Kaestner for comments. We thank the National Institute on Aging for funding. All errors are ours. The views expressed herein are those of the author(s) and do not necessarily reflect the views of the National Bureau of Economic Research.

ing of how, or even whether, individuals respond to changes in food prices. Regardless of whether municipalities intend to influence health, there may be health effects that need to be quantified. To meet this public policy need, a literature on food prices and obesity has emerged in health economics. Chou, Grossman, and Saffer (2004) found that the real fast-food restaurant price, the real food-at-home price, and the real full-service restaurant price were negatively associated with weight in an adult population. Lakdawalla and Philipson (2002) found qualitatively similar, but larger, effects on a population of young adults. Another study found that the real price of fast-food is negatively related to body weight among adolescents, while the real price of fruits and vegetables food is positively associated (Auld and Powell 2008). Among U.S. children from kindergarten to the third grade, lower real food prices of fruits and vegetables are significantly associated with lower weight gain (Sturm and Datar 2005, 2008).

Economic theory suggests that food prices affect food intake. Biology suggests that food intake affects both the level of current weight, and the rate at which weight changes. Therefore, manipulating the price of food may have both short- and long-run consequences for body weight. This effect is reinforced by inertia in body weight (Heo, Faith, and Pietrobelli 2002).

Most of the economic literature to date has examined the contemporaneous relationship between food prices and body weight either in a cross-sectional setting or panel data setting.[1] However, the long-run consequences of food prices may be quite different.

To fill this gap in the literature, we study the short- and long-run body weight consequences of changing food prices. We use the Health and Retirement Study (HRS), a panel of U.S. adults aged fifty and over. The use of the HRS is motivated both by its panel features, which facilitate the study of long-run consequences, and by the particular importance of studying health and health care expenditures in this population.

The rest of the chapter is organized as follows: Section 3.2 outlines the conceptual framework. Section 3.3 describes the data, and Section 3.4 the methods. Section 3.5 reports the results, and Section 3.6 concludes.

3.2 Conceptual Framework

We conceptualize the determination of body weight as a dynamic problem, with body weight as a state variable and food intake as a control variable. Consider an individual who maximizes lifetime utility by choosing food consumption and nonfood consumption, subject to a budget constraint. Changes in body weight are driven by current food intake, and current body weight. Current body weight directly affects utility either by affecting health or body image. This problem is formalized as:

---

1. Exceptions are the studies by Sturm and Datar (2005, 2008).

$$\max \int_{t_0}^{t_1} e^{-rt} U(W(t), F(t), C(t)) dt$$

$$s.t.\ W.' = \frac{dW}{dt} = g(W(t), F(t))$$

(1)
$$W(t_0) = W_0$$

$$t_0, t_1\ \text{fixed}$$

$$C(t) + P_t F(t) \leq I_t.$$

Variable r is the one-period discount rate; $W(t)$ is body weight at time t; $F(t)$ is the amount of food intake at time t; p_t is the relative price of food. Variable $C(t)$ is the nonfood consumption at time t; I_t is the income; $C(t)$ can be written as $I_t - p_t F(t)$.

We assume that utility is concave in food intake ($U_{FF} < 0$), that eating more leads to weight gain ($g_F > 0$), and that a given level of food intake results in less weight gain for heavier people ($g_W < 0$).

The Hamiltonian for this optimal control problem is:

(2) $$H(t, W, F, \lambda) = e^{-rt} U(W(t), F(t), I_t - p_t F(t)) + \lambda g(W(t), F(t)).$$

If $W^*(t)$ and $F^*(t)$ maximize the objective function, the necessary conditions include:

(3) $$H_F = e^{-rt}(U_W W_F + U_F - p_t U_C) + \lambda g_F = 0.$$

The second-order condition can be written as:

(4) $$H_{FF} = e^{-rt}(U_{WF} W_F + U_W W_{FF} + U_{FF} - p_t U_{CF}) + \lambda g_{FF} < 0.$$

It is straightforward to show that the demand for food is downward-sloping in this model, or that $\partial F^*/\partial p_t < 0$.[2] Second, since $g_F > 0$, weight gain will be larger as $F^*(t)$ increases. Finally, the steady-state body weight will also rise with food consumption.[3]

Based on the analysis above, we raise the following two hypotheses that will be subject to empirical test:

1. Increases in the relative price of food are associated with lower rates of body weight gain.

2. Increases in the relative price of food are associated with lower steady-state level of body weight.

---

2. Computing the derivative of equation (3) with respect to p_t, we obtain $H_{FF} \partial F^*/\partial p_t = e^{-rt} U_C$. According to (4), $H_{FF} < 0$. Since $U_C > 0$, it implies that $\partial F^*/\partial p_t < 0$.

3. Since $g_w < 0$, body weight W_s will increase at a diminishing rate until it reaches a steady state. This steady-state body weight W_s will satisfy $g(W_s, F^*(t)) = 0$. Differentiating this expression with respect to $F^*(t)$ yields: $g_F(W_s, F^*(t)) + g_w(W_s, F^*(t)) \partial W_s/\partial F^*(t) = 0$. Since $g_F(W_s, F^*(t)) > 0$, and $g_w(W_s, F^*(t)) < 0$, it must be true that $\partial W_s/\partial F^*(t) > 0$.

3.3   Data

3.3.1   Health and Retirement Study Data

We use the Health and Retirement Study (HRS), a biennial survey of the population over age fifty, to carry out the analysis. The original HRS cohort—first interviewed in 1992—was a nationally representative sample of approximately 7,600 households ($n = 12,654$ individuals) with at least one member who was born between 1931 and 1941. In every interview wave, HRS respondents are asked detailed questions about demographics, employment, occupation, income and wealth, and health insurance. Questions were also asked about self-reported general health status, prevalence and incidence of chronic conditions, functional status and disability, and self-reported body height and weight. County residence is available also, on a restricted-use basis; this allows us to link geographical information on food prices, as discussed below.

Body mass index (BMI) in HRS is constructed from self-reported weight and height. Earlier research has identified systematic error in measurement for these variables; to address this issue, we employ the correction method developed by Cawley (1999). The Cawley procedure relies on the availability of external data on both actual and self-reported heights and weights. The relationship between the self-reported and actual numbers is then used to adjust the self-reported values.

Objectively measured height and weight data are available for a subsample of the HRS. In the year 2006, HRS randomly selected half its households and measured their weight and height. The self-reported weight and height is also available for these households. Using these variables, we run linear regressions of actual weight on reported weight and its square, age, and age squared, separately for the following eight subgroups: white male non-Hispanic, white female non-Hispanic, black male non-Hispanic, black female non-Hispanic, Hispanic male, Hispanic female, other male, and other female. Figure 3A.1 through 3A.4 show the relationship between predicted weight and height versus self-reported weight and height. Non-Hispanic white (male and female) and black female tend to underreport weight when self-reported weight is high. There is a slight overreport of height across all race-gender groups, especially among "other male."

3.3.2   Food Price Data

We obtain prices for food and other goods from the ACCRA Cost of Living data, published quarterly by the American Chamber of Commerce Researchers Association (ACCRA), for more than 200 cities. We use data from 1992 to 2003.

The ACCRA collects prices for fifty-nine distinct but standardized items, which are all listed in tables 3B.1 to 3B.3. Of the items listed, twenty-two are at-home food. Some examples include: 5 lb bag of sugar, cane or beet; 3 lb can of Crisco brand shortening; and 12 oz can of Minute Maid brand frozen concentrated orange juice. Prices for three fast-food items are reported, which include: a quarter-pound patty with cheese (McDonald's Quarter-Pounder with Cheese, where available); 12″ to 13″ thin crust cheese pizza (Pizza Hut or Pizza Inn, where available); and thigh and drumstick, with or without extras (Kentucky Fried Chicken or Church's where available). For each city, ACCRA collects mean prices for each of the fifty-nine items. It also reports the expenditure weight of each item in the budget of a nationally representative household with a "middle-management" lifestyle.

Since the ACCRA data are reported quarterly, we average prices over the available quarters to obtain annual prices. The ACCRA reports prices at the level of metropolitan areas, but the HRS data codes residence at the county level. Therefore, we use the population-weighted averages of city prices to construct prices at the county level. We calculate "real" prices by deflating using the Bureau of Labor Statistics (BLS) consumer price index for all goods.

Using the ACCRA data, we calculate the following prices: price per calorie, price of cigarettes, and price of gasoline.

Individual Item Prices

We use the price of cigarettes and of gasoline, as collected by ACCRA. The price of gasoline is the cash price at a self-service pump, if available, for one gallon of regular unleaded, national brand gasoline, inclusive of all taxes. The price of cigarettes is calculated as the price of a carton of Winston king-size (85mm) cigarettes.

Price Per Calorie

A composite food price index like the price of food at home does not take into account differential impacts on body weight of consuming various foods. For example, using this price index, the impact of a 10 percent price increase in vegetables on body weight would be equal to that of a 10 percent increase in the price of butter, if the expenditure shares of the two goods are the same. A better alternative is to put more weight on foods that are more calorie-dense than others. Therefore, we construct a measure of the price per calorie. Increases in this index we interpret as relative increases in the price of high-calorie foods.

To construct the price per calorie variable, we first construct price per calorie for each food item in the ACCRA basket. This is given by the price per unit of food, divided by calories per unit of food. We obtain the data on calories from the United States Department of Agriculture (USDA) web site of "What's In The Foods You Eat *Search Tool.*"[4] For example, 100

4. http://www.ars.usda.gov/Services/docs.htm?docid=17032.

grams of ground beef contain 254 calories, and 100 grams of bananas have 90 calories.

The item prices are then aggregated to form a composite index of price per calorie. This index weights each food item by its share of calorie contribution to the mean basket of food consumption reported by ACCRA in its 1992 data. The index aggregates across all at-home food and fast-food items, using this weighting scheme.

Define calprice$_{gt}$ as the index for price per calorie, for area g at time t. This index aggregates across our twenty-five food items, indexed by j. Time measurement is normalized so that the base year of 1992 is written as $t = 0$. Before describing the mathematical expression for the index, it helps to define the following auxiliary terms:

p_{gjt}: Price per unit of food j, in area g, at time t
k_j: calories per unit of food j
w_{j0}: expenditure share for food j, in base year

We can then define the calorie share of item j, in area g, during the base year, as follows:

$$c_{gj0} \equiv \frac{[(W_{j0}/p_{gj0})k_j]}{\sum_{j=1}^{25}(W_{j0}/p_{gj0})k_j}.$$

Finally, this allows us to write the calorie-price index as:

$$(5) \qquad \text{calprice}_{gt} = \sum_{j=1}^{25}\frac{p_{gjt}}{k_j}c_{gj0}.$$

3.3.3   Analytic Sample

We begin with 9,733 HRS respondents born between 1931 and 1941, first interviewed in 1992, and with positive HRS sampling weight. Those who did not die or drop out of the sample were followed biennially until 2004. Due to the nature of the analysis, we exclude several segments of the sample. First, we exclude individuals residing in counties for which ACCRA collects no data. Second, we exclude individuals with missing values for any of the variables used in the regression analysis. Third, we exclude observations with nonadjacent waves of data. For example, if an individual was interviewed in wave 1, wave 3, and wave 4, we exclude the wave 1 data, but retain the data from waves 3 and 4. Finally, we exclude individuals who moved from one county to another. These individuals moved at some point between interviews, which are spaced twenty-four months apart. Given the substantial between-city variation in food prices, this induces considerable error in measuring the "true" price that the individual faces over the relevant time frame. The detailed sample selection process is shown in figure 3.1. There are 3,111 individuals included in the final analytic sample. Below, we investigate the possibility of sample selection bias.

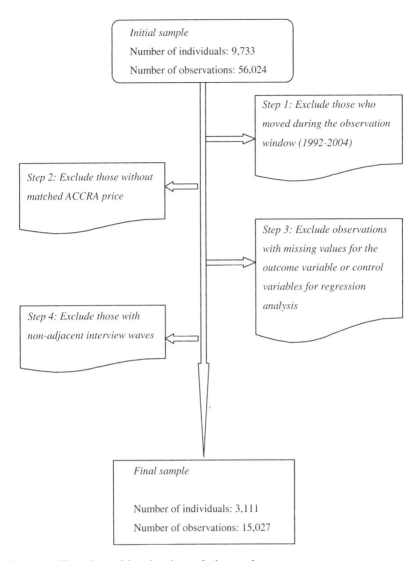

Fig. 3.1   Flow chart of forming the analytic sample

3.4   Methods

3.4.1   Econometric Analysis

The conceptual framework implies that current body weight is a function of past body weight, and factors that affect energy intake and energy expenditure. A reduced-form equation is the following dynamic linear panel model:

$$(6) \quad W_{igt} = \beta_0 + \sum_{k=0}^{t-1} \gamma_k W_{ig,k} + P_{gt}\beta_1 + Z_{gt}\beta_2 + X_{igt}\beta_3 + \alpha_i + \tau_t + \varepsilon_{igt}.$$

Variable W_{igt} is the weight for individual i in geographic region g at time t. Variables $W_{ig,k}$ are body weight in previous periods; more than one previous period could affect current body weight, but including too many periods will greatly reduce the sample size. We minimize the number of periods to include, while ensuring there is no serial correlation in the error term ε_{igt}, which is a necessary assumption for the model estimation we will use. Variable P_{gt} represents food prices; Z_{gt} stands for other regional variables; α_i is individual fixed effect; while τ_t are year fixed effects. Since HRS is a biennial survey, to reflect prices during a two-year period, P_{gt} is calculated as the average of the prices for the current year t and the year before. There is one exception: the last year of HRS data in our analytic sample is 2004, but the latest available ACCRA data we could obtain is for year 2003. As a result, the prices P_{gt} for the HRS survey year 2004 are calculated using only the 2003 ACCRA data.

To estimate equation (6), we use system generalized method of moments (GMM) (Arellano and Bond 1991; Arellano and Bover 1995; Blundell and Bond 1998), which combines the moment conditions of the differenced equation with moment conditions for the model in levels. The following moment conditions are jointly estimated using the "xtabond2" command in Stata 10:

$$(7) \quad E(W_{ig,k}\Delta\varepsilon_{igt}) = 0, k = 1,2,\ldots t - 2, t = 1,\ldots T$$

$$E(\Delta W_{ig,q}(\alpha_i + \varepsilon_{igt})) = 0, q = 1,2,\ldots t - 1$$

$$E(\Delta P_{gt}\Delta\varepsilon_{igt}) = 0$$

$$E(\Delta Z_{gt}\Delta\varepsilon_{igt}) = 0$$

$$E(\Delta X_{igt}\Delta\varepsilon_{igt}) = 0.$$

County Characteristics

Apart from the food price vectors, we include the following county-level characteristics in the regressions: log of price of cigarettes, log of price of gasoline, and log of price of nonfood goods (excluding cigarettes and gasoline).

Following Chou, Grossman, and Saffer (2004), we include cigarette prices in the weight equation, since cigarettes may serve a weight control function. If smoking reduces weight, cheaper cigarettes might contribute to weight reduction, holding food prices constant.

The effects of the gasoline price are more complex. On the one hand, this affects the cost of transportation and the incentives for exercise. For instance, in areas where gasoline is expensive, people may choose to live closer to work, and take public transportation, both of which involves more exercise than driving. The price of gasoline is also correlated with the cost of agricultural output. In principle, this could also absorb some of the cost-driven variation in the price of food: increases in the price of gasoline may increase the cost of producing and transporting food; this may have different effects in different parts of the country. In practice, however, including the price of gasoline had little impact on the estimated effects of food price variation.

Finally, the price of nonfood goods captures the substitution and income effects that occur when the overall cost of living rises.

Individual Characteristics

We include the following time-varying individual characteristics in our regression models: age, self-reported diagnosis of chronic conditions (cancer, diabetes, heart disease, hypertension, lung disease, stroke, arthritis, mental problems), whether self-rated health is fair or poor; marital status, whether the respondent is working for pay, total household income, total household wealth, and health insurance status.

3.4.2   Correction for Sample Attrition Bias

Since we include only 32.0 percent of the initial sample (3,111 out of 9,733 unique individuals) in our analysis, sample selection bias may be an issue, in the sense that our analytic sample may no longer be representative of the study population. In particular, the question is whether our sample selection criteria are correlated with food price and weight changes.

To address sample selection bias, we adjust the sampling weights to account for our secondary selection criteria. We first estimate a probit model of whether an individual in the study sample will appear in the analytic sample. Regressors include demographics, health, and economic status at the 1992 interview. We then predict the probability of sample inclusion for those in the analytic sample, and multiply the sampling weight by the inverse of the predicted probability. All descriptive and regression analyses are carried out using the modified sampling weight. This procedure addresses selection bias on the basis of observables, but we may still suffer from selection on the basis of unobservables (Wooldridge 2002).

The selection model is presented in table 3.1. It shows that residing in rural areas greatly decreases the probability of being included in the analytic sample. This is because the ACCRA price data is only collected in cities. Even though we aggregate data at the county level, those in rural counties are excluded. Individuals with diabetes at the baseline interview are also less likely to appear in the analytic sample. In addition, non-Hispanic blacks, Hispanic, and those with less than high school education are more likely to be included. Finally, those with higher household wealth are also more likely to appear in the analytic sample.

The original sampling weight has a mean of 2,340, standard deviation of 1,048, a minimum of 563 and a maximum of 7,710. After multiplying by the

Table 3.1   **Probit model of whether being included in the analytic sample**

Covariate	Being included in the analytic sample
Male	−0.025
	(0.029)
Non-Hispanic black	0.303***
	(0.039)
Hispanic	0.374***
	(0.051)
Less than high school	0.095**
	(0.037)
Some college and above	0.044
	(0.032)
Suburban area	−0.038
	(0.031)
Rural area	−0.775***
	(0.036)
Initial cancer	0.094
	(0.063)
Initial diabetes	−0.105**
	(0.048)
Initial heart disease	−0.015
	(0.047)
Initial hypertension	0.002
	(0.030)
Initial lung disease	0.020
	(0.061)
Initial stroke	−0.085
	(0.088)
Initial arthritis	0.026
	(0.030)
Initial psyche problems	0.019
	(0.054)
Initial current smoking	−0.006
	(0.031)
Initial self-rated health is fair/poor	0.001
	(0.040)
Initial physical activity	−0.013
	(0.034)
Initial age	0.426***
	(0.161)
Initial age squared	−0.004***
	(0.001)
Initial log of household income	−0.010
	(0.011)
Initial non-positive household wealth	0.042
	(0.111)
Initial log of household wealth	0.022**
	(0.010)
Initial widowed	−0.022
	(0.059)

Table 3.1   (continued)

Covariate	Being included in the analytic sample
Initial single	0.080**
	(0.039)
Initial R working for pay	0.014
	(0.033)
Initial any health insurance	-0.017
	(0.041)
Constant	−12.266***
	(4.460)
N	9,492

Source: Health and Retirement Study 1992-2004, ACCRA 1992-2003.

Note: A probit model is used to model the probability that a HRS respondent who is born between year 1931 and 1941 is included in the analytic sample.

***$p < 0.01$

**$p < 0.05$

*$p < 0.10$

inverse of the probability, the mean is raised to 5,813, the standard deviation 3,560, the minimum 921, and the maximum is 26,687. Descriptive statistics of the analytic sample are shown in table 3.2.

3.5   Results

The key outcome variable is either BMI or its natural logarithm. When the outcome variable is BMI (or log BMI), we include in equation (6) the individual's BMI (or log BMI) in the previous two periods as right-hand side control variables. Including two periods is the minimum necessary for an error term without autocorrelation. All regressions also include the following variables: log of price of cigarettes, log price of gasoline, log price of nonfood goods excluding cigarettes and gasoline, self-reported diagnosis of chronic conditions, self-rated health, marital status, whether working for pay, total household income, total household wealth, health insurance status, and time dummies.

In addition to average effects, we are also interested in examining whether there will be heterogeneous food price effects across demographic and socioeconomic subgroups. First, we examine whether the price-weight relationship is stronger for individuals who are obese (BMI $\geq$ 30 kg/m^2) at baseline. If so, this is consistent with the hypothesis that food tax policy better targets those with unhealthy weight. We add baseline obesity interacted with price to equation (6). It is also possible that the poor may be more price-elastic. We thus interact placement in the bottom tercile of baseline household wealth with food prices.

Table 3.2   **Summary statistics**

Variable	Mean	Standard deviation
Body mass index (kg/m²)	28.65	6.01
Prices		
Price per 1,000 calories	0.79	0.07
Price per 100 grams of fat	1.79	0.21
Price of cigarettes	15.16	4.74
Price of gasoline	0.78	0.08
Price of nonfood items excl.cigarettes and gasoline	229.39	91.41
Demographics		
Age at interview	61.4	4.9
Male	46.6%	49.9%
Hispanic	6.8%	25.1%
Non-Hispanic black	11.2%	31.5%
Less than high school	21.6%	41.2%
Some college and above	40.3%	49.1%
Widowed	9.7%	29.5%
Single	16.9%	37.5%
Health conditions		
Cancer	9.1%	28.8%
Diabetes	14.2%	34.9%
Heart disease	16.8%	37.4%
Hypertension	43.3%	49.6%
Lung disease	7.4%	26.2%
Stroke	4.2%	20.0%
Arthritis	48.1%	50.0%
Psyche problems	11.2%	31.5%
Self-rated health is fair/poor	22.8%	41.9%
Economic conditions		
R working for pay	51.4%	50.0%
Any health insurance	91.3%	28.2%
HH total income	36,407	49,739
HH wealth	242,413	1,201,071

Source: HRS 1992-2004, ACCRA 1992-2003.

Note: Number of individuals: 3,111; Number of observations: 15,027.

3.5.1   Price Per Calorie and BMI

First, we examine the relationship between price per calorie and our BMI measures. Table 3.3 analyzes the impact of price per calorie on BMI. The first column shows model estimation without any interaction effects. Current BMI is strongly associated with its two lagged values, demonstrating the persistence of BMI. The coefficient on log price per calorie is negative and statistically significant at the 10 percent level. A 10 percent reduction in price per calorie is associated with a BMI increase of approximately 0.26 units within two years. Coefficients for the other price variables are insignificant.

The second column of table 3.3 shows estimation results with interaction

Table 3.3   **Effect of price per calorie on BMI**

Independent variable	Model specification		
	I	*II*	*III*
BMI two years ago	0.672***	0.651***	0.657***
	(0.031)	(0.036)	(0.031)
BMI four years ago	0.210***	0.195***	0.206***
	(0.026)	(0.027)	(0.024)
Log of price per calorie	–2.568*	–2.308*	–1.734
	(1.406)	(1.395)	(1.675)
Log of price per calorie · (obese at baseline)		0.979	
		(4.038)	
Log of price per calorie · (poor at baseline)			–1.771
			(2.936)
Log of cigarettes price	0.566	0.464	0.573
	(0.694)	(0.645)	(0.693)
Log of cigarettes price · (obese at baseline)		0.387	
		(0.523)	
Log of cigarettes price · (poor at baseline)			–0.215
			(0.453)
Log of gasoline price	0.006	–0.268	0.302
	(1.065)	(0.936)	(1.085)
Log of gasoline price · (obese at baseline)		0.849	
		(1.559)	
Log of gasoline price · (poor at baseline)			–0.425
			(1.325)
Log of nonfood price	0.652	0.354	0.243
	(0.579)	(0.515)	(0.588)
Log of nonfood price · (obese at baseline)		-0.702	
		(0.475)	
Log of nonfood price · (poor at baseline)			0.807*
			(0.477)
N	8,231	8,231	8,231

Source: Health and Retirement Study, 1992–2004, ACCRA price data, 1992–2003. Models are estimated using system GMM. All models also include the following variables: self-rated health, chronic conditions, working status, marital status, household income and household wealth, health insurance status, and year dummies.

***$p < 0.01$

**$p < 0.05$

*$p < 0.10$

terms between being obese at baseline and price variables. The main effect of price per calorie remains significant but the interaction term is insignificant, suggesting statistically similar food price-BMI relationships for the obese and nonobese. Estimation in the last column of table 3.3 includes interaction terms between being poor at baseline—defined as being at the bottom tercile of the household distribution—and price variables. Both the main and interaction term of log of per calorie are negative, but insignificant.

Table 3.4 shows the effect of price per calorie on log BMI. The coefficients can be interpreted as elasticities. The first column shows the estimation without any interaction terms. The coefficient on the log of price per calorie is negatively and statistically significant at 10 percent level. Quantitatively, a 10 percent reduction in price per calorie is associated with a 0.77 percent reduction in BMI within two years. The next two columns confirm the results

Table 3.4   **Effect of price per calorie on log BMI**

	Model specification		
Independent variable	I	II	III
Log of BMI two years ago	0.654***	0.593***	0.641***
	(0.030)	(0.048)	(0.031)
Log of BMI four years ago	0.195***	0.171***	0.200***
	(0.023)	(0.025)	(0.023)
Log of price per calorie	−0.077*	−0.074	−0.047
	(0.046)	(0.048)	(0.054)
Log of price per calorie · (obese at baseline)		0.032	
		(0.116)	
Log of price per calorie · (poor at baseline)			−0.089
			(0.094)
Log of cigarettes price	0.020	0.015	0.020
	(0.022)	(0.022)	(0.022)
Log of cigarettes price · (obese at baseline)		0.013	
		(0.014)	
Log of cigarettes price · (poor at baseline)			−0.009
			(0.014)
Log of gasoline price	−0.006	−0.015	−0.002
	(0.032)	(0.031)	(0.034)
Log of gasoline price · (obese at baseline)		0.029	
		(0.043)	
Log of gasoline price · (poor at baseline)			0.003
			(0.041)
Log of nonfood price	0.019	0.016	0.003
	(0.018)	(0.018)	(0.018)
Log of nonfood price · (obese at baseline)		−0.026*	
		(0.014)	
Log of nonfood price · (poor at baseline)			0.028**
			(0.014)
N	8,231	8,231	8,231

Source: Health and Retirement Study, 1992-2004, ACCRA price data, 1992-2003. Models are estimated using system GMM. All models also include the following variables: self-rated health, chronic conditions, working status, marital status, household income and household wealth, health insurance status, and year dummies.
***$p < 0.01$
**$p < 0.05$
*$p < 0.10$

in table 3.4 that the food price effect does not differ by either baseline BMI status or baseline household wealth.

Even if the entire estimated effect is causal, the short-term effect of price per calorie on BMI appears relatively small. A one-standard deviation, or 10 percent, reduction in price is associated with a BMI increase of 0.26 units, or 0.77 percent. By way of comparison, clinical guidelines suggest 10 percent BMI reductions as the minimum necessary for clinically meaningful health benefits to overweight individuals.

The long-run effect of price per calorie may be larger, but still below the threshold of clinical significance. Once again presuming that our entire estimate is causal, figure 3.2 and figure 3.3 show the simulated changes in BMI, both in levels and in percentages, due to a permanent 10 percent reduction in price per calorie. After ten years, the price reduction will be associated with a BMI increase of 1.05 units (or 2.5 percent). If we extrapolate to the model's implied long-run steady-state, these figures rise to 2.2 units of BMI (or 5.1 percent), still quite modest from a clinical perspective. Of course, applied to the entire population, this is a nontrivial effect, compared to the total growth in mean BMI over the last several decades.

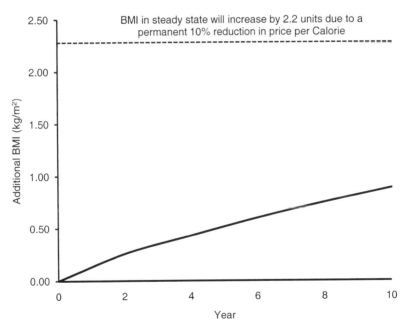

Fig. 3.2   Additional BMI due to a permanent 10 percent reduction in price per calorie

Note: This figure shows the simulated effect of a permanent 10 percent reduction in price per calorie on BMI trajectory over ten years, based on the estimates shown in the first column of table 3.3.

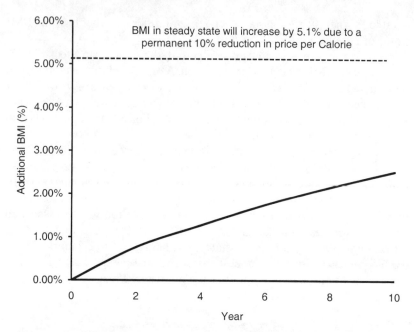

Fig. 3.3   Additional BMI as a percentage of total BMI due to a permanent 10% reduction in price per calorie

Note: This figure shows the simulated effect of a permanent 10 percent reduction in price per calorie on additional BMI as a percentage of total BMI, over ten years, based on the estimates shown in the first column of table 3.4.

3.5.2   Comparisons to the Previous Literature

The majority of the previous literature has examined the short-term effects of food prices on body weight. Our results for the short-term relationship between prices and BMI appear to be roughly in line with the literature that focuses on other subpopulations. We estimate that the short-term elasticity between the price of calories and body weight is –0.077. For at-home food, Chou, Grossman, and Saffer (2004) estimated a price elasticity of –0.04. Gelbach, Klick, and Stratmann (2007) find that doubling the price of "unhealthy" food is associated with about 1 percent less BMI.

We found that the effect of food prices on weight grow over time. Sturm and Datar (2008) also found that the effect of food prices on body weight gain among children became larger during a five-year period, relative to the effect during a three-year period.

3.5.3   Identification

Our models are identified by local trends in food prices. The data reveal substantial variation across regions in local price trends. It is natural to inquire into the sources of these, but quite difficult to pinpoint an exact origin. We investigated several hypotheses.

Several studies have found that store formats are important in explaining cross-sectional regional price variations. One study found that food sold at Walmart is on average about 15 percent to 25 percent cheaper than traditional supermarkets (Hausman and Leibtag 2004). Another study examined the effects of Walmart entry on the city-level prices of several nonfood retail items, including aspirin, cigarettes, soft drinks, detergent, and others. The author found negative price effects of Walmart entrance (Basker 2005). Motivated by this result, we assessed whether geographic variation in the appearance of Walmart entry generated significant differences in local price trends. This failed to provide much, if any, explanatory power.

Second, we tested the hypothesis that some areas were more exposed to increases in transportation costs for food. To test this, we tested for systematic price trend differences across states with large and small shares of agricultural land. To be sure, this is a fairly crude measure of local transportation costs. Perhaps due to this error in measurement, we failed to find systematic differences in price trends across areas with more or less agricultural land and agricultural output.

A third option, related to transportation costs, exploits variation in the price of gasoline (Gelbach, Klick, and Stratmann 2007). The Gelbach et al. study has found that census-region level price variation in gasoline influence, the relative price of healthy food. Moreover, while gasoline can affect incentives to exercise, its effects on the cost of transporting goods should vary systematically across the country, depending on how far retailers are from production sites. This serves as a source of identification that "nets out" the common impact on exercise, and isolates the impact on transportation costs.

Following this reasoning, we used the interactions of gasoline price and approximate measures of per capita food production (proportion of population employed in food manufacturing, and per capita farm area, proportion of land arable) as the instruments for food prices. First-stage results were roughly consistent with our assumptions—the interactions of gasoline price and per capita food output measures have significant and negative effects on price per calorie. However, including the interactions as instruments in the system GMM estimation raised the standard error substantially, and the effect of price per calorie becomes positive and statistically insignificant. One interpretation is that the gasoline instrument introduces too much noise to be useful.

The failure to identify a clean source of variation begs the question of whether price trends are correlated with other economic or social factors that also influence weight. As a partial test of this, we assessed the impact of including observable health and economic factors on the price coefficients of interest. We reestimated models for the effect of price per calorie on BMI by dropping all health and economic factors. The results are shown in table 3C.1. They are very similar to those in table 3.3. The effect of price per calorie on log BMI is also very robust to inclusion or exclusion of health and economic factors (results not shown).

3.5.4   Limitations

First, as discussed earlier, local variation in food prices might not be exogenous. If the supply of food is upward-sloping (i.e., if food prices are not primarily cost-driven), the resulting simultaneity between supply and demand would create downward bias in our estimated price effects. Testing this possibility would require a plausibly valid instrument, but these are in short supply here. We explored several candidates. First, fuel prices may influence the supply of food and ultimately body weight. However, they may also influence incentives for exercise, and thus the demand for weight. Moreover, the first-stage relationships between local trends in fuel prices and local trends in food prices are—perhaps not surprisingly—quite weak. A second candidate is local weather variation, particularly extreme weather events. These may affect the costs of distribution and transportation of food. However, such major events also have a variety of additional causal effects that can impact exercise, metabolism, and economic status. In the absence of an instrument, we have presented evidence that observed variation in economic and demographic factors are unrelated to local trends in price. It remains possible that unobserved variation in these factors is still correlated with price.

As a result of these issues, it is possible that our effects combine both selective and causal factors. In discussing the implications of our findings, we have presumed that selection is likely to enlarge our estimates, which would then be upper bounds on the causal impacts. The idea is that heavier individuals will be likely to select into areas with cheaper food. If this assumption fails, it is possible that the causal impact of price on BMI is much larger than we have estimated.

One concern here is the possibility of measurement error in food prices. As is typically the case with the analysis of price effects, measurement error is another important issue. The ACCRA price data are based on sampling a number of local stores, but intracity price variation may not be adequately captured. More generally, it is quite difficult to measure the basket of prices faced by a particular individual who lives in a particular part of a city. This may result in downward bias that could partially, or even completely, offset the effects of selection.

Finally, we have the common problem of measurement error in weight. Our approach was to correct for self-reporting bias using a subsample of HRS respondents for whom data are available on measured weight and self-reported weight. Following Cawley (1999), we impute the expected measurement error in self-reported weight for the rest of the sample. Naturally, this strategy does not purge the measurement error; it merely mitigates it, to the extent that our imputation contains some relevant information. This would be a problem if error in reporting were correlated with price trends. Unfortunately, we cannot test this directly, because we do not have a panel of data on reporting error, which is only measured in one wave of the HRS data.

3.6   Conclusions

We examined both the short-term and long-term relationships between food prices of various kinds and body weight. We found very modest short-term relationships between price per calorie on body weight, and the magnitudes align with the previous literature. We do not find differential effects of price per calorie by baseline obesity or baseline household wealth. The long-term effect is larger, but still below the threshold of clinical significance. Within ten years, a 10 percent permanent reduction in price per calorie would be associated with a BMI increase of 1.05 units (or 2.5 percent). The maximum long-run effect implied by the model is still modest, at 2.2 units of BMI (or 5.1 percent).

From a policy perspective, these results suggest that policies raising the price of calories may have little effect on weight in the short term. They may curb the rate of growth somewhat more over a longer period of time. From 1980 to 2000, the average BMI of American adults increased by about 2.7 BMI units (Chou, Grossman, and Saffer 2004). Based on our estimates, a 10 percent increase in the price per calorie would have the potential to roll back 38 percent of this growth within ten years. As we have emphasized, however, caution is warranted in inferring causality from our estimates.

At a minimum, policymakers interested in reducing body weight will not find a fat tax to be a quickly effective solution. Indeed, significant weight reductions are likely to postdate the decision-making horizon of an elected official. However, from a positive point of view, our results suggest the importance of treating weight as a dynamic process, and emphasize the cumulative effects of economic incentives on body weight.

Appendix A

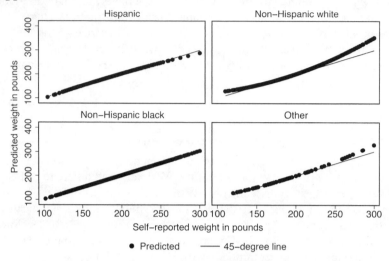

Fig. 3A.1 Compare predicted and self-reported weight among females (graphs by race/ethnicity)

Notes: Weight prediction is based on the ordinary least squares (OLS) regressions of measured weight against self-reported weight and self-reported weight squared, age and age squared, and predicted at the mean age, by gender and race. The estimation sample includes respondents aged 52 and over in the 2006 HRS survey and with both self-reported and measured weight. Height prediction is based on the OLS regressions of measured height against self-reported height and self-reported height squared, age and age squared, and predicted at the mean age, by gender and races. The estimation sample includes respondents aged 52 and over in the 2006 HRS survey and with both self-reported and measured height.

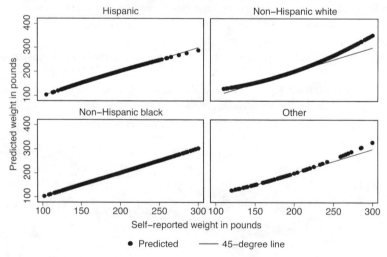

Fig. 3A.2 Compare predicted and self-reported weight among males (graphs by race/ethnicity)

Note: See notes to figure 3A.1.

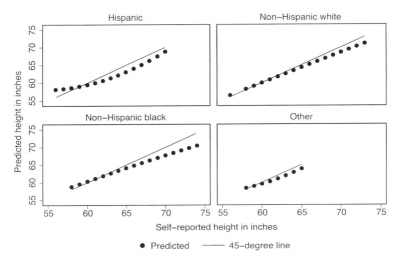

Fig. 3A.3 Compare predicted and self-reported height among females (graphs by race/ethnicity)

Note: See notes to figure 3A.1.

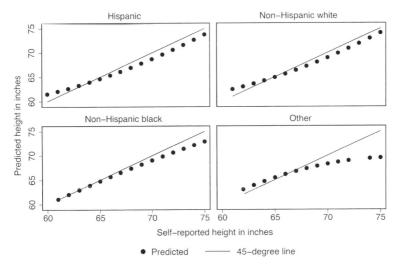

Fig. 3A.4 Compare predicted and self-reported height among males (graphs by race/ethnicity)

Note: See notes to figure 3A.1.

Appendix B

Table 3B.1   Items, descriptions, and expenditure shares for ACCRA data collected in year 1992

Expenditure share within each category	Item	Item description
Grocery (expenditure share 13%)		
0.0527	T-Bone steak	Price per pound
0.0527	Ground beef or hamburger	Price per pound, lowest price
0.0492	Sausage	Price per pound; Jimmy Dean 100% pork
0.0371	Frying chicken	Price per pound, whole fryer
0.0306	Chunk light tuna	6.125-6.5 oz can, Starkist or Chicken of the Sea, packed in oil
0.0494	Whole milk	Half-gallon carton
0.009	Eggs	One dozen, grade A, large
0.0376	Margarine	One pound, cubes, Blue Bonnet or Parkay
0.0376	Parmesan cheese, grated	8 oz. canister, Kraft brand
0.0228	Potatoes	10 pound sack, white or red
0.0474	Bananas	Price per pound
0.0228	Iceberg lettuce	Head, approximately 1.25 pounds
0.0818	Bread, white	24 oz. loaf, lowest price, or prorated 24-oz. equivalent, lowest price
0.0748	Cigarettes	Carton, Winston, king-size (85 mm.)
0.0513	Coffee, vacuum-packed	13 oz. can, Maxwell House, Hills Brothers, or Folgers
0.0314	Sugar	5 pounds, cane or beet, lowest price
0.0419	Corn flakes	18 oz., Kellogg's or Post Toasties
0.0072	Sweet peas	15-17 oz. can, Del Monte or Green Giant
0.0072	Tomatoes	14-1/2 oz. can, Hunt's or Del Monte
0.0333	Peaches	29 oz. can, Hunt's, Del Monte, or Libby's, halves or slices
0.0221	Facial tissues	175-count box, Kleenex brand
0.0417	Washing powder	42 oz. ("Ultra"), Tide, Bold, or Cheer
0.0184	Shortening	3 pound can, all-vegetable, Crisco brand
0.0384	Frozen orange juice	12 oz. can, Minute Maid brand
0.0072	Frozen corn	10 oz. can, whole kernel, lowest price
0.056	Baby food	4-4.5 oz. jar, strained vegetables, lowest price
0.0384	Soft drink	2 liter Coca-Cola, excluding any deposit
Housing (expenditure share 28%)		
0.2631	Apartment, monthly rent	Two-bedroom, unfurnished, excluding all utilities except water, 1-1/2 baths, approximately 950 sq. ft.
	Total purchase price	1,800 sq. ft. living area new house, 8,000 sq. ft. lot, urban area with all utilities
	Mortgage rate	Effective rate, including points and origination fee, for 30-year conventional fixed- or adjustable-rate mortgage
0.7369	Monthly payment	Principal and interest, using mortgage rate from item 29B and assuming 25% down payment

Table 3B.2   **Items, descriptions, and expenditure shares for ACCRA data collected in year 1992**

Expenditure share within each category	Item	Item description
Utilities (expenditure share 9%)		
0.9	Total home energy cost	Monthly cost, at current rates, for average monthly consumption of all types of energy during the previous 12 months for the type of home specified in item 29A
	Electricity	Average monthly cost for all-electric homes is shown in column 30A; average monthly cost for homes using other types of energy as well is shown in column 30B
	Other home energy	Average monthly cost at current rates for natural gas, fuel oil, coal, wood, and any other forms of energy except electricity
0.1	Telephone	Private residential line; customer owns instruments. Price includes: basic monthly rate; additional local use charges, if any, incurred by a family of four; Touch Tone fee; all other mandatory monthly charges, such as long distance access fee and 911 fee; and all taxes foregoing
Transportation (expenditure share 10%)		
0.1	Commuter fare	One-way commuting fare, up to ten miles
0.3541	Auto maintenance	Average price to computer—or spin balance—one front wheel
0.5459	Gasoline	One gallon regular unleaded, national brand, including all taxes; cash price at self-service pump if available
Health Care (expenditure share 5%)		
0.175	Hospital room	Average cost per day for semiprivate room
0.3509	Office visit, doctor	American Medical Association procedure 90050: general practitioner's routine examination of established patient
0.3509	Office visit, dentist	American Dental Association procedure 1110 (adult teeth cleaning) and 0120 (periodic oral examination)
0.1232	Aspirin	100 table bottle, Bayer brand, 325 mg. tablets

Table 3B.3   **Items, descriptions, and expenditure shares for ACCRA data collected in year 1992**

Expenditure share within each category	Item	Item description
Miscellaneous (expenditure share 35%)		
0.095	Hamburger sandwich	1/4 pound patty with cheese, pickle, onion, mustard, and catsup. McDonald's Quarter-Pounder with Cheese, where available
0.095	Pizza	12″–13″ thin crust cheese pizza. Pizza Hut or Pizza Inn, where available
0.095	Fried chicken	Thigh and drumstick, with or without extras, whichever is less expensive. Kentucky Fried Chicken or Church's where available
0.0174	Haircut	Man's barber shop haircut, no styling
0.0174	Beauty salon	Woman's shampoo, trim, and blow dry
0.0174	Toothpaste	6 oz–7 oz. tube, Crest or Colgate
0.0174	Shampoo	15 oz. bottle, Alberto VO-5
0.0174	Dry cleaning	Man's two-piece suit
0.115	Man's dress shirt	Arrow, Enro, Van Heusen, or J.C. Penney's Stafford. White, cotton/polyester blend (at least 55% cotton), long sleeves
0.0523	Boy's underwear	Package of three briefs, size 10-14, cotton, lowest price
0.115	Man's denim jeans	Levi's brand, 501s or 505s, rinsed, washed, or bleached, size 28/30–34/36
0.0742	Major appliance repair	Home service call, clothes washing machine; minimum labor charge, excluding parts
0.0271	Newspaper subscription	Daily and Sunday home delivery, large-city newspaper
0.459	Movie	First-run, indoor, evening, no discount
0.459	Bowling	Price per line (game), evening rate
0.0654	Tennis balls	Can of three extra duty, yellow, Wilson or Penn Brand
0.0384	Board game	Parker Brothers "Monopoly," no. 9 edition
0.0163	Liquor	J&B Scotch, 750 ml. bottle
0.0162	Beer	Budweiser or Miller Lite, 6-pack, 12 oz. containers, excluding any deposit
0.0163	Wine	Gallo chablis blanc, 1.5 L bottle

Source: Council for Community and Economic Research (C2ER)—formerly known as ACCRA.

Appendix C

Table 3C.1   **Effect of price per gram of calorie on log BMI, without controlling for health or demographic variables**

	Model specification		
Independent variable	*I*	*II*	*III*
BMI two years ago	0.680***	0.653***	0.664***
	(0.029)	(0.034)	(0.030)
BMI four years ago	0.216***	0.198***	0.210***
	(0.025)	(0.027)	(0.024)
Log of price per calorie	−2.571*	−2.518*	−1.811
	(1.409)	(1.381)	(1.709)
Log of price per calorie · (obese at baseline)		2.041	
		(3.983)	
Log of price per calorie · (poor at baseline)			−1.237
			(2.974)
Log of cigarettes price	0.544	0.401	0.581
	(0.709)	(0.650)	(0.701)
Log of cigarettes price · (obese at baseline)		0.257	
		(0.525)	
Log of cigarettes price · (poor at baseline)			−0.395
			(0.442)
Log of gasoline price	−0.107	−0.233	0.193
	(1.076)	(0.945)	(1.106)
Log of gasoline price · (obese at baseline)		0.640	
		(1.567)	
Log of gasoline price · (poor at baseline)			−0.306
			(1.308)
Log of nonfood price	0.768	0.422	0.259
	(0.592)	(0.517)	(0.588)
Log of nonfood price · (obese at baseline)		−0.753*	
		(0.452)	
Log of nonfood price · (poor at baseline)			0.976**
			(0.446)
N	8,231	8,231	8,231

Source: Health and Retirement Study, 1992–2004, ACCRA price data, 1992–2003.

Notes: All models also include the following variables: year dummies, self-rated health, chronic conditions, working status, marital status, household income and household wealth.

***p < 0.01

**p < 0.05

*p < 0.10

References

Arellano, M., and S. Bond. 1991. Some tests of specification for panel data: Monte Carlo evidence and an application to employment equations. *Review of Economic Studies* 58 (2): 277–97.

Arellano, M., and O. Bover. 1995. Another look at the instrumental variable estimation of error-components models. *Journal of Econometrics* 68 (1): 29–51.

Auld, M., and L. Powell. 2008. Economics of food energy density and adolescent body weight. *Economica* 76 (304): 719–40.

Basker, E. 2005. Selling a cheaper mousetrap: Wal-Mart's effect on retail prices. *Journal of Urban Economics* 58 (2): 203–29.

Blundell, R., and S. Bond. 1998. Initial conditions and moment restrictions in dynamic panel data models. *Journal of Econometrics* 87 (1): 115–43.

Cawley, J. 1999. *Obesity and addiction.* Phd diss. University of Chicago, Chicago, IL.

Chou, S.-Y., M. Grossman, and H. Saffer. 2004. An economic analysis of adult obesity: Results from the behavioral risk factor surveillance system. *Journal of Health Economics* 23 (3): 565–87.

Gelbach, J. B., J. Klick, and T. Stratmann. 2007. Cheap donuts and expensive broccoli: The effect of relative prices on obesity. Available at SSRN: http://ssrn.com/abstract-976484.

Hausman, J., and E. Leibtag. 2004. CPI bias from supercenters: Does the BLS know that Wal-Mart exists? NBER Working Paper no. 10712. Cambridge, MA: National Bureau of Economic Research, August.

Heo, M., M. S. Faith, and A. Pietrobelli. 2002. Resistance to change of adulthood body mass index. *International Journal of Obesity* 26 (10): 1404–5.

Jacobson, M. F., and K. D. Brownell. 2000. Small taxes on soft drinks and snack foods to promote health. *American Journal of Public Health* 90 (6): 854–7.

Lakdawalla, D. N., and T. J. Philipson. 2002. Technological change and the growth of obesity. NBER Working Paper no. 8946. Cambridge, MA: National Bureau of Economic Research, May.

Nestle, M., and M. F. Jacobson. 2000. Halting the obesity epidemic: A public health policy approach. *Public Health* 115 (1): 12–24.

Sturm, R., and A. Datar. 2005. Body mass index in elementary school children, metropolitan area food prices and food outlet density. *Public Health* 119 (12): 1059–68.

———. 2008. Food prices and weight gain during elementary school: 5-year update. *Public Health* 122 (11): 1140–3.

Wooldridge, J. M. 2002. *Econometric analysis of cross section and panel data.* Cambridge and London: MIT Press.

4

Outcomes in a Program that Offers Financial Rewards for Weight Loss

John Cawley and Joshua A. Price

4.1 Introduction

A variety of approaches are being used to treat obesity and encourage weight loss. One promising strategy based on psychology and behavioral economics is to offer financial incentives for weight loss. Obesity is costly to health insurance companies (Finkelstein, Fiebelkorn, and Wang 2003) and employers (Cawley, Rizzo, and Haas 2007), so for either or both of those organizations to offer monetary incentives for enrollees or employees to lose weight could be mutually beneficial.

This chapter studies data from a firm that coordinates a program of financial incentives for weight loss in various work sites in the United States. We study attrition and weight loss in three types of incentive programs: one that offers no financial rewards for weight loss, one that offers quarterly payments that rise in value with the amount of weight loss, and a third that takes deposits (bonds) that are only refunded if the employee achieves a specific weight loss goal, and also includes a quarterly lottery for those who have lost weight. Relative to previous studies of weight loss in response to financial incentives, strengths of this study include a large sample size (2,407) and a long intervention (one year).

John Cawley is an associate professor in the Department of Policy Analysis and Management at Cornell University, and a research associate of the National Bureau of Economic Research. Joshua A. Price is assistant professor of economics at the University of Texas at Arlington.

The authors thank Company X for providing their data and for the generosity of their time in explaining their intervention and discussing the data. For helpful comments, the authors thank Dan Benjamin, Dhaval Dave, Ron Ehrenberg, Michael Grossman, Naci Mocan, and participants in a Cornell work-in-progress seminar, the NBER Preconference and Conference on Economic Aspects of Obesity. We thank the USDA Economic Research Service for financial support through its Behavioral Health Economics Research Program.

A 2007 Institute of Medicine report on obesity prevention set the immediate next step—which it described as an essential priority action for the near future—as "learning what works and what does not work and broadly sharing that information." (Institute of Medicine 2007, 410). It also notes that "All types of evaluation can make an important contribution to the evidence base upon which to design policies, programs, and interventions." (IOM 2007, 4). This chapter makes a contribution to that effort by documenting enrollment, attrition, and weight loss in one interesting and promising intervention. This chapter presents basic patterns in the data; a subsequent chapter will estimate regression models to test specific hypotheses about attrition and weight loss.

4.2   Conceptual Framework and Previous Literature

For obese people, weight loss would likely result in substantial benefits.[1] For example, the health benefits of modest weight loss (defined as 5 to 10 percent of starting weight) include decreased blood pressure and cholesterol, and a 25 percent reduction in mortality risk for type 2 diabetics (Vidal 2002). Weight loss may also improve quality of life (Ford et al. 2001). There may also be financial benefits. Cawley (2004) finds a causal impact of weight on wages, and that obese white females earn roughly 11 percent less than healthy-weight white females. Finkelstein, Fiebelkorn, and Wang (2003) calculate that, relative to the healthy weight, the obese incur $125 higher annual out-of-pocket health care costs. With two-thirds of Americans overweight or obese (Ogden et al. 2006), and given these potential benefits of weight loss, it may not be surprising that 46 percent of all American women and 33 percent of all American men are trying to lose weight (Bish et al. 2005).

Most people fail in their attempts to lose weight,[2] and many of those who are successful in losing weight regain it in a short period of time.[3] For ex-

---

1. There are two ways researchers have sought to measure the benefits of weight loss. The first is to examine changes in outcomes associated with losing weight. The second is to compare the outcomes of individuals of different weight, and assume that the difference in outcomes is due to the difference in weight. Each has its limitations: weight loss studies often lack power, and comparisons across weight levels are confounded by differences in unobserved characteristics. Vidal (2002) assesses the evidence on the benefits of weight loss and concludes that modest weight loss (5 to 10 percent of initial body weight) improves cardiovascular risk factors and helps prevent or delay the onset of type 2 diabetes and hypertension.

2. Some obese individuals are able to lose weight by modifying their behaviors: eating less and exercising more. In the select group enrolled in the Weight Control Registry, all of whom have lost at least thirty pounds and kept it off for at least one year, 44.6 percent report losing the weight entirely on their own, that is, without the help of a commercial program, physician, or nutritionist (Wing and Phelan 2005). Clearly, such statistics do not generalize to the population; anyone who failed at initial weight loss is ineligible for this registry of people who maintained weight loss for a year.

3. Conventional wisdom is that virtually no one succeeds at maintaining weight loss. This perception has been traced back to a 1959 study of 100 obese individuals in which only 2 percent maintained loss of twenty pounds or more two years after the treatment (Stunkard and

ample, in one community-based study of weight gain prevention (Crawford, Jeffery, and French 2000), most (53.7 percent) participants *gained* weight in the first twelve months, three-quarters gained weight over three years, and only 4.6 percent lost weight and maintained the loss for three years.

Theory and evidence from psychology and behavioral economics provide several explanations for why so many weight loss attempts fail. First, the benefits of weight loss are not salient. For example, foregone quality of life and lost wages are not visible and therefore they are frequently unrecognized as opportunity costs (Bastiat 1850).

A second possible explanation for repeated failure at weight loss is that the benefits of weight loss may not be immediate. Improvements in health and labor market outcomes may not occur for some time after weight loss, and Ainslie (1975) finds consistent evidence that there is a decline in the effectiveness of rewards as the rewards are delayed from the time of choice.

A third explanation for repeated failure at weight loss is that, contrary to the standard economic model of discounted utility (Samuelson 1937), people may discount hyperbolically, which produces time-inconsistent preferences (Ainslie 1975). In this context, time-inconsistent preferences mean that people want to do what is in their long-run interest (lose weight), but they consistently succumb to the temptation to eat and be sedentary. Thaler and Shefrin (1981) describe individual decision making as a battle between a farsighted planner (who in this context wants to diet) and a myopic doer (who in this context wants to eat and be sedentary).

One intervention, financial rewards for weight loss, may offer a solution to the problems of salience, immediacy, and time-inconsistency. Financial rewards, even though they may be dwarfed in value by the other benefits of weight loss, have the benefit of being salient, with their amount and delivery date known with certainty in exchange for clearly defined objectives. Even small financial incentives can be effective because research has found that people tend not to compare payoffs to their income or wealth but instead "bracket" them—consider them in isolation (Read, Loewenstein, and Rabin 1999; Kahneman and Tversky 1979). Lotteries may be particularly cost-effective incentives for healthy behavior. People tend to overweight the probability of unlikely events and underweight the probability of likely events (Kahneman and Tversky 1979), implying that lotteries can be more attractive than certain payments, even if the two have equal expected values. Financial rewards can also be paid immediately, before other benefits of weight reduction may be realized.

Financial rewards can also be structured to help people with time-

McLaren-Hume 1959; Wing and Phelan 2005). However, the 1959 study was based on a crude diet intervention with negligible support or follow-up so its poor results may not generalize to today's much more intensive interventions.

inconsistent preferences stay committed to weight loss. In general, pre-commitment devices may help people with time-inconsistent preferences empower their farsighted planner (Strotz 1955–1956; Laibson 1997). In this context, one could allow people to post a bond that is automatically forfeited if they fail to achieve their weight loss goals. Such a bond allows a person to influence their own future decisions by increasing the punishment for suc-cumbing to short-run temptation. People tend to exhibit loss aversion—they dislike losing their own money more than they like winning an equal amount of someone else's money (Tversky and Kahneman 1991; Camerer 2005), which suggests that a posted bond may be more effective than a reward of the same size. Using a bond to increase adherence to a weight loss regimen does not guarantee success. Even individuals who are aware of their time-inconsistent preferences may still be partially naive in that they overestimate their future willpower (O'Donoghue and Rabin 2001), and as a result may either post too small a bond or have too much faith in the bond as a precom-mitment device.

Motivated by these theories and findings, several businesses now help employers offer financial incentives for employee weight loss. In addition, several businesses help consumers post bonds that are only refunded if one achieves specific weight loss goals. The William Hill betting agency in the U.K. books wagers that the bettor cannot achieve a specified weight loss in a specific period of time and verifies the weight loss with a medical examina-tion (Burger and Lynham 2008).[4] A company named stickK.com[5] that was founded by Yale economists Ian Ayres and Dean Karlan allows people to post bonds that are forfeited if they fail to meet their weight loss goal. How-ever, verification is weak: success in achieving one's goal is determined (and refunds are made) based on either the honor system or through verification by a third party chosen by the bettor, and if the third party does not submit a report the self-report of the bettor is accepted.

The contribution of this chapter is to examine outcomes in a program that offers various financial rewards (including certain payments, lotteries, and refundable bonds) for weight loss. The outcomes we examine include attrition and weight loss, both in pounds and as a percentage of baseline weight.

A substantial literature confirms that financial incentives influence healthy behaviors. Kane et al. (2004) review forty-two studies of the effect of eco-nomic incentives on preventive behaviors such as immunization, smoking cessation, and exercise; they find that the economic incentives were effective at changing behavior in 73 percent of studies. Financial incentives form the basis for an innovative substance abuse treatment program known as

---

4. This market is relatively small—the annual number of applications for such bets is roughly 200 (Burger and Lynham 2008).

5. The web site's Frequently Asked Questions page states that the company's name includes two K's because "K" often symbolizes "contract" in legal writing.

contingency management. A meta-analysis found overwhelming evidence that such incentives raise compliance (drug abstinence) by an average of 30 percent (Lussier et al. 2006). Consistent with bracketing, even small financial incentives have proven effective; for example, as little as $2.50 for a single negative test result for cocaine (Higgins, Allesi, and Dantona 2002).

Specific to the current context, there is mixed empirical evidence on the extent to which weight loss is responsive to financial rewards. A recent review and meta-analysis (Paul-Ebhohimhen and Avenell 2007) identified nine published randomized controlled trials (RCTs) that used guaranteed financial incentives (i.e., certain payments, not lotteries) for weight loss, with a follow-up of at least one year. The meta-analysis was unable to reject the null hypothesis of no effect of financial rewards on weight loss; it calculated a mean weight loss of 0.4 kg at twelve months, which was not statistically significant. A broader set of studies (including, e.g., those with nonrandomized designs or shorter follow-up) are listed in appendix table 4A.1.[6]

Relative to past studies, ours has several advantages. This study has a relatively large sample size (2,407); for comparison, the sample size of all published RCTs of financial incentives for weight loss combined totals 424 (treatment $N = 252$, control $N = 172$) (Paul-Ebhohimhen and Avenell 2007). The intervention studied by this chapter also covers a relatively long time period (one year). Moreover, we examine data from a real-world intervention rather than one constructed by, and overseen by researchers, which is important because a criticism of studies of weight loss programs is that it is unclear how the results of pilot programs generalize to real-world implementation. A limitation of this study, however, is that it is opportunistic data; individuals were not randomly assigned to different incentive schedules for weight loss.

4.3 Description of the Intervention

Our data come from a company (that we will call Company X) that helps employers provide financial incentives for their employees to lose weight; specifically, it monitors employee weight loss and pays the rewards. After an employer contracts with Company X, Company X has a kickoff event in the workplace that explains the program to the employees and encourages them to sign up. Participation is optional. Those who sign up select a physical activity regimen at either the foundation (easiest), intermediate, or advanced level. The program consists of several elements: (a) daily e-mail coaching that includes information about healthy and effective methods of weight loss such as decreasing calorie intake and increasing physical activity in a manner consistent with the regimen the enrollee chose at baseline;

---

6. There are other studies that offer financial rewards for exercise or for attending weight loss programs, but appendix table 4A.1 is limited to studies of financial rewards for weight loss.

(b) call center support; (c) weigh-ins at least once a quarter; and (d) financial incentives for achieving specific weight loss targets. Only employees who are overweight (body mass index [BMI] of at least 25) are eligible to receive financial rewards, and no financial rewards will be paid once an employee's BMI falls below 25 (i.e., when the employee falls into the "healthy weight" category).

The weigh-ins take place in kiosks that are compliant with the Health Insurance Portability and Accountability Act of 1996 (HIPAA)[7] and which Company X installs in the employer's workplace. Employees enter the privacy-protected kiosk and stand on a scale; their body mass index is recorded and sent over an Internet connection to their personal web page as well as to Company X's database. Participants can weigh themselves as often as they like, and the lowest recorded weight will be counted as that quarter's weight. Financial rewards are paid based on percent of baseline weight lost.[8]

Company X has a standard set of incentives that it proposes, but employers can modify it. In our data, there are three incentive schedules. The first is Company X's standard set of incentives: the employee participants pay no fee (all costs are paid by the employer), and employees receive quarterly payments determined by percent of baseline weight lost to date. Table 4.1 lists the standard set of incentives: payment thresholds occur at each percentage point of weight loss up to 5 percent (1, 2, 3, 4, 5), then thresholds occur every 5 percentage points (5, 10, 15, 20, 25, 30) up to 30 percent of weight loss. The payment associated with these thresholds varies; for the first seven (1, 2, 3, 4, 5, 10, 15) the reward is a dollar per percentage point of weight loss. Then the per-percentage-point rewards increase: $25 for losing 20 percent, $35 for losing 25 percent, and $50 for losing 30 percent. These are monthly amounts that are paid quarterly, so someone who loses 5 percent of his weight and keeps it off for three months receives a $15 check for the quarter ($5 monthly payment × 3 months). Five employers (with a total of thirteen work sites participating) used this standard incentives schedule.

The second ("modified") incentive schedule, used by one employer (with two work sites participating), is shown in table 4.2 and includes both a lottery and a deposit contract (bonds). The lottery takes place each quarter and the prizes are gift certificates (ten $50 gift cards and ten $50 salon vouchers); only

7. The Health Insurance Portability and Accountability Act (HIPAA) regulates the disclosure of health information.

8. We asked Company X whether people game the system by trying to weigh more at baseline (from which future weight losses are judged). They said that through the cameras installed in their kiosks they do not see people wearing heavier clothes to the baseline weigh-in than to later weigh-ins; in all cases people seem for vanity reasons to remove shoes and sweaters before weighing in. However, Company X acknowledges that they have no way to know if people, for example, hid weights in their pockets or shoes before the baseline weigh-in. If people engage in such deception then we would expect to see significant drops in weight at the first weigh-in after baseline, but we do not find this pattern in the data.

Table 4.1   **Financial rewards based on weight loss, "standard incentives"**

Weight loss (as % of baseline weight)	Dollar reward per month (Paid quarterly)
1	1
2	2
3	3
4	4
5	5
10	10
15	15
20	25
25	35
30	50

Notes: Only participants with BMI over 25 (that is, those who are overweight or obese) are eligible to receive incentives. Moreover, people can only get incentives for weight loss down to a BMI of 25—there is no financial incentive for anyone in the healthy weight (18.5 to 25) or underweight (< 18.5) BMI categories to lose weight.

Table 4.2   **Financial rewards based on weight loss, "modified incentives"**

Weight loss (as % of baseline weight)	Reward
Greater than zero	Entered into quarterly drawing for gift certificates: ten $50 gift cards each quarter and ten $50 salon vouchers each quarter.
5	Complete reimbursement of monthly fees (11 * $9.95 = $109.45), paid at end of year
10	Complete reimbursement of monthly fees (11 * $9.95 = $109.45) plus $100 bonus, paid at end of year
"Biggest loser" (as % of baseline) at work site	$250 gift certificate, awarded at end of year, plus the appropriate award listed above for the specific amount of weight loss

Notes: Only participants with BMI over 25 (that is, those who are overweight or obese) are eligible to receive incentives. Moreover, people can only get incentives for weight loss down to a BMI of 25—there is no financial incentive for anyone in the healthy weight (18.5 to 25) or underweight (< 18.5) BMI categories to lose weight.

those who had lost some weight since baseline are eligible for the drawing. The deposit contract is that employees must pay $9.95 per month (except the first month, which is free), all of which (11 × $9.95 or $109.45) is refunded at the end of the year if the respondent loses at least 5 percent of baseline weight by year's end. If the respondent loses 10 percent or more of their baseline weight, they receive in addition to their refunded fees ($109.45) a $100 bonus, for a total of $229.40. In addition, the "biggest loser" (as a percent of baseline weight) receives a $250 gift certificate at the end of the year.

   We refer to the monthly fees as a bond because the participant posts his or her own money, which is returned contingent on achieving certain weight loss goals. However, the bond is paid in monthly installments, which may generate different behavior than if it was paid in full before beginning the program. A participant needs just a single moment of willpower to post an up-front bond, but must exercise willpower eleven times to pay all of the fees in this schedule. Before paying each of those monthly fees, the respondent may consider his likelihood of losing sufficient weight to receive a refund, and thus whether to continue participating. For this reason, attrition may be higher for refundable monthly fees than it would be for a single up-front bond.

Whether a participant would receive a higher payoff in the standard or modified group depends on both quarter and magnitude of weight loss. In quarters one through three, the standard incentives are more generous than the modified incentives at all levels of weight loss, with the exception that those losing between 0.1 percent and 0.9 percent of baseline weight receive no reward in the standard incentives group, but are eligible for the lottery for gift cards in the modified incentives group. In quarter four, the standard incentives are more generous for weight loss of between 1 percent and 4 percent, but the modified incentives are more generous for weight loss of 5 percent or more.

The third ("control") schedule, used by one employer (with a total of two work sites), offered no incentives for weight loss, but did include one modest incentive to not attrite: participants were promised $20 if they participated for the entire year (i.e., weighed in at least once in each of the four quarters). This group received all of the features of the Company X intervention (daily e-mails, call center access, weigh-ins at the kiosk) but were offered no incentives for weight loss, making it useful both as a control group for measuring the impact of financial incentives isolated from all the other program elements, and for estimating the impact of the Company X treatment minus the financial incentives.

Figure 4.1 presents a flow diagram of attrition and analysis for all three groups (standard incentives, modified incentives, control) combined.

4.4   Hypotheses

Part of our purpose in this chapter is exploratory—to measure enrollment, attrition, and weight loss in these programs. We focus in particular on attrition and weight loss as outcomes because the National Institutes of Health (NIH) Technology Assessment Conference Panel (1993) recommends using the percentage of all beginning participants who complete the program, and the percentage of those completing the program who achieve various degrees of weight loss as measures of program success. The NIH considers a loss of 10 percent of baseline weight in six months to one year to be good progress for an obese individual (USDHHS 2000).

Another purpose of this chapter is to test the following hypotheses.

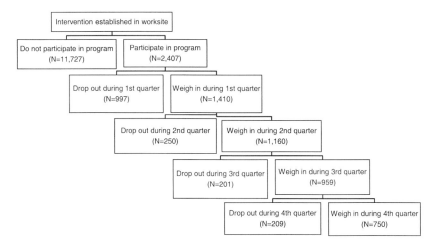

Fig. 4.1   Flow diagram of attrition and analysis

4.4.1   Hypotheses Regarding Enrollment

There will be lower enrollment in the program that required people to post forfeitable bonds. The law of demand states that the quantity demanded falls with price. The program that requires people to post a forfeitable bond raises the expected price of participation, assuming that not all possible participants expect a 100 percent probability of success (and therefore the return of their bond). The published literature confirms that, all else equal, enrollment in weight loss programs is lower if people are asked to post forfeitable bonds (e.g., Jeffery, Thompson, and Wing 1978).

Those who are willing to post a forfeitable bond will be better motivated or prepared for weight loss than those not required to post such a bond. In other words, we expect differential selection—those unwilling to post a forfeitable bond because they expect little weight loss are excluded from the modified incentives group, but are not excluded from the control group or standard incentives group. As a result, we expect that the modified incentives group will be better prepared or motivated for weight loss than the other groups.

4.4.2   Hypotheses Regarding Attrition

There will be lower attrition in the program that required employees to post bonds that are refundable based on achievement of weight loss goals. Those willing to post a bond are expected to be more motivated or determined to lose weight. Selection aside, bonds may also increase retention.

Those who attrite will have been relatively unsuccessful at weight loss. Participants enroll with incomplete information about certain costs and benefits of participating. Those that lose relatively little weight may update their prior beliefs and conclude that it is utility maximizing for them to drop out of the intervention. This is especially true of those in the modified incentives group, who are charged a monthly fee for participation that will not be refunded if year-end weight loss is less than 5 percent of baseline weight.

4.4.3   Hypotheses Regarding Weight Loss

Weight loss will be greater for those offered financial rewards for weight loss. Both the standard incentives group and the modified incentives group were offered financial rewards for weight loss, whereas the control group was not offered any. In other words, we hypothesize that financial rewards are effective in promoting weight loss.

In quarter four, weight loss will be greater in the modified incentives group than in the standard incentives group.

This prediction is based on the magnitude of the incentives; the modified incentives group has much greater incentives for 5 percent and 10 percent weight loss by the end of quarter four. Specifically, the modified incentives group receives a refund of their $119.40 bond if at least 5 percent of weight is lost, with an additional bonus of $100 if 10 percent of weight is lost. Moreover, those achieving very high weight loss will be in competition for the $250 bonus for being the "biggest loser." In contrast, the standard incentives group is paid $5 per month for losing 5 percent of starting weight and $10 per month for losing 10 percent of starting weight (triple those amounts for the entire quarter). Relative to the standard incentives, the modified incentives create greater incentives for weight loss by the end of quarter four.

In addition, there are two reasons that the relative performance of the modified incentives group by the end of quarter four might be better than one would expect based on the magnitude of the rewards alone. First, we expect differential selection—those willing to post a bond are likely better prepared or more motivated for weight loss. Second, the research literature on loss aversion indicates that people are more motivated by a risk of losing their own money (as in the modified incentives group) than they are by the prospect of winning someone else's money (as in the standard incentives group).

In quarters one through three, weight loss will be greater in the standard incentives group than in the modified incentives group.

This prediction is also based on the magnitude of the incentives. In quarters one through three, the standard incentives group is offered $5 per month for 5 percent weight loss, and $10 per month for 10 percent weight loss (see table 4.1 for the full schedule of financial rewards). In contrast, there is no marginal reward for 5 percent or 10 percent weight loss in any of the first three quarters for the modified incentives group (those losing any weight at all are eligible for lottery prizes, but there is no additional reward for any weight loss above the trivial amount that makes one eligible for the lottery).

However, there are three reasons that the relative performance of the modified incentives group in quarters one through three might be better than one would expect based on the magnitude of the rewards alone. The first reason is differential selection. The second reason is loss aversion; the fear of losing one's money at year's end may motivate members of the modified incentives group to lose weight in the early quarters, even when there are no quarter-specific rewards for doing so. Third, it may take more than one quarter to achieve 5 percent or 10 percent weight loss, so in order to meet their year-end goals members of the modified incentives group may have to lose weight in earlier quarters, even though they have no financial incentives for meaningful weight loss in those quarters.

4.5   Methods and Data

A limitation of our data is that they are not the result of a randomized controlled trial. They are opportunistic data, provided to us by Company X. As a result, we face two challenges: (a) assignment to the three treatment groups is nonrandom: the incentive schedules were chosen by the employers; (b) the participation of employees is voluntary; there is selection by employees.

Regarding problem number one (selection by employers into different incentive schedules), we assume that this is ignorable. In other words, we assume that employer preference for incentive structure is uncorrelated with unobserved employee characteristics that affect attrition and weight loss. Company X told us that the reason that one employer requested the modified incentives schedule (with forfeitable bonds) is because the company didn't want to pay for cash rewards. In contrast, it would be problematic if the modified schedule was requested because the employer thought it would be more effective for their particular employees.

A related problem is that unobserved employee characteristics may vary systematically across the three groups. Company X designed this intervention for office employees who spend their days in front of computers; it is they, for example, who are most likely to read the daily e-mails regarding nutrition and physical activity. For the most part, enrollees fit this description. Table 4.3 lists the industries of the employers. The five employers (with a total of thirteen work sites) in the standard incentive group include a Health Maintenance Organization (HMO) office, an HMO clinic (in which enrollees are nurses), two bank offices, and an insurance company. The one employer (with a total of two work sites) that instituted the modified incentive schedule is an insurance company, and the one employer (with a total of two work sites) in the control group is the administrative office of a grocery chain. Company X tells us that the nurses (who face the standard incentive schedule) have generally been least compliant with the program; they specu-

Table 4.3   Description of employers

Employer	Description	Incentive schedule
1	HMO clinic—nurses	Standard
2	Banking office	Standard
3	HMO office	Standard
4	Banking office	Standard
5	Insurance office	Standard
6	Insurance company	Modified
7	Grocery administrative office	Control

late that it may be because they do not work in front of computers all day and thus derive less benefit from the daily e-mails and the online tracking of measured weight.

Regarding problem number two (selection by employees into participation), we consider this to be a limitation for generalizing results to the entire population, but not a problem in the sense that any similar intervention is also likely to be optional, and so the findings for a set of volunteers is most relevant. All of the studies in appendix table 4A.1 are based on volunteers recruited to participate in a weight loss program, and are likewise not a random sample of the general population.

An additional problem when studying weight loss is that there is attrition from the program. Weight loss interventions in general (even those without financial rewards) typically have substantial attrition (Ware 2003; Gadbury, Coffey, and Allison 2003). There are several strategies for handling the attrition when evaluating interventions. The definitive is the intent-to-treat analysis, which includes all patients in their groups, regardless of whether they received the treatment, deviated from the protocol, or withdrew (Ware 2003). However, to implement this one must have follow-up data on all of the dropouts, which is not available in this case. Another option is to conduct a "completers" analysis, which examines data only for those who completed the study. This is likely to be biased toward showing an impact of the treatment, as those most likely to quit are probably those for whom the intervention was least effective (Ware 2003). Another option is last-observation-carried-forward, which assumes that the dropouts remained at their last measured weight. This also likely results in upward bias in estimates of program effectiveness, as weight regain is common (Ware 2003; Serdula et al. 1999). Another option is baseline-carried-forward, which assumes that after attriting the subjects return to their baseline weight. This may cause downward bias in the estimate of efficacy, as weight regain may be incomplete or slow. We present findings for completers analysis, last-observation-carried-forward, and baseline-carried-forward.

The total number of employees in the data set is 2,407: 1,513 facing the standard incentives, 765 facing the modified incentives, and 129 in the control group with no financial incentives. The data cover 2004 to 2008. We drop from the sample participants with baseline BMI below twenty-five because they were not eligible for financial rewards. Thirteen participants in the control group were dropped because they were simultaneously participating in another workplace weight loss intervention.

We estimate attrition rates by quarter and group. We graph the distribution of weight loss by group and quarter, both for a completers analysis (ignoring dropouts), assuming that dropouts stayed at their last measured weight (last-observation-carried-forward) and assuming that dropouts return to baseline (baseline-carried-forward). We also calculate the unconditional mean loss in pounds and percent of baseline weight lost by group and quarter, for a completers analysis, last-observation-carried-forward, and baseline-carried-forward.

4.6   Empirical Results

4.6.1   Descriptive Statistics

Table 4.4 presents the summary statistics for participants by group. Our overall sample ($N = 2,407$) consists of 1,513 participants in the standard incentives group, 765 participants in the modified incentives group, and 129 participants in the control group.

In each of these groups, men are a minority: 15.7 percent of the standard incentives group, 21.2 percent of the modified incentives group, and 35.7 percent of the control group. Average age ranges from 43.0 to 46.2 across groups, and average baseline BMI ranges between 31.3 and 32.8 across groups. In each group there is a strikingly high prevalence of morbid obesity (BMI of greater than or equal to forty). In the United States as a whole, the morbidly obese constitute 4.8 percent of the population and 7.3 percent of all overweight Americans (Ogden et al. 2006). In contrast, the morbidly obese constitute 28.7 percent of the standard incentives group, 30.5 percent of the modified incentives group, and 22.5 percent of the control group.

4.6.2   Enrollment

We hypothesized that: *There will be lower enrollment in the program that required people to post forfeitable bonds.* Table 4.5 lists the percent of the workforce that enrolled in the program, by incentive schedule. Ideally, we would know the number of employees with BMI of twenty-five or higher, because only they are eligible for financial rewards for weight loss. Instead, for the denominator we know only the total number of employees (i.e., those of all BMI). As a result, these are likely to be underestimates of the percentage of those eligible for financial rewards who enrolled in the program. Percent enrollment was 18.6 percent for the modified incentives (which required a bond), 24.8 percent for the standard incentives, and 20.3 percent

Table 4.4   Summary statistics by group

Variable	Standard incentives			Modified incentives			Control group		
	Obs.	Mean	Std. dev.	Obs.	Mean	Std. dev.	Obs.	Mean	Std. dev.
Initial BMI	1513	32.8	6.24	765	32.8	6.00	129	31.3	5.72
Male	1513	0.157	0.364	765	0.212	0.409	129	0.357	0.481
Age	1513	46.2	10.4	765	43.0	8.8	129	44.4	10.6
Height	1513	65.5	3.41	765	66.1	3.42	129	66.7	4.25
Overweight (30 > BMI > = 25)	1513	0.412	0.492	765	0.382	0.486	129	0.519	0.502
Obese (40 > BMI > = 30)	1513	0.301	0.459	765	0.314	0.464	129	0.256	0.438
Morbidly obese (BMI > = 40)	1513	0.287	0.452	765	0.305	0.461	129	0.225	0.419
Foundation exercise regimen	1513	0.601	0.490	765	0.550	0.498	129	0.488	0.502
Intermediate exercise regimen	1513	0.337	0.473	765	0.374	0.484	129	0.426	0.496
Advanced exercise regimen	1513	0.062	0.241	765	0.076	0.265	129	0.085	0.280
E-mail open rate	740	45.7	36.41	765	51.0	35.09	129	28.7	32.47

Table 4.5   **Enrollment rates**

	Control group (1)	Standard incentive group (2)	Modified incentive group (3)	*p*-value (1) equals (2)	*p*-value (1) equals (3)	*p*-value (2) equals (3)
Mean	0.203	0.248	0.186	0.613	0.839	0.477
(Std. dev.)	(0.100)	(0.115)	(0.024)			

Note: Enrollment rates are calculated by the fraction of those who enroll in the program by the total population of the workplace. Individuals with BMI < 25 may enroll in the program, but receive no payouts.

for the program that offered no financial rewards for weight loss but all of the other program elements (i.e., the control group). The point estimates of enrollment are consistent with our prediction that the requirement of a bond would result in lower enrollment, but the differences are not statistically significant.

We also hypothesized that: *Those who are willing to post a forfeitable bond will be better motivated or prepared for weight loss than those not required to post such a bond.* There are two variables that can give us information about the degree of such differences in selection. The first variable is the level of exercise regimen that the employee chose at the beginning of the program. If those willing to pay the monthly fees in the modified incentives group are more motivated or prepared to lose weight, one should find that they are less likely to choose the easiest exercise regimen. This is confirmed by the data. Table 4.4 indicates that the easiest exercise regimen (called Foundation) was chosen by 60.1 percent of the standard incentives group but only 55.0 percent of the modified incentives group, a difference significant at the 1 percent level. We also expected that the control group, offered $20 if they participated for the full year, would be less motivated on average and, therefore, more likely to choose the easiest exercise regimen than those in the modified incentives group, but we do not find this—an even lower percentage of the control group than the modified incentives group (48.8 percent versus 60.1 percent) chose the easiest exercise regimen, but the difference is not statistically significant.

The second variable that sheds light on difference in selectivity is the percentage of the program e-mails that enrollees read. If those willing to pay the monthly fees in the modified incentives group are more motivated or prepared to lose weight, one should find that they read a higher percentage of the program e-mails. That prediction is confirmed by the data—table 4.4 indicates that the average percentage of e-mails read was 51.0 percent for members of the modified incentives group compared to 45.7 percent for members of the standard incentives group, a difference significant at the 1 percent level. (A caveat is that this variable is missing for 51.1 percent of the standard incentives group—it simply wasn't recorded for certain employers in certain years.)

The control group, being paid to participate, had the lowest e-mail open rate of 28.7 percent, which is significantly different from both other groups at the 1 percent level. It is interesting that the control group had the lowest percentage choosing the easiest exercise regimen (which suggests more motivation or better preparation) but the lowest e-mail open rate (which suggests lower commitment).

Overall, the patterns of both exercise regimen and e-mail opening suggest that the group required to post a bond (i.e., the modified incentives group) was selected to be better prepared and more serious about weight loss than the standard incentives group, and therefore should be less likely to attrite and more likely to lose weight.

4.6.3   Attrition

Table 4.6 lists the cumulative percentages dropping out, by quarter, for each group. In the standard incentives group, 51.2 percent of baseline participants have dropped out by the end of quarter one, and cumulative attrition rises in the three subsequent quarters to 62.1 percent, 72.0 percent and 76.4 percent. In the modified incentives group, attrition is lower: 24.8 percent after one quarter, rising in the three subsequent quarters to 33.5 percent, 39.3 percent, and 57.4 percent. Even in the control group, where participants are promised $20 if they weigh in every quarter for a year, attrition is substantial: 25.6 percent after one quarter, rising in the three subsequent quarters to 39.5 percent, 45.0 percent, and 48.1 percent. When considering the levels of attrition, one should keep in mind that enrollees were already a select sample. Participation was optional, and most employees declined to enroll.

Attrition is typically substantial in weight loss interventions of all kinds (Ware 2003; Gadbury, Coffey, and Allison 2003). However, the attrition in these groups is particularly high. For example, a recent review (Paul-Ebhohimhen and Avenell 2007) of RCTs involving financial rewards for weight loss found that the maximum attrition in any such study was 57.9 per-

Table 4.6	Cumulative attrition, by group and quarter		
Quarter	Standard incentives (%)	Modified incentives (%)	Control group (%)
1	51.2[a,b]	24.8	25.6
2	62.1[a,b]	33.5	39.5
3	72.0[a,b]	39.3	45.0
4	76.4[a,b]	57.4[a]	48.1

[a]represents significant difference with the control group at the 5% level
[b]represents significant difference between standard and modified incentive groups at the 5% level

cent at thirteen months, far below what the standard incentives group experienced in twelve months (76.4 percent, but roughly equal to what the modified incentives group experienced at twelve months (57.4 percent). This suggests that real-world interventions may experience far higher rates of attrition than those overseen by researchers (who for the purposes of data quality undertake extensive efforts to keep enrollees from attriting), which raises questions about how well the results of pilot studies such as those in appendix table 4A.1 can be duplicated on a larger scale.

We hypothesized that: *There will be lower attrition in the program that required employees to post bonds that are refundable based on achievement of weight loss goals.* The data are consistent with this hypothesis; in every quarter, attrition is significantly lower in the modified than the standard incentives group. For example, table 4.6 shows that, by the end of quarter one, attrition in the modified incentives group is only half that in the standard incentives group (24.8 percent versus 51.2 percent). It is impossible to tell from our data whether the difference in attrition is due to selection or loss aversion. Selection was evident in the earlier finding that those in the modified incentives group were more likely to choose an advanced physical activity regimen and tend to open more program e-mails; before entering the program they may have been better prepared and more motivated to lose weight. On the other hand, those in the modified incentives group have "skin in the game" in the form of their deposits, and loss aversion may motivate them to stay in the program.

We also hypothesized that: *Those who attrite will have been relatively unsuccessful at weight loss.* Table 4.7 lists the weight loss (in pounds) by quarter, categorized by whether the participant dropped out in the following quarter or persisted in the program through the following quarter. The table is divided vertically into four panels: full sample, standard incentives group, modified incentives group, and control group. Among the full sample, those who drop out in the subsequent quarter have significantly lower average weight loss than those who persist through the next quarter, in quarters one, two, and three. For example, in the full sample, those who stay in the program through quarter two had quarter one weight loss of 4.67 pounds on average, whereas those who dropped out during quarter two had quarter one weight loss of 3.49 pounds on average. For the full sample in each quarter, the difference in mean weight loss to date is statistically significant at better than the 1 percent level. When we divide the sample by incentive schedule, the same pattern exists for those in the modified incentives group: in each of the first three quarters, weight loss to date is significantly lower among those who drop out in the following quarter than those who persist through the following quarter. Note that those in the modified incentives group have the greatest incentive to drop out if they are not making progress, because to persist requires paying monthly fees that may be forfeited. The pattern is weaker for the standard incentives group; in quarter two future dropouts

Table 4.7   **Weight loss by future attrition status**

Quarter	Persist in next quarter	Dropout next quarter	*t*-test *p*-value
	Full sample		
1	4.67	3.49	0.004
	(2.3%)	(1.8%)	
2	5.73	3.33	0.000
	(2.8%)	(1.7%)	
3	6.38	4.23	0.008
	(3.1%)	(2.0%)	
	Standard incentive group		
1	4.90	4.07	0.122
	(2.5%)	(2.1%)	
2	6.67	3.99	0.003
	(3.2%)	(2.0%)	
3	6.93	8.96	0.128
	(3.2%)	(4.3%)	
	Modified incentive group		
1	4.66	1.03	0.000
	(2.3%)	(0.6%)	
2	5.36	0.76	0.001
	(2.6%)	(0.3%)	
3	6.77	−1.91	0.000
	(3.4%)	(−1.0%)	
	Control group		
1	3.42	3.54	0.929
	(1.8%)	(1.5%)	
2	3.46	1.36	0.325
	(1.9%)	(0.6%)	
3	1.82	7.99	0.041
	(0.9%)	(4.0%)	

Note: Weight loss in pounds (percent weight loss in parentheses).

have significantly lower weight loss than those who persist through the next quarter, but the difference is not statistically significant. In quarter one and in quarter three, the sign is in the opposite direction and the difference is not statistically significant. For the control group, in no quarter do future dropouts have significantly lower weight loss to date than those who will persist in the program. On the whole, these results suggest that, for the full sample as well as for the modified incentive group in particular, those who attrite are those who have been relatively unsuccessful at weight loss. In other words, the participants who are relatively successful at losing weight are more likely to remain in the program.

4.6.4   Weight Loss

The distribution of percent weight loss at the end of the program (end of quarter four), is shown in figure 4.2 (for the standard incentives group), figure

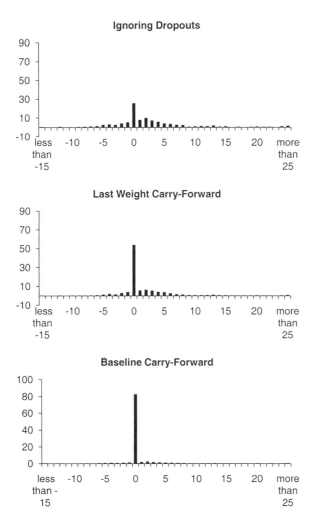

Fig. 4.2   Distribution of percent weight loss under standard incentives, quarter 4

4.3 (for the modified incentives group), and figure 4.4 (for the control group). The horizontal axis shows the percent of baseline weight lost (rounded down to the nearest percentage point[9]) and the vertical axis indicates the percentage of that sample. Each figure consists of three graphs: the top graph is the distribution of weight loss in a completers analysis that ignores dropouts, the

9. We round down so that everyone indicated as having a specific percent weight loss received exactly the reward associated with that percent weight loss. If we rounded to the nearest percentage point, a participant who lost 4.6 percent of her starting weight would be rounded to 5 percent even though she would not have qualified for the financial reward associated with achieving 5 percent weight loss.

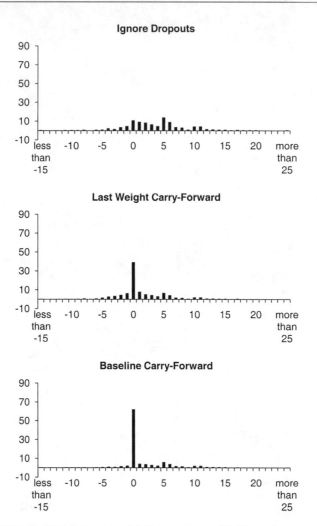

Fig. 4.3   Distribution of percent weight loss under modified incentives, quarter 4

middle graph is from a last-observation-carried-forward analysis in which dropouts are assumed to have stayed at their last measured weight, and the bottom graph is the distribution of weight loss in a baseline-carried-forward analysis that assumes that every dropout returned to their baseline weight. A comparison of the top, middle, and bottom graphs confirms that how attrition is handled has a substantial impact on estimated weight loss. In the top graphs (the completers analysis), the distribution of outcomes seems more favorable (although the modal outcome is usually zero weight loss), but in the middle and bottom graphs that include information on dropouts, by far the most common outcome is that respondents lost zero weight (largely driven by the assumption of setting dropouts at baseline weight).

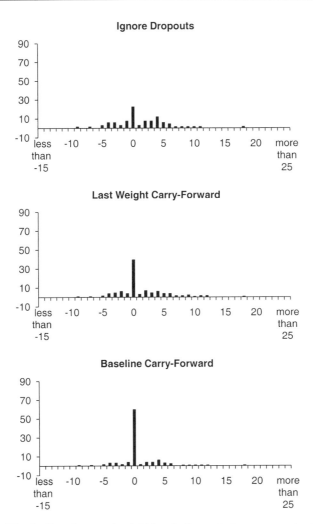

Fig. 4.4   Distribution of percent weight loss in the control group, quarter 4

Each of the graphs in figure 4.3 indicates that more people in the modified incentives group are just over the thresholds of 5 percent weight loss (at which participants are refunded their year's worth of fees, or $109.46) and 10 percent weight loss (at which they also receive a $100 bonus), than just under the thresholds. Moreover, such heaping is not apparent in the distribution associated with the standard incentive schedule, which has more continuous reward thresholds. This suggests that people may be pushing to achieve the substantial payoffs associated with losing 5 percent or 10 percent of baseline weight.

We next discuss the evidence regarding our hypotheses regarding weight loss.

Weight loss will be greater for those offered financial rewards for weight loss.
We test for differences in unconditional means of weight loss in pounds and
percent of baseline weight by quarter and group. We then test for differences
in unconditional probability of losing 5 percent and 10 percent of baseline
body weight. Note that the differences between the treatment groups and
the control group can be interpreted as the effect of the financial incentives,
distinct from all of the other program elements (e.g., daily e-mails and call
center support) shared by the control group, with the caveat that there may
be differential selection by employers to incentive schedules, and that there
may be differential selection by workers into participation that differs by
incentive schedule.

Table 4.8 lists weight loss in pounds and percent of baseline weight, by
group and quarter. The cells also list the minimum and maximum weight
loss (a negative minimum weight loss indicates weight gain) for that group in
that quarter (the minimum and maximum are not affected by how dropouts
are treated, so they are entered in only the leftmost column for each group).
Because so many participants drop out, and attrition is correlated with
weight loss success, estimates of average weight loss are extremely sensitive
to how attrition is handled. We focus here on the baseline-carried-forward
analysis, which assumes that everyone who dropped out went back to their
baseline weight.

In the baseline-carried-forward analysis, average weight loss in the control group totals 2.6 pounds (1.29 percent) by the end of the first quarter,
1.9 pounds (0.98 percent) by the end of the second quarter, 1.7 pounds (0.82
percent) by the end of the third quarter, and 1.7 pounds (0.87 percent) by
the end of the fourth quarter. These can be interpreted as the unconditional
average effect of the program elements other than financial rewards (e.g.,
e-mails, call center access, and weigh-ins), because in a previous randomized experiment, a control group that received no treatment of any kind
experienced virtually no change in average weight after six or twelve months
(Jeffery et al. 1993). This suggests that changes in weight observed in the
control group measure the effect of all elements of Company X treatment
except financial rewards.

In the standard incentives group, average weight loss totaled 2.2 pounds
(1.13 percent) by the end of the first quarter, 2.1 pounds (1.04 percent) by
the end of the second quarter, 2.2 pounds (1.03 percent) by the end of the
third quarter, and 1.4 pounds (0.64 percent) by the end of the fourth quarter.
We fail to reject the null hypothesis of no difference between the control and
standard incentives group; in fact, average weight loss is consistently lower
in the standard incentives group than in the control group.

Despite the small average weight loss in the standard incentives group,
there are some substantial success stories; the maximum weight lost since
baseline is 58.8 lbs. in quarter one, 89.4 lbs. in quarter two, 109.2 lbs. in
quarter three, and 116.8 lbs. in quarter four. For any given mean, success

Table 4.8   Weight loss in pounds and percent of baseline weight, by group and quarter

Quarter	Standard incentives			Modified incentives			Control group		
	Ignoring dropouts	Last weight carry-forward	Baseline carry-forward	Ignoring dropouts	Last weight carry-forward	Baseline carry-forward	Ignoring dropouts	Last weight carry-forward	Baseline carry-forward
1	4.6 (2.31%) Min = −12.6 Max = 58.8	2.2[b] (1.13%)	2.2[b] (1.13)	4.2 (2.06%) Min = −11.6 Max = 34.6	3.2 (1.55%)	3.2 (1.55%)	3.4 (1.73%) Min = −6.0 Max = 19.6	2.6 (1.29%)	2.6 (1.29%)
2	5.5[a,b] (2.73%) Min = −19.8 Max = 89.4	2.7 (1.34%)	2.1[b] (1.04%)	4.9 (2.38%) Min = −18.4 Max = 52.8	3.3 (1.64%)	3.3 (1.58%)	3.1 (1.62%) Min = −8.8 Max = 30.2	2.4 (1.21%)	1.9 (0.98%)
3	7.77[a,b] (3.68%) Min = −25.4 Max = 109.2	3.2 (1.54%)	2.2 (1.03%)	4.1 (2.00%) Min = −29.8 Max = 53.6	2.6 (1.27%)	2.5 (1.21%)	3.0 (1.49%) Min = −22.2 Max = 32	2.2 (1.06%)	1.7 (0.82%)
4	6.1[b] (2.75%) Min = −25.6 Max = 116.8	3.2 (1.52%)	1.4[b] (0.64%)	8.4[a] (4.15%) Min = −30.6 Max = 61.2	3.3 (1.61%)	3.6[a] (1.77%)	3.2 (1.68%) Min = −13.8 Max = 30.8	2.9 (1.47%)	1.7 (0.87%)

Notes: A positive number indicates weight lost. A negative number (e.g., for the minimum weight loss) indicates weight gain.
[a]Represents significant difference with the control group at the 5% level.
[b]Represents significant difference between standard and modified incentive groups at the 5% level.

stories are balanced by failures; for example, the maximum weight *gain* is 12.6 lbs. in quarter one, 19.8 lbs. in quarter two, 25 lbs. in quarter three, and 25.6 lbs. in quarter four.

In the modified incentives group, average weight loss totaled 3.2 pounds (1.55 percent) by the end of the first quarter, 3.3 pounds (1.58 percent) by the end of the second quarter, 2.5 pounds (1.21 percent) by the end of the third quarter, and 3.6 pounds (1.77 percent) by the end of the fourth quarter. In quarter four (but not earlier quarters) the difference between the modified incentives group and the control group in average weight loss is statistically significant.

We also measure weight loss by success in reaching certain benchmarks. Table 4.9 lists the percent of participants losing 5 percent of baseline weight, by group and quarter, for completers, last-observation-carried-forward, and baseline-carried-forward analyses. In the baseline-carried-forward analysis, the percentage of the control group that lost 5 percent of their baseline weight, by quarter, was: 9.3 percent, 7.8 percent, 13.2 percent, and 10.1 percent.

Relative to the control group, it is generally the case that smaller percentages of the standard incentives group achieved 5 percent weight loss in each quarter (8.3 percent, 8.2 percent, 7.9 percent, and 5.4 percent); the difference is statistically significant in quarters three and four.

Relative to the control group, higher percentages of the modified incentives group achieved 5 percent weight loss in each quarter (12.6 percent, 16.5 percent, 14.0 percent, 19.5 percent); the differences are statistically significant in quarters two and four.

We also examine the probabilities of losing 10 percent of baseline weight, the outcome that the USDHHS (2000) recommends for evaluating weight loss programs. Table 4.10 lists the unconditional probabilities of losing 10 percent of baseline weight by group and quarter, for completers, last-observation-carried-forward, and baseline-carried-forward analyses. Assuming that dropouts returned to their baseline weight, the percentage of the control group that lost 10 percent of baseline weight, by quarter, was 0.0 percent, 2.3 percent, 2.3 percent, and 3.1 percent. These are comparable to the corresponding percentages for the standard incentives group (1.2 percent, 2.0 percent, 2.9 percent, and 2.4 percent; the differences are not statistically significant. Relative to the control group, higher percentages of the modified incentives group achieved 10 percent weight loss in each quarter (2.1 percent, 4.3 percent, 3.8 percent, and 6.5 percent), but the differences are not statistically significant.

We hypothesized that: *In quarter four, weight loss will be greater in the modified incentives group than in the standard incentives group.* This is true for the unconditional means in table 4.8. Assuming dropouts return to their baseline weight (baseline-carried-forward), average year-end weight loss is 3.6 pounds (1.77 percent) in the modified incentives group compared to

Table 4.9   Percent of respondents losing 5% of baseline weight, by group and quarter

	Standard incentives			Modified incentives			Control group		
Quarter	Ignoring dropouts (%)	Last weight carry-forward (%)	Baseline carry-forward (%)	Ignoring dropouts (%)	Last weight carry-forward (%)	Baseline carry-forward (%)	Ignoring dropouts (%)	Last weight carry-forward (%)	Baseline carry-forward (%)
1	17.1	8.3[b]	8.3[b]	16.7	12.6	12.6	12.5	9.3	9.3
2	21.6	10.8[b]	8.2[b]	24.8[a]	16.9	16.5[a]	12.8	10.1	7.8
3	28.1	13.0	7.9[a,b]	23.1	15.0	14.0	23.9	15.5	13.2
4	22.7[b]	13.3[b]	5.4[a,b]	45.7[a]	20.9	19.5[a]	19.4	17.8	10.1

[a]Represents significant difference with the control group at the 5% level.
[b]Represents significant difference between standard and modified incentive groups at the 5% level.

Table 4.10   Percent of respondents losing 10% of baseline weight, by group and quarter

	Standard incentives			Modified incentives			Control group		
Quarter	Ignoring dropouts (%)	Last weight carry-forward (%)	Baseline carry-forward (%)	Ignoring dropouts (%)	Last weight carry-forward (%)	Baseline carry-forward (%)	Ignoring dropouts (%)	Last weight carry-forward (%)	Baseline carry-forward (%)
1	2.4	1.2	1.2	2.8	2.1	2.1	0.0	0.0	0.0
2	5.2	2.2[b]	2.0[b]	6.5	4.3	4.3	3.8	2.3	2.3
3	10.4[b]	3.8	2.9	6.3	4.1	3.8	4.2	2.3	2.3
4	10.1[b]	4.4[b]	2.4[b]	15.3[a]	6.8	6.5	6.0	4.7	3.1

[a]Represents significant difference with the control group at the 5% level.
[b]Represents significant difference between standard and modified incentive groups at the 5% level.

1.4 pounds (0.64 percent) in the standard incentives group, a difference significant at the 1 percent level. Table 4.9 indicates that at the end of quarter four, 19.5 percent of the modified incentives group had lost 5 percent or more of their baseline weight, compared to only 5.4 percent of the standard incentives group, a difference significant at the 1 percent level. Table 4.10 shows that the percent losing 10 percent or more of baseline weight was 6.5 percent in the modified incentives group and only 2.4 percent in the standard incentives group, a difference significant at the 1 percent level.

In quarters one through three, weight loss will be greater in the standard incentives group than in the modified incentives group.

Contrary to our prediction, weight loss is greater in the modified incentives group than in the standard incentives group in quarters one through three. Table 4.8 shows that those in the modified incentives group lost an average of 3.2, 3.3, and 2.5 pounds in the first three quarters, compared to the standard incentives group average losses of 2.2, 2.1, and 2.2 pounds. This difference is statistically significant at the 1 percent level in quarters one and two. Table 4.9 shows that in each case a higher proportion of the modified incentives group than the standard incentives group achieved 5 percent weight loss: 12.6 percent versus 8.3 percent in quarter one, 16.5 percent versus 8.2 percent in quarter two, and 14.0 percent versus 7.9 percent in quarter three; in each case these differences are statistically significant at the 1 percent level. Table 4.10 shows that the probability of losing 10 percent or more of baseline weight is consistently higher in the modified incentives group than the standard incentives group, and the difference is statistically significant in quarter two.

These results suggest that the effect of greater financial incentives for the standard incentives group is swamped by some combination of more favorable selection into the modified incentives group, loss aversion, and the necessity of starting early to achieve 5 percent or 10 percent weight loss by the end of quarter four.

4.7   Discussion

A 2007 Institute of Medicine report on preventing obesity set the immediate next step—which it described as an essential priority action for the near future—as "learning what works and what does not work and broadly sharing that information." (IOM 2007, 410). It also notes that "All types of evaluation can make an important contribution to the evidence base upon which to design policies, programs, and interventions." (IOM 2007, 4). This chapter makes a contribution to that effort by documenting attrition and weight loss in a large program that offers financial incentives for weight loss.

The program studied is of particular interest because it is a real-world intervention, not a pilot program designed and monitored by researchers.

As a result, the data are informative about how such interventions work in the real world. However, because it is a real-world intervention, it suffers the limitations of selection by employers of incentive schedule, and a relatively small control group (129 out of a total sample of 2,407).

We study the two outcomes recommended by the NIH for evaluating weight loss interventions: attrition and weight loss. We find higher attrition (up to 76.4 percent after one year) than virtually all previous studies (see appendix table 4.1 and Paul-Ebhohimhen and Avenell 2007). Another recent study of real-world wagers on own weight loss also found 80 percent failure (Burger and Lynham 2008).

We find that the financial rewards in this program are associated with modest weight loss. After one year, it averages 1.4 pounds for those in the standard incentives group, 1.7 pounds for those in the control group, and 3.6 pounds for those in the modified incentives group, under the assumption that dropouts experienced no weight loss. (The additional 1.9 pounds lost by the modified incentives group relative to the control group is statistically significant, but the weight loss of the standard incentives group is not significantly different from that of the control group.) The NIH considers a loss of 10 percent of baseline weight in six months to one year to be good progress for an obese individual (USDHHS 2000). By this standard, very few participants in this program achieve good progress toward weight loss: just 2.4 percent of the standard incentives group, 3.1 percent of those in the control group, and 6.5 percent of the modified incentives group lost 10 percent of their starting weight in twelve months (neither the standard incentives nor modified incentives group is significantly different from the control group on this measure). By most measures, participants in the modified incentives group had twelve-month weight loss that was greater than those in the standard incentives group, but it is not clear how much of this is due to selection and how much is due to the difference in incentives (e.g., bonds) controlling for selection.

The weight loss associated with the program we examine is generally smaller than that documented in the previous literature. (This is especially true when one considers that selection of firms into specific incentive schedules and selection of employees into participation that differs by incentive schedule may imply that even the modest effects found here may be optimistic.) For example, Volpp et al. (2008) estimate mean sixteen-week weight loss to be 13.1 lbs. when rewards take the form of a lottery with a daily expected value of $3, and 14.0 lbs. when the rewards take the form of deposit contracts or bonds, whose amount is chosen by the enrollee but can vary between $0 and $3 per day and is matched 1:1 if the weight loss goal is achieved.

Our findings are closer to those of Finkelstein et al. (2007), who find modest weight loss (between 2.0 and 4.7 lbs.) at three months, but no significant weight loss at six months, associated with financial rewards that varied between $7 and $14 per percentage point of weight lost after six months.

Likewise, Butsch et al. (2007) find no significant difference in twelve-week weight loss between a treatment group offered a $150 refund of their enroll-ment fee if they lost 6 percent of their initial weight, and a control group which was not eligible for such a refund.

Overall, our findings regarding attrition and weight loss suggest that the experience of pilot programs (such as those described in appendix table 4A.1) may be overly optimistic about what can be achieved on a larger scale.

To put our findings in a broader context of what works to promote weight loss, a literature review (Douketis et al. 2005) found that dietary and lifestyle therapy tends to result in less than 5 kg weight loss after two to four years, pharmacologic therapy results in 5 to 10 kg weight loss after one to two years, and surgical therapy results in 25 to 75 kg weight loss after two to four years. At this point, financial rewards remain an intriguing approach to weight loss but it remains to be seen whether they can be as effective as traditional medical approaches.

This chapter presents the basic patterns in the data. Our follow-up work will estimate hazard models of attrition and estimate regression models of weight loss to measure the change in weight associated with the incentive schedules, controlling for the observable characteristics of participants. Future research in this area should also focus on the optimal design of financial incentives for maximizing loss of excess weight, finding ways to decrease attrition, whether offering extrinsic rewards decreases intrinsic motivation, and whether weight loss is maintained after financial incentives for weight loss are removed.

Appendix

Table 4A.1   Previous literature on financial incentives for weight loss

Study	Study design	Intervention and incentives	Sample size and population	Duration	Weight loss	Attrition
Volpp et al. (2008)	Randomized controlled trial	3 groups: Deposits contract of $0–$3/day matched 1:1 Lottery for daily prize with E[V] = $3 Self-reported daily weight $20 for monthly weigh-in, unconditionally	N = 57 (19 in each of 3 groups) Patients at Philadelphia Veterans Affairs Medical Center with BMI 30–40	16 weeks	Mean weight loss: Lottery: 13.1 lbs Deposit contracts: 14.0 Control: 3.9 lbs	8.8%
Burger and Lynham (2008) working paper	Opportunistic data from William Hill betting agency for 1993–2006	Maximum bet of $65. William Hill offered odds ranging from 5:1 to 50:1; potential payoff averaged $1,926 Average duration of bet is 8 months, weight to be lost ranges from 28–168 lbs Each bettor weighed at start and end of bet by physician No control group	N = 51 Self-selected members of British population	Average of 8 months	Approximately 80% of people betting on their weight loss lose the bet	Approximately 80% of people betting on their weight loss lose the bet
Finkelstein et al. (2007)	Randomized trial, no control group	Three groups: Back loaded: $0 at 3 months, $14 per % point lost at 6 months Front loaded: $14 per % point lost at 3 months, $0 at 6 months Steady payment: $7 per % point lost at both 3 months and 6 months Weigh-ins at 3 months and 6 months Incentives only up to 10% weight loss ($140)	N = 207 (72 in back loaded, 64 in front loaded, 71 in steady payment) Overweight and obese employees at one university and 3 community colleges in NC	6 months	Mean weight loss 3 months: 2 lbs for back loaded, 4.7 lbs for front loaded, 3 lbs for steady payment Mean weight loss at 6 months not significantly different from zero	54% in back loaded, 45% in front loaded, 31% in steady payment
Butsch et al. (2007)	Sequential control-intervention, not randomized	Treatment group eligible for 50% reimbursement of enrollment fee ($150 of $300) if lose 6% of initial weight and attend 10 of 12 group sessions Control group was not eligible for reimbursement	N = 401 (241 intervention of which 59 enrolled, 160 control of which 40 enrolled) Participants in Univ. of Alabama at Birmingham EatRight lifestyle program BMI 30 and over	12 weeks	Mean weight loss: 2.25% in control group, 3.27% in intervention group; difference not statistically significant	Not stated

(continued)

Table 4A.1 (continued)

Study	Study design	Intervention and incentives	Sample size and population	Duration	Weight loss	Attrition
Hubbert et al. (2003)	Propensity score matching of 4 controls to each member of intervention group	Treatment group eligible for 50% of cost of program fees ($150 of $300) if lose 6% of initial weight and attend 10 of 12 group sessions Control group was not eligible for reimbursement	N = 125: 25 in intervention group, 100 in control group Participants in Univ. of Alabama at Birmingham EatRight lifestyle program and members of UAB-owned HMO BMI 30 and over	12 weeks	Mean weight loss: 7.3 kg (6.1%) in intervention group, 4.0 kg (3.9%) in control group; both differences are statistically significant	Not stated
Jeffery, Forster, et al. (1993)	Block-randomized controlled experiment (work sites randomized)	Work sites divided evenly between treatment and control groups Treatment (Healthy Worker Project) consisted of health education classes and payroll deductions that served as bonds—refunded if achieve weight loss goals or donated to charity otherwise Goals chosen by employee and ranged from minimum of 0 lb and maximum of 1% body weight loss each week Participants chose amount of payroll deduction (minimum of $5 biweekly) 200 employees surveyed at baseline and again after 2 years (cohort) Another 200 employees surveyed after 2 years (cross-section) Weight self-reported but corrected for reporting error	32 work sites in Minneapolis / St. Paul metropolitan area Of 10,000 employees in treatment work sites, 2,041 employees participated in weight control program	2 years	No treatment effect was found for weight In cohort survey, average change in BMI was 0.08 units for control group, −0.02 units for treatment group; not statistically significant In cross-sectional survey, average change in BMI was −0.05 in both the treatment and control groups	No attrition of worksites
Jeffery, Wing, et al. (1993)	Randomized controlled experiment	Five groups: 1) control; 2) standard behavioral therapy (SBT); 3) SBT plus food provision; 4) SBT plus incentives; 5) SBT plus food provision plus incentives Weekly incentives: $0 if gained weight, $2.50 if did not gain weight; $12.50 if weight loss was 50% of goal, $25 if weight loss reached goal Weight-loss goals could be either 14, 18, or 23 kg during course of program Weight measured at baseline, 6, 12, and 18 months. There were also optional weekly weigh-ins	N = 202 men and women from Pittsburgh and Minneapolis-St. Paul, of which 40 to 41 were in each of the 5 groups Had to be 14-32 kg overweight	18 months	No effect of financial incentives or the interaction of financial incentives with food provision	11% attrition at 6 months, 13% at 12 months, 15% at 18 months

Study	Design	Description	Duration	Results	Notes
Jeffery, Hellerstedt, and Schmid (1990)	Randomized experiment	Two groups: 1) offered a weight control newsletter program for price of $5; 2) offered the same program for free but requiring a $60 deposit that would be refunded based on (proportional to) success in weight loss Individuals chose weight loss goals of not more than 4 lb a month Weight self-reported (questionnaire, telephone survey). For subset of respondents, validation of self-report through measurement of weight	$N = 1,304$ residents of Bloomington, Minnesota: 1,190 in the $5 newsletter program group and 114 in newsletter plus incentive program group	6 months	Weight loss averaged about 4 lbs for $5 program and 8 lbs for incentive program	3.8% did not return survey
Kramer et al. (1986)	Randomized controlled experiment	Three groups: 1) monthly financial contingencies for weight maintenance; 2) monthly financial contingencies for participation in training sessions to solidify behavioral changes; 3) no treatment $120 deposit. For each of 12 sessions not attended, participant forfeited $10. Refund also withheld if weighed more than "baseline" (post-first-treatment) weight. Withheld refunds (forfeited moneys) were distributed among those who were at or below "baseline" weight at final session Weight measured at "baseline" and at one year	$N = 85$ individuals who had already lost 10% or more of their body weight through a 15-week weight loss program	1 year	Incentives had no impact on weight maintenance/ amount of weight regained. Average weight regain: 10.3 lbs in control group, 11.9 lbs. in group with incentives	6 of 28 (21%) of the incentives group refused to attend final weigh-in. They self-reported weight, and 5 lbs was added to account for underreporting
Jeffery et al. (1984)	Randomized controlled experiment	Three groups 1) regular contract, 2) difficulty-grade contract; 3) no contract (control) All deposited $150. Immediately refunded to control group Regular contract group received $30 for each 5-lb increment of weight loss Difficulty-grade contract group received $5 for first 5 lbs lost, $10 for second, $20 for third, $40 for fourth, and $75 for fifth	$N = 113$ Roughly half recruited from population sample and the other half from newspaper advertisements	15 weeks	Average weight loss: 26.2 lbs (12.8%) in difficulty-grade contract 21.7 lbs (10.8%) in regular contract 17.7 lbs (8.5%) in control group	11 subjects (10%) refused to attend final weigh-in. They self-reported weight, and 5 lbs was added to account for underreporting.

(*continued*)

Table 4A.1   (continued)

Study	Study design	Intervention and incentives	Sample size and population	Duration	Weight loss	Attrition
Jeffery et al. (1983)	Randomized experiment	Six treatment groups: 3 levels of deposit ($30, $150, $300) times two types of payoff criteria: individual weight loss or mean group weight loss All received 15-week behaviorally oriented program. Goal was 30 pounds lost Cash refunds per week at rate of $1, $5, or $10 per pound up to 2 pounds per week Monies not refunded for weight loss by end of program were distributed equally among those who achieved the 30-pound weight loss goal Participants were weighed weekly	N = 89 Men in the Minneapolis area with self-reported weight at least 30 pounds above the ideal	15 weeks	Individuals rewarded for group performance lost on average 5 lbs more weight. This difference was maintained over 1 year follow-up No significant effects of contract size	None
Coates et al. (1982)	Randomized experiment	Four treatment groups: 2 incentivized behaviors (weight loss or decrease in calorie consumption) by 2 frequencies of therapeutic contact (5 times or 1 time per week) Deposits were equal to 15 weeks' allowance or 50% of earnings from part-time work; amounts varied from $15–$240 (mean = $67.75). Source of payment: parents (51.5%), subjects (39.4%), shared (9.1%) Weight loss goal was 1 lb per week, or caloric reduction necessary to lose 1 lb per week. Monetary reward was delivered either once per week or once per week at treatment center Weighed at each clinic visit. Food records checked	N = 36 Adolescents at least 10% above average weight-for-height	15 weeks	The treatment group receiving rewards for weight loss and coming to the clinic 5 times per week was the only group to significantly reduce the percent over-weight. Treatment effects maintained over a 6-month follow-up period Significant correlation between initial monetary deposit and percent overweight lost No significant difference based on whether parents or subject paid the deposit	None

Jeffery, Thompson, and Wing (1978)	Randomized controlled experiment	Three treatment groups: deposits were returned contingent on either attendance, calorie restriction, or weight loss. Also a control group Each of the three treatment groups deposited $200. One group paid $20 for losing 2 lbs per week. Another paid $20 for calorie restrictions calculated to cause loss of 2 lbs per week. Third group paid $20 for weekly attendance	N = 31 Respondents to newspaper advertisement for people who need to lose 50 lbs or more	10 weeks	Groups rewarded for weight loss or calorie reductions lost an average of 20 lbs, significantly more weight loss than either the group rewarded for attendance (8.6 lbs) or the control group (12.4 lbs)	4 of 7 in control group quit
Mann (1972)	Single-subject reversal design	Subjects deposited a large number of valuables (e.g., money, jewelry, medals) with the researcher and signed a Contingency Contract allowing the researcher to switch them from treatment to control conditions, with the treatment being valuables being either returned or forfeited based on weight loss One valuable was returned for each 2 lb weight loss over a 2-week period. Subjects weighed every Monday, Wednesday, and Friday.	N = 8 Respondents to newspaper advertisement. All agreed to lose 25 pounds or more and had physician approval	Durations of treatments varied: total study ran at least 400 days	Average weekly weight loss of 1.6 to 1.7 pounds during treatment, regain of 1.4 pounds per week when incentives removed	None

References

Ainslie, G. 1975. Specious reward: A behavioral theory of impulsiveness and impulse control. *Psychological Bulletin* 82 (4): 463–96.

Bastiat, M. F. 1850. *That which is seen, and that which is not seen: The unintended consequences of government spending.* West Valley City, Utah: Waking Lion Press, 2006.

Bish, C. L., H. M. Blanck, M. K. Serdula, M. Marcus, H. W. Kohl III, and L. K. Khan. 2005. Diet and physical activity behaviors among Americans trying to lose weight: 2000 behavioral risk factor surveillance system. *Obesity Research.* 13 (3): 596–607.

Burger, N. and J. Lynham. 2008. Betting on weight loss . . . and losing: Personal gambles as commitment mechanisms. University of California Santa Barbara. Working Paper.

Butsch, W. S., J. D. Ard, D. B. Allison, A. Patki, C. S. Henson, M. M. Rueger, K. A. Hubbert, G. L. Glandon, and D.C. Heimberger. 2007. Effects of a reimbursement incentive on enrollment in a weight control program. *Obesity* 15 (11): 2733–38.

Camerer, C. 2005. Three cheers-psychological, theoretical, empirical—For loss aversion. *Journal of Marketing Research* 42 (5): 129–33.

Cawley, J. 2004. The impact of obesity on wages. *Journal of Human Resources* 39 (2): 451–74.

Cawley, J., J. A. Rizzo, and K. Haas. 2007. Occupation-specific absenteeism costs associated with obesity and morbid obesity. *Journal of Occupational and Environmental Medicine* 49 (12): 1317–24.

Coates, T. J., R. W. Jeffery, L. E. Slinkard, J. D. Killen, and B. G. Danaher. 1982. Frequency of contact and monetary reward in weight loss, lipid change, and blood pressure reduction with adolescents. *Behavior Therapy* 13:175–85.

Crawford, D., R. W. Jeffery, and S. A. French. 2000. Can anyone successfully control their weight? Findings of a three year community-based study of men and women. *International Journal of Obesity* 24:1107–10.

Douketis, J. D., C. Macie, L. Thabane, and D. F. Williamson. 2005. Systematic review of Long-term weight loss studies in obese adults: Clinical significance and applicability to clinical practice. *International Journal of Obesity* 29:1153–67.

Finkelstein, E. A., I. C. Fiebelkorn, and G. Wang. 2003. National medical spending attributable to overweight and obesity: How much, and who's paying? *Health Affairs* Web Exclusive, W3-219.

Finkelstein, E. A., L. A. Linnan, D. F. Tate, and B. E. Birken. 2007. A pilot study testing the effect of different levels of financial incentives on weight loss among overweight employees. *Journal of Occupational and Environmental Medicine* 49 (9): 981–89.

Ford, E. S., D. G. Moirarty, M. M. Zack, A. H. Mokdad, and D. P. Chapman. 2001. Self-reported body mass index and health-related quality of life: Findings from the behavioral risk factor surveillance system. *Obesity Research* 9 (1): 21–31.

Gadbury, G. L., C. S. Coffey, and D. B. Allison. 2003. Modern statistical methods for handling missing repeated measurements in obesity trial data: Beyond LOCF. *Obesity* 4:175–84.

Higgins, S. T., S. M. Alessi, and R. L. Dantona. 2002. Voucher-based incentives: A substance abuse treatment innovation. *Addictive Behaviors* 27:887–910.

Hubbert, K. A., B. F. Bussey, D. B. Allison, T. M. Beasley, C. S. Henson, and D.C. Heimburger. 2003. Effects of outcome-driven insurance reimbursement on short-term weight control. *International Journal of Obesity* 27:1423–29.

Institute of Medicine. 2007. *Progress in preventing childhood obesity: How do we measure up?* Washington, DC: National Academies Press.

Jeffery, R. W., W. M. Bjornson-Benson, B. S. Rosenthal, C. L. Kurth, and M. M. Dunn. 1984. Effectiveness of monetary contracts with two repayment schedules on weight reduction in men and women from self-referred and population samples. *Behavior Therapy* 15:273–79.

Jeffery, R. W., J. L. Forster, S. A. French, S. H. Kelder, H. A. Lando, P. G. McGovern, D. R. Jacobs, and J. E. Baxter. 1993. The healthy worker project: A work-site intervention for weight control and smoking cessation. *Journal of Public Health* 83 (3): 395–401.

Jeffery, R. W., W. M. Gerber, B. S. Rosenthal, and R. A. Lindquist. 1983. Monetary contracts in weight control: Effectiveness of group and individual contracts of varying size. *Journal of Consulting and Clinical Psychology* 51 (2): 242–8.

Jeffery, R. W., W. L. Hellerstedt, and T. L. Schmid. 1990. Correspondence programs for smoking cessation and weight control: A comparison of two strategies in the Minnesota Heart Health Program. *Health Psychology* 9 (5): 585–98.

Jeffery, R. W., P. D. Thompson, and R. R. Wing. 1978. Effects on weight reduction of strong monetary contracts for calorie restriction or weight loss. *Behavior Research and Therapy* 16:363–9.

Jeffery, R. W., R. R. Wing, C. Thorson, L. R. Burton, C. Raether, J. Harvey, and M. Mullen. 1993. Strengthening behavioral interventions for weight loss: A randomized trial of food provision and monetary incentives. *Journal of Consulting and Clinical Psychology* 61:1038–45.

Kahneman, D., and A. Tversky. 1979. Prospect theory: An analysis of decision under risk. *Econometrica* 47 (2): 263–92.

Kane, R. L., P. E. Johnson, R. J. Town, and M. Butler. 2004. A structured review of the effect of economic incentives on consumers' preventive behavior. *American Journal of Preventive Medicine* 27 (4): 327–52.

Kramer, F. M., R. W. Jeffery, M. K. Snell, and J. L. Forster. 1986. Maintenance of successful weight loss over one year: Effects of financial contracts for weight maintenance or participation in skills training. *Behavioral Therapy* 17 (3): 295–301.

Laibson, D. 1997. Golden eggs and hyperbolic discounting. *Quarterly Journal of Economics* 112 (5): 443–77.

Lussier, J. P., S. H. Heil, J. A. Mongeon, G. J. Badger, and S. T. Higgins. 2006. A meta-analysis of voucher-based reinforcement therapy for substance use disorders. *Addiction* 101:192–203.

Mann, R. A. 1972. The behavior-therapeutic use of contingency contracting to control an Adult behavior problem: Weight control. *Journal of Applied Behavior Analysis* 5 (2): 99–109.

National Institutes of Health (NIH) Technology Assessment Conference Panel. 1993. Methods for voluntary weight loss and control. *Annals of Internal Medicine* 119 (7): 764–70.

O'Donoghue, T., and M. Rabin. 2001. Choice and procrastination. *Quarterly Journal of Economics* 116 (1): 121–60.

Ogden, C. L., M. D. Carroll, L. R. Curtin, M. A. McDowell, C. J. Tabak, and K. M. Flegal. 2006. Prevalence of overweight and obesity in the United States, 1999–2004. *Journal of the American Medical Association* 295:1549–55.

Paul-Ebhohimhen, V., and A. Avenell. 2007. Systematic review of the use of financial incentives in treatments for obesity and overweight. *Obesity Reviews* 9:355–67.

Read, D., G. Loewenstein, and M. Rabin. 1999. Choice bracketing. *Journal of Risk and Uncertainty* 19 (1-3): 171–97.

Samuelson, P. A. 1937. A note on measurement of utility. *Review of Economic Studies* 4:155–61.

Serdula, M. K., A. H. Mokdad, D. F. Williamson, D. A. Galuska, J. M. Mendlein, and G. W. Heath. 1999. Prevalence of attempting weight loss and strategies for controlling weight. *Journal of the American Medical Association* 282 (14): 1353–58.

Strotz, R. H. (1955–1956). Myopia and inconsistency in dynamic utility maximization. *Review of Economic Studies* 23 (3): 165–80.

Stunkard, A., and M. McLaren-Hume. 1959. The results of treatment for obesity. *Archives of Internal Medicine* 103:79–85.

Thaler, R. H., and H. M. Shefrin. 1981. An economic theory of self-control. *Journal of Political Economy* 89 (2): 392–406.

Tversky, A., and D. Kahneman. 1991. Loss aversion in riskless choice: A reference-dependent model. *Quarterly Journal of Economics* 106:1039–61.

U.S. Department of Health and Human Services, National Institutes of Health. 2000. *The practical guide: Identification, evaluation, and treatment of overweight and obesity in adults.* NHLBI Obesity Education Initiative, NIH no. #00-4084.

Vidal, J. 2002. Updated review on the benefits of weight loss. *International Journal of Obesity* 26 (Suppl 4): S25–S28.

Volpp, K. G., L. K. John, A. B. Troxel, L. Norton, J. Fassbender, and G. Loewenstein. 2008. Financial incentive based approaches for weight loss: A randomized trial. *Journal of the American Medical Association* 300 (22): 2631–37.

Ware, J. H. 2003. Interpreting incomplete data in studies of diet and weight loss. *New England Journal of Medicine* 348 (21): 2136–37.

Wing, R. R., and S. Phelan. 2005. Long-term weight loss maintenance. *American Journal of Clinical Nutrition* 82 (supplement): 222S–225S.

Economic Contextual Factors and Child Body Mass Index

Lisa M. Powell and Frank J. Chaloupka

5.1 Introduction

Over the past few years, public health officials and state legislatures have increasingly introduced a number of bills and enacted laws with the aim of reducing childhood obesity (Cawley and Liu 2008). Much of this legislation has been in the area of improving school nutrition standards and increasing physical education requirements. In addition to these policy areas, given the success in other public health areas such as tobacco, there has been much discussion on the potential of implementing fiscal pricing policies (such as soda and "fat" taxes, or subsidies to fruits and vegetables) to address the problem of obesity, generally (Jacobson and Brownell 2000; Marshall 2000; Leicester and Windmeijer 2004; Caraher and Cowburn 2005; Kim and Kawachi 2006; Powell and Chaloupka 2009). The idea here is to change the relative costs of consuming unhealthy, energy dense food versus more healthy, less dense foods with the aim of shifting consumption patterns to achieve a healthier weight outcome. Indeed, the price of a calorie has been shown to be substantially cheaper when obtained from energy dense versus more healthful, less dense foods (Drewnowski and Specter 2004; Drewnowski and Darmon 2005). It is argued that technological change has contributed to the United

Lisa M. Powell is a research professor in the Department of Economics and a senior research scientist at the Institute for Health Research and Policy at the University of Illinois at Chicago. Frank J. Chaloupka is distinguished professor of economics and director of the Health Policy Center of the Institute for Health Research and Policy at the University of Illinois at Chicago, and a research associate of the National Bureau of Economic Research.

This research was supported by the National Research Initiative of the U.S. Department of Agriculture Cooperative State Research, Education and Extension Service, grant number 2005-35215-15372. We also are grateful to the Robert Wood Johnson Foundation Bridging the Gap ImpacTeen project for making the price and outlet density data available to us. We thank Zeynep Isgor for her excellent research assistance.

States obesity epidemic by altering incentives such that the relative price of consuming a calorie has fallen over time, while production efficiency has raised the cost of physical activity, and work has become more sedentary (Lakdawalla and Philipson 2002; Philipson and Posner 2003; Cutler, Glaeser, and Shapiro 2003; and Lakdawalla, Philipson, and Bhattacharya 2005). Recent evidence suggests that rising obesity is primarily the result of overconsumption of calories associated both with technological innovations as well as changes in sociodemographic factors (Bleich et al. 2008).

A growing body of research has sought to provide evidence on the extent to which economic factors such as food prices and food-related outlet availability are related to weight outcomes. Among adults, cross-sectional analyses have found higher fast-food prices and food-at-home prices (Chou, Grossman, and Saffer 2004) and higher prices of sugar (Miljkovic and Nganje 2008) to be statistically significantly associated with lower weight outcomes; although another study did not find evidence of a statistically significant association between fast-food prices and weight for adults, and found higher fruit and vegetable prices to be positively associated with adult body mass index (BMI) (Beydoun, Powell, and Wang 2008).

A number of recent studies have examined economic factors and children's and adolescents' weight. Higher fast-food prices have been statistically significantly associated with lower BMI and obesity among adolescents using cross-sectional data (Chou, Rashad, and Grossman 2005, 2008; Monheit, Vistnes, and Rogowski 2007; Powell et al. 2007a; Auld and Powell 2009) and statistically significantly related to lower adolescent BMI based on longitudinal models (Powell 2009; Powell and Bao 2009). Fast-food prices, however, have not been found to be statistically significantly related to weight outcomes among younger children (Sturm and Datar 2005, 2008; Powell and Bao 2009). On the other hand, these same studies on younger children (Sturm and Datar 2005, 2008; Powell and Bao 2009) which have used longitudinal data, have found higher fruit and vegetable prices to be statistically significantly related to higher weight outcomes among children. Further, a recent study also found adolescents' weight to be sensitive to the price of fruits and vegetables (Auld and Powell 2009). The magnitude of the price effects where significant have generally been quite small, although a number of studies have found larger effects for low-socioeconomic status (SES) children (Sturm and Datar 2005; Powell and Bao 2009) and for children and adolescents at risk of overweight (Sturm and Datar 2005; Auld and Powell 2009). Thus, the existing literature does provide some evidence that fiscal food pricing interventions may improve weight outcomes among children and adolescents.

The relationship between fast-food or full-service restaurant availability and child or adolescent weight outcomes has not been found to be statistically significant (Chou, Rashad, and Grossman 2005, 2008; Sturm and Datar 2005; Monheit, Vistnes, and Rogowski 2007; Powell et al. 2007a; Auld and

Powell 2009; Powell 2009; Powell and Bao 2009). In addition, the existing evidence on the effects of supermarket availability is mixed; whereas Sturm and Datar (2005) did not find a statistically significant relationship between supermarket availability and child weight, a recent study by Powell and Bao (2009) found that increased supermarket availability was statistically significantly negatively associated with child BMI when availability was assessed on a per land area basis rather than on a per capita basis. Among older children, Powell et al. (2007b) and Auld and Powell (2009) found that greater per capita local area supermarket availability was statistically significantly associated with lower adolescent BMI, but Powell (2009) found no significant association between supermarket availability and adolescent BMI.

The purpose of this study is to provide empirical evidence on the extent to which we can expect fiscal policy interventions in the area of food pricing or other interventions that reduce the relative cost of obtaining healthy foods by, for example, increasing access to outlets such as supermarkets, to improve weight outcomes among U.S. children. Previous studies using longitudinal data whose samples included younger children controlled for individual-level random, but not fixed, effects. This study builds on the previous literature by using fixed effects panel data methods to account for individual-level unobserved heterogeneity. We draw on longitudinal data from the Child Development Supplement of the Panel Study of Income Dynamics (CDS PSID) combined at the zip code level with food price data from the American Chamber of Commerce Researchers Association (ACCRA) and food-related outlet density data obtained from Dun & Bradstreet (D&B). We examine the relationship between child weight and the real price of energy dense foods such as fast-foods, the real price of healthy foods such as fruits and vegetables, fast-food and full-service restaurant availability, and access to food store outlets such as supermarkets, grocery stores, and convenience stores. We estimate both cross-sectional and individual-level fixed effects models to account for individual-level unobserved heterogeneity. We also examine whether the relationships between child weight and food prices and food-related outlet availability differ by households' SES by examining differences in estimates by household income.

5.2 Data

5.2.1 Individual-Level Data

The CDS-PSID data were collected by the University of Michigan's Institute for Social Research as a supplement to focus on children of the PSID sample, which is a nationally representative longitudinal sample of adults and their families collected since 1968. This study draws on two waves of the CDS, CDS-I collected in 1997 and CDS-II collected in 2002 to 2003.

The 1997 CDS gathered data on children aged 0 to 12 of PSID parents, providing information on 3,563 children from 2,394 participating families. The 2003 CDS contains follow-up data on 2,908 of the children sampled in the previous wave, now aged six to nineteen years old, from 2,017 families. The main interviews were conducted with each child's primary caregiver. Information on parents' income, education, and work-related variables was drawn from the 1997 and 2003 PSID waves and linked to the CDS data by household identifiers.

Our outcome measure for child weight is based on the gender-age-specific BMI percentile ranking. The BMI is calculated as (weight(lb)/height(in)^2) × 703. The child's weight was measured by the interviewers in both CDS data waves, while the child's height was reported by the child's primary caregiver in the first data wave and measured in an in-person assessment interview in the second data wave. We used the Centers for Disease Control's SAS program based on gender-age specific growth charts to obtain the age-gender specific BMI percentile rankings (Kuczmarski, Kuczmarski, and Najjar 2001). Table 5.1 shows that, on average, children were in the sixty-first percentile of the BMI distribution. Children's weight increased over the sample period moving them, on average, from the fifty-eighth percentile in 1997 to the sixty-third percentile of the BMI distribution in 2003 (not shown in tables). Children with a BMI greater than the eighty-fifth percentile are defined to be at risk of overweight, and those with a BMI greater than the ninety-fifth percentile are overweight (or, more commonly, referred to as obese).

A rich set of individual- and household-level demographic variables are used as controls in the empirical models. The descriptive statistics of these variables are reported in table 5.1 and they include: gender, race/ethnicity (white, African American, Hispanic, other race), whether the child was breastfed as a baby, child's birthweight (in pounds), child's age, marital status of the family head (married, never married, divorced/separated/widowed), mother's education (less than high school, completed high school, some college, college graduate or more, missing), mother's work status (not working, working part-time, working full-time, missing), family income (indicators for income quintiles) and year of the interview wave (1997, 2003). We also control for the degree of urbanization of the children's zip code of residence based on data from the Census 2000 that measure population size within a zip code inside urbanized areas, outside urbanized areas (referred to as suburban areas), and in rural areas. We calculate the percentages of a zip code's population by degree of urbanization and then define a zip code's level of urbanization by the category making up the largest percentage of its population. For instance, if in a zip code, the largest percentage of its population lives in urbanized areas, we define the zip code to be urban. Dichotomous indictors based on the Census 2000 are thus created for residences in urban, suburban, or rural areas, which are then merged with the CDS-PSID by the zip code-level geocode identifier. We also draw on Census

Table 5.1	Summary statistics: Economic contextual, outcome and control variables

	Mean/frequency
Contextual economic variables	
Price of fruits & vegetables ($1982–1984)	0.7319
	(0.0996)
Price of fast-food ($1982–1984)	2.7261
	(0.1669)
Fast-food restaurants	2.0887
	(3.5712)
Non-fast-food restaurants	10.4009
	(21.2717)
Supermarket stores	0.5236
	(1.4346)
Convenience stores	1.1863
	(2.2738)
Grocery stores	4.5306
	(26.3830)
Median household income ($2000)	45,049.89
	(17,503.81)
Outcome variable	
BMI percentile	61.1043
	(31.4631)
Control variables	
Male	49.53%
White[a]	68.24%
African American	15.07%
Hispanic	10.29%
Other race	6.39%
Age	10.1694
	(4.2366)
Birth weight (in pounds)	7.3276
	(1.6405)
Child breastfed	59.98%
Family income ($1982–1984)	39,925.36
	(46,763.53)
Head is married[a]	75.58%
Head is never married	8.66%
Head is widowed/divorced/separated	15.76%
Mother less than high school[a]	13.91%
Mother completed high school	26.91%
Mother completed some college	28.28%
Mother completed college or more	24.25%
Mother's education missing	6.65%
Mother does not work[a]	20.56%
Mother works part-time	37.43%
Mother works full-time	40.08%
Mother's work hours missing	1.94%
Urban[a]	66.39%
Suburban	12.96%
Rural/farm	20.65%
N	3258

Notes: Summary statistics are weighted. Standard deviations are shown in parentheses for continuous variables.

[a]Denotes omitted categories in regression models. Food outlets are defined per 10,000 capita per 10 squares miles.

2000 data to include a continuous measure of zip code-level median household income, which also is merged to the CDS-PSID by the zip code-level geocode identifier.

We limit the sample to children who are at least two years of age in the CDS-I in 1997, and at most eighteen years of age in CDS-II in 2003. In addition, girls who reported to be pregnant at the time of the interviews are excluded from the estimation sample. The final estimation sample based on nonmissing data includes a balanced sample of 3,258 observations on 1,629 children.

5.2.2   Food Price Measures

The ACCRA price data contain quarterly information on prices across more than 300 U.S. cities. The price data are matched to the CDS-PSID sample based on the closest city match available in the ACCRA using the zip code-level geocode indicator. The closest city match is determined by the shortest straight line distance between the centroid point of the child's zip code and the centroid point of the ACCRA price city. We created a match quality variable based on this distance in miles that we control for in all regression analyses. Based on the items available in the ACCRA data, we create two food-related price indices: a fruit and vegetable price index and a fast food price index. All prices are deflated by the Bureau of Labor Statistics (BLS) Consumer Price Index (CPI) (1982 to 1984 = 100).

The fruit and vegetable price index is based on the prices available for the following food items: bananas, lettuce, potatoes, canned sweet peas, canned tomatoes, canned peaches, and frozen corn. The ACCRA reports weights for each item based on expenditure shares derived from the BLS Consumer Expenditure Survey. These weights are used to compute a weighted fruit and vegetable price index based on the product prices of the seven food items noted earlier. The fast food price is based on the following three items included in the ACCRA data: a McDonald's Quarter-Pounder with cheese, a thin crust regular cheese pizza at Pizza Hut and/or Pizza Inn, and fried chicken (thigh and drumstick) at Kentucky Fried Chicken and/or Church's Fried Chicken. The fast-food price index is computed as an average of these three product prices given that they have equal weights. As shown in table 5.1, the average real ($1982 to 1984) price of the fruit and vegetable index is 73 cents and the average real price of a fast-food meal is $2.73. The ACCRA price data are not without their limitations: the data are collected only in a limited number of cities and metropolitan statistical areas, and they do not provide price data at lower geographic units; the data are based on establishment samples that reflect a mid-management (a higher) standard of living; ACCRA does not always continuously sample the same cities and, hence, the data are not fully comparable over time; and, a small number of food items are surveyed and, hence, the data are limited in their representativeness across food groups. The extent to which the limited number of food items available in the ACCRA data yields a nonrepresentative market basket will bias downwards any associations. Despite these limitations, given the national coverage of these price data, they have been similarly used in a number of previous studies (Chou, Grossman, and Saffer 2004; Chou, Rashad, and Grossman 2005, 2008; Lakdawalla, Philipson, and Bhattacharya 2005; Sturm and Datar 2005, 2008; Powell et al. 2007a; Auld and Powell 2009; Powell and Bao 2009).

5.2.3   Outlet Density Measures

Data on food store and restaurant outlets were obtained from a business list developed by D&B available through its MarketPlace software (Dun and Bradstreet 2005). MarketPlace contains information on more than fourteen million businesses in the United States and is compiled and updated quarterly through directories, government registries, web sites, and interviews; nonetheless, these commercial data have limitations as they are subject to count and/or classification error. MarketPlace allows sorting by multiple criteria such as location and Standard Industry Classification (SIC) codes of business types. Facilities may be listed by both primary and secondary SIC codes. We draw on the primary SIC code listing only in creating the list of outlets used for this analysis. Outlet density data are matched by year at the zip code level to the CDS-PSID, and are computed as the number of available outlets per 10,000 capita per ten square miles using Census 2000 zip code-level population and land area estimates. That is, the availability of food outlets is defined to take into consideration accessibility both in terms of congestion (per capita) and distance (per land area).

Data on restaurant outlets are available from D&B under the four-digit SIC code of "Eating Places." Fast-food restaurants were defined by the full set of eight-digit SIC codes (excluding coffee shops) that fell under the six-digit SIC code of "Fast food restaurants and stands," plus the two eight-digit SIC codes for chain and independent pizzerias. Non–fast-food restaurants, referred to as full-service restaurants, were defined as the total number of "Eating Places" minus fast-food restaurants and excluding coffee shops, ice cream, soft drink and soda fountain stands, caterers, and contract food services. Information on the number of food store outlets by type were extracted at the six-digit SIC code level to allow us to examine the availability of three types of food store outlets: (a) supermarkets, (b) grocery stores, and (c) convenience stores. Table 5.1 shows that the average number of food-related outlets per 10,000 capita per ten squares miles per zip code was 2.09 fast-food restaurants, 10.40 full-service restaurants, 0.52 supermarkets, 1.19 convenience stores, and 4.53 grocery stores.

5.3   Empirical Model

We empirically examine the importance of economic contextual and individual- and household-level factors on child weight following an economic framework where weight outcomes depend on marginal costs and benefits related to behaviors such as food consumption (Cutler, Glaeser, and Shapiro 2003; Chou, Grossman, and Safer 2004; Auld and Powell 2009). Higher costs of healthful foods through direct monetary prices (i.e., fruit and vegetables prices) and limited access (i.e., lower supermarket availability) are expected to decrease healthful food consumption and increase weight outcomes. Lower costs of unhealthy, energy dense food (i.e., fast-food prices) and increased access (i.e., greater availability of fast-food restaurant or convenience stores) are expected to increase the consumption of energy dense foods and raise energy intake and related weight. Thus, our empirical model examines the importance of the direct monetary prices of foods such as fruits and vegetables and fast-food. In addition, we proxy the opportunity cost of the time spent acquiring the food and the preparation and cleanup time by examining measures of restaurant (including full-service and fast-food restaurant) and food store (including supermarket, grocery stores, and convenience stores) availability. We also control for zip code-level neighborhood median household income. Controlling for neighborhood contextual variables helps to remove zip code-level heterogeneity that may be correlated with general neighborhood socioeconomic patterns, and to control for potential unobserved zip code-level time-varying heterogeneity.

We estimate a reduced form empirical model of children's BMI percentile of the following form:

$$(1) \qquad BMI_{ist} = \beta_0 + \beta_1 PRICE_{st} + \beta_2 OC_{st} + \beta_3 X_{it} + \beta_4 D_t + \varepsilon_{ist},$$

where $PRICE_{st}$ is a vector that measures fruit and vegetable and fast-food prices faced by individuals in geographic area s at time t. This vector also includes our price match quality measure of the distance in miles between the centroid of the zip code and the closest ACCRA city match. The OC_{st} is a vector of other contextual factors including measures of the availability (per 10,000 capita per ten square miles) of full-service and fast-food restaurants and supermarkets, grocery stores, and convenience stores, and neighborhood median income in geographic area s at time t; X_{it} is a vector of individual and household characteristics as described earlier, and D_{it} is a year dummy variable; β are conformable vectors of parameters to be estimated, and ε_{ist} is a standard residual term. We begin by estimating cross-sectional ordinary least squares (OLS) BMI percentile models.

However, cross-sectional estimates based on equation (1) may be biased, and standard errors may be underestimated if there exist unobserved individual-level effects. Therefore, $\varepsilon_{ist} = v_i + w_{ist}$ is rewritten and Equation (1) then can be rewritten as:

$$(2) \qquad BMI_{ist} = \delta_0 + \delta_1 PRICE_{st} + \delta_2 OC_{st} + \delta_3 X_{it} + \delta_4 D_t + v_i + w_{ist},$$

where v_i is the constant individual-specific residual, and w_{ist} is a standard residual. Hence, to account for unobserved individual-level heterogeneity, an individual-level fixed effects (FE) model is estimated. In this model, any explanatory variable that is constant over time for individual i gets swept away by the fixed effects. The FE panel estimation allows v_i to be arbitrarily correlated with the independent variables and the time-invariant covariates in the vector X_i, and the constant individual-specific residual v_i are differenced out and within person equation estimates are provided (Wooldridge 2002).

We assess the robustness of the price effects by estimating alternative model specifications that exclude restaurant outlets, food store outlets, and neighborhood median household income. We also provide separate estimates for our price and food-related outlet density contextual factors by SES on the basis of family income.

5.4   Results

In table 5.2, we present the results from the cross-sectional OLS model (as described in equation [1]) and the longitudinal individual-level FE model (as described in equation [2]) on the relationship between children's BMI percentile ranking and economic contextual factors controlling for individual- and household-level covariates. Controlling for all other covariates, the cross-sectional results show that higher prices of fruits and vegetables have a statistically significant positive effect on children's BMI percentile: a one-dollar increase in the price of fruit and vegetables is associated with a 20.28 percentage point increase in the child's BMI percentile ranking. In elasticity terms, a 10 percent increase in the price of fruit and vegetables increases BMI percentile by 2.4 percent (see table 5.5). The fruit and vegetable price estimate from the FE model is similar to the OLS estimates, but loses some statistical power (p-value = 0.052 in the FE model compared to p-value = 0.012 in the OLS model). The corresponding price elasticity from the FE model is 0.25. The price of fast-food is negatively associated with children's BMI percentile in the cross-sectional model, but the point estimate does not achieve statistical significance. The fast-food price estimate is positive and insignificant in the FE model. These price results are consistent with study findings by Sturm and Datar (2005, 2008) and Powell and Bao (2009) who found statistically significant but inelastic fruit and vegetable price effects on children's weight and statistically insignificant fast-food price effects. The results presented in table 5.3 suggest that the price estimates found in both the cross-sectional OLS and longitudinal FE models are robust to the exclusion of the restaurant outlets, the food store outlets, and neighborhood median household income.

With regard to our measures of food-related outlet availability, as shown in table 5.2, the results from the OLS model do not reveal any statistically significant associations between these variables and children's weight status. Similarly, food-related outlet availability generally is not found to be related

Table 5.2   **Regression analysis results: Children's BMI percentile ($N = 3258$)**

Outcome variable: BMI percentile	Cross-sectional estimates no contextual variables	Cross-sectional estimates	Longitudinal estimates (individual fixed effects)
Price of fruits and vegetables		20.2776**	21.0400*
		(8.0568)	(10.8226)
Price of fast-food		–3.6060	5.4151
		(4.4974)	(4.9435)
Fast-food restaurants		0.1236	0.3944
		(0.2867)	(0.3028)
Non-fast-food restaurants		–0.0126	–0.0939**
		(0.0356)	(0.0462)
Supermarket stores		–0.2140	–0.1684
		(0.2231)	(0.2376)
Convenience stores		–0.3129	0.2483
		(0.2831)	(0.2339)
Grocery stores		–0.0031	0.0189
		(0.0055)	(0.0317)
Median household income		–0.0873*	–0.0242
		(0.0503)	(0.0740)
Male	1.5451	1.4693	(dropped)
	(1.2430)	(1.2425)	
African American	4.4327**	3.1101	(dropped)
	(1.8975)	(1.9827)	
Hispanic	8.1319***	7.7714**	(dropped)
	(3.0906)	(3.0951)	
Other race	5.5369	4.9150	(dropped)
	(3.5307)	(3.5120)	
Birth weight (in pounds)	1.6655***	1.6750***	(dropped)
	(0.4065)	(0.4085)	
Child breastfed	–0.7231	–0.5559	(dropped)
	(1.5367)	(1.5413)	
Head is never married	–3.7116	–3.8735	–2.2316
	(2.5931)	(2.6024)	(3.2516)
Head is widowed or divorced or separated	–2.6509	–2.6575	0.7069
	(1.9013)	(1.8875)	(2.3822)
Mother completed high school	–3.0285	–3.2304	–4.9001
	(2.2139)	(2.2187)	(4.7511)
Mother completed some college	–1.6435	–1.6471	–0.2415
	(2.2979)	(2.3010)	(5.1319)
Mother completed college or more	–4.9301*	–4.8597*	–8.9546
	(2.5593)	(2.5795)	(6.4289)
Mother works part-time	0.5693	0.3511	–0.9054
	(1.8443)	(1.8411)	(1.9367)
Mother works full-time	3.9109**	3.7915**	–1.9903
	(1.9194)	(1.9206)	(2.3075)
Near-low income	–2.1566	–2.4044	0.0792
	(2.0678)	(2.0723)	(2.1217)
Middle income	–3.5365	–3.8377	–0.2233
	(2.3985)	(2.4028)	(2.4056)
Near-high income	–4.4337*	–4.5977*	0.2579
	(2.5597)	(2.5733)	(2.7047)

Table 5.2 (continued)

Outcome variable: BMI percentile	Cross-sectional estimates no contextual variables	Cross-sectional estimates	Longitudinal estimates (individual fixed effects)
High income	−3.8202	−3.5809	−1.1944
	(2.7775)	(2.8687)	(3.2423)
Suburban	1.1933	0.3371	−4.8939
	(2.3209)	(2.4081)	(3.4668)
Rural/farm	3.2431*	2.3262	−2.9525
	(1.8266)	(2.1341)	(3.0506)
Year 2003 dummy	3.8706**	2.0669	4.9493***
	(1.5491)	(1.7500)	(1.4001)

Notes: All regression models include but do not report on: constant term, price match quality measure of miles to nearest price match, and missing indicators for mother's education, mother's work hours and family income. The cross-sectional models also include controls for age and age squared. The restaurant and food store outlet density measures are defined per 10,000 capita per 10 square miles. Standard errors are reported in parentheses and are robust and clustered at the zip code level.

***Significant at the 1 percent level.
**Significant at the 5 percent level.
*Significant at the 10 percent level.

Table 5.3 Alternative model specifications: Robustness checks

	Model 1	Model 2	Model 3	Model 4
Cross-sectional estimates				
Price of fruits and vegetables	20.2776**	16.9609**	16.9906**	16.4896**
	(8.0568)	(7.8465)	(7.8223)	(7.7673)
Price of fast-food	−3.6060	−3.8484	−3.7404	−4.0236
	(4.4974)	(4.5145)	(4.5149)	(4.4758)
Restaurant outlet controls	Yes	Yes	Yes	No
Food store outlet controls	Yes	Yes	No	No
Median household income control	Yes	No	No	No
Longitudinal estimates (individual fixed effects)				
Price of fruits and vegetables	21.0400*	20.7912*	20.5488*	21.4464**
	(10.8226)	(10.7549)	(10.7596)	(10.8027)
Price of fast-food	5.4151	5.4685	5.1798	4.4782
	(4.9435)	(4.9281)	(4.9179)	(4.9119)
Restaurant outlet controls	Yes	Yes	Yes	No
Food store outlet controls	Yes	Yes	No	No
Median household income control	Yes	No	No	No

Notes: Cross-sectional and longitudinal fixed effects models include but do not report on variables shown in table 5.2 plus the additional variables described in the notes of table 5.2. Standard errors are reported in parentheses and are robust and clustered at the zip code level.

***Significant at the 1 percent level.
**Significant at the 5 percent level.
*Significant at the 10 percent level.

to children's weight in the FE model, with the exception of a statistically significant negative relationship between full-service restaurant availability and BMI percentile.

Turning to the results for the individual- and household-level covariates shown in table 5.2, the OLS results show that after controlling for the contextual economic factors, African American children are no longer statistically significantly heavier than their white counterparts, and the magnitude of the difference in the BMI percentile gap falls by 30 percent (from 4.43 to 3.11). These results suggest that local area economic contextual factors explain part of the BMI gap between African American and white children. However, the economic contextual factors do not appear to explain any of the differences in weight between Hispanic and white children with Hispanic children being, on average, 7.77 percentiles higher in the BMI distribution even after controlling for the economic contextual factors and all other individual-level and household-level characteristics. In terms of other time-constant individual-level covariates, higher birth weight is associated with a significantly higher BMI ranking.

With regard to parents' SES and work status, having a mother who has completed college or more is weakly statistically significantly associated with being approximately 5 percentiles lower in the BMI distribution compared to children whose mothers do not have a high school education. Children living in households with higher levels of income also are found to have a weakly statistically significantly lower BMI percentile ranking compared to those children living in lower income households. A number of previous studies have found a significant association between higher maternal education and a lower prevalence of child obesity, but a statistically insignificant relationship between household income and child obesity (Anderson, Butcher, and Levine 2003; Classen and Hokayem 2005; Powell and Bao 2009). With respect to mothers' work status, consistent with the previous literature (Anderson, Butcher, and Levine 2003; Classen and Hokayem 2005; Liu et al. 2009), having a mother who works full-time is associated with a higher weight outcome. However, none of these parental characteristics are found to be statistically significantly associated with child weight outcomes in the FE model.

Table 5.4 presents cross-sectional and longitudinal estimates to examine potential differences in the relationship between the economic contextual factors and children's BMI percentile ranking across populations of different SES measured by household income. Table 5.5 presents the price elasticities for the low-income populations (we do not report price elasticities for the high-income populations since none of those estimates are statistically significant). The results reveal that low-income children's BMI percentile ranking is more sensitive to the price of fruits and vegetables than their high-income counterparts, particularly in the FE model. For low-income children, the BMI percentile fruit and vegetable price elasticity based

Table 5.4 Contextual variables and children's BMI percentile by household income

	Price of fruits and vegetables	Price of fast-food	No. of fast-food restaurants	No of Non-fast-food restaurants	No. of supermarket stores	No. of convenience stores	No. of grocery stores
				Cross-sectional estimates			
Full sample	20.2776**	−3.6060	0.1236	−0.0126	−0.2140	−0.3129	−0.0031
	(8.0568)	(4.4974)	(0.2867)	(0.0356)	(0.2231)	(0.2831)	(0.0055)
By income status							
Low-income	24.0650*	−18.2990**	−0.3450	0.0533	−0.5748**	−0.2212	−0.0024
(N = 1,257)	(13.5821)	(7.2544)	(0.3845)	(0.0552)	(0.2251)	(0.2984)	(0.0054)
High-income	16.5493	3.6396	0.5648	−0.1814*	0.8223	−1.2652*	0.3246
(N = 1,255)	(12.0265)	(6.8268)	(0.4334)	(0.1076)	(0.8544)	(0.7474)	(0.2258)
				Longitudinal estimates (individual fixed effects)			
Full sample	21.0400*	5.4151	0.3944	−0.0939**	−0.1684	0.2483	0.0189
	(10.8226)	(4.9435)	(0.3028)	(0.0462)	(0.2376)	(0.2339)	(0.0317)
By income status							
Low-income	53.0907**	−4.9697	0.0612	−0.0561	−0.5025***	0.8212***	−0.0139
(N = 1,257)	(22.5951)	(9.1495)	(0.3349)	(0.0408)	(0.1642)	(0.3150)	(0.0144)
High-income	−2.5056	−0.3097	0.9313	−0.2953	0.7702	−1.4087	0.2841
(N = 1,255)	(21.7981)	(8.8108)	(1.0181)	(0.3242)	(0.6903)	(1.1468)	(0.4098)

Notes: Low-income population is defined by the bottom two income quintiles and high-income includes the top two quintiles. Cross-sectional and longitudinal fixed effects models include but do not report on variables shown in table 5.2 plus the additional variables described in the notes of table 5.2. Standard errors are reported in parentheses and are robust and clustered at the zip code level.

***Significant at the 1 percent level.

**Significant at the 5 percent level.

*Significant at the 10 percent level.

Table 5.5   Price elasticities: Full sample and low-income sample

	Cross-sectional		Longitudinal	
	Full sample	Low income	Full sample	Low income
Price of fruits & vegetables	0.2395**	0.2720*	0.2485*	0.6001**
Price of fast-food	–0.1579	–0.7693**	0.2372	–0.2089

Notes: Elasticities are calculated based on the regression estimates presented in table 5.4 and mean fast-food prices, fruit and vegetable prices, and BMI percentile within each subsample.
**Significant at the 5 percent level.
*Significant at the 10 percent level.

on the FE models is 0.60, more than twice that of the sample as a whole (full sample elasticity of 0.25). Whereas the price of fast-food is not found to be statistically significantly associated with children's weight in the full sample in either the OLS or FE model, fast-food prices are found to be statistically significantly negatively associated with low-income children's weight in the OLS model, with a BMI percentile fast-food price elasticity of –0.77. However, the negative effect in the FE model is not statistically significant.

There also exist some interesting differences in results with respect to availability of food stores among the low- and high-SES populations. In particular, greater availability of supermarkets is related to a statistically significant but small reduction in BMI percentile ranking among low-income children: one additional supermarket (per 10,000 capita per ten squares miles) in the zip code is related to roughly a one-half percentage point reduction in children's BMI percentile ranking. This result is found for both the cross-sectional OLS model and the longitudinal FE model. Also in the FE model, greater convenience store availability increases low-income children's BMI percentile ranking. In the cross-sectional model among high-income children, greater availability of full-service restaurants and convenience stores is weakly statistically significantly associated with lower BMI percentile, but the effect is not statistically significant once we control individual-level heterogeneity in the FE model.

5.5   Discussion and Conclusions

As policymakers consider the adoption of fiscal pricing interventions such as food taxes on less healthy foods and subsidies for relatively healthy foods, it is important for them to be able to draw on evidence based on longitudinal models of the relationship between food prices and weight outcomes. This study builds on the previous literature in this area by providing new evidence on the relationships between economic contextual factors such as food prices and outlet availability and child weight using longitudinal fixed effects methods to control for individual-level heterogeneity. The results from the FE models showed that higher fruit and vegetable prices were statistically significantly related to a higher BMI percentile ranking among children, with larger effects for children in low-SES families. The fruit and vegetable price elasticity for BMI percentile ranking was estimated to be 0.25 for the full sample, and 0.60 among low-income children. These results are consistent with previous study findings based on individual-level random effects models that found children's BMI to be sensitive to the price of fruits and vegetables with greater effects for low-SES children (Sturm and Datar 2005, 2008; Powell and Bao 2009). This growing body of evidence suggests that subsidies to healthful foods such as fruits and vegetables, in particular subsidies targeted to low-income families, may help to reduce children's weight and reduce the likelihood that they fall into the at risk for overweight or overweight categories of the BMI distribution.

Fast-food prices were not found to be statistically significantly related to children's weight outcomes in either the cross-sectional OLS or longitudinal FE models for the full-sample. The cross-sectional results suggested that higher fast-food prices were associated with lower BMI among low-income children, but estimates from comparable FE models were not statistically significant. Powell and Bao (2009) found that fast-food prices were statistically significantly associated with lower BMI among low-SES children aged six to seventeen and among youths aged thirteen to seventeen, but not among the full sample of children aged six to seventeen. In addition, a number of cross-sectional studies (Chou, Rashad, and Grossman 2005, 2008; Monheit, Vistnes, and Rogowski 2007; Powell et al. 2007a; Auld and Powell 2009) and one FE longitudinal study (Powell 2009) have found significant relationships between fast-food prices and adolescents' BMI and overweight prevalence suggesting that fast-food taxes may be an effective tool for curbing overweight among this population. Unfortunately, repeated observations during adolescence are not available in the CDS-PSID and, hence, we cannot provide FE estimates separately for teenagers.

Our study results also suggest that in addition to the potential for effective fiscal pricing interventions, it is also important, particularly among low-income populations, to help ensure adequate access to food stores such as supermarkets that are more likely to provide a greater selection of, and lower prices for, a range of healthier food options. Greater availability of supermarkets was shown to have small but statistically significant negative effects on low-SES children's weight. A limited number of recent studies similarly have found statistically significant associations between supermarket availability and BMI among adolescents (Powell et al. 2007b; Auld and Powell 2009) and children (Powell and Bao 2009). Given that a number of studies in the public health literature have documented the limited availability of supermarkets in low-income and minority neighborhoods (Morland et al. 2002; Shaffer 2002; Moore and Diez Roux 2006; Powell et al. 2007c), the results in this study suggest that in addition to fiscal food pricing policies, interventions aimed at improving access through zoning or other incentives such as tax breaks to encourage the location of supermarkets in areas that are underserved can contribute to reducing childhood obesity. Also, the study results suggest that policy instruments that reduce the relative costs of healthy versus unhealthy foods both in terms of monetary costs and access will help to reduce the BMI-gap between African American and white children and, in turn, reduce health disparities in the United States.

Although food in the United States is subsidized for low-income individuals and families through a number of programs such as Food Stamps, the Women, Infant, and Children (WIC) Nutrition Program, the Child and Adult Care Food Program, and the National School Lunch and Breakfast Programs, food subsidies directed at the consumer have not traditionally existed for specific food items. However, some benefits, such as WIC, can only be used for certain foods and others are delivered through the provision of regulated foods such as school breakfasts and lunches. In particular, changes were recently made within the WIC program with the addition of monthly cash-value vouchers specifically for fruits and vegetables in the amount of $10 for fully breastfeeding women, $8 for nonbreastfeeding women, and $6 for children (Oliveira and Frazão 2009). Further, the USDA undertook a "Healthy Purchase" pilot program in California that targeted subsidies within the food stamp program such that for each dollar of food stamps spent on fresh produce, participants were subsidized a portion of the cost (Guthrie et al. 2007). Similarly, food taxes have not generally been introduced or increased with the aim of modifying consumption behavior as they have been used in other public health areas such as tobacco. Food taxes are currently imposed on selected categories of food such as soft drinks, candy, and snacks in grocery stores and vending machines, but at quite low tax rates (Chriqui et al. 2008). Evaluations of programs and pilot projects that subsidize healthful foods, and studies that examine the relationship between food taxes and energy intake and weight outcomes, in particular using longitudinal data, will further contribute to the evidence required by policymakers to assess the potential effectiveness of using pricing policies to curb the obesity crisis among children and adolescents in the United States.

Estimates of price elasticities among children and youth are particularly important—if such elasticities are higher than among the general population, then we can expect to see more beneficial changes in behavior and related weight outcomes among these younger groups. This evidence is critical given the development of obesity-related health risks among children, that food consumption patterns become more permanent as we age, and that childhood obesity has been shown to track into adulthood.

Reference

Anderson, P. M., K. F. Butcher, and P. B. Levine. 2003. Maternal employment and overweight children. *Journal of Health Economics* 22 (3): 477–504.

Auld, M. C., and L. M. Powell. 2009. Economics of food energy density and adolescent body weight. *Economica* 76 (304): 719–40.

Beydoun, M. A., L. M. Powell, and Y. Wang. 2008. The association of fast food, fruit and vegetable prices with dietary intakes among U.S. adults: Is there modification by family income? *Social Science & Medicine* 66 (11): 2218–29.

Bleich, S., D. Cutler, C. Murray, and A. Adams. 2008. Why is the developed world obese? *Annual Review of Public Health* 29:273–95.

Caraher, M., and G. Cowburn. 2005. Taxing food: implications for public health nutrition. *Public Health Nutrition* 8 (8): 1242–9.

Cawley, J., and F. Liu. 2008. Correlates of state legislative action to prevent childhood obesity. *Obesity* 16 (1): 162–7.

Chou, S. Y., M. Grossman, and H. Saffer. 2004. An economic analysis of adult obesity: Results from the behavioral risk factor surveillance system. *Journal of Health Economics* 23 (3): 565–87.

Chou, S. Y., I. Rashad, and M. Grossman. 2005. Fast-food restaurant advertising on television and its influence on childhood obesity. NBER Working Paper no. 11879. Cambridge, MA: National Bureau of Economic Research, December.

———. 2008. Fast-food restaurant advertising on television and its influence on childhood obesity. *Journal of Law and Economics* 51 (4): 599–618.

Chriqui, J. F., S. S. Eidson, H. Bates, S. Kowalczyk, and F. Chaloupka. 2008. State sales tax rates for soft drinks and snacks sold through grocery stores and vending machines, 2007. *Journal of Public Health Policy* 29:226–49.

Classen, T., and C. Hokayem. 2005. Childhood influences on youth obesity. *Economics and Human Biology* 3 (2): 165–87.

Cutler, D. M., E. L. Glaeser, and J. M. Shapiro. 2003. Why have Americans become more obese? *The Journal of Economic Perspectives* 17 (3): 93–118.

Drewnowski, A., and N. Darmon. 2005. Food choices and diet costs: An economic analysis. *Journal of Nutrition* 135 (4): 900–4.

Drewnowski, A., and S. E. Specter. 2004. Poverty and obesity: The role of energy density and energy costs. *American Journal of Clinical Nutrition* 79 (1): 6–16.

Dun and Bradstreet. 2005. *The DUNSright quality process: The power behind quality information.* Waltham, MA: Dun and Bradstreet.

Guthrie, J., E. Frazão, M. Andrews, and D. Smallwood. 2007. Improving food choices—Can food stamps do more? *Amber Waves* 5 (2): 22–8.

Jacobson, M. F., and K. D. Brownell. 2000. Small taxes on soft drinks and snack foods to promote health. *American Journal of Public Health* 90 (6): 854–7.

Kim, D., and I. Kawachi. 2006. Food taxation and pricing strategies to "thin out" the obesity epidemic. *American Journal of Preventive Medicine* 30 (5): 430–7.

Kuczmarski, M. F., R. J. Kuczmarski, and M. Najjar. 2001. Effects of age on validity of self-reported height, weight, and body mass index: Findings from the Third National Health and Nutrition Examination Survey, 1988–1994. *Journal of the American Dietetic Association* 101 (1): 28–34.

Lakdawalla, D., and T. Philipson. 2002. The growth of obesity and technological change: A theoretical and empirical examination. NBER Working Paper no. 8946. Cambridge, MA: National Bureau of Economic Research, December.

Lakdawalla, D., T. Philipson, and J. Bhattacharya. 2005. Welfare-enhancing technological change and the growth of obesity. *American Economic Review* 95 (2): 253–7.

Leicester, A., and F. Windmeijer. 2004. *The 'fat tax': Economic incentive to reduce obesity, Briefing Note 4.* London: Institute for Fiscal Studies.

Liu, E., C. Hsiao, T. Matsumoto, and S. Chou. 2009. Maternal full-time employment and overweight children: Parametric, semi-parametric, and non-parametric assessment. *Journal of Econometrics* 152 (1): 61–9.

Marshall, T. 2000. Exploring a fiscal food policy: The case of diet and ischaemic heart disease. *British Medical Journal* 320:301–5.

Miljkovic, D., and W. Nganje. 2008. Regional obesity determinants in the United States: A model of myopic addictive behavior in food consumption. *Agricultural Economics* 38:375–84.

Monheit, A. C., J. P. Vistnes, and J. A. Rogowski. 2007. Overweight in adolescents: Implications for health expenditures. NBER Working Paper no. 13488. Cambridge, MA: National Bureau of Economic Research, October.

Moore, L. V., and A. V. Diez Roux. 2006. Associations of neighborhood characteristics with the location and type of food stores. *American Journal of Public Health* 96 (2): 325–31.

Morland, K., S. Wing, R. A. Diez, and C. Poole. 2002. Neighborhood characteristics associated with the location of food stores and food service places. *American Journal of Preventative Medicine* 22 (1): 23–9.

Oliveira, V., and Frazão, E. 2009. *The WIC program background, trends, and economic issues, 2009 edition.* Economic Research Report no. 73. U.S. Department of Agriculture, Economic Research Service.

Philipson, T. J., and R. A. Posner. 2003. The long-run growth in obesity as a function of technological change. *Perspectives in Biology and Medicine* 46 (3): S87.

Powell, L. M. 2009. Fast food costs and adolescent body mass index: Evidence from panel data. *Journal of Health Economics* 29:963–70.

Powell, L. M., M. C. Auld, F. J. Chaloupka, P. M. O'Malley, and L. D. Johnston. 2007a. Access to fast food and food prices: Relationship with fruit and vegetable consumption and overweight among adolescents. *Advances in Health Economics and Health Services Research* 17:23–48.

———. 2007b. Associations between access to food stores and adolescent body mass index. *American Journal of Preventive Medicine* 33 (4, Supplement 1): S301–07.

Powell, L. M., and Y. Bao. 2009. Food prices, access to food outlets and child weight outcomes. *Economics and Human Biology* 7:64–72.

Powell, L. M., and F. J. Chaloupka. 2009. Food prices and obesity: Evidence and policy implications for taxes and subsidies. *The Milbank Quarterly* 87 (1): 229–57.

Powell, L. M., S. Slater, D. Mirtcheva, Y. Bao, and F. J. Chaloupka. 2007c. Food store availability and neighborhood characteristics in the United States. *Preventive Medicine* 44 (3): 189–95.

Shaffer, A. 2002. *The persistence of LA's grocery gap: The need for a new food policy and approach to market development.* Los Angeles: Center for Food and Justice, Urban and Environmental Policy Institute, Occidental College.

Sturm, R., and A. Datar. 2005. Body mass index in elementary school children, metropolitan area food prices and food outlet density. *Public Health* 119 (12): 1059–68.

———. 2008. Food prices and weight gain during elementary school: 5-year update. *Public Health* 122 (11): 1140–43.

Wooldridge, J. M. 2002. *Econometric analysis of cross section and panel data.* Cambridge, MA: MIT Press.

6

The Relationship between Perceptions of Neighborhood Characteristics and Obesity among Children

Bisakha Sen, Stephen Mennemeyer, and Lisa C. Gary

Overweight and obesity are among the most important of these new health challenges. Our modern environment has allowed these conditions to increase at alarming rates and become highly pressing health problems for our Nation. At the same time, by confronting these conditions, we have tremendous opportunities to prevent the unnecessary disease and disability that they portend for our future.
—Secretary of Health and Human Services, Tommy G. Thompson[1]

6.1 Introduction

It is a well-established fact that the prevalence of obesity among adults and children has increased markedly in the United States over the last three decades, and is considered to be a health problem of epidemic proportions. Given the scale of this problem, it is imperative to decipher the factors that influence the likelihood of obesity. The "Let's Move" campaign by First

Bisakha Sen is an associate professor in the Department of Health Care Organization and Policy at the University of Alabama at Birmingham. Stephen Mennemeyer is a professor in the Department of Health Care Organization and Policy at the University of Alabama at Birmingham. Lisa C. Gary is an assistant professor in the Department of Healthcare Organization and Policy at the University of Alabama at Birmingham.

We thank Susan Averett, Michael Grossman, Naci Mocan, the attendees at the NBER Obesity Conference, and the NBER and University of Chicago Press reviewers for valuable comments. We thank Laura Argys for her generous help in constructing the body weight variables in this. The responsibility for all errors and opinions is ours.

1. "The Surgeon General's call to action to prevent and decrease overweight and obesity" (2002). http://www.surgeongeneral.gov/topics/obesity/calltoaction/toc.htm.

Lady Michelle Obama has prioritized the goal of reduction of childhood obesity, thus further emphasizing the need for understanding factors that influence childhood obesity from a policy-making perspective. A report from the National Center for Environmental Health (Cummins and Jackson 2004) recognizes that community and neighborhood can potentially play important roles in child health—including obesity. However, the report also emphasizes that there has been relatively limited research that actually documents the nature of the relationship between community, neighborhood, and various aspects of child health, and concludes that "This new research field is wide open." Particularly, we were able to identify just one study that explored the relationship between neighborhood quality and obesity in children, using data from ten cities (Lumeng et al. 2006).

In this study, we extend extant research by exploring the relationship between children's body mass index (BMI) as well as probability of obesity with different aspects of the neighborhood as reported by the mother using linked data from the National Longitudinal Survey of Youth 1979 (NLSY79) and the Children of NLSY79 (CoNLSY). We also analyze the extent to which hitherto unexplained differences in the prevalence of obesity between non-Hispanic white children and minority children may be explained by the differences in neighborhood quality. We use several years of data where the mothers in the NLSY79 are asked about how they rate their neighborhood as a place to raise children, and are also asked about several specific characteristics about their neighborhood, such as whether run-down buildings, lack of jobs, lack of police, inadequate transport, indifferent neighbors, and so forth are a problem. Our results find that overall maternal rating of the neighborhood as a place to raise children is a significant predictor of the child's BMI or obesity risk in some models, but that these results are not robust, nor are they statistically significant in models that control for unobserved heterogeneity via fixed effects. However, one key neighborhood characteristic as perceived by the mother—namely, whether she believes that there is sufficient police protection in the neighborhood,—plays a significant role in predicting child BMI and remains robust across a range of model specifications.

6.2   Background

6.2.1   Neighborhood Characteristics, Physical Activity, Obesity

There is an emerging consensus in the scientific community that environmental factors play a role in the obesity epidemic, and that environmental solutions will be needed to address the problem. Thus, there is growing interest in understanding what is an "obesogenic environment" (Glass, Rasmussen, and Schwartz 2006), with a focus both on characteristics of the built environment—such as transportation or availability of physical activity facilities—as well as socioeconomic deprivation at the community level. This literature has been encouraged, in part, by work indicating that moving to a better neighborhood impacts educational outcomes for minority children, though the results are different for boys versus girls (Leventhal, Fauth, and Brooks-Gunn 2005). Several studies have explored the relationship between neighborhood characteristics and physical activity, though the results have not always been consistent. For example, a report from the Centers for Disease Control and Prevention (1999) using data from the Behavioral Risk Factor Surveillance System found that higher levels of perceived neighborhood safety correlated with higher levels of physical activity for adults. In contrast, Romero et al. (2001) found that children's own perceptions of neighborhood safety were actually inversely related to self-reported physical activity and BMI. Another study, by Brownson et al. (2001), found no statistical correlation between neighborhood crime rates and adult physical activity. A review of nineteen quantitative studies by Humpel, Owen, and Leslie (2002) found that neighborhood safety had positive associations with physical activity in some studies, and no statistical association in others, though no negative association was found in any study. In a relatively recent study, Gordon-Larsen et al. (2006) found that inequality in access to physical-activity facilities were a major predictor of obesity risk as well as physical activity, and that low socioeconomic status neighborhoods as well as high-minority population neighborhoods were less likely to have good access to physical-activity facilities. Glass, Rasmussen, and Schwartz (2006) used data on elderly adults in the Baltimore area, and found that residents of neighborhoods that ranked high in psychosocial hazards had higher BMI, less physical activity, and less healthy diets than their peers in neighborhoods ranking lower in psychosocial hazards, even after controlling for race-ethnicity, education, household wealth, and substance use. However, one problem that few of these studies have been able to address is the potential endogeneity between neighborhood characteristics and either physical activity or obesity. Namely, that the neighborhood that people reside in is at least partly due to their own choice, and persons with unmeasured personal or cultural propensities for greater physical activity and energy-balanced lifestyles might be more likely to live in neighborhoods that facilitate that physical activity and lifestyle.

We are aware of only two studies that directly test the relationship between neighborhood perceptions and obesity. The first of these is by Burdette, Wadden, and Whitaker (2006), and use data from the Fragile Families and Child Wellbeing study. Perceptions of the mothers in that survey about the neighborhood are measured using two separate indexes—a "neighborhood safety/social disorder" scale based on eight items, like how often the women saw loitering people, drunks/drug dealers, gang activities, and disorderly/misbehaving people in the neighborhood, and a "collective efficacy" scale based on whether the mothers felt that their neighbors could be trusted, and whether the neighbors would intervene in situations like a fight breaking out in the near vicinity or children loitering around. The study finds that mothers living in neighborhoods that they perceived to be relatively unsafe were more likely to be obese than counterparts living in neighborhoods they perceived to be safe, after controlling for indicators of socioeconomic status (SES) like income, education, race/ethnicity, and marital status. The second study, by Lumeng et al. (2006), uses a sample of 768 children from ten cities in the United States, who were part of the National Institute of Child Health and Human Development Study of Early Child Care and Youth Development. They obtain neighborhood quality perceptions using a sixteen-item measure of neighborhood characteristics, that was completed by the mother and at least one other adult guardian in the household (father, stepfather, grandparent) when the child was in the first grade. The items are then divided into two scales—the neighborhood safety subscale, and the neighborhood social involvement subscale. They find that, among seven-year-old-children, those residing in neighborhoods where the perceived neighborhood safety index was in the lowest quartile had a higher risk of being obese than counterparts in other neighborhoods, and this relationship held after controlling for parental marital status, education, race/ethnicity, and child's participation in after-school activities. This study is based on a relatively small sample of children that is 85 percent white, thus its results may not be generalizable.

Finally, extant studies have found a correlation between the time spent watching television and obesity among children (Dietz and Gortmaker 1985; Robinson et al. 1993; Robinson 1999). If there is a correlation between neighborhood quality and the time spent by children in sedentary, indoor activities like watching television, then this could be a potential pathway through which perceived neighborhood quality affects children's body weight. However, we are not aware of any study that explores the relationships between parental neighborhood perceptions and the amount of time children spend watching television.

6.2.2 Race-Ethnicity, Socioeconomic Status (SES), and Obesity among Children

It is well established that obesity disproportionately affects certain minority youth populations. Results from the 1999 to 2002 National Health and Nutrition Examination Survey (NHANES) found that African American and Mexican American adolescents aged twelve to nineteen were more likely to be overweight (21 percent and 23 percent, respectively) than non-Hispanic white adolescents (14 percent). Among children six to eleven years old, 22 percent of Mexican American children and 20 percent of African American children were overweight, compared to 14 percent of non-Hispanic white children (National Center for Health Statistics 2008). Furthermore, the rate of increase in obesity prevalence among children has been more pronounced among minority children than white children. For example, between 1986 and 1998, obesity prevalence among African Americans and Hispanics increased 120 percent, as compared to a 50 percent increase among non-Hispanic whites (Strauss and Pollack 2001).

A comprehensive review of literature by Sobal and Stunkard (1989) finds that, among adults, there is a consistent negative relationship between higher socioeconomic status (SES) (as measured by income, education, or occupation status) and being obese, but the relationship appears weaker and less consistent in children. While many studies included in the aforementioned review find that SES is negatively associated with children's obesity risk, other research suggests that this relationship varies by ethnicity. Specifically, the negative relationship between better SES and prevalence of obesity seems more apparent among white children and adolescents, but much less apparent among black or Mexican American (and presumably other Latino) adolescents (Troiano and Flegal 1998). In other words, black and Latino children from families with higher SES are no less likely to be overweight or obese than those in families with lower socioeconomic status. It has been speculated that the difference in the relationship between SES and obesity may be driven by cultural differences in eating habits, as well as attitudes towards body weight (Strauss & Knight 1999). We speculate that one other factor may play a role—specifically, neighborhood quality. Extant research finds that white families are more likely than black and Latino families to move into better and nonpoor neighborhoods, even after accounting for income (South and Crowder 1997; Hango 2002), and that black families are less likely than nonblack families to convert dissatisfaction with neighborhood to an actual move (South and Deane 1993). If better neighborhood quality is negatively related to the risk of childhood obesity, then the racial and ethnic differences in neighborhood quality among families of comparable SES might explain some of the racial and ethnic differences in children's obesity among families of comparable SES.

6.3   Data and Methods

6.3.1   Theoretical Framework and Empirical Models

Essentially the approach we take here is to assume that there exists a simple "production function" of a child's BMI percentile (or, alternatively, a binary indicator of whether the child is obese or not) as a function of caloric intake and energetic versus sedentary activities, and these in turn are determined by the mother's perception of the neighborhood, as well as other familial, demographic, and socioeconomic characteristics that might have a bearing on the child's exercise and eating patterns.

We posit a very simple model that is broadly within the framework of Grossman's model of health, where parents attempt to optimize healthy weight for the child, where the arguments in the production function for healthy weight include the child's caloric intake, and caloric expenditure through exercise and activity. Thus, the child's BMI can be written as a production function of these inputs:

(1) $$\text{BMI} = F(C_{(+)}, E_{(-)}, S_{(+)}; R),$$

where C represents caloric intake, E represents time spent in energetic activity, and S represents time spent in sedentary activities. Arguably, the two groups of activities are mutually exclusive and exhaustive; however, we choose to explicitly include both in the production function. Variable R represents other residual unobserved factors, including genetics. The signs in parentheses indicate whether each of these components is expected to increase or decrease BMI. Fully specifying and expanding the model— which would yield demand functions for caloric intake and types of activities as functions of the market prices of the inputs, shadow prices of time, and income—is beyond the scope of this chapter. However, we can posit that neighborhood quality is a factor in the demand functions of each of the components of the production function, since it arguably plays a role in determining the "price" of each of the components.

Specifically,

(2) $$C = C(N, X); E = E(N, X); S = S(N, X),$$

where N is a measure of neighborhood characteristics that for simplicity is termed neighborhood quality, and X represents other demographic and socioeconomic characteristics that play a role in determining market or shadow prices, as well as income and preferences.

Poor-quality and dangerous neighborhoods are likely to make outdoor activities—be it playing outdoors or walking to schools and recreational facilities—hazardous and, hence, more costly. Thus, children may be made to spend more time indoors by parents, and thus spend more time in sedentary occupations. Poor-quality and dangerous neighborhoods could also make it more difficult for parents to acquire healthy foods like fresh produce, which in turn could contribute to an unhealthy diet by the children. On the other hand, it could be argued that, if older children in particular had more license to be outdoors and to walk to various places, then they may also be able to go to stores or fast-food establishments and buy calorically dense foods without their parents' supervision. Furthermore, it could be argued that other built environment characteristics—for example, the lack of sidewalks—could make the issue of outdoor activities moot even if the neighborhood was otherwise perceived as high-quality and safe. Thus, it is difficult to predict a priori what effects neighborhood quality will have on each of the arguments in the production function for healthy weight, and thus, ultimately, how neighborhood quality will affect a child's weight. Hence, this question must be empirically determined.

To explore this empirically, we start by substituting equation (2) into equation (1) and creating a reduced-form BMI production function as

(3) $BMI = F(N, X, R)$.

Based on equation (3), we posit a simple linear specification model such that the BMI of the ith child in the tth period is expressed as

(4) $BMI_{it} = \alpha N_{it} + X_{it}\beta + R_{it} + \varepsilon_{it}$.

Empirical studies on children's weight often use dichotomous models to investigate what covariates influence the odds of children being obese or overweight. However, a recent study by Field, Cook, and Gillman (2005) reports that, simply being in the upper half of the age and gender specific BMI distribution is a good predictor of becoming obese as an adult, as well as developing health problems like hypertension in early adulthood. This suggests that, in addition to investigating what factors correlate with the risk of obesity/overweight in children, researchers should also be concerned about what factors simply predict a higher BMI in children. Hence, we estimate models with continuous measures of BMI (specifically, the BMI percentile score as well as the BMI-z score), in addition to linear probability models when the dependent variable is a binary indicator of whether the child is obese or not. To account for the fact that there are repeated observations for each child, as well as multiple children of the same mother in the data, standard errors are clustered at the maternal level.

We face the standard dilemma here that R_{it}, which represents unobserved determinants of the child's obesity, may also be correlated to the variable used to measure neighborhood quality. Neighborhood characteristics are not purely exogenous. For example, it may be speculated that families who have unobserved preferences for sedentary pastimes may disproportionately select into neighborhoods that are not conducive to outside activities. If the mother has a genetic predisposition towards obesity that she passes on to her children, then that predisposition towards obesity could also impose wage penalties upon her (Cawley 2004), and in turn decide the nature of the neighborhood that she can afford to live in. Thus, failing to account for these unobservables are likely to result in biased estimates of the effects of neighborhood quality on child body weight. Finally, in a situation where the neighborhood quality is measured based on the mother's perceptions of the neighborhood with no other external validation, there is the added issue that R_{it} may include unmeasured maternal characteristics that correlate both with such perceptions and her children's health outcomes. For example, a mother who is suffering from depression or other mental health problems may perceive the neighborhood as being an unsafe and hostile place, and at the same time she may also be less capable of properly monitoring the caloric intake and physical activities of her children to ensure their healthy weight.

We initially approach this problem by explicitly controlling for past maternal BMI in the model. The argument here is that past maternal BMI may serve both as a proxy for the genetic endowments in the family as well as the mother's unobserved preferences for caloric intake and physical activity, but it will not in itself be affected by current neighborhood quality (though one might argue that some mothers will continue to be in neighborhoods that are identical or very similar to the ones they grew up in themselves). Thereafter, we also use the fairly standard methods of fixed effects models, where we first estimate the models after including mother-level fixed effects, and thereafter we estimate them including child-level fixed effects. We have a slight preference for the former. Given that our measures of neighborhood quality are based entirely on the mother's reports, arguably the primary concern is the existence of maternal unobserved characteristics that correlate both with her perceptions about the neighborhood as well as her children's body weight outcomes. We also attempt a "propensity score regression method" where we calculate the probability of the mother living in a neighborhood of a certain quality based on an extensive list of her characteristics, and include that probability as a specific control variable in the regression equation (give cites). We recognize the inherent shortcomings of all of these methods. For example, the fixed effects methods fail to account for unobservables that may be time variant over the period of study, tend to accentuate the effects of measurement error, and can lead to the loss of statistical power. Propensity score regressions account for mother-level observables, but will not eliminate the bias in results that arise from variables that remain unobservable and unmeasured. Nonetheless, we believe that these are the best tools that we have to minimize the effects of bias-inducing unobservables in this study, even if we cannot altogether eliminate that bias.[2]

One of the specific contributions of this chapter is to explore whether differences in maternal perceptions of neighborhood quality can explain any of the hitherto unexplained differences in BMI and obesity risk between minority and nonminority children. To do this, we start by estimating the following empirical model:

$$(5) \qquad N_{it} = M_i\mu + X_{it}\lambda + u_{it},$$

where M_i are binary indicators of the race-ethnicity of the mother—one binary indicator to denote whether she is black, and one binary indicator to denote whether she is of Hispanic origin. The symbol X_{it} is now defined (with slight abuse of notation) as a vector of indicators of socioeconomic and demographic status other than race-ethnicity. The purpose is to statistically test whether the above minority populations are likely to have worse perceptions of their neighborhood compared to their white peers after controlling for the other socioeconomic and demographic characteristics.

We follow this up with a Oaxaca-Blinder decomposition (Blinder 1973;

---

2. We debated using instrumental-variable techniques, but were not aware of any viable instruments that would correlate to maternal perceptions of the neighborhood, but not have any direct bearing on the BMI of her children.

Oaxaca 1973), which is a technique that was originally used in labor market analysis to compare mean differences between two groups in the dependent variable of a regression model—typically wages. Here we use the technique to examine mean differences in the BMI percentile score of groups of children. We compare non-Hispanic whites (hereafter, "whites") to African Americans (hereafter "blacks") and, later, whites to Hispanics using the approach discussed in Jann (2008).

The Oaxaca-Blinder decomposition can be summarized with the expression

(6) $$R = \{E(X_w) - E(X_b)\}' B_w + \{E(X_b)' (B_w - B_b)\}.$$

This can be abbreviated as

(7) $$R = Q + U,$$

where:

(8) $$Q = \{E(X_w) - E(X_b)\}' B_w,$$

(9) $$U = \{E(X_b)' (B_w - B_b)\}.$$

Assume that we estimated a linear model for the BMI percentile score for whites (subscript w) and then again for blacks (subscript b). Here, Q represents the difference in the mean values of right hand-side regressors $E(X_w) - E(X_b)$ (i.e., the "endowments") multiplied by the regression coefficients B_w of the white group, against whom it is assumed that there is no discrimination (or alternatively, for whom it can be assumed that the coefficient estimates represent the correct response of the dependent variable to a change in the independent variable). Thus, for our analysis, Q is the part of the differential in the BMI percentile score that is explained by group differences in the levels of the regressors (the "quantity effect"). The symbol U is the unexplained part of the differential. In the labor market literature, U is often interpreted to be the part due to discrimination, as well as the effect of any unobserved differences between the two groups. In our analysis, we interpret U as the effect of unobserved differences between the two groups.

6.3.2   Data

The primary sources of data for this project are the National Longitudinal Survey of Youth 1979 cohort (NLSY79) and the Children of the NLSY79 (CoNLSY). We use survey year data from 1992 to 2000, which are the only years when questions were asked about neighborhood quality.

The NLSY79 is a multipurpose panel survey that originally included a sample of 12,686 individuals who were within the age range of 14 to 21 years of age on December 31, 1978. This original sample consists of three subsamples: a cross-sectional sample of 6,111 individuals representative of the noninstitutionalized civilian U.S. population within the prescribed age range; a supplemental sample designed to oversample Hispanics, blacks, and economically disadvantaged white U.S. population within the prescribed age range; and a sample of 1,280 respondents designed to represent U.S. military personnel within the prescribed age range.

Annual interviews were conducted beginning in 1979, with a shift to a biennial interview mode after 1994. The NLSY79 provides extensive information on all its respondents, including labor force activities, demographic characteristics, marital status, income, education, spousal characteristics, health status, and other socioeconomic characteristics. In year 2000, 4,113 of the original 6,283 female respondents remained in the sample. Of the missing 2,170, 441 were members of a military over-sample dropped in 1984, 890 were from an over-sample of economically disadvantaged white people dropped in 1990, and 105 were deceased. The remainder is lost due to attrition.

The CoNLSY sample is comprised of all children born to NLSY79 female respondents who live with their mother full-time or at least part-time, who have been independently followed and interviewed in various ways biennially, starting in 1986. Children who cease to live with their mothers altogether following a divorce are no longer included. The records from NLSY79 and CoNLSY can be easily linked via the mother's sample identification number. As of 2000, a total of 11,205 children had been identified as having been born to the original 6,283 NLSY79 female respondents, mostly during the years that they have been interviewed (of course, an unknown number of additional children may have been born to respondents after they attritioned or were dropped from the sample). Given the design of the CoNLSY survey, not all the children are assessed in each survey year. Children enter the data set after they are born, and once they reach the age of fifteen, they are dropped from this survey.[3] Given this design, there are more very young children entering the CoNLSY data set in the early years, when the mothers in the NLSY79 are in their peak childbearing years; whereas, in the later years, there are fewer children in the data set overall (since more have exceeded the age of fifteen), and fewer very young children are entering the dataset since fewer NLSY79 female respondents are giving birth.

Neighborhood perceptions: In 1992, the NLSY79 started to include a series of questions addressed to the mothers in the data set about their perceptions about their neighborhood. They were asked how they rated their neighborhoods overall as a place to raise children, with potential answers being "excellent," "very good," "good," "fair," and "poor." Thereafter, the respondents are specifically asked about selected neighborhood features, including neighbors lacking respect for law and order, crime and violence,

---

3. Once the children are over the age of fifteen, they leave the CoNLSY and enter another survey called the NLSY79 Young Adults.

abandoned and run-down buildings, lack of police protection, lack of public transportation, parents who do not supervise children, neighbors who are indifferent about other neighbors, and people unable to find jobs. For each of these issues, respondents state whether they consider it "a big problem," "somewhat of a problem," or "not a problem" in their neighborhoods. These questions were discontinued after the 2000 survey.

We use this information to create binary variables for overall neighborhood quality—namely, whether the mother qualifies the neighborhood as being an excellent or very good place to bring up children, and whether she qualifies it as only a fair or a poor place to bring up children. Thereafter, we create a series of binary indicators for the specific characteristics to indicate whether the mother considers each of those characteristics to be at least somewhat of a problem in the neighborhood.

Height and weight information: The CoNLSY survey covers numerous developmental and health aspects of the children. For all children below the age of fourteen, the child's height and weight at the time of the interview are recorded. In the majority (approximately 65 percent) of cases, interviewers measure height by tape measure and weight using a scale. In the remaining cases, height and weight are reported by the child's mother. We include all child-observations, regardless of whether the height and weight were mother-reported or interviewer-measured. However, we do include an explicit binary indicator to identify those cases where height and weight were interviewer-measured.

While the previously mentioned height and weight information can be used to create a conventional BMI score using the standard formula of (weight in lbs $\times$ 703)/(height in inches)^2, it should be noted that, unlike adults, absolute BMI scores carry less meaning for growing-age children in terms of health markers. Therefore, we follow the convention in the literature and alternately use BMI-z scores and BMI-percentile scores, which show how the child's BMI compares with his or her age and gender specific BMI distribution.[4] Equation (4) is estimated using both BMI-z and BMI-percentile scores. We also follow the convention of denoting a child to be obese if his or her BMI is at or above the ninety-fifth percentile of the age and gender specific BMI distribution of the reference period.

Other variables: We draw upon the rich array of information on socioeconomic and demographic characteristics that are available in the NLSY79 and CoNLSY for all respondents to control for other familial characteristics. Since current maternal BMI may also be a function of contemporane-

---

4. The BMI-z and BMI-percentile scores were created using Statistical Analysis Software (SAS) programs provided by the Centers for Disease Control and Prevention (CDC) at http://www.cdc.gov/nccdphp/dnpa/growthcharts/resources/sas.htm. We acknowledge our debt to Laura Argys, who played a key role in using the programs and generating the BMI-z and BMI-percentile values. These scores were initially created for use in an ongoing project by Argys and Sen (2008).

ous neighborhood quality (since poor neighborhood quality may also limit adult physical activity), we use maternal BMI based on height and weight information from the first time it was asked in the NLSY79—in the 1981 survey. Finally, we include information from the NLSY79 Geocode data to identify the counties where each mother lives in each survey year, and use this information to merge in county characteristics likely to be associated with neighborhood perceptions. Specifically, we used FBI Uniform crime statistics aggregated at the county level. Variables included murders, forcible rapes, robberies, aggravated assaults, burglaries, larcenies, motor vehicle thefts, and arsons each defined per hundred thousand of population in the county. These data are available annually. We used the collection from the University of Virginia (U.S. Federal Bureau of Investigation 2004). Other descriptors of the county include the percentages of the county population that was black and Hispanic, the percent of households with a female head, and income per capita were obtained from Area Resource File using data from the U.S. Census for 1900 and 2000 (and for 1995 for per capita income) and interpolated from intervening years (U.S. Bureau of Health Professions 2007). County annual unemployment rates were obtained from the Bureau of Labor Statistics (U.S. Bureau of Labor Statistics 1992–2000).

6.4   Results and Discussion

6.4.1   Maternal Perceptions of Neighborhood Characteristics and Child Body Weight

Table 6.1 presents descriptive statistics for the full sample, by race-ethnicity, and by neighborhood quality rating. The mean BMI-percentile in the pooled full sample is 56.9, and the obesity rate is about 17 percent. About 56 percent of the mothers in the pooled full sample report that their neighborhood is a "very good" or "excellent" place for children (hereafter referred to as "very good"), while 23 percent rate it as "fair" or "poor" (hereafter referred to as "not good"). The remaining mothers rate it as "good." Among the specific characteristics, the one that is perceived as at least somewhat of a problem by the largest fraction of responding mothers is unsupervised children (45.6 percent), followed by lack of respect for law and order (36.7 percent), jobless people (35.2 percent), indifferent neighbors (33.2 percent), crime and violence (30.4 percent), lack of transport (30.1 percent), lack of police protection (25.4 percent), and run-down buildings (19.9 percent). Not surprisingly, the black and Hispanic subsamples rate their neighborhoods more poorly and report more problems than does the white subsample. This is probably due, at least in part, to the fact that the black and Hispanic subsamples also have lower family income, lower levels of educational attainment, and higher proportions of them live in central cities compared to the white subsample. It can also be seen that the subsample living in "not good"

Table 6.1   Descriptive statistics

Variable	Description	Full sample (N = 12256) mean	White (N = 6434) mean	Black (N = 3431) mean	Hispanic (N = 2391) mean	Poor neighborhood[a] (N = 2805)	Good neighborhood[b] (N = 9451)
bmipct	Child BMI percentile	56.904 (34.508)	55.021 (34.002)	60.457 (34.608)	56.871 (35.318)	59.191 (34.043)	56.22 (34.543)
bmiz	Child BMI-z score	0.134 (1.881)	0.056 (1.783)	0.287 (1.950)	0.125 (2.022)	0.205 (2.081)	0.112 (1.810)
vow	Binary indicator child is obese	0.171	0.144	0.214	0.180	0.190	0.164
ngh_rate_n~d	Neighborhood rates fair / poor	0.230	0.123	0.386	0.292	n.a.	n.a.
ngh_rate_v~d	Neighborhood rates excellent / very good	0.563	0.702	0.381	0.452	n.a.	n.a.
ngh_nolaw	No respect for law & order a problem	0.367	0.283	0.504	0.394	0.778	0.244
ngh_crime	Crime and violence a problem	0.304	0.191	0.473	0.365	0.670	0.190
ngh_bldg	Run-down buildings a problem	0.199	0.139	0.307	0.206	0.454	0.123
no_police	Lack of police protection a problem	0.252	0.165	0.365	0.323	0.522	0.171
no_trans	Lack of transport a problem	0.301	0.262	0.373	0.299	0.330	0.291
no_super	Unsupervised children a problem	0.456	0.394	0.571	0.459	0.778	0.360
no_care	Uncaring neighbors a problem	0.332	0.263	0.426	0.383	0.623	0.244
no_jobs	Too many jobless people a problem	0.354	0.213	0.556	0.443	0.679	0.258
male	Child is male	0.505	0.506	0.489	0.526	0.528	0.498
Black	Mother is African-American	0.281	n.a.	n.a.	n.a.	0.472	0.224
Hisp	Mother is Hispanic	0.195	n.a.	n.a.	n.a.	0.247	0.179
childage	Child's age	7.197 (2.531)	7.017 (2.535)	7.469 (2.518)	7.291 (2.503)	7.400 (2.481)	7.135 (2.542)

(*continued*)

Table 6.1   (continued)

Variable	Description	Full sample (N = 12256) mean	White (N = 6434) mean	Black (N = 3431) mean	Hispanic (N = 2391) mean	Poor neighborhood[a] (N = 2805)	Good neighborhood[b] (N = 9451)
scaletape	BMI from scale & tape measures by interviewer	0.697	0.679	0.730	0.700	0.700	0.696
mom_age	Mother's age	26.585	27.169	25.766	26.196	25.711	26.840
		(3.881)	(3.752)	(3.935)	(3.881)	(3.821)	(3.860)
no_smsa	Does not live in MSA	0.173	0.207	0.158	0.103	0.141	0.182
cen_city	Lives in central city	0.164	0.079	0.294	0.207	0.285	0.128
momnowork	Mother not employed outside home	0.215	0.199	0.220	0.250	0.287	0.193
dadpresent	Father in household	0.628	0.772	0.347	0.647	0.396	0.699
tnfaminc_r~1	Annual family income (real)	60883.07	73692.61	40655.15	55639.23	37762.99	67772.79
		(104320.20)	(118856.40)	(72355.05)	(96230.12)	(49040.12)	(114903.40)
momed12_15	Mother has some college	0.700	0.680	0.737	0.701	0.721	0.692
momed16_20	Mother has at least 4 yrs of college	0.189	0.264	0.116	0.096	0.061	0.226
mombmi81	Mother's BMI, 1981	21.887	21.388	22.604	22.196	22.470	21.715
		(3.509)	(3.270)	(3.857)	(3.387)	(3.875)	(3.373)

Note: n.a. = not applicable.

[a]Those who rate neighborhood as fair or poor.

[b]Those who rate neighborhood as good or higher.

neighborhoods have higher mean BMI-percentile for their children as well as higher rates of obesity. Not surprisingly, higher proportions of this sub-sample are minorities, more likely to live in the inner city, be single-parent households, have lower family income, have mothers who are not working and with lower educational attainment, and have mothers who had higher BMI themselves in 1981, compared to their counterparts living in better neighborhoods. Living in "not good" neighborhoods also correlates with reporting higher rates of specific neighborhood problems. With the exception of lack of transportation—where the proportions across the two groups are somewhat comparable—those living in "not good" neighborhoods are substantially more likely to answer in the affirmative about the existence of specific problems in the neighborhood. The Cronbach's alpha for the eight specific dimensions of neighborhood quality is 0.84, indicating high internal consistency. Therefore, these eight items reliably represent the construct of perceived neighborhood quality.

Table 6.2 presents three sets of results from regressing measures of the child's body weight (BMI-percentile, BMI-z score, and a binary indicator of obesity) upon the overall neighborhood rating and other characteristics. The initial specification includes demographic and geographic characteristics, but no other indicators of socioeconomic status. The second specification includes measures of socioeconomic status—maternal education, presence of a father in the household, total family income, and maternal employment status. The third and final specification additionally includes maternal BMI as measured in 1981. Perceived neighborhood quality is captured by two binary indicators of "very good" and "not good," with the basis for comparison being whether the neighborhood is "good." It can be seen that being in a "not good" neighborhood is associated with a higher BMI-percentile in the first two model specifications, and with a higher BMI-z score in the first model specification. However, once the full range of familial socioeconomic characteristics as well as maternal BMI from 1981 are controlled for, no further statistical associations remain between any of the outcome variables and the overall neighborhood quality measures. Models using maternal fixed effects and child fixed effects also failed to find any statistical relationship between the outcome variables and the neighborhood quality measures. Those results are available upon request.

We repeated the estimations after substituting each of the eight specific neighborhood characteristics (that is, the binary indicator for whether a specific issue was at least somewhat of a problem) in place of the general rankings. For brevity, only the results pertaining to the neighborhood characteristics are presented (table 6.3). Most of the specific characteristics do not have any significant relationship to the BMI outcomes or obesity risk—with the exception of the problems of indifferent neighbors and inadequate police protection. The children of mothers who report that indifferent neighbors are a problem on average belong to a 1.84 higher BMI-percentile and

Table 6.2   Regression results for child BMI, obesity risk and overall neighborhood ratings

	Model 1			Model 2			Model 3		
	BMI-percentile	BMI-z score	Obese	BMI-percentile	BMI-z score	Obese	BMI-percentile	BMI-z score	Obese
ngh_rate_n~d	2.421**	0.024**	0.059	2.350**	0.017	0.072	1.710	0.043	0.011
	(2.24)	(2.25)	(0.98)	(2.13)	(1.56)	(1.21)	(1.57)	(0.73)	(0.99)
ngh_rate_g~d	0.999	0.017*	0.029	0.792	0.011	0.027	0.309	0.005	0.006
	(1.03)	(1.70)	(0.56)	(0.81)	(1.08)	(0.53)	(0.32)	(0.11)	(0.61)
male	0.306	0.028***	0.058	0.413	0.029***	0.064	0.567	0.071*	0.030***
	(0.37)	(3.28)	(1.41)	(0.51)	(3.34)	(1.55)	(0.70)	(1.73)	(3.59)
Black	4.461***	0.070***	0.200***	4.052***	0.064***	0.196***	2.613**	0.130**	0.050***
	(3.64)	(5.52)	(3.20)	(3.18)	(4.79)	(3.02)	(2.08)	(2.03)	(3.78)
Hisp	2.261	0.046***	0.101	2.064	0.039***	0.103	1.173	0.062	0.030**
	(1.63)	(3.55)	(1.42)	(1.47)	(2.96)	(1.45)	(0.86)	(0.90)	(2.29)
childage	1.379***	-0.007***	0.068***	1.314***	-0.007***	0.066***	1.058***	0.054***	-0.010***
	(5.76)	(-2.83)	(5.46)	(5.46)	(-2.97)	(5.22)	(4.44)	(4.24)	(-4.14)
scaletape	-7.114***	-0.085***	-0.369***	-7.135***	-0.085***	-0.368***	-7.04***	-0.364***	-0.084***
	(-9.36)	(-9.97)	(-8.93)	(-9.41)	(-10.06)	(-8.96)	(-9.34)	(-8.87)	(-10.04)
mom_age	0.155	0.000	0.005	0.193	0.001	0.005	-0.001	-0.004	-0.001
	(0.71)	(-0.07)	(0.43)	(0.87)	(0.44)	(0.47)	(0.00)	(-0.32)	(-0.47)
no_smsa	0.361	0.006	0.049	0.220	0.002	0.047	-0.431	0.017	-0.005
	(0.28)	(0.50)	(0.71)	(0.17)	(0.16)	(0.69)	(-0.35)	(0.26)	(-0.38)
cen_city	1.423	0.011	0.055	1.359	0.010	0.056	0.874	0.034	0.005
	(1.18)	(0.80)	(0.88)	(1.13)	(0.76)	(0.89)	(0.74)	(0.55)	(0.42)

	(1)	(2)	(3)	(4)	(5)	(6)	(7)	(8)	(9)
momnowork				-4.605***	-0.028***	-0.231***	4.386***	-0.221***	-0.026***
				(-4.40)	(-2.85)	(-4.01)	(-4.22)	(-3.83)	(-2.68)
dadpresent				-0.872	-0.002	-0.009	-0.900	-0.011	-0.003
				(-0.83)	(-0.20)	(-0.17)	(-0.86)	(-0.20)	(-0.24)
tnfaminc_r~1				0.000	0.000***	0.000	0.000	0.000	0.000
				(-0.73)	(-2.81)	(-1.05)	(-0.38)	(-0.69)	(-2.47)
momed12_15				-0.702	-0.011	0.018	-0.086	0.046	-0.005
				(-0.47)	(-0.67)	(0.21)	(-0.06)	(0.52)	(-0.33)
momed16_20				-1.797	-0.051***	-0.006	-0.623	0.047	-0.039**
				(-0.96)	(-2.59)	(-0.06)	(-0.34)	(0.46)	(-2.06)
mombmi81							1.470***	0.067***	0.015***
							(10.05)	(8.72)	(9.97)
R^2	0.07	0.06	0.04	0.08	0.06	0.05	0.10	0.07	0.06
F	60.23	44.77	23.87	47.64	34.49	20.83	54.67	35.76	26.29

Notes: Data shows β values, with *t*-statistics in parentheses. All models also include region fixed effects and year fixed effects. Standard errors clustered upon mothers.

***$p < 0.01$

**$p < 0.05$

*$p < 0.10$

Table 6.3   **Child BMI, obesity risk, and specific neighborhood characteristics**

		BMI-percentile	Obese
ngh_nolaw	No respect for law and order a problem	0.94	–0.004
		(1.11)	(–0.50)
ngh_crime	Crime and violence a problem	1.13	0.007
		(1.27)	(0.82)
no_super	Unsupervised children a problem	0.27	–0.001
		(0.33)	(–0.33)
ngh_bldg	Run-down buildings a problem	0.44	–0.005
		(0.43)	(–0.49)
no_jobs	Too many jobless people a problem	1.09	0.01
		(1.19)	(0.99)
no_trans	Lack of transport a problem	0.39	–0.003
		(0.52)	(0.39)
no_care	Uncaring neighbors a problem	1.84**	0.02**
		(2.23)	(2.31)
no_police	Inadequate police protection a problem	3.65***	0.03***
		(3.98)	(2.82)

Notes: Data shows β values, with *t*-statistics in parentheses. All models also control for the variables included in model 2, table 6.2, as well as region and year fixed effects. Standard errors clustered upon mothers.
***$p < 0.01$
**$p < 0.05$
*$p < 0.10$

are at a 2 percent higher risk of obesity compared to children whose mothers do not report it as a problem. The children of mothers who report that inadequate police protection is a problem on average belong to a 3.65 higher BMI-percentile and are at a 3 percent higher risk of obesity compared to children whose mothers do not report it as a problem.

Thereafter, we used only these two characteristics to estimate further models, including those that controlled for the mother's BMI from 1981, and those that included maternal and child fixed effects. We found that there no longer remained any significant relationship between the problem of indifferent neighbors and the outcomes. However, inadequate police protection continued to have a significantly negative effect both on the BMI-percentile and BMI-*z* scores in almost all the model specifications, though not always on the risk of obesity per se (table 6.4). We also ran models that included the full set of specific neighborhood characteristics, in addition to other characteristics, and there, too, inadequate police protection continued to be statistically significant in almost all models, thus alleviating the concern that the estimated effects of inadequate police protection when included only by itself was simply picking up the effects of other neighborhood characteristics omitted from the model.

Table 6.4   **Different models for child BMI, obesity risk, and lack of police protection, full sample and by race-ethnicity**

	BMI-percentile	Risk of Obesity
Full sample		
Models excluding mother's BMI	3.65***	0.03***
	(3.98)	(2.82)
Models including mother's BMI	3.10***	0.02**
	(3.46)	(2.27)
Models with maternal fixed effects	2.44***	0.016
	(2.64)	(1.45)
Models with child fixed effects	1.93**	0.01
	(2.04)	(1.08)
Models including maternal propensity scores	3.22***	0.02**
	(3.47)	(2.40)
Full sample, includes other neighborhood characteristics		
Models excluding mother's BMI	3.77***	0.03***
	(3.76)	(2.70)
Models including mother's BMI	3.44***	0.03***
	(3.47)	(2.44)
Models with maternal fixed effects	2.37**	0.01
	(2.41)	(1.33)
Models with child fixed effects	1.93**	0.01
	(2.04)	(1.14)
Models including maternal propensity scores	3.49***	0.02**
	(3.42)	(2.45)
Non-Hispanic whites		
Models excluding mother's BMI	2.45*	0.02*
	(1.64)	(1.94)
Models including mother's BMI	1.72	0.02
	(1.18)	(1.46)
Models with maternal fixed effects	1.26	0.02
	(0.89)	(1.11)
Models with child fixed effects	0.51	0.01
	(0.37)	(0.60)
Models including maternal propensity scores	1.81	0.02
	(1.18)	(1.57)
Blacks		
Models excluding mother's BMI	3.09**	0.02
	(2.14)	(1.34)
Models including mother's BMI	2.65*	0.01
	(1.91)	(0.79)
Models with maternal fixed effects	2.97*	0.02
	(1.86)	(0.94)
Models with child fixed effects	2.94**	0.02
	(1.96)	(0.91)
Models including maternal propensity scores	3.01**	0.02
	(2.06)	(1.18)

(*continued*)

Table 6.4   (continued)

	BMI-percentile	Risk of Obesity
Hispanics		
Models excluding mother's BMI	5.32***	0.03
	(2.84)	(1.52)
Models including mother's BMI	4.67**	0.03
	(2.51)	(1.29)
Models with maternal fixed effects	3.68*	0.01
	(1.85)	(0.46)
Models with child fixed effects	2.64	0.01
	(1.36)	(0.44)
Models including maternal propensity scores	4.55**	0.02
	(2.41)	(0.83)

Notes: Data shows β values, with *t*-statistics in parentheses. The second set of models control for the full array of specific neighborhood characteristics in addition to inadequate police protection. All models also control for the variables included in model 2, table 6.2, as well as region and year fixed effects. Standard errors clustered upon mothers.
***$p < 0.01$
**$p < 0.05$
*$p < 0.10$

Upon rerunning the analyses separately for (non-Hispanic) whites, blacks and Hispanics, we found that inadequate police protection typically had larger and more significant effects on BMI-percentile of black and Hispanic children compared to whites, but that for all the subsamples, the effects on the risk of obesity per se tended to be statistically imprecise. These results are also in table 6.4.

As mentioned earlier, we used one further approach to test the robustness of the results pertaining to inadequate police protection—a propensity scores approach. This method, described by D'Agostino (1998), and used in previous studies like Sen and Swaminathan (2007), essentially involves estimating first stage binary regressions for the treatment in question using as control all available and relevant observable characteristics; obtaining the predicted probabilities of being subject to the treatment; and finally, including that predicted probability (i.e., the propensity for the treatment) as an added control in the final outcomes regression, which also includes the binary indicator of treatment. While propensity scores, by definition, only control for observable factors, if one is able to use a wide range of observables that directly measure or adequately proxy for the potential confounders to construct these scores, then arguably the omitted variable bias in the coefficient estimate of the binary treatment is substantially reduced. The advantages of including the propensity score in the final regression rather than attempting a more conventional propensity score matching method proposed by Rosenbaum and Rubin (1984) is that it prevents the loss of sample size since we do not have to omit observations from the control group that do not closely match members from the treated group, and also helps avoid the problems regarding which particular matching technique is the appropriate one.

We estimate initial probit equations on perceptions of inadequate police protection using the following maternal characteristics: whether she grew up in an intact parental family herself, whether either parent was an immigrant and a foreign language was spoken at home, her religious attendance as reported in the first survey year, whether her mother was employed outside the home, proxy variables for the importance of education in the home environment in form of whether newspapers came to the house and whether the family had a library card when she was fourteen, whether she reported binge drinking in a past survey (the question is asked in the 1985 survey), whether anyone in her family had a problem with alcohol, her family's poverty status in 1978, and whether in the 1982 survey she reported facing discrimination when looking for a job based on sex, race, or nationality, whether she faced discrimination based on age (i.e., considered too young), and finally, her self-esteem score based on the ten-item Rosenberg Self-Esteem Scale based on the individual's self-evaluation. Higher scores on this scale are indicative of greater self-esteem.[5] The NLSY79 administered these questions and created the scale in the 1980 and 1987 interviews. We use the information from 1987. Of our selected variables, being in poverty in 1978 and binge drinking significantly increases the probability of reporting inadequate police protection, whereas maternal employment, newspapers, and a library card in the house when she was fourteen, and higher self-esteem significantly reduces the probability of reporting inadequate police protection. Living in an intact parental family herself reduces the probability of reporting inadequate police protection with weak statistical significance, while religious attendance, parental immigrant status, or alcohol problems among other family members do not have any significant effect. Full results are available upon request. As explained above, we then create the predicted probabilities (i.e., the propensity scores) of reporting inadequate police protection from the probit model, and then use that as an added control in our equations for the child's body weight. We find that the relationship between inadequate police protection and child's BMI-percentile as well as likelihood of being obese remain comparable to earlier findings using maternal fixed effects—namely, inadequate police protection significantly increases both BMI-percentile and risk of obesity for the full sample, but for subsamples by race-ethnicity, the effects on risk of obesity

5. The scale is short, widely used, and has accumulated evidence of validity and reliability. It contains ten statements of self-approval and disapproval with which respondents are asked to strongly agree, agree, disagree, or strongly disagree. Of these, on five items disagreeing is indicative of higher self-esteem, while on the remaining five disagreeing is indicative of lower self-esteem, and thus must be reversed when the items are added.

tend to be statistically imprecise, and the effects on BMI-percentile appear to be larger and more significant for blacks and Hispanics compared to whites.[6]

It would be useful to be able to explore the causal pathways between perceived inadequate police protection and children's body weight. Unfortunately, the CoNLSY data sets provide very limited information on either energetic versus sedentary activities or diet quality. The only pathway we were able to consider from this data is the sedentary activity of television watching, an activity that has been found to be associated with increased risk of obesity in previous studies (Dietz and Gortmaker 1985; Robinson et al. 1993; Robinson 1999). We estimate the relationship between maternal perceptions of inadequate police protection and reported average hours of television watching per day by the children during weekdays and during weekends, in models with and without controls for the other neighborhood characteristics, mother-level fixed effects, child-level fixed effects, and the previously calculated propensity scores. The results are reported in table 6.5. Maternal reports of inadequate police protection are associated with increases in the children's television watching by 0.36 to 0.47 hours during weekdays and 0.26 to 0.42 hours on weekends in the models without fixed effects. When maternal fixed effects are included, estimated impact on television watching on weekdays is about 0.32 hours, and continues to be statistically significant. When child fixed effects are included, the estimated effect falls to about 0.20 hours and becomes statistically insignificant. In models with maternal or child fixed effects, the relationship between inadequate police protection and TV watching during weekends is statistically insignificant, and the sign on the effect is counterintuitive. Furthermore, we are concerned regarding the validity of the results because of possible measurement error in the television watching variable in the CoNLSY data set. A number of respondents reported watching television for more than twenty hours a day on weekdays and weekends, and some reported watching television for more than twenty-four hours a day. Hence, there is likely to be measurement error in the hours of television watching variable, and whether this affects the estimates of interest depends on the nature of the measurement error. If the measurement error is uncorrelated to the actual value of hours of television (classical measurement error), then it will not bias

---

6. It has been argued that propensity score regressions yield results similar to those yielded by including all mother-level characteristics in the final model individually, with the only advantage being that fewer degrees of freedom are lost when including a single propensity score rather than an array of individual variables (Bhattacharya and Vogt 2007). Indeed, when we repeated the regression models for child BMI-percentile and obesity risk after explicitly including all maternal characteristics instead of the predicted propensity score, our results stayed very similar.

Table 6.5   **Television watching on weekdays and weekends, and lack of police protection**

	Hours of TV watched during weekdays	Hours of TV watched during weekends
Full sample		
Models excluding mother's BMI	0.470***	0.420***
	(3.15)	(3.48)
Models including mother's BMI	0.452***	0.407***
	(3.04)	(3.30)
Models with maternal fixed effects	0.316**	–0.016
	(2.29)	(–0.15)
Models with child fixed effects	0.201	–0.033
	(1.32)	(–0.28)
Models including maternal propensity scores	0.437***	0.385***
	(2.81)	(3.08)
Full sample, includes other neighborhood characteristics		
Models excluding mother's BMI	0.373**	0.275**
	(2.25)	(2.09)
Models including mother's BMI	0.363**	0.268**
	(2.29)	(2.02)
Models with maternal fixed effects	0.324**	–0.133
	(2.21)	(–1.15)
Models with child fixed effects	0.193	–0.182
	(1.20)	(–1.46)
Models including maternal propensity scores	0.372**	0.261*
	(2.27)	(1.94)

Notes: Data shows β values, with *t*-statistics in parentheses. The second set of models control for the full array of specific neighborhood characteristics in addition to inadequate police protection. All models also control for the other variables included in table 6.4, as well as region and year fixed effects. Standard errors clustered upon mothers.

***p < 0.01
**p < 0.05
*p < 0.10

the model estimates, though it may increase the standard errors. However, if the measurement error is uncorrelated with the reported value but correlated with the true value of the outcome variable, then model estimates will be biased towards zero (Hyslop and Imbens 2001). The most complex scenario is when the measurement error in the outcome variable is potentially correlated with the inadequate police protection (for example, respondents who report the more outlying values of television hours may do so because they have relatively low cognitive abilities, and this in turn may be correlated to how they perceive their neighborhood), whereby the bias in the estimate could be large and its direction nondecipherable without more information. (Hyslop and Imbens 2001). Thus, we treat these results with some skepticism. Ultimately, the issue of pathways through which neighborhood quality perceptions influence body weight must be addressed using other data sets that provide more thorough and better measures of energetic/sedentary activities and diet quality.[7]

Finally, as a prelude to exploring whether differences in police protection can explain any part of the variation in children's body weight across race-ethnicity, we first verify that there exist differences in levels of (perceived) police protection between white mothers, black mothers and Hispanic mothers that cannot be explained by differences in socioeconomic factors such as income, education, presence of a husband in the household, and so forth. Table 6.6 reports results from linear probability models based on equation (5), where the lack of police protection, as well as a general rating of the neighborhood as not good, are regressed on race-ethnicity as well as all the socioeconomic and geographic controls in the other models. Results show that, compared to white mothers, black mothers have a 13 percent higher probability, and Hispanic mothers have an 8.2 percent higher probability of reporting that lack of police protection is a problem in their neighborhood. Moreover, compared to white mothers, black mothers have about a 16.3 percent higher probability, and Hispanic mothers have about an 8.3 percent higher probability of reporting that the overall quality of the neighborhood was not good. Hence, there exist differences across race-ethnicity in neighborhood quality that are not explained away by differences in socioeconomic status across race-ethnicity. This provides justification for doing Oaxaca-Blinder decomposition.

6.4.2   Oaxaca-Blinder Decomposition

Table 6.7 shows the Oaxaca-Blinder decomposition based on ordinary least squares (OLS) models with robust standard errors, and table 6.8 shows the Oaxaca-Blinder decomposition based on models with mother-level fixed effects. For brevity, we mostly confine our detailed discussion to the results presented in table 6.7. The left-hand-side of the table (columns [2] to [4]) has the (non-Hispanic) white versus blacks comparison; the right-hand (columns [5] to [7]) is the (non-Hispanic) white versus Hispanic comparison. In case of whites versus blacks, for example, the mean predicted BMI percentile scores are respectively 55.06 and 60.46 with a statistically significant difference (at 1 percent) of −5.40 BMI percentile points. This difference can be broken down in columns (3) and (4), respectively, into the total explained

---

7. We debated about the possibility of regressing BMI on television watching in a two-stage least squares (2SLS) framework with inadequate police protection serving as an instrument for television watching. We eventually decided against this. An objective, external measure of neighborhood safety would have probably served as a good instrument. But we have concerns about whether mother-reported perceptions of police protection could in some cases be correlated with certain maternal emotional and mental health issues that could also affect her maternal skills and, thus, her child's body weight. Under the circumstances, we do not believe that maternal perceptions of inadequate police protection would satisfy the characteristics of a good instrument.

Table 6.6   Reported lack of police protection, poor neighborhood quality and
                   respondent characteristics

	Lack of police protection a problem	Overall neighborhood rating fair or poor
Black	0.129***	0.163***
	(7.07)	(9.03)
Hisp	0.083***	0.082***
	(3.77)	(4.09)
childage	0.003	–0.004
	(1.03)	(–1.22)
mom_age	–0.001	–0.003
	(–0.32)	(–1.10)
no_smsa	0.047**	–0.029*
	(2.49)	(–1.85)
cen_city	0.119***	0.116***
	(6.52)	(6.20)
momnowork	0.044**	0.056***
	(2.51)	(3.58)
dadpresent	–0.035	–0.125***
	(–2.33)	(–8.61)
tnfaminc_r~1	0.000***	0.000***
	(–2.91)	(–5.63)
momed12_15	–0.108***	–0.115***
	(–4.11)	(–4.59)
momed16_20	–0.180***	–0.191***
	(–6.18)	(–7.07)
R^2	0.09	0.150
F	21.03	42.93

Notes: Data shows β values, with t-statistics in parentheses. All models also control for region and year fixed effects. Standard errors clustered upon mothers.
***$p < 0.01$
**$p < 0.05$
*$p < 0.10$

part that is due to differences in the levels of the regression variables—that is, Q in equation (7)—which is –2.73 ($z = 2.75$), and the total unexplained part, U in equation (7), which is –2.67 ($z = 1.91$). The rest of the entries in columns (3) and (4) show the decomposition at the level of the individual variables.

A comparison of the previous models with Oaxaca-Blinder decomposition models that exclude perceived police protection finds that, in absence of controlling for police protection, of the –5.40 BMI percentile points gap between whites and blacks, –2.50 ($z = 2.57$) is explained, and –2.90 ($z = 2.09$) is unexplained. Of the –1.90 BMI percentile points gap between whites and Hispanics –1.66 ($z = –1.86$) is explained and –0.244 ($z = 0.17$) is unexplained in absence of controlling for police protection (full results from these models

Table 6.7   **Oaxaca-Blinder decomposition of BMI-percentile difference**

	White vs. black			White vs. Hispanic		
	Differential	Explained	Unexplained	Differential	Explained	Unexplained
Prediction_1	55.059***			55.059***		
	(80.442)			(80.439)		
Prediction_2	60.462***			56.966***		
	(69.952)			(52.198)		
Difference	−5.402***			−1.907		
	(−4.900)			(−1.480)		
no_police2		−0.348	−0.339		−0.268	−0.944
		(−1.173)	(−0.458)		(−1.165)	(−1.244)
mombmi81		−1.809***	2.927		−1.192***	−3.488
		(−4.720)	(0.405)		(−3.555)	(−0.402)
male		0.009	0.406		−0.012	−0.655
		(0.474)	(0.433)		(−0.486)	(−0.599)
childage		−0.295*	−5.336		−0.180*	−6.996
		(−1.946)	(−1.334)		(−1.811)	(−1.542)
scaletape		0.411***	−0.921		0.172	0.621
		(3.807)	(−0.675)		(1.628)	(0.449)
mom_age		0.187	8.511		0.130	−0.056
		(0.422)	(0.676)		(0.421)	(−0.004)
no_smsa		0.001	0.088		0.002	0.387
		(0.012)	(0.184)		(0.012)	(0.974)
cen_city		0.094	0.148		0.058	−0.477
		(0.214)	(0.186)		(0.214)	(−0.700)
momnowork		0.126	−0.311		0.274*	−0.901
		(1.185)	(−0.616)		(1.879)	(−1.298)
dadpresent		−0.450	0.228		−0.130	−1.247
		(−0.688)	(0.266)		(−0.683)	(−0.739)
tnfaminc_real		−0.078	−0.066		−0.041	−0.089
		(−0.501)	(−0.177)		(−0.498)	(−0.225)
momedu		−0.462	−3.414		−0.597	−2.369
		(−1.416)	(−1.113)		(−1.296)	(−0.791)
region		−1.050**	4.571*		−0.992	6.045*
		(−2.390)	(1.799)		(−1.614)	(1.801)
years		0.934***	−4.374**		1.003***	−1.632
		(4.174)	(−2.255)		(4.163)	(−0.722)
Total		−2.729***	−2.673*		−1.771*	−0.136
		(−2.756)	(−1.910)		(−1.955)	(−0.093)

Note: Data shows β values, with *t*-statistics in parentheses. The Oaxaca-Blinder decompositions use the Oaxaca command in STATA 10, which also calculates variance estimates for the components of the Oaxaca-Blinder decomposition.

***$p < 0.01$v

**$p < 0.05$

*$p < 0.10$

Table 6.8	Oaxaca-Blinder decomposition of BMI-percentile difference with fixed effects					
	White vs. black			White vs. Hispanic		
	Differential	Explained	Unexplained	Differential	Explained	Unexplained
Prediction_1	55.059***			55.059***		
	(155.273)			(155.273)		
Prediction_2	60.462***			56.966***		
	(112.723)			(90.582)		
Difference	−5.402***			−1.907***		
	(−8.402)			(−2.641)		
no_police2		−0.256	−0.626		−0.197	−0.773
		(−0.887)	(−0.796)		(−0.886)	(−0.985)
male		0.022	0.722		−0.027	−1.580
		(1.052)	(0.849)		(−1.094)	(−1.558)
childage		0.040	3.403		0.025	−10.358
		(0.086)	(0.236)		(0.086)	(−0.656)
scaletape		0.324***	0.196		0.136**	0.560
		(4.321)	(0.154)		(2.035)	(0.425)
mom_age		−0.968	32.948		−0.673	−18.572
		(−0.665)	(0.663)		(−0.664)	(−0.331)
no_smsa		−0.033	−0.639		−0.073	−0.182
		(−0.373)	(−0.989)		(−0.374)	(−0.390)
cen_city		0.230	0.993		0.142	−0.911
		(0.537)	(1.122)		(0.537)	(−1.244)
momnowork		0.062	−0.100		0.135	0.311
		(1.434)	(−0.163)		(1.611)	(0.387)
dadpresent		−0.043	2.369**		−0.012	−1.053
		(−0.055)	(1.994)		(−0.055)	(−0.466)
tnfaminc_real		0.116	−0.161		0.061	0.291
		(0.790)	(−0.372)		(0.786)	(0.499)
momedu		−0.820	0.233		−0.800	6.560
		(−0.692)	(0.025)		(−0.521)	(0.750)
region		0.241	2.836		2.931*	−19.614*
		(0.205)	(0.374)		(1.690)	(−1.832)
years		1.300***	−7.084		1.382***	1.009
		(2.584)	(−1.116)		(2.598)	(0.143)
Total		0.215	−5.618***		3.029	−4.936**
		(0.107)	(−2.688)		(1.268)	(−1.991)

Note: Data shows β values, with *t*-statistics in parentheses. The Oaxaca-Blinder decompositions use the Oaxaca command in STATA 10, which also calculates variance estimates for the components of the Oaxaca-Blinder decomposition.

***$p < 0.01$

**$p < 0.05$

*$p < 0.10$

are available upon request). Thus, accounting for the differences in the levels of perceived police protection explains part of the otherwise unexplained gap in BMI between the groups in our sample. Table 6.7 shows that the differences in perceived police protection between blacks and whites account for somewhat more than 12 percent (–0.348 of –2.729) of the explained gap between the two groups, and between whites versus Hispanics, the differences in the level of police protection account for almost 15 percent (–0.2681 of –1.771) of the explained gap between the two groups. However, the corresponding z-statistics, which are derived based on the assumption that both the coefficient estimates and the sample means of the X variables are subject to sampling variation (Jann 2008), indicate that the results are statistically imprecise. Thus, we cannot say whether differences in perceived police protection can help explain the BMI gap between white and black or Hispanic children in the general population.

The differences in the mother's BMI contributes significantly to the explained gap between both whites and blacks and whites and Hispanics. Some other variables that are significant but have no practical implications are a variable that summaries the effects of the various year dummies and a binary indicator of whether the child's height and weight were measured by the survey interviewer (rather than being based on the mother's report).

The differences in the levels of police protection are not statistically significant in the Oaxaca-Blinder decompositions based on fixed effects models, either. However, one factor that is significant in these fixed effects models and worth commenting on is the presence of the father in the household. A father's presence in the household has an important effect on the weight of a black child, but no discernible effect for white children. For a black child, a father's presence has a statistically significant effect that on average reduces a child's weight by almost 7 percentile points. For a white child, a father's presence has a small (1/10 of a BMI percentile point) and statistically insignificant effect on the child's weight. (Detailed regression results for these effects are not reported here but are available from the authors.) White children in the NLSY sample have more fathers present than black children (77 percent v. 35 percent). The Oaxaca decomposition says that, for two otherwise identical white and black children, if a black father had acted like (i.e., had the same regression coefficient as) a white father, then the child would be heavier by about 2.3 BMI percentile points. Further, if as many black children had fathers present as white children and if the fathers acted like white fathers, this would have no statistically significant effect on the average weight of black children. Thus, when they are present, black fathers have an important and favorable influence on their children's weight.

In the white versus Hispanic comparison, the presence of a father does not appear to play a statistically significant role in explaining differences between the two groups.

Our main regression analysis found that mothers who are concerned about a lack of police in their neighborhoods tend to have heavier children. We also found that minority mothers reported greater lack of police protection than their white counterparts even after accounting for other family characteristics. Nonetheless, the Oaxaca-Blinder decompositions show that this difference in perceived police protection is not able to explain away the difference in the average body weight of minority children compared to white children. Hence, we conclude that there are other unobserved factors that largely account for these group differences.

6.4.3   Correlates of Perceived Neighborhood Quality

One issue in this chapter is that the neighborhood quality variables are based purely on the mother's reports, and there is no external validation. Thus, this raises the question about what factors may play a role in affecting the mother's perceptions. This is a particularly important issue, especially if the larger policy implication here is that one method to address the childhood obesity epidemic might be to improve neighborhoods that they reside in.

While we have no objective measures of neighborhood characteristics, we can identify the counties that the respondents reside in using the NLSY79 Geocode data.[8] One hypothesis is that women who live in counties that have high crime and where the population has low socioeconomic status will, ceteris paribus, express more concern about poor neighborhood quality and inadequate police protection (we make this hypothesis with the caveat that there may be immense within-county variation in quality of neighborhoods). To examine this issue, use the county identifier to link each responding mother to crime statistics and other variables, we have attempted to link the mothers' perceptions to official crime data and other variables describing the county in which the mother lived at the time of the NLSY surveys.

We estimate linear probability regressions for whether or not the mother reports inadequate police protection after including all county-level characteristics as well as mother-level characteristics that are potentially time-variant, both without (model one) and with (model two) mother-level fixed effects, for the full sample and separately by race-ethnicity. Results are in table 6.9.

We find that the crime variables have mixed effects on the probability of mothers reporting inadequate police protection. In fact, none of the variables yield estimated effects that are consistent in terms of direction and significance across the two sets of models. For example, rape and aggravated assault increase the probability for the full sample in model one, but are not consistent across the subsamples. In model two, rape has a counterintuitive

---

8. Unfortunately, the Geocodes are not able to do the linkage for finer resolution such as a census track, which might be linked to data from individual police departments.

Table 6.9   Lack of police protection and county and respondent characteristics by race-ethnicity

	Models without fixed effects				Models with fixed effects			
	All	Whites	Blacks	Hispanic	All	Whites	Blacks	Hispanic
murder100k	-0.000	-0.000	-0.003**	-0.002	0.003	0.002	0.004	-0.002
	(-0.289)	(-0.154)	(-2.570)	(-0.722)	(1.451)	(0.744)	(1.336)	(-0.353)
rape100k	0.000*	0.000	0.001	0.000	-0.000	-0.001*	0.003**	-0.004***
	(1.921)	(0.769)	(1.401)	(0.220)	(-0.374)	(-1.730)	(2.191)	(-2.614)
rob100k	0.000	0.000	0.000*	0.000	0.000	0.000	-0.000	0.000
	(1.338)	(0.184)	(1.800)	(0.709)	(1.040)	(0.964)	(-0.084)	(0.944)
aggas100k	0.000*	-0.000	0.000***	0.000	0.000	0.000	0.000	-0.000
	(1.702)	(-0.169)	(3.328)	(0.815)	(0.635)	(0.616)	(0.598)	(-0.019)
burg100k	-0.000	0.000*	-0.000	0.000	-0.000	0.000	-0.000*	0.000
	(-0.417)	(1.669)	(-0.986)	(0.030)	(-1.244)	(0.173)	(-1.722)	(0.941)
larc100k	-0.000***	-0.000	-0.000***	-0.000	0.000	-0.000	0.000	0.000
	(-3.061)	(-1.108)	(-3.031)	(-0.718)	(0.528)	(-0.768)	(1.186)	(1.459)
mvtheft100k	0.000	-0.000	0.000	0.000	0.000	0.000	0.000	-0.000
	(0.468)	(-0.800)	(0.690)	(0.611)	(0.123)	(0.325)	(0.756)	(-1.299)
arson100k	0.000	0.000	0.000	0.000	0.001***	0.001	0.001	0.000
	(1.362)	(1.055)	(0.631)	(1.208)	(2.967)	(1.574)	(0.703)	(1.133)
unemplyrate	-0.001	0.004*	0.009*	-0.007**	-0.007	-0.004	-0.003	0.004
	(-0.760)	(1.801)	(1.799)	(-2.330)	(-1.194)	(-0.568)	(-0.168)	(0.352)
pctBlack	0.000	-0.001	-0.001	-0.001	-0.020*	-0.016	-0.035	0.039
	(0.465)	(-1.033)	(-1.043)	(-0.435)	(-1.795)	(-1.033)	(-1.624)	(0.812)
pcthisp	0.001***	0.001**	-0.005***	0.001	-0.005	0.008	-0.019	0.005
	(3.048)	(2.117)	(-4.683)	(0.923)	(-0.730)	(0.884)	(-1.415)	(0.234)
pctfemhead	0.008***	0.004*	0.009***	0.008**	0.025	-0.002	0.061	0.031
	(4.817)	(1.844)	(2.896)	(1.995)	(1.312)	(-0.093)	(1.599)	(0.612)

pcincome	-0.000***	-0.000***	0.000	-0.000***	-0.000	0.000	-0.000	-0.000
	(-4.751)	(-4.311)	(0.801)	(-3.412)	(-0.461)	(1.170)	(-0.406)	(-1.142)
mom_age	-0.002*	0.001	-0.005*	-0.005	-0.002	0.001	-0.005	-0.001
	(-1.949)	(0.751)	(-1.866)	(-1.531)	(-1.429)	(0.238)	(-1.617)	(-0.211)
no_smsa	0.044***	0.027*	0.063**	-0.021	0.001	-0.014	0.001	-0.060
	(3.600)	(1.910)	(2.235)	(-0.556)	(0.027)	(-0.405)	(0.017)	(-0.632)
cen_city	0.081***	0.036**	0.109***	0.020	0.121***	0.067**	0.151***	0.007
	(6.713)	(1.960)	(4.910)	(0.752)	(5.679)	(2.215)	(3.758)	(0.150)
momnowork	0.037***	0.033***	-0.003	0.075***	0.035*	0.033	-0.010	0.092*
	(3.882)	(2.848)	(-0.162)	(3.222)	(1.920)	(1.416)	(-0.288)	(1.941)
dadpresent	-0.051***	-0.043***	-0.048***	0.026	-0.039**	-0.024	-0.035	0.025
	(-6.034)	(-3.745)	(-2.705)	(1.211)	(-2.520)	(-1.078)	(-1.174)	(0.652)
tnfaminc_real	-0.000***	-0.000***	-0.000*	-0.000*	-0.000***	-0.000**	-0.000	-0.000
	(-3.922)	(-2.606)	(-1.751)	(-1.652)	(-2.730)	(-2.311)	(-1.270)	(-0.665)
momed12_15	-0.121***	-0.128***	-0.171***	-0.015	-0.101***	-0.118***	-0.110**	-0.018
	(-9.530)	(-6.304)	(-7.092)	(-0.598)	(-3.699)	(-2.717)	(-2.272)	(-0.359)
momed16_20	-0.196***	-0.193***	-0.248***	-0.067*	-0.165***	-0.154***	-0.189***	-0.027
	(-12.623)	(-8.707)	(-7.216)	(-1.645)	(-5.276)	(-3.367)	(-2.945)	(-0.332)
R^2	0.087	0.043	0.102	0.031	0.172	0.215	0.180	0.118
F	47.252	12.507	16.503	3.903	6.388	2.671	2.897	1.309

Notes: Data shows β values, with *t*-statistics in parentheses. All models also control for region and year fixed effects. Standard errors clustered upon mothers.

***$p < 0.01$

**$p < 0.05$

*$p < 0.10$

negative sign for almost all the groups. We speculate that one reason for the counterintuitive negative signs is that certain types of violent crime could lead to the deployment of more police in the county, so that police presence may actually become more visible in the immediate aftermath of an increase in crime. The county characteristics that seem to consistently affect the probability of reported inadequate police protection in model one are the percent of female-headed households and the per capita income in the county, with the former increasing and the latter decreasing the probability of reported inadequate police protection. Higher unemployment rates increase the probability of reported inadequate police protection for whites and blacks, but surprisingly, seem to decrease it for Hispanics. In model two, the directions of the effects remain the same, but they become statistically imprecise, possibly because of the lack of variation in these county-level variables over the period of the study.

With regard to the personal maternal characteristics that affect maternal reports of inadequate police protection, the ones that remain significant in model two, even after accounting for unobserved mother-level time-invariant heterogeneity, are the variables indicating the mother's education level. Residing in central city is significant for all groups except Hispanics, while total family income is only significant for non-Hispanic whites. We repeated the analyses using maternal fixed effects and the mother-level characteristics, but omitted the county level characteristics, and found very similar results.

A final question may be whether changes in perceptions about police protection are driven by changes in the quality of the existing neighborhood or by an actual relocation to a different neighborhood. About 35 percent of the sample of mothers change their reports about adequacy of police protection at least once over the period of study. Unfortunately, once again, the Geocode data does not permit us to identify how many of these women actually changed neighborhoods, but only if their county of residence changed between one survey and the next. About 28 percent of our sample changes their counties of residence at least once within the period of study. However, of those who reported a change in adequacy of police protection, only 27 percent also reported a change in county of residence, and of those who did change their county of residence, 66.7 percent reported no change in adequacy of police protection. We emphasize again that we are not able to capture changes in residential locations that occur within a county in this data set, but the above findings do suggest that most of the reported variation in police protection cannot be explained by relocations to new neighborhoods in different counties.

6.5   Conclusion

Our chapter addresses the relatively unexplored question of the effects of contextual factors—such as neighborhood quality—on children's body weight and obesity risk. The main advantages of this study include the nationally representative nature of the data, as well as the longitudinal nature of the data, which allows us to control for time-invariant confounding factors at the maternal level. In summary, our chapter finds that overall maternal perceptions of neighborhood quality is not a particularly strong determinant of children's body weight outcomes. However, one specific neighborhood characteristic—the perceived lack of police protection, is a significant determinant of such body weight outcomes. Moreover, there are significant differences in perceived lack of police protection between white and minority women, though it is arguable whether this can explain part of the hitherto unexplained gap in body weight between non-Hispanic white and minority children in the population.

It is not entirely clear why police protection in particular plays a significant role in effecting children's body weight, when other neighborhood characteristics—such as crime and violence, or lack of respect for law and order, do not. One might speculate that, at the margin, visible police presence might reduce certain activities that would make parents fearful of letting their children outdoors—such as drug-peddling, loitering, or physical violence and bullying on the playground.

The chapter has several shortcomings. The most important of these is our inability to completely control for time-variant unobservable factors that might both influence the mother's perceptions of police protection as well as the child's weight. Furthermore, the key variables of interest—overall neighborhood quality and specific neighborhood characteristics—are based purely on mother reports, with no external validation. Also, we are not able to account for any characteristics of the child's school, including the quality of physical education programs or of school lunches in those schools, since the CoNLSY does not include that information. Insofar as children from low-quality neighborhoods are also more likely to go to schools were meal plans are of a lower quality and physical education programs are substandard, this could exacerbate the detrimental effects of poor neighborhood quality on body weight. Finally, we are not able to adequately explore what causal pathways might lead from perceptions of inadequate police protection to increased child body weight.

Since this is one of the first papers to explore the relationship between neighborhood perceptions and children's body weight outcomes using a national-level data set, and since the previously mentioned limitations preclude us from determining a definitive causal link between actual neighborhood quality and children's BMI, it seems premature to make policy recommendations before these results are validated via further research. One suggested direction for future research is to explore the extent to which perceptions of neighborhood characteristics, such as adequate police protection, are correlated to objective measures of neighborhood characteristics. If perceptions of police protection are driven by the actual number of police personnel available to the neighborhood, then, arguably, providing resources to increase police protection in low-income and minority neighborhoods, or providing housing subsidies that allows a low-income individual to move into a higher socioeconomic neighborhood with better police protection, will improve these perceptions, and may eventually improve child obesity outcomes.[9] However, if the perceptions of inadequate police protection are influenced by more complex issues such as whether neighborhood residents believe that, even though the police are present, they are indifferent or even hostile towards the residents, then addressing this problem becomes considerably more challenging. The NLSY data are inadequate to explore these issues, and hence these questions must be further investigated using more appropriate data sets.

References

Argys, L., and B. Sen. 2008. Parental time, income and children's BMI. Department of Healthcare Organization & Policy, University of Alabama at Birmingham. Working paper.

Bhattacharya, J., and W. B. Vogt. 2007. Do instrumental variables belong in propensity scores? NBER Working Paper no. 343. Cambridge, MA: National Bureau of Economic Research, September.

Blinder, A. S. 1973. Wage discrimination: Reduced form and structural estimates. *Journal of Human Resources* 8:436–55.

Brownson, R. C., E. A. Baker, R. A. Housemann, L. K. Brennan, and S. J. Bacak. 2001. Environmental and policy determinants of physical activity in the United States. *American Journal of Public Health.* 91:1995–2003.

Burdette, H. L., T. A. Wadden, and R. C. Whitaker. 2006. Neighborhood safety, collective efficacy, and obesity in women with young children. *Obesity* 14:518–25.

Cawley, J. 2004. The impact of obesity on wages. *Journal of Human Resources* 39 (2): 451–74.

Centers for Disease Control and Prevention. 1999. Neighborhood safety and the prevalence of physical inactivity: Selected states, 1996. Morbidity and Mortality Weekly Report 48:143–6.

Cummins, S. K. and R. J. Jackson. 2004. The built environment and children's health. *Pediatric Clinics of North America* 48 (5): 1241–52.

D'Agostino, R. B. 1998. Tutorial in biostatistics: Propensity score methods for bias reduction in comparison of a treatment to a non-randomized control group. *Statistics in Medicine* 17:2265–81.

Dietz, W. H., and S. Gortmaker. 1985. Do we fatten our children at the television set? Obesity and television viewing in children and adolescents. *Pediatrics* 75:807–12.

Field, A. E., N. R. Cook, and M. W. Gillman. 2005. Weight status in childhood as a predictor of becoming overweight or hypertensive in early adulthood. *Obesity* 13:163–9.

---

9. We could not explore this issue with the NLSY because, while it does report on the receipt of housing subsidies, it does not distinguish between living in a public housing facility in a low-income neighborhood or living in freestanding rental space in a better neighborhood.

Glass, T., M. Rasmussen, and B. Schwartz. 2006. Neighborhoods and obesity in older adults: The Baltimore memory study. *American Journal of Preventative Medicine* 31 (6): 455–63.

Gordon-Larsen, P., M. C. Nelson, P. Page, and B. M. Popkin. 2006. Inequality in the built environment underlies key health disparities in physical activity and obesity. *Pediatrics* 117:417–24.

Hango, D. W. 2002. The anchoring of American families to their homes and neighbourhoods: Determining factors of residential mobility. Ohio State University, Department of Sociology. Working Paper.

Humpel, N., N. Owen, and E. Leslie. 2002. Environmental factors associated with adults' participation in physical activity: A review. *American Journal of Preventative Medicine* 22 (3): 188–99.

Hyslop, D. R., and G. W. Imbens. 2001. Bias from classical and other forms of measurement error. *Journal of Business and Economic Statistics* 19 (4): 475–81.

Jann, B. 2008. A stata implementation of the Blinder-Oaxaca decomposition. Swiss Federal Institute of Technology Zurich. ETH Zurich Sociology Working Paper no. 5.

Leventhal, T., Fauth, R. C., and Brooks-Gunn, J. 2005. Neighborhood poverty and public policy: A 5-year follow-up of children's educational outcomes in the New York City moving to opportunity demonstration. *Developmental Psychology* 41 (6): 933–52.

Lumeng, J. C., D. Appugliese, H. J. Cabral, R. H. Bradley, and B. Zuckerman. 2006. Neighborhood safety and overweight status in children. *Archives of Pediatrics and Adolescent Medicine* 160:25–31.

National Center for Health Statistics. 2008. Prevalence of overweight among children and adolescents: United States, 1999–2002. Available at: http://www.cdc.gov/nchs/products/pubs/pubd/hestats/overwght99.htm.

Oaxaca, R. 1973. Male-female wage differentials in urban labor markets. *International Economic Review* 14:693–709.

Robinson, T. N. 1999. Reducing children's television viewing to prevent obesity: A randomized controlled trial. *Journal of the American Medical Association* 282 (16): 1561–67.

Robinson, T. N., L. D. Hammer, J. D. Killen, H. C. Kraemer, D. M. Wilson, C. Hayward, and C. B. Taylor. 1993. Does television viewing increase obesity and reduce physical activity? Cross-sectional and longitudinal analyses among adolescent girls. *Pediatrics* 91 (2): 499–501.

Romero, A., T. Robinson, H. Kraemer, S. Erickson, H. Haydel, F. Mendoza, and J. Killen. 2001. Are perceived neighborhood hazards a barrier to physical activity in children? *Archives of Pediatrics and Adolescent Medicine* 155:1143–48.

Rosenbaum, P. R., and D. B. Rubin. 1984. Reducing bias in observational studies using subclassification on the propensity score. *Journal of the American Statistical Association* 79:516–24.

Sen, B., and S. Swaminathan. 2007. Maternal prenatal substance use and behavior problems among children in The U.S. *Journal of Mental Health Policy and Economics:* 189–206.

Sobal, J., and A. J. Stunkard. 1989. Socioeconomic status and obesity: A review of the literature. *Psychological Bulletin* 105:260–75.

South, S. J., and K. D. Crowder. 1997. Escaping distressed neighborhoods: Individual, community, and metropolitan influences. *American Journal of Sociology* 102 (4): 1040–84.

South, S. J., and G. D. Deane. 1993. Race and residential mobility: Individual determinants and structural constraints. *Social Forces* 72 (1): 147–67.

Strauss, R. S., and J. Knight. 1999. Influence of the home environment on the development of obesity in children. *Pediatrics* 103 (6): 85.

Strauss, R. S., and H. A. Pollack. 2001. Epidemic increase in childhood overweight, 1986–1988. *Journal of the American Medical Association* 280 (22): 2845–48.

Troiano, R. P., and K. M. Flegal. 1998. Overweight children and adolescents: Description, epidemiology, and demographics. *Pediatrics* 101 (3): 497–504.

U.S. Bureau of Health Professions. 2007. *Area resource file (Arf)*. Rockville, MD: Department of Health and Human Services Health Resources and Services Administration.

U.S. Bureau of Labor Statistics. 2009. Labor force data by county, 1992–2000. http://www.bls.gov/Lau/#Data Date.

U.S. Federal Bureau of Investigation. 2004. Uniform crime reports county data. Available at: http://Fisher.Lib.Virginia.Edu/Collections/Stats/Crime/.

7

Studying the Child Obesity Epidemic with Natural Experiments

Robert Sandy, Gilbert Liu, John Ottensmann, Rusty Tchernis, Jeff Wilson, and O. T. Ford

7.1 Introduction

One of the broad strategies for reducing child obesity is to alter the built environment near children's homes to either promote calorie expenditures or reduce calorie consumption. Some of the proposals in this built environment strategy are to: (a) build sidewalks, (b) construct recreational amenities such as pools, soccer fields, basketball courts, and trails (c) require mixes of residences and retail outlets through zoning laws, (d) locate schools within walking distance of homes, and (e) limit fast-food restaurants (King et al. 1995; Sallis, Bauman, and Pratt 1998; Margetts 2004; Committee on Environmental Health 2009). The two crucial questions in implementing this built-environment strategy are which proposals will reduce child obesity, and the degree to which crime counteracts any benefits of changing the built environment.

This chapter uses clinical data from 1996 to 2006 to estimate the effect of

Robert Sandy is assistant executive vice president of Indiana University and professor of economics at Indiana University–Purdue University Indianapolis (IUPUI). Gilbert Liu is assistant professor of pediatrics at the Indiana University School of Medicine. John Ottensmann is professor of public and environmental affairs and director of Urban Policy Research at Indiana University-Purdue University Indianapolis (IUPUI). Rusty Tchernis is associate professor of economics at the Andrew Young School of Policy Studies, Georgia State University, and a faculty research fellow of the National Bureau of Economic Research. Jeff Wilson is associate professor and chair of the department of geography at Indiana University-Purdue University Indianapolis (IUPUI). O. T. Ford is a graduate student in the department of geography at the University of California, Los Angeles.

We thank Shawn Hoch, Zhang Ya, Megan McDermott, Bikul Tulachan, and Jonathan Raymont for research assistance. This study was funded under NIH NIDDK grant R21 DK075577-01. We thank the participants at the Purdue University Department of Agricultural Economics seminar, and at the NBER preconference and conference on Economic Aspects of Obesity for many helpful comments, and Kristen Butcher for a careful and insightful review.

changes in nearby physical environment and crime levels on child weight. Electronic medical records for patients who received care at a large academic health care system in Indianapolis between 1996 through 2006 provide anthropometric, demographic, and geographic data for over 60,000 children between the ages of three and sixteen years of age. The identifying assumption in our research design is that changes in the physical environment are exogenous to children who were at the same address before and after the change. This natural experiment approach addresses a major limitation of cross-sectional studies of the associations between environment and child obesity. Cross-sectional associations are confounded when families select their locations. For example, families that highly value exercise are more likely to live near a recreation trail. In cross-sectional regressions, a variable for proximity to a recreation trail could pick up the unobserved effects of the selection.

Controlling for selection is important in identifying the determinants of body weight. For example, in the adult body weight context there are many cross-sectional studies that find that urban sprawl is associated with obesity. However, these results were not supported by studies of migrants between high- and low-sprawl cities (Plantinga and Bernell 2007) and for cities that changed their sprawl levels over time (Ewing, Brownson, and Berrigan 2006). In the child obesity context sprawl was associated with a higher probability of overweight in cross-sectional data, but the initial level of sprawl did not have a significant effect on weight gains over three years (Ewing, Brownson, and Berrigan 2006).

The built environment changes we study are fast-food restaurants, convenience stores, supermarkets, recreation trails, and thirteen publicly accessible recreational amenities, such as public outdoor basketball courts and outdoor pools. We also studied the direct effect of crime levels on child obesity and interactions between changes in crime levels and the built environment on obesity. We test our exogeneity assumption by comparing the trend in body mass index (BMI) for children who will gain an amenity in the future to the trend for children who never gain an amenity. We use the term "amenities" to mean any built environment factor, desirable or undesirable. We found that, except for supermarkets, all of the amenities had largely the same trends for children who would in the future gain an amenity and those who would not.

The remaining sections of the chapter are a literature review, a description of the data, the estimation strategy, results, and conclusions.

7.2   Literature Review

Although the entire literature on the effect of the built environment on child obesity is quite recent, it is growing rapidly. A comparison of three literature review articles published in 2005, 2007, and 2010 illustrates this rapid growth. The 2005 review article by Booth, Pinkston, and Carlos Poston covers the years 1998 and 2004, and includes two studies on child obesity/overweight and the built environment. The 2007 review article by Papas and colleagues discusses six articles published over a four-year period, beginning in 2002. A 2010 review article by Galvez, Pearl, and Yen describes fifteen studies published over a twenty-month period beginning in January of 2008. All of the child obesity and built environment studies in these review articles use cross-sectional data. Based on these three review articles, the rate of production of articles increased from 0.33 per year in 1998 to 2004, to 1.5 per year in 2002 to 2006, and to nine per year in 2008 through the first eight months of 2009.

In light of the aforementioned three review articles, this section will only highlight a few important studies and make three observations about the literature that connect to this study. The first observation is a need for weight or weight status as an outcome. Second, there is a lack of understanding as to what are the distances between homes and amenities that should be considered in defining the relevant built environment surrounding a child's residence. Third, analyses should be of specific amenities rather than aggregations of amenities. The review article by Galvez, Pearl, and Yen describes thirty-three additional articles that estimate associations between the built environment and behaviors thought to affect weight, for example, walking to school. A behavioral response to a change in the built environment is a necessary, but not a sufficient, condition for changes in body weight. For example, a potential weight loss due to behavior observed at a recreation amenity can be offset if the child either reduces other exercise or eats more. Measures of body weight are required to confirm that observed behaviors do reduce body weight. A related problem with many studies of behaviors tied to specific environmental amenities is that, because they are expensive, they are usually done at a small scale. An example of small-scale observations of behavioral responses is using trained observers to record activity levels in three city parks and categorize whether the children's play is sedentary, moderate, or vigorous (Tester and Baker 2009). Even if body weight measures were available in such small-scale studies it would be difficult to detect a statistically significant effect.

While some nationally representative data sets only include self-reported or parent-reported height and weight data (e.g., the Youth Behavioral Risk Factor Surveillance System), there are a few that include directly measured height and weight (e.g., National Health and Nutrition Examination Survey). However, these national data sets have severe limitations for studies examining associations between weight status and environment. One limitation, due to restrictions on providing home address information in these data sets, is the requirement to summarize amenities at relatively large geographies around the center of an area known to include the child's home. Many studies have found that children are unlikely to walk or bike to school if the distance is beyond a mile (McDonald 2007; Timperio et al. 2004; Schloss-berg et al. 2006; Merom et al. 2006). Presumably, recreational amenities need to be within a mile of the child's home to generate frequent usage by children who walk or ride bicycles. If being driven or taking public trans-portation is the primary mode for children to access an amenity, then the transportation time is much more important than the Euclidean distance. A study by Gordon-Larsen et al. (2006) illustrates the coarse spatial resolu-tions that arise from limitations in national probability samples for health surveillance. They were restricted to locating study subjects based on Census block groups, and then defined amenities as relevant if they were within a five-mile radius of the Census block group. Census block groups vary widely in size based on density of settlement, but optimally contain approximately 1,500 persons.

Another problem in studies that use national data sets is the necessity of combining different types of recreational amenities when developing vari-ables to the point where there is little chance of being able to discern which amenity types are beneficial. Singh, N. Siahpush, and M. D. Kogan (2010) combine parent/guardian-reported data on availability of (a) sidewalks and walking paths, (b) parks and playgrounds, (c) recreation centers, commu-nity centers, and boys' and girls' clubs, and (d) libraries and bookmobiles into an index of built environment resources. They found that higher values of this index were associated with a lower probability of overweight. The inclusion of libraries and bookmobiles is puzzling in that they seem to be resources that encourage reading, a sedentary activity. Even if libraries and bookmobiles somehow reduced body weight, the index approach blurs that effect with those of the other amenities.

The effect of fast-food restaurants on obesity has probably received more public attention than any other food or recreation amenity. The presumed link between fast-food and child obesity has prompted a ban on new restau-rants in parts of Los Angeles (Los Angeles Times 2008). This link, however, may reflect in part decisions to locate fast-food restaurants in areas in which residents have a higher than average taste for high-caloric foods, and hence a larger than average percentage of the population is overweight. Anderson and Matsa (2007) have one of the few obesity papers that address the endo-geneity of location issue for any type of amenity. However, it is for adults living in rural areas. They used location near an interstate highway exit as an instrument for fast-food location. Their conclusion is that fast-food has no causal effect on adult BMI.

A second paper on fast-food restaurants and obesity that addresses endo-geneity is Currie et al. (2009). They have 3.06 million student-year observa-tions for ninth graders in California over the years 1999 and 2001 through 2007, with precise locations of their schools and the fast-food restaurants. They do not have data on individual children. Obesity rates are reported for all ninth graders in a school. The measurements on the children are taken during the spring semester and represent approximately thirty weeks of exposure to any near-to-the-school fast-food restaurant for a child entering high school. They find a 5.2 percent increase in the incidence of obesity, relative to the mean of 32.9 percent, for schools that have a fast-food restaurant within 0.1 miles. They found no effect for fast-food within analytic buffers of 0.25, 0.5, and 1.0 miles from the school. They attribute the statistically significant and economically important effect within 0.1 miles as being due to the ninth graders having to be able to quickly walk to the fast-food restaurants for it to influence their weight status.

Since Currie and colleagues have no data on individuals, they cannot know if the children who gained a nearby fast-food restaurant by enrolling in a particular high school had also recently gained a fast-food restaurant near their homes. They also could not exclude the possibility that a higher proportion of the children whose schools have fast-food restaurants within 0.1 miles entered the ninth grade being already obese. Going across years, they find no trend in obesity rates at schools that will gain a fast-food restaurant in the future. However, they have very little temporal variation at the level of the school in the number of fast-food restaurants within 0.1 miles.

The Currie and colleagues paper shows the importance of being able to define highly precise specifications of the environment around a child's home when studying how the built environment is associated with obesity. The first law of geography according to Waldo Tobler is, "Everything is related to everything else, but near things are more related than distant things" (Tobler 1970). The likelihood of children interacting with amenities is probably inversely proportional to the cost of travel to them. Or stated slightly differently, physical activity or eating opportunities that are very nearby likely have stronger influence than those opportunities that are as far as five Euclidean miles distant.

Summing up this literature review section, several of the gaps in the existing literature are addressed in our study. We address the endogeneity of location issue. We draw tight circles of 0.1, 0.25, 0.5, and 1.0 miles around the child's home. We estimate the individual effects of different types of recreational amenities and food vendors. We utilize directly measured heights and weights, which are much more reliable than parent/guardian-reported heights and weights. We do not, however, have observations on child behavior. To our knowledge, no study to date has a comparably large sample, direct observations of behavior at recreation and food amenities, and the geographic resolution needed to analyze the effect of amenities near children's residences. Privacy concerns in national data sets plus the expense of either directly observing child behavior or administering a survey about exactly what amenities children utilize would make doing such a study difficult.

7.3   Data

The main sources of our data are: (a) clinical records from pediatric ambulatory visits to the Indiana University Medical Group between 1996 and 2006; (b) annual inspections by the Marion County Health Department of all food establishments; (c) aerial photographs, used to identify and verify recreational amenities; (d) reports of violent crimes from the Indianapolis Police Department and the Marion County Sheriff's Department; (e) birth certificates; and (f) the U.S. Census. These six data sources are described in more detail below.

7.3.1   Clinical Records From Well-Child Visits

The Indiana University Regenstrief Medical Records System (RMRS), in existence since 1974, is an electronic version of the paper medical chart. It has now captured and stored 200 million temporal observations for over 1.5 million patients. Because RMRS data are both archived and retrievable, investigators may use these data to perform retrospective and prospective research. The RMRS is distributed across three medical centers, thirty ambulatory clinics, and all of the emergency departments throughout the greater Indianapolis region. The RMRS supports physician order entry, decision support, and clinical noting, and is one of the most sophisticated and most evaluated electronic medical record systems in the world.

Using the RMRS, we identified medical records in which there are simultaneous assessments of height and weight in outpatient clinics for children aged three to eighteen years inclusive. We then decided to exclude children above the age of sixteen for reasons described in the section on descriptive statistics. For these clinic visits, we extracted the visit date, date of birth, gender, race, insurance status, and visit type (e.g., periodic health maintenance versus acute care). We found that too few patients had private insurance for this variable to have any predictive power. Because height and weight measurements are routinely performed as part of pediatric health maintenance, these measures should be present for virtually all children receiving preventive care at each of the study sites. The data generated by pediatric visits in the RMRS include higher representation of low-income and minority households compared to the demographics of the study area because the associated clinics serve a population that is mostly publicly insured or has no insurance. The overrepresentation of minorities and low-income households in the RMRS, we contend, is a decided advantage. Poorer households are more sensitive to their immediate neighborhood because they face financial constraints against motorized transit (e.g., reduced car ownership, less money for gasoline or bus fares). Indianapolis has a vestigial public transportation system. It has been described as the worst city system in the Midwest (Quigley 2003). If the built environment has any effect on child weights it should be most readily observed in poorer households in a city with minimal public transportation. Moreover, obesity is more prevalent in poorer households and among poorer children. Knowing what interventions reduce and exacerbate child overweight in this population would be valuable.

National guidelines for well-child visits advocate annual visits for ages three to six years and at least biannual visits thereafter. We extracted ICD-9 codes or other diagnoses list data for identifying children who may have systematic bias in growth or weight status (i.e., pregnancy, endocrine disorders, cancer, congenital heart disease, chromosomal disorders, and metabolic disorders), and excluded observations for such children. We also excluded patient encounters prior to 1996 because the RMRS did not archive address data before this date.

7.3.2   Food Establishment Data

We received annual inspection data on 8,641 food service establishments in Indianapolis that received permits from the Marion County Board of Health between 1993 and 2007, inclusive. Of these, 5,550 are restaurants and 1,507 are in the grocery category. Fast-food establishments have been a particular focus of research on adult obesity and child overweight. Defining and identifying fast-food restaurants is problematic. Fast-food establishments in our study have been defined in two ways. Chou, Rashad, and Grossman (2008) identified a set of forty-one national fast-food chains when they studied the effect of local advertising on child overweight. We will refer to that as the "national chains" list. The national chains are of special interest because they advertise more than local restaurants and local chains, and their restaurants are generally larger, in higher-traffic locations, and more likely to have a drive-up window. The second method of identifying fast-food relied on the Census Bureau's counts of restaurants by Standard Industrial Classification (SIC) codes. Chou, Grossman, and Saffer (2004) used the Census Bureau data for state-level counts of establishments in the SIC 5812/40. These are establishments with a limited menu of items such as pizza, barbecue, hotdogs, and hamburgers. We refer to these restaurants as limited-service restaurants. Full-service restaurants (SIC 5812/10), in contrast, have at least fifteen seats, table service, and serve prepared food from a full menu.

We have 735 establishments in Indianapolis on the national chains list and 1,138 establishments on the broader limited-service list. Data-cleaning challenges included repeated counting due to slight changes in names of restaurants at the same address. Of the 735 fast-food restaurants on the national chains list, 393 were opened between 1994 and 2004, which allows a natural experiment investigating change in food environment as a possible cause of change in child body mass index.

There were 1,507 retail food establishments in the data. Again, we had to do some data cleaning. From the perspective of a Marion County food inspector, a sushi retailer that rents space in a supermarket is a separate inspection entity, but from the consumer's perspective it is part of the supermarket. After a first cut at data cleaning, there were 114 supermarkets. The Indianapolis market, not atypically, has been roiled by the entry of supermarket chains, as well as discount stores with embedded supermarkets such as Meijer, Walmart, and Target. The city's largest chain, Kroger, has had a substantial expansion. Some of the entrants failed, such as Cub Foods, and have left behind stores that are still empty. Among supermarkets there is even more variation, proportionally, than among the national chains' fast-food establishments. Fifty of the 114 supermarkets would satisfy the temporal requirement for a natural experiment because they opened after the first year, closed before 2004, or both.

7.3.3   Recreational Amenities

The study began with a geographic database of recreational amenities and associated features (such as parking lots), in vector form, developed from 2001 data provided by the Indianapolis Parks and Recreation Department. Each individual amenity, such as a basketball court or soccer field, was included as a feature in the database. We incorporated three other similar databases for later periods, also provided by the Indianapolis Parks and Recreation Department.

Additional recreational amenities were identified for the years 1995 through 2006 through the interpretation of aerial photographs. We chose thirteen specific recreational amenities for identification. These were thought to be the most likely to be used by children in the study population and to be amenable to identification from aerial photographs, as well as sufficiently numerous to measure an effect. The chosen categories and their quantifications within 0.1, 0.25, 0.5, and 1 mile buffers centered on the child's home are:

1. Baseball and softball fields, count of fields in buffer
2. Outdoor basketball courts, count of hoops in buffer
3. Family centers (indoor recreation center), area of facilities in buffer
4. Fitness courses, area in buffer
5. Football fields, count of fields in buffer
6. Kickball fields, count of fields in buffer
7. Playgrounds without permanent equipment, area in buffer
8. Playgrounds with permanent equipment, area in buffer
9. Swimming pools, area of water in buffer
10. Soccer fields, total area available for playing in buffer
11. Tennis courts, count of courts in buffer
12. Track and field facilities, area of facilities in buffer
13. Volleyball courts, count of courts in buffer

Nine photo interpreters participated in the process; they were assigned specific areas of the county, generally strips half a mile wide running north-to-south. To control for quality of interpretation, amenities lying on the borders of assigned interpretation areas were to be analyzed by both relevant interpreters. The resulting border features were then compared to each other and to the photographs. Where the features differed, the more accurate interpretation was selected for the final data set, and corrected if necessary. Additionally, errors that appeared in this process were treated as potential systematic errors; the other features interpreted by the responsible interpreter were examined for evidence of the same error repeated. If present, such errors were corrected, and if errors were found while the process was ongoing, the interpreter was retrained to avoid the error. An appendix contains the full details of the photo interpretation process.

7.3.4   Crime Data

When the city limits of Indianapolis were expanded to the border of Marion County in 1970 (while excluding certain small municipalities), the original police jurisdictions were not affected. Therefore, during the study period, the primary law enforcement responsibility for Marion County was divided between the Indianapolis Police Department (IPD), which had responsibility for the area within the original Indianapolis boundary, the Marion County Sheriff's Department (MCSD), which had responsibility for most of the outlying areas of the county, and the police departments of the four small excluded municipalities of Speedway, Lawrence, Southport, and Beech Grove. In 2007, the Indianapolis Police Department and the Marion County Sheriff's Department were merged into the Indianapolis Metropolitan Police Department

From the Indianapolis Police Department, for the IPD service area in which they had primary responsibility, we have a data set of the geocoded locations of all crimes reported for the Federal Bureau of Investigation's Uniform Crime Reports (UCR), from 1992 through 2005. From the Marion County Sheriff's Department, for the area in which they had primary responsibility, we have a data set on the point locations of a wide range of crimes and other incidents, including the UCR crimes, from 2000 through 2005. We are using information on the crimes from both data sets that are included in the UCR violent crime categories: criminal homicides, rapes, robberies, and aggravated assaults. The data set includes the date and time of the crime, and more detailed information on the specific type of crime within each of those four categories. Because of the manner in which these data have been assembled, we have reason to believe that these are accurate locations and that the classification of the type of crime is accurate.

To summarize, we have the following coverage for violent crimes:

1. Through 1999, for the IPD service area only.
2. From 2000 through 2005, for both the IPD service area and the MCSD jurisdiction.

No crime data are available for any time period for the jurisdictions of the four small excluded municipalities that are within Marion County.

7.3.5   Birth Certificate Data From the Marion County Health and Hospital Corporation

We matched children's clinical data with Marion County Health and Hospital Corporation data on birth certificates by date of birth, gender, mother's surname, and child's given name. We were able to match 34.3 percent of the children in the clinical data. For a match to be possible, the child must have been born in Marion County. The birth certificate data include birth weight, sex, race, mother's age and intention to breastfeed, parents' marital status, and one or both parents' education, race, and eligibility for Women, Infants, and Children (WIC) aid (all, of course, at time of birth). In the few cases where reported race changed between the birth certificate and the clinical record, we used the race identified in the clinical record.

7.3.6   Neighborhood Characteristics

Neighborhood characteristics were estimated for 0.5 mile and 1.0 mile buffers surrounding each residence. These include five variables derived from Census 2000 data: population density, proportion African American, proportions graduated from high school and from college, and median family income. The first two are estimated from the block data, the remainder from the block group data. Two additional neighborhood characteristics are measures of the density and of the interconnectedness of the road network. Land use diversity in the area is represented by the proportion of land in commercial and residential use. Detailed information on the data sources and procedures used to create these variables are provided in an appendix.

Data Cleaning

In examining the height and weight data from the clinical records we found highly improbable patterns, such as a child shrinking five inches in height from one well-child visit to the next. We calculated z-scores for height and weight measures based on year 2000 U.S. Centers for Disease Control and Prevention (CDC) growth charts. We used CDC statistical programs to identify biologically implausible values for heights and weights (Centers for Disease Control and Prevention 2000). Figure 7.1 shows the histograms of heights and weights, excluding biologically implausible values with z-scores greater than $+ 3.0$.

Visually, there is a small amount of truncation for the heights in the right tail of its distribution. As can be seen in the second graph, the truncation in the right tail of the body weight distribution is substantial. The CDC Growth Chart reference population spans the period 1963 to 1994, and thus does not fully cover the epidemic in child obesity of the past two decades. Another visual indicator of the extent of the epidemic is how much the distribution has shifted to the right relative to the mean of the reference population. We

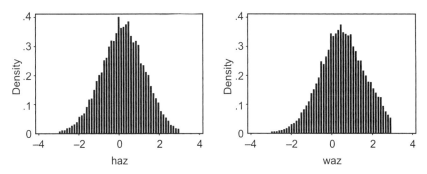

Fig. 7.1   Histograms of standardized height (haz) and weight (waz) scores after dropping observations with z-scores at or above 3

dropped observations with weight-for-height, weight-for-age z-scores, and BMI z-scores either below –3 or above + 5.0 as under the assumption that they were likely due to data entry error or measurement errors.

7.4   Descriptive Statistics

The histogram of the ages of all children at the time of their well-child visits is shown in figure 7.2. Since well-child visits for preschool-age children are more frequent, the higher bars for ages three, four, and five were expected, as well as the steady decline thereafter. Prior to age sixteen the genders at the well-child visits are split nearly fifty-fifty. For age seventeen, the ratio is more than eighty-twenty females-to-males. One of the authors of this chapter works as a pediatrician in these clinics. His explanation for the high ratio of females-to-males among the sixteen- and seventeen-year-olds is the requirement that the girls must have physicals before they can obtain birth control pills.

The sixteen- and seventeen-year-olds are clearly a different population. To simplify our analysis, we restricted our sample to children under the age of sixteen. The literature on child obesity and the built environment has papers on a variety of age ranges. There is no established basis for splitting up our broad range of ages into subsamples. There is not an obvious age at which children in the range of three through fifteen gain significantly more control over their food and exercise choices. Although obtaining a driver's license does give a child much more independence, our exclusion of children aged sixteen or greater eliminates this factor. Lacking any a priori or literature comparison basis for splitting the sample by age, our split was dictated by the data. Almost exactly 50 percent of our observations are below age eight. For each amenity, we tested whether the coefficients for children younger than eight were the same as for children eight or older. Some of our amenities are clearly suited for younger children, such as playground equipment,

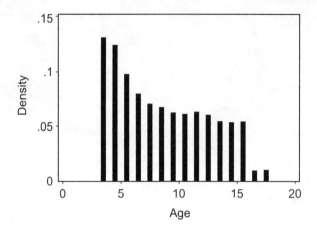

Fig. 7.2   Histogram of age at time of clinic visit

and others for older children, such as volleyball courts, tennis courts, and football fields.

Most studies of child weight determinants use the body mass index percentile compared to the pre-epidemic population sampled in the National Health and Nutrition Examination Survey (NHANES) I from 1971 to 1974. Absolute thresholds for overweight or obesity are not applied to children because the amount of body fat changes with age and differs between girls and boys. The mean body mass index percentile in our data is 65.5. A disadvantage to using the percentiles of the reference population is truncation. For the 205 well-child visits in our sample that were at the one-hundredth percentile, we would not be able to observe any responses to amenities that increase their weight. For the 5,049 well-child visits at or above the ninety-ninth percentile, there would be limited ability to observe weight increase responses. To avoid the truncation problem inherent in the percentiles, we used the BMI z-score as the dependent variable.

Table 7.1 has the descriptive statistics for the data used in the cross-sectional analysis. The definitions and procedures used to create the neighborhood characteristics variables are in an appendix. Again, all of the data were restricted to children whose age was under sixteen, and who had an absolute value of the z-score of height relative to the reference population less than three, a z-score of weight relative to the reference population between −3 and 5, and a z-score of BMI relative to the reference population also between −3 and 5.

Table 7.2 has the environmental variables that are based on the annual Marion County food establishment inspections, Indianapolis Department of Parks and Recreation records, the Indianapolis and Marion County crime reports, and our photo interpretation of recreational amenities. These are reported within buffers of 0.1 mile, 0.1 to 0.25 miles, 0.25 to

Table 7.1   **Descriptive statistics for the cross-sectional analysis**

	Clinical observations by year				
	Year	N			
	1996	1,811			
	1997	10,744			
	1998	13,437			
	1999	13,289			
	2000	12,242			
	2001	12,034			
	2002	11,945			
	2003	11,502			
	2004	8,135			
	2005	7,795			
	N	Mean	St. d.	min.	max.
Clinical data					
BMI z	102,955	0.68	1.17	−2.99	4.99
Well-child visit	102,955	0.82	0.38	0.00	1.00
Female	100,937	0.48	0.50	0.00	1.00
White	102,955	0.29	0.45	0.00	1.00
Black	102,955	0.53	0.50	0.00	1.00
Hispanic	102,955	0.13	0.33	0.00	1.00
Neighborhood characteristics					
Population density	102,955	9.32	4.23	0.00	27.35
Percent black	102,954	0.43	0.35	0.00	0.98
Percent high school	102,954	0.70	0.13	0.38	1.00
Percent college	102,954	0.12	0.11	0.00	0.85
Median family income	102,954	37,540	12,302	11,202	157,951
Road network density	102,955	3.60	1.24	0.00	9.27
Number of road intersections	102,955	25.10	15.78	0.00	109.00
Commercial land use	102,955	0.07	0.09	0.00	0.89
Residential land use	102,955	0.64	0.21	0.00	1.00
Marion County birth certificate data:					
Child's birth weight (g)	54,066	3141.55	630.21	170.00	5443.00
Father's age	26,827	27.23	7.37	14.00	91.00
Father's years of education	25,562	11.66	2.10	1.00	26.00
Mother's age	54,171	23.10	5.64	11.00	50.00
Mother's education	53,095	11.21	1.90	1.00	24.00
Intention to breastfeed	50,487	0.22	0.41	0.00	1.00
Marital status (1 = married)	54,986	0.28	0.45	0.00	1.00
WIC Eligibility (1 = yes)	50,890	0.74	0.44	0.00	1.00

0.5 miles, and 0.5 to 1 mile. The table reports the average values by buffer over the study period. The definitions of the recreational amenities are in an appendix.

One striking number from the descriptive statistics is the amount of crime. The violent crimes included are criminal homicides, rapes, robberies,

Table 7.2   **Amenity variables**

	Mile radius	Mean	St. d.	min.	max.	N
Fast-food restaurants	.1	0.03	0.20	0.00	4.00	98,541
	.1–.25	0.22	0.66	0.00	7.00	98,541
	.25–.5	0.87	1.40	0.00	11.00	98,541
	.5–1	3.44	2.99	0.00	20.00	98,541
Supermarkets	.1	0.01	0.08	0.00	1.00	98,541
	.1–.25	0.06	0.25	0.00	3.00	98,541
	.25–.5	0.22	0.48	0.00	4.00	98,541
	.5–1	0.78	0.82	0.00	4.00	98,541
Convenience stores	.1	0.03	0.18	0.00	2.00	98,541
	.1–.25	0.17	0.43	0.00	3.00	98,541
	.25–.5	0.54	0.83	0.00	7.00	98,541
	.5–1	1.98	1.85	0.00	11.00	98,541
Trails (m)	.1	12.72	106.14	0.00	2100.67	102,955
	.1–.25	108.83	478.02	0.00	7110.42	102,955
	.25–.5	503.92	1323.73	0.00	12646.57	102,955
	.5–1	2419.53	4091.35	0.00	40526.93	102,955
Violent crimes (annual)	.1	4.18	5.37	0.00	49.00	98,541
	.1–.25	16.09	17.56	0.00	135.00	98,541
	.25–.5	47.16	49.13	0.00	354.00	98,541
	.5–1	155.80	144.66	0.00	739.00	98,541
Baseball diamonds	.1	0.07	0.35	0.00	7.00	102,955
	.1–.25	0.47	1.05	0.00	12.00	102,955
	.25–.5	1.67	2.09	0.00	16.00	102,955
	.5–1	6.31	4.09	0.00	27.00	102,955
Basketball hoops	.1	0.25	0.78	0.00	9.00	102,955
	.1–.25	0.98	1.63	0.00	18.00	102,955
	.25–.5	3.05	2.97	0.00	21.00	102,955
	.5–1	10.40	5.94	0.00	56.00	102,955
Family centers (m²)	.1	1.43	34.52	0.00	1430.10	102,955
	.1–.25	13.72	130.18	0.00	3483.40	102,955
	.25–.5	88.92	389.36	0.00	3483.40	102,955
	.5–1	357.66	755.85	0.00	5517.90	102,955
Fitness areas (m²)	.1	2.37	63.89	0.00	4099.10	102,955
	.1–.25	23.09	266.94	0.00	5423.90	102,955
	.25–.5	69.10	462.40	0.00	11786.00	102,955
	.5–1	390.63	1343.81	0.00	11786.00	102,955
Football fields	.1	0.02	0.16	0.00	2.00	102,955
	.1–.25	0.10	0.34	0.00	5.00	102,955
	.25–.5	0.27	0.61	0.00	8.00	102,955
	.5–1	1.03	1.19	0.00	11.00	102,955
Kickball diamonds	.1	0.01	0.11	0.00	3.00	102,955
	.1–.25	0.06	0.26	0.00	4.00	102,955
	.25–.5	0.21	0.50	0.00	5.00	102,955
	.5–1	0.65	1.01	0.00	7.00	102,955
Playgrounds, no equipment (m²)	.1	72.99	316.35	0.00	4559.50	102,955
	.1–.25	309.05	684.31	0.00	10268.30	102,955
	.25–.5	982.75	1300.46	−0.10	12972.40	102,955
	.5–1	2981.93	2373.51	0.00	14253.70	102,955

Table 7.2   (continued)

	Mile radius	Mean	St. d.	min.	max.	N
Playgrounds with equipment (m²)	.1	133.70	372.93	0.00	6818.80	102,955
	.1–.25	486.26	797.68	0.00	10165.20	102,955
	.25–.5	1408.51	1617.50	–0.10	15141.80	102,955
	.5–1	5170.40	3557.66	0.00	21986.30	102,955
Pools (m²)	.1	22.24	85.19	0.00	1717.80	102,955
	.1–.25	69.27	193.09	0.00	2825.10	102,955
	.25–.5	201.78	344.25	0.00	5526.10	102,955
	.5–1	710.51	811.61	0.00	7247.30	102,955
Soccer (m²)	.1	39.42	464.84	0.00	23207.30	102,955
	.1–.25	481.89	2275.35	0.00	77155.50	102,955
	.25–.5	1937.60	6346.88	0.00	137783.10	102,955
	.5–1	8364.20	15137.73	0.00	193082.40	102,955
Tennis	.1	0.10	0.51	0.00	12.00	102,955
	.1–.25	0.45	1.18	0.00	32.00	102,955
	.25–.5	1.48	2.67	0.00	35.00	102,955
	.5–1	5.41	5.63	0.00	47.00	102,955
Track and field (m²)	.1	47.92	467.45	0.00	15158.00	102,955
	.1–.25	394.62	1725.75	0.00	19316.10	102,955
	.25–.5	1052.36	2940.19	0.00	25371.70	102,955
	.5–1	4024.17	6037.80	0.00	39704.60	102,955
Volleyball	.1	0.03	0.17	0.00	2.00	102,955
	.1–.25	0.10	0.35	0.00	4.00	102,955
	.25–.5	0.30	0.61	0.00	5.00	102,955
	.5–1	0.92	1.12	0.00	9.00	102,955

and aggravated assaults. The maximum value for the tenth-mile buffer was forty-nine.

7.5 Estimation Strategy

Our initial data set consists of fixed information on the child (race, sex, family composition at birth), changing information on the child (height, weight, and age at each clinic visit), fixed information on the parents (race, mother's and possibly father's education at the child's birth), changing information on the family (residence), the built environment near the residence in each year, crime counts by year within buffers around the child's home, and some information on neighborhood characteristics for buffers around each residence, including information on the road network, and land use, and the population density from the census.

As was mentioned earlier, to control for the variations in BMI as the child ages, we use age-sex adjusted base-period BMI z-scores as the dependent variable. We estimate two main types of models, Ordinary Least Squares (OLS) and Fixed Effects (FE) for a child at a stable address across serial clinic visits.

For the FE estimation we assume that households that stay at the same location after an amenity is placed near their residence retain the same preferences they had before the amenity was added. Under this assumption, the household fixed effect would remove constant-over-time preferences for location amenities and any other unobserved variables that did not change for each household. For example, the parents' discount rate over future consumption by either themselves or their children and their altruism toward their children would wash out in the fixed effects specification.

The key potential criticism of the FE estimation is that there are unobserved variables common to households that are located near the new amenity. If the households in a neighborhood lobbied the parks department to obtain the playground or pool built near them, then there would be some common-to-the-neighborhood but unobserved-to-the-econometrician interest in exercise that would bias the estimates. A pool placed near a neighborhood where the parents had lobbied (presumably because they were anxious to have their children use the new pool) would have a smaller effect on child overweight. This is the endogeneity problem in another guise.

More problematic is the location of privately owned amenities such as fast-food restaurants or supermarkets. These types of firms often employ market researchers to identify areas where households will be the most receptive to a fast-food outlet or the most likely to buy fresh produce. We can use robust estimators that yield consistent estimates of the standard errors when there are common-but-unobserved differences at a neighborhood level, but without the original information that was in the hands of the market researchers, we cannot fully control for differences among households in receptiveness to fast-food or fresh produce. At least the direction of any potential bias is clear. We will have upper-bound estimates on child overweight effect of these privately owned amenities. Thus, if any of them turn out to have a negligible estimated effect, we can be confident that public policy aimed at increasing or reducing these amenities would have no impact. Further, by looking at the trends in BMI z-score (BMI z) before amenities such as fast-food arrived, we can test whether the children who will gain an amenity in the future differ from those who will not.

7.6   Results

To see how much of the variation in BMI z can be accounted for by the fixed mother and child characteristics, BMI z was regressed on all of the variables in table 7.3, using robust standard errors clustered on the child's identification data (ID). Three of the year-indicator variables were significant at the 10 percent level, but these are omitted. The results are also reported separately for children under age eight and over age eight. Age is measured at the time of the clinic visit and is a continuous variable.

Table 7.3   OLS regression of fixed mother and child characteristics and
neighborhood characteristics

Variable	All ages	Age < 8	Age ≥ 8
Age	0.098***	0.218***	0.220***
Age squared	−0.003***	−0.014***	−0.008***
Well-child visit	−0.052*	−0.035	−0.074*
Female	0.027	−0.050*	0.140***
White	−0.155**	−0.125*	−0.156
Black	−0.066	−0.083	−0.034
Hispanic	0.356***	0.336***	0.251
Mother's weight gain	0.001	0.001	0.001
Mother's age	0.009***	0.008***	0.012***
Birth weight	0.379***	0.434***	0.293***
WIC	0.033	0.016	0.063
Mother's marital status	0.012	0.006	0.02
Intention to breastfeed	0.008	0.02	−0.023
Mother's education	−0.015*	−0.025***	0.003
Population density	0.004	0.005	0.003
Proportion black	−0.146***	−0.226***	−0.021
Proportion high school grad.	−0.208	−0.165	−0.249
Proportion college grad.	0.268	0.340*	0.148
Median family income	−0.004**	−0.004*	−0.004*
Road network density	−0.014	−0.015	−0.018
Number of road nodes	0.457	1.395	−0.248
Prop. commercial land	0.007	0.081	−0.094
Prop. residential land	0.055	0.018	0.099
Constant	−0.890***	−1.271***	−1.581***
Observations	42,890	25,436	17,420
R^2	0.07	0.08	0.05

Note: Robust standard errors in parentheses.
***Significant at the 1 percent level.
**Significant at the 5 percent level.
*Significant at the 10 percent level.

About 7.4 percent of the overall variation in BMI z can be accounted for by fixed child characteristics, mother's characteristics, and neighborhood characteristics. The explanatory power is 8 percent for the younger children and 5 percent for the older children. The increased explanatory power of the model for younger children may be attributable to the birth certificate data more accurately representing the current socioeconomic environment of the study subject. The well-child visit indicator is significant overall and for the older children; the sign is negative. The negative association between child weight and well-child care is counterintuitive. The well-child variable, in theory, represents the health status of the child, with poorer-health-status children having systematically lower body mass index. Recall that visits with diagnostic codes known to affect body weight were dropped from the data set (pregnancy, endocrine disorders, cancer, congenital heart disease, chromosomal disorders, and metabolic disorders).

The well-child variable may reflect behavior practices of the child's caregivers. Caregivers who less frequently access routine health maintenance for their children, or primarily bring their children in for sick-child visits, may be less supportive of child health behaviors associated with optimal child weight (e.g., promoting routine physical activity or a nutritious diet). A health maintenance organization (HMO) study found that overweight children were less likely to have well-child visits (Estabrooks and Shetterly 2007).

Relative to the reference population, BMI z is increasing rapidly with age. As children age from the sample minimum of three to the maximum of sixteen years, their predicted BMI z increases by 0.6. The mean BMI z-score for children in the age range three to four is 0.43, while for children in the age range fifteen to sixteen it is 0.85. The age and age squared specification is parsimonious, but a histogram, in Figure 7.3, suggests a rapid increase up to age thirteen, and level BMI z thereafter.

The BMI z gain appears to be largely a permanent cumulative process. Children (Wilfley et al. 2007) and adults (Jeffery et al. 2000) are often able to lose weight in the short-term, but find it much more difficult to sustain any loss from their peak weight over a long period. Large recorded z-score gains are rarely reversed at later visits.

To assess how often large gains in weight were reversed, we looked at the subset of children with large BMI z-gains, defined as + 0.5 in BMI z from the first visit to the second visit. At the mean of the reference population a z-score gain of 0.5 would be 27 percentile points. The count of big gainers that have at least three visits was 3,381. Among these big gainers, the count of those who were above their initial z score by the third visit was 2,743. The big gainers who were at or below their first-visit z-score by the third visit was 638. Only 19 percent of the big gainers recovered.

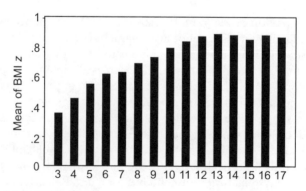

Fig. 7.3   Mean BMI z by age

There is some noise in the weight and the height data that are likely due to data entry or measurement errors at the clinics. If observations of big gainers between the first and second visits were primarily due to such errors, we would expect them to largely disappear by the next visit. Because only a small proportion of the big gains were reversed, we can be confident that they are not primarily due to recording errors. Further, the irreversibility of most of the big gains supports our conclusion that the weight gains are largely cumulative.

The age effect, due to tendency of children to accumulate weight relative to the reference population and rarely lose any of it, is quite strong. Consequently, we will include age and age squared in subsequent regressions, which always have a maximum age of sixteen. What these regressions can tell us is the extent to which the addition or removal of an amenity can alter the pronounced BMI z-age pattern.

The birth certificate variables are available for only one third of the data set. This is too small a sample size to detect many amenity effects. In table 7.4, we drop the birth certificate variables and add the amenity variables.

The amenities that are significant show up at various distances. There is no reason to expect the real effects of different amenities to operate over the same distance. Also, in the smaller circles there may be real effects but too few observations to yield statistically significant results. In discussing the results in table 7.4, we concentrate on the signs and significance levels rather than the values of the coefficients. We do this because we are primarily interested in how the OLS results contrast with the FE results. We think the OLS results are telling us more about who chooses to live near an amenity, such as a school with open recreational facilities or a fast-food restaurant that is near a major road.

Age and age squared are highly significant in every OLS regression. In cross-section, the well-child visit indicator is always negative. It is significant in six of the nine regressions, including all of the regressions on the over age eight children. The female indicator variable should not be significant because the BMI z variable adjusts for gender in the reference population. The consistent negative and significant coefficients for the younger children and the positive and significant coefficients for the older children indicate that relative to boys in the same age range, the younger girls are not gaining BMI z as fast while the older girls are gaining BMI z faster than older boys. The differential may be due to a trend toward an earlier age of puberty for girls.

In terms of racial differences, the striking result is the high BMI z values for Hispanics relative to the omitted category—Asian and other. There are two variables related to African Americans. One refers to the race of the child. Older black children are significantly heavier than the omitted category and than whites. The second variable refers to the neighborhood. Other things equal, living in a neighborhood with a higher proportion of

Table 7.4 OLS with birth certificate variables excluded

Variables	Tenth of mile			Quarter mile			Half mile			One mile		
	All ages	Age < 8	Age > 8	All ages	Age < 8	Age > 8	All ages	Age < 8	Age > 8	All ages	Age < 8	Age > 8
Age	0.093***	0.185***	0.217***	0.093***	0.185***	0.216***	0.093***	0.184***	0.217***	0.093***	0.188***	0.212***
Age squared	-0.003***	-0.012***	-0.008***	-0.003***	-0.012***	-0.008***	-0.003***	-0.012***	-0.008***	-0.003***	-0.012***	-0.008***
Well-child visit	-0.026	-0.001	-0.053**	-0.027	-0.001	-0.054***	-0.028*	-0.003	-0.054***	-0.028*	-0.004	-0.054***
Female	0.002	-0.072***	0.081***	0.002	-0.071***	0.080***	0.003	-0.070***	0.081***	0.002	-0.071***	0.079***
White	0.02	-0.013	0.078**	0.018	-0.017	0.078**	0.02	-0.012	0.076**	0.022	-0.009	0.077**
Black	0.007	-0.089**	0.114***	0.005	-0.094**	0.117***	0.005	-0.091**	0.115***	0.01	-0.087**	0.119***
Hispanic	0.366***	0.371***	0.298***	0.367***	0.369***	0.300***	0.368***	0.372***	0.300***	0.365***	0.371***	0.295***
Population density	0.004	0.004	0.003	0.004*	0.003	0.006*	0.004	0.004	0.005	0.007***	0.008***	0.007**
Proportion black	-0.110***	-0.221***	0.01	-0.122***	-0.228***	-0.003	-0.108***	-0.216***	0.017	-0.141***	-0.217***	-0.053
Proportion with college	-0.057	-0.038	-0.08	-0.065	-0.048	-0.063	-0.026	0.029	-0.063	-0.215*	-0.148	-0.275
Family income	-0.002*	-0.001	-0.002*	-0.001	-0.001	-0.002*	-0.001	-0.001	-0.002	-0.001	-0.001	-0.001
Proportion residential	-0.061	-0.087	-0.052	-0.062	-0.069	-0.076	-0.073*	-0.091*	-0.08	-0.057	-0.073	-0.058
Fast-food	0.082**	0.041	0.134***	0.019*	0.01	0.030**	0.003	0.002	0.003	-0.003	-0.004	-0.002
Supermarkets	-0.185**	-0.195**	-0.168	-0.013	-0.036	0.021	0.023	0.027	0.019	0.011	0.015	0.006
Convenience stores	0.07	0.022	0.121**	-0.02	-0.01	-0.03	0.012	0.012	0.015	-0.007	-0.003	-0.011
Trails	-0.746	-1.321*	-0.066	-0.266**	-0.331**	-0.128	-0.053	-0.032	-0.043	0.030*	0.035	0.028
Crime	-0.009	0.21	-0.171	0.033	0.084	-0.015	0.009	0.015	0.003	0.003	0.001	0.006
Baseball/softball	0.006	-0.02	0.037	-0.002	-0.001	-0.003	0.002	-0.001	0.006	-0.003	-0.008***	0.003
Basketball	-0.004	0.01	-0.018	-0.002	0.005	-0.010*	0.003	0.009***	-0.003	0.001	0.001	0.002
Family centers	-1.544	0.038	-3.811	0.614	0.402	0.736	0.645***	0.871***	0.342	0.204**	0.370***	0.002

Fitness areas	−0.716	−1.539*	0.318	0.25	0.071	0.442	0.124	−0.068	0.355*	0.029	−0.002	0.067
Football	−0.078	−0.046	−0.119	0.016	0.031	−0.002	0.009	0.022	−0.006	0.001	0.007	−0.006
Kickball	0.112	0.172*	0.038	0.042	0.073**	0.005	0.007	0.016	−0.007	0.006	0.001	0.01
Playgrounds (no equipment)	−0.329	−0.355	−0.238	−0.056	−0.063	−0.056	−0.043	−0.026	−0.082	−0.036	0.008	−0.085*
Playgrounds (with equipment)	−0.042	−0.301	0.311	0.018	0.024	0.34	0.001	−0.026	0.028	−0.022	−0.001	−0.038
Pool	−0.808	−1.292	−0.08	−0.517	−0.119	−0.329*	−0.215	−0.267	−0.126	0.154	0.144	0.151
Soccer	0.055	0.237	−0.134	0.002	−0.014	0.315	−0.009	−0.004	−0.01	0.002	0.004	0.002
Tennis	−0.014	−0.029*	0.004	−0.002	−0.005	−0.301	−0.003	−0.003	−0.004	−0.003**	−0.002	−0.004**
Track and field	0.294	0.09	0.729***	0.004	−0.007	0.222	−0.013	−0.011	−0.016	0.011	0.022	−0.002
Volleyball	0.068*	0.094**	−0.031	0.009	0.002	0.21	0.016	0.008	0.018	0.009	−0.001	0.019**
Constant	0.242***	0.053	−0.557**	0.235**	0.043	−0.550**	0.196**	0.008	−0.605***	0.164	0.041	−0.620***
N (observations)	96,522	50,503	45,951	96,522	50,503	45,951	96,522	50,503	45,951	96,522	50,503	45,951
R^2	0.03	0.04	0.01	0.03	0.04	0.01	0.03	0.04	0.01	0.03	0.04	0.01

Notes: Robust standard errors in parentheses.

***Significant at the 1 percent level.

**Significant at the 5 percent level.

*Significant at the 10 percent level.

blacks is associated with a lower BMI z. Since proportions run from 0 to 1, the interpretation of the coefficient is straightforward. For children under the age of eight, hypothetical neighborhoods with no African Americans have higher BMI z, by about 0.22, than neighborhoods that are entirely African American. The proportion of residents in the neighborhood with a college education is almost never significant (one of nine at the 0.10 level). The median family income in the neighborhood and proportion of dwellings that are residential are similar (both have two of nine at the 0.10 level). In the neighborhoods our children live in, college education is rare and incomes are generally low.

The fast-food variable is significant in four of the nine OLS regressions. The significant coefficients are always positive. This positive effect on BMI is the conventional result for fast-food in cross-sectional regressions. The significant coefficients are for the closer buffers, within 0.1 and 0.25 miles. The supermarket variable (OLS) also has the conventional result that supermarkets are associated with lower BMI z when they are close. The signs on the first five coefficients are negative. Of those, just two are significant. Supermarkets also tend to be located on major roads that are on commuting routes. Households that live near a supermarket are likely to differ from households that live far from the nearest supermarket. The convenience store variable has little explanatory power in the OLS regression. Only one of the nine coefficients is significant. Crime is never significant in the OLS regressions.

Very few of the recreational amenities have a significant negative sign. These include trails ($<$ 8 at 0.1 miles, all ages at 0.25 miles, and $<$ 8 at 0.25 miles), baseball/softball ($<$ 8 for 1.0 mile), pools ($>$ 8 at 0.25 miles), and tennis ($<$ 8 at 0.1 miles, all ages at 1.0 miles). Even some of the results that do have a negative and significant sign are counterintuitive; for example, how many children under eight play tennis?

The problems with the OLS results are that they have little explanatory power, most of the demographic variables have limited policy implications, and most importantly, it is impossible to know if the associations are causal. For example, track and field facilities and football fields are almost all located at middle schools and high schools. Even if they had been statistically significant, would the BMI z differences associated with these variables be due to children using these amenities, or simply to unobserved differences in the families that chose to live near these schools? The fast-food restaurants, supermarkets, and even convenience stores tend to be located on major roads that are commuting routes from the city center to the suburbs. Later, we provide some clear maps showing these amenities lined up on the commuting routes. Are the BMI z associations of these amenities due to proximity to these food sources or to unobservable differences in households living near major roads?

Table 7.5   Counts of children having any change by amenity and by buffer

	0.1 mile	0.25 mile	0.5 mile	1 mile
Fast-food	29	342	1,446	4,980
Supermarkets	8	79	337	1,290
Convenience stores	33	270	1,066	3,686
Trails	73	258	715	2,085
Crime	14,643	17,782	18,923	19,946
Baseball/softball	50	371	1,168	4,252
Basketball	179	1,041	3,519	9,655
Family centers	0	16	429	614
Fitness	18	39	271	477
Football fields	4	64	232	1,070
Kickball	35	187	622	2,112
Playgrounds no equipment	143	572	3,596	5,764
Playground with equipment	483	1,942	7,561	13,601
Pools	93	329	2,702	3,447
Soccer fields	19	192	1,733	3,847
Tennis	84	250	734	2,133
Track and field	7	28	835	939
Volleyball	14	78	299	1,019

7.6.1   FE Regressions

Before reporting the FE regressions we report in table 7.5 following how many children had changes in each of the amenities.

The large number of children having changes in the amounts of crime is due to the underlying variable counting individual crimes. At the smallest buffer, within 0.1 miles, many of the amenities have so few children facing changes that it is unlikely we would observe any effect. These include supermarkets, family centers, fitness areas, football fields, soccer fields, track and field, and volleyball courts. Except for the family centers, by the 0.25-mile buffer there are enough children with observed changes that if changes in the amenity indeed had an effect on BMI, at that distance we would have a good chance of observing the effect. We added the 0.1-mile buffer for all amenities because the Currie and colleagues paper found a fast-food effect within 0.1 miles of a child's school. The vast majority of the changes in amenities that are in counts were a gain or loss of one unit; for example, one fast-food restaurant. Of these, the modal change was from 0 to 1 unit with the next most frequent being from 1 unit to 0.

Data on individual children have more variation than data on the average of the all ninth graders in high schools. Our sample of children is 3.2 percent of the Currie and colleagues sample. Their sample is based on observations of 3.06 million student-years, and our data on 98,541 clinic visits among children with two or more visits while residing at the same address. We have twenty-nine changes in the number of fast-food restaurants within the 0.1-mile buffer compared to twenty-two in the Currie and colleagues sample.

In the FE regressions reported in table 7.6, we dropped all variables that are constant at the level of the child. Again, this sample is restricted to observations in which a child remains at the same address between clinic visits. The same restrictions on age and biologically implausible values of BMI z, height, and weight used in the cross-section regression are applied in the FE regressions. The covariates to the environmental/amenity variables are age and age squared, year of clinic visit indicator variables, an indicator for a well-child visit, and crime.

Again, the coefficients on the year dummy variables are not reported. In the FE regressions, the children under eight years of age are gaining BMI z faster relative to the reference population than the children over age eight, roughly by 0.13 BMI z units a year. This younger versus older child differential did not appear in the OLS regressions. The well-child variable is now positive and significant at the 10 percent level for all children. This FE result sharply contrasts with the OLS result for the well-child visit variable, which was always negative, and significant in six of the nine OLS regressions. Thus, for a given child a non–well-child visit is associated with a lower weight than a well-child visit.

There are very few overlaps from the OLS to the FE results of the same amenity being significant at the same distance. Adding a fast-food restaurant within a quarter mile of the same child appears to significantly *reduce* the child's BMI z. Recall that in the cross-sectional results at the tenth-mile buffer, the association between BMI z and fast-food was positive.

From a public policy perspective, the FE results for the recreational amenities are somewhat discouraging. The variables with negative and significant coefficients are fitness areas for all children and younger children at 0.25 miles; kickball for all children and younger children at 0.1 mile, all children at 0.25 miles, and older children at the 0.5 and 1.0 mile buffers; playgrounds without equipment for younger children at 0.5 miles; tennis for older children at 0.25 miles; and volleyball for older children at the 0.1 mile buffer and older children at the mile buffer. The division across amenities that might be associated with reducing BMI z in younger versus older children appears plausible; for example, younger children use playgrounds and kickball fields, while the older ones use volleyball courts.

As a check on whether their estimated fast-food effects on percentages of boys in a high school who were overweight (defined as the eighty-fifth percentile) could plausibly be due to the calories from an extra fast-food meal per day, Currie and colleagues calculated the weight *gain* required for a median height fourteen-year-old boy to move from the eightieth to the eighty-fifth percentile of the BMI distribution. This weight gain was 3.6 pounds. To get a sense of what our estimated coefficients imply for weight gains we will use boys, to match Currie and colleagues, but change the age to

Table 7.6   **Fixed effects regressions**

Variables	Tenth of mile			Quarter mile			Half mile			One mile		
	All ages	Age < 8	Age > 8	All ages	Age < 8	Age > 8	All ages	Age < 8	Age > 8	All ages	Age < 8	Age > 8
Age	0.117***	0.279***	0.151***	0.117***	0.280***	0.153***	0.117***	0.280***	0.153***	0.118***	0.279***	0.155***
Age squared	-0.003***	-0.017***	-0.005***	-0.003***	-0.017***	-0.005***	-0.003***	-0.017***	-0.005***	-0.003***	-0.017***	-0.005***
Well-child visit	0.014*	0.019	0.007	0.014*	0.02	0.008	0.013*	0.018	0.008	0.013*	0.017	0.007
Fast-food	-0.134	-0.074	-0.109	-0.077***	-0.084	-0.038	-0.021*	-0.037	-0.012	0.015**	0.024**	0.003
Supermarkets	0.052	-0.169	-0.255	-0.046	-0.054	-0.096	0.028	0.044	0.042	0.01	0.028	0.043***
Convenience stores	0.009	-0.096	-0.004	0.029	0.024	0.011	0.004	0.036	-0.025*	0.013*	0.036**	-0.007
Trails	-0.557	-1.214	1.802*	0.014	-0.333	0.368**	0.04	-0.056	0.088	0.017	0.023	0.033*
Crime	-0.098	0.069	-0.186	-0.096**	-0.162**	-0.057	-0.050***	-0.088**	-0.023	-0.013	-0.031**	0.002
Baseball/softball	0.081*	0.187**	-0.008	0.013	-0.006	0.026	-0.001	0.015	-0.011	-0.005	-0.013	0.008
Basketball	0.001	0.01	-0.035	-0.01	-0.007	-0.015	-0.003	-0.007	0.004	0.001	-0.002	0.004*
Family centers	—	—	—	-0.812	-6.09	0.659	1.099	1.124	1.122	-0.818*	-0.184	-0.18
Fitness areas	-12.278	-62.440**	25.365	-2.262***	-4.813***	0.651	0.095	-0.247	0.385	0.07	0.182	0.077
Football	0.433	0.507	-0.082	0.09	0.074	-0.007	0.104***	0.116*	0.015	-0.006	-0.001	-0.01
Kickball	-0.322***	-0.416**	-0.049	-0.084**	-0.103	-0.046	0.008	0.04	-0.047**	-0.004	0.013	-0.048***
Playgrounds (no equip.)	-0.28	-1.434	2.643***	0.08	-0.571	0.464**	-0.007	-0.478**	0.296**	-0.056	-0.112	-0.013
Playgrounds (with equip.)	0.516	1.365	-0.257	0.851***	1.291***	0.393	0.416***	0.706***	0.072	0.029	0.113	-0.037
Pool	-1.49	-3.33	-2.08	-1.149	-2.097	-0.169	-0.147	-0.12	-0.949	0.458	1.228*	-0.205
Soccer	-0.067	0.042	-0.133	0.016	-0.059	0.024	0.015	0.027	0.003	0.015**	0.026**	0.006
Tennis	-0.014	0.004	-0.008	-0.003	0.014	-0.027**	0.005	0.014	-0.003	0.005	0.001	0.006
Track and field	8.515	12.495	—	-0.076	0.193	-0.029	0.156	0.364*	0.143	0.091*	0.201**	0.073
Volleyball	0.09	0.113	-0.904***	-0.018	-0.073	-0.074	0.038	0.051	-0.021	-0.013	-0.026	-0.030*
Constant	-0.218	-0.622*	-0.343***	-0.174	-0.497***	-0.369***	-0.310***	-0.739***	-0.373***	-0.304***	-0.844***	-0.440***
N (observations)	98,541	50,521	47,952	98,541	50,521	47,952	98,541	50,521	47,952	98,541	50,521	47,952
N (child/address)	54,823	30,304	26,615	54,823	30,304	26,615	54,823	30,304	26,615	54,823	30,304	26,615
R^2	0.02	0.02	0.02	0.02	0.02	0.02	0.02	0.02	0.02	0.02	0.02	0.02

Note: Standard errors in parentheses. Dashed cells indicate that the variable was dropped because there were no children who gained or lost a family center within a tenth of a mile from their home.

***Significant at the 1 percent level.

**Significant at the 5 percent level.

*Significant at the 10 percent level.

8, which is the median for our data. We will start at the eighty-fifth percentile, their end point, and calculate the implied weight *loss* for some amenities that were estimated to statistically significant effect in reducing weight. Adding a kickball diamond within a tenth of a mile is associated (based on the equation for all ages) with a reduction of 2.8 pounds. The weight reduction for adding a playground within a half mile (based on the under age eight regression) is 4.1 pounds. The weight reduction for adding a volleyball court within a tenth of a mile (based on the age eight or over regression) is 6.9 pounds. Recreational amenities that could reduce the weights of overweight eight-year-old boys within a year of being located near their homes by anything in the range of 2.8 to 6.9 pounds would be economically significant.

Switching to the statistically significant effects for food vendors, at a mile distance the addition of a fast-food restaurant was associated (in the all-ages regression) with a tiny weight gain, 0.14 pounds. The addition of a supermarket within a mile (all-ages regression) is associated with a gain of 0.42 pounds. The addition of a convenience store within a mile (under age eight regression) was associated with a gain of 0.36 pounds. The weight changes associated with adding a food vendor, even when statistically significant, are smaller than the weight losses associated with the few recreational amenities that have negative and significant coefficients.

Some of our results are counterintuitive. Fast-food is associated with weight reduction for all ages at a quarter mile. Trails are only significant for the older children. This trails result is partly intuitive because younger children walking on the trails could wander into the paths of runners, bicyclists, and in-line skaters. We see more young children riding in strollers or in bicycle carriers or on tandem bicycles than those traveling entirely on their own power. However, the counterintuitive part is that all of the coefficients that are significant have a positive sign.

If the reported results were causal effects, then BMI z-reducing policy would be to build fast-food restaurants within a quarter mile of the child's home and surround the child's home with a fitness area, a kickball diamond, and a playground, all at their respective optimal distances. Before much credence can be given to these estimates, the issue of the endogeneity of the placement of these amenities must be addressed.

The FE framework allows for separate consideration of gains and losses in amenities. We tested whether the coefficient on a gain was the same as for a loss for every amenity, and could not reject the null hypothesis of equality in a single case. Also, we looked at assumption of linearity of effects; for example, that a gain from 0 to 1 is the same as a gain from 1 to 2. A very high fraction of all of the changes we observed in counts of amenities is in the range of 0 to 1 or from 1 to 0. We could not reject the null hypothesis of linearity largely because we observed too few higher-order changes.

7.6.2   Endogeneity of Amenity Location

The sharp differences in significance levels and signs between the OLS and FE regressions raise questions about the endogeneity of the location of food vendors. As pointed out in the literature review, vendors may choose to open new fast-food restaurants, for example, in areas in which a larger percentage of the population is overweight. Figures 7.4, 7.5, 7.6, and 7.7 shed light on this issue by showing fast-food, supermarket, limited-service restaurant, and convenience store locations and changes in location, respectively. Some background on the geography of Indianapolis is necessary to interpret these figures. The borders of Indianapolis and Marion County are the same. The metropolitan area includes the surrounding counties, which are not shown in these figures. The population of the metropolitan area in 2006 was 1.66 million. The city proper had a population of 786,000 in same year. The city has a single central business district located at its geographic center. The original street plan for the city had major roads set at angles that can be interpreted as time on a clock. For example, the road running from the center straight north to 12:00, Meridian Street, is the main commuting route from suburbs directly north of the city. The one running from 3:00 to the center of town, East Washington Street, is the major commuting artery for suburbs directly to the east of the city. The roads at approximately 12:30,

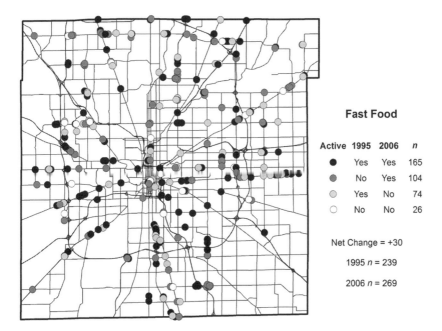

Fig. 7.4   Fast-food locations and changes in Indianapolis

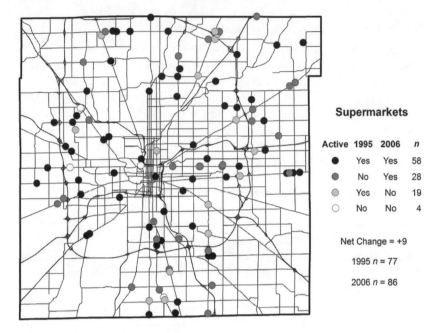

Fig. 7.5   Supermarket locations and changes in Indianapolis

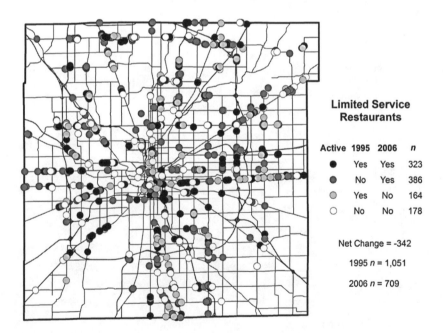

Fig. 7.6   Limited-service restaurant locations and changes in Indianapolis

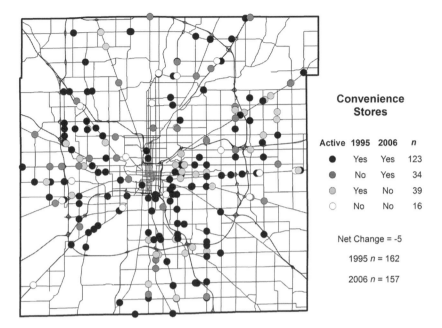

Fig. 7.7   Convenience store locations and changes in Indianapolis

1:30, 4:40, 5:50, 7:30, 8:30, 9:00, 10:30, and 11:00 are also major commuting routes supporting the large traffic to and from the suburbs.

Recall that we defined the fast-food establishments as belonging to national chains. These high-volume restaurants are clearly concentrated on the major surface roads leading in and out of the city center. Traffic flow data would be useful as an instrument to predict fast-food location. Unfortunately, public traffic flow data are outdated and have limited and highly uneven coverage.

The supermarkets, shown in the map in figure 7.5, are also located primarily along major streets. The difference between the supermarkets and the fast-food restaurants is a relative dearth in the inner city (the poorest area). This supermarket "desert" is a residential area immediately north of the central business district. In contrast, the fast-food restaurants are well represented in the inner city.

Figures 7.6 and 7.7 depict locations and changes of limited-service restaurants and convenience stores. The southwest and southeast corners of the county are still largely rural. Other than in those undeveloped areas, there are limited-service restaurants and conveniences stores widely distributed across the county.

One means of addressing the endogeneity of amenity locations is to examine the relationship between the arrival of new amenities in year T and children's BMI z-levels and trends in years prior to that year. Under the assumption that the future cannot cause the past, significant relationships indicate that location decisions depend on the body weight of potential customers. To accomplish this, we ran two sets of regressions as follows:

(1) $$\text{BMI}z_{i,t} = \alpha + \beta X_{i,T} + e_i, \qquad t = 1, \ldots T\text{-}1,$$

(2) $$\text{BMI}z_{i,t} = \alpha + \beta X_{i,T} + \gamma t + \lambda\,(t * X_{i,T}) + e_i,$$

where X_{iT} is a dichotomous indicator that equals 1 if, for example, a fast-food restaurant opened in the area in which the ith child resides in year T. A positive and significant value of β in equation (1) means that the restaurant is more likely to open in an area in which children had high BMIs in the past. A positive and significant value of λ in equation (2) means that the opening of a new restaurant is more likely in an area in which children's BMI had been growing more rapidly in the past.

The results are reported in table 7.7. For each amenity, the top line reports the sign of the estimate of β from equation (1) provided it was significantly different from zero at a 5 percent significance level. Similarly, the second line of each panel reports the sign of significant estimates of λ from equation (2). The results show that only the location of supermarkets is preceded by differences in children's weight, as well as differences in trajectories of children's weight gain.

The positive trends observed at all four buffers for supermarkets undercut the claim that their new locations were selected independently of the prior changes in children's BMI z. Thus, the FE results that supermarkets increase children's weights at the half-mile buffer are suspect. Fast-food restaurants appear to be entering areas with higher child BMI z values and higher rates of child obesity, at least for the quarter- and half-mile buffers. However, these initial differences in levels may not predict the change that will occur after the arrival of a new fast-food restaurant. Our assumption is that gains in BMI z will be the same for a given stimulus over a broad range of initial BMI z. We believe having the same trend in BMI z for children with and without future fast-food gives us an unbiased estimate of the response to the arrival of an amenity. Our negative coefficient quarter-mile fast-food result along with no difference in BMI z trends prior to arrival of the fast-food align with the Anderson and Matsa result cited earlier. While fast-food meals are notoriously calorie-dense, they can have no BMI z effect if children or adults offset the additional calories by eating less food at other meals or by eating fewer meals. Alternatively, there may be so much fast-food in Indianapolis that any child so inclined could readily access a fast-food restaurant whether one was within a tenth of a mile or a quarter mile or not. Either way, as a means of attacking the child obesity epidemic, the Los Angeles freeze on new fast-food restaurants mentioned in the introduction may be misplaced.

Table 7.7   **Signs of significant coefficients for future amenities**

		Radius			
		.1	.1–.25	.25–.5	.5–1
Fast-food restaurants	BMI z		+	+	
	Trend				
Trails	BMI z		+		
	Trend			+	
Supermarkets	BMI z		+	+	+
	Trend	+	+	+	+
Convenience stores	BMI z		+	+	
	Trend			+	
Parks	BMI z	–	–	–	–
	Trend	+		–	–
Baseball/softball diamonds	BMI z	–			+
	Trend				+
Basketball courts	BMI z				–
	Trend		+	+	
Family centers	BMI z				–
	Trend				
Fitness centers	BMI z				–
	Trend				+
Football fields	BMI z				
	Trend			+	
Kickball diamonds	BMI z		+		–
	Trend	+		+	
Playgrounds with no equipment	BMI z				
	Trend				
Playgrounds with equipment	BMI z				
	Trend				
Pools	BMI z		+		
	Trend	–			
Soccer fields	BMI z				
	Trend	+			
Tennis courts	BMI z			+	+
	Trend				
Track and field	BMI z				
	Trend				
Volleyball courts	BMI z				
	Trend		+		–

Fast-food and supermarkets are the highest-profile amenities. Of the remaining sixty trend terms (fifteen amenities times four buffers), eleven are significant. These are scattered such that none of the other amenities has a significant trend term for more than one buffer. Either the locations of these remaining amenities are not being selected on the basis of differences in BMI z trends, or we do not have enough data to detect differences in BMI z trends.

7.7   Conclusion

Our first conclusion is that cross-sectional results differ dramatically from the FE results. We believe that the cross-sectional results tell us more about who chooses to live near an amenity than what adding that amenity might do. In cross-section, nearby (tenth-mile) fast-food increases children's BMI z. Our cross-section regression has controls for child's age, race, gender, mother's age at child's birth, mother's education, WIC eligibility, intention to breastfeed, and many neighborhood characteristics. These are as comprehensive a set of covariates as we have seen for child BMI regressions. Other study strengths include directly measured height and weight data for a large sample size that includes high proportions of African American and Hispanic children. Still, in the fixed effects framework, nearby (quarter-mile) fast-food appears to reduce children's weights, with no difference in the trend of BMI z gain prior to the arrival of the fast-food. While we doubt that fast-food really reduces children's BMI z, the results of the fixed effects models cast doubt on the highly publicized policies to reduce fast-food exposure as interventions for preventing obesity.

A second conclusion is that if the arrival of amenities (other than supermarkets) is unrelated to prior trends in BMI z, then there appears to be little in the way of surefire interventions for reducing children's BMI z, through either recreational amenities or food vendors. The best candidates appear to be fitness areas, kickball fields, and volleyball courts. Weight reductions for overweight children (defined as at the eighty-fifth percentile of the pre-epidemic distribution) in the range of three to six pounds, as estimated for eight-year-old boys for these amenities, would be valuable results for an intervention.

Our results look at the short-term. They look for BMI z responses within the year the amenity arrives. It may be that a recreational amenity does have a BMI z-reducing effect on nearby children if it is measured years after its arrival. However, we have few observations with long runs of time after the arrival of an amenity.

Further, our study demonstrates the benefits of an interdisciplinary team of economists, a physician, an urban planner, and geographers. It would have been impossible to assemble these data without the interdisciplinary collaboration.

7.7.1   Future Work

The present chapter is our first effort in using these data. We mentioned earlier that our estimated effects were short-term, specifically within a year, and that we intend to look for persistent effects from changing amenities.

A general assumption of our methods used in this chapter is that proximity is a proxy for exposure to amenities. We do not have direct observational data on whether or not children and their families use (or are even aware of) the amenities we measured. In future prospective work, we hope to collect detailed observational data on spatial and temporal interaction with amenities through survey and global positioning system (GPS) tracking. This may allow us to better infer causal effects of the built environment on children's weight.

National Institutes of Health (NIH)-funded R21 studies are meant to test the feasibility of a new research design. Our study demonstrates that it is feasible to collect detailed longitudinal data on selected components of the built environment surrounding the homes of a large sample of children in a metropolitan area. In total, it took our team about twenty months to assemble and clean the built-environment data used in the analytical portion of this study. As spatial information technologies continue to become more widespread and agencies (such as police, parks, and food safety departments) increasingly collect and organize data on amenities in forms that are easily extended to spatial analysis, it should be easier to extend the methods used in this study both spatially (to include larger populations in multiple cities) and temporally (to include longer-term longitudinal experiments). We plan to seek funding for a six-city extension of the present study. A six-fold increase in the sample size over different regions of the country would provide much more reliable results.

Our study examined associations between BMI z and proximity to amenities within four buffer distances. We used relatively simple methods to measure spatial proximity—straight line (Euclidean) buffers. In future work we will explore more complex measures of proximity, including network buffers and travel time models that consider movement along street networks. This will allow us to test other specifications for built-environment variables, including specific distances or travel times to individual amenities, average distance or time to the closest three amenities of a given type, and more general measures of accessibility to amenities.

Appendix A
Photo Interpretation

Orthorectified aerial photograph mosaics were available for most study years. The primary exception was 1996, for which no photographs of Marion County were available. Small, scattered areas were missing from the 1995 photographs. Photographs were available for 1998 for most of the county. Owing to a problem with the initial flight for 1998, no photography was available for a narrow band of the county running north to south through the center. This area was reflown in early 1999 using the same techniques; the resulting photographs were treated differently in this study from the 1998 photographs, as well as from a complete set of photographs taken later in 1999 using different techniques.

The photographs varied greatly in quality; only the last four years were in color, and later years were generally of higher spatial resolution than earlier years, though the 1998 (and matching early 1999) photographs were significantly coarser than other years. Contrast was also starker and thus of lower quality in earlier years, particularly in 1995.

All photographs were provided to a team of photo interpreters in digital format. In one case, 2005, images were available from Indiana University's spatial data portal, representing the same original photography as the 2005 file photographs, but reproduced at higher resolution. Photographs were examined on computer display in ArcMap 9.2, generally at scales of 1:1000 to 1:2500. Accompanying this was a copy of the amenities database (described earlier in the section on data), in which interpreters were to save any changes.

The county was divided into interpretation areas, usually consisting of a linear strip half a mile wide, running north to south; each area was assigned to a particular interpreter, though much of the county was eventually analyzed by more than one interpreter. The tasks of the interpreter were two: first, to locate recreational amenities of the selected types and add them to the database (through heads-up digitizing), and second, to determine during which years each amenity was present. This information was recorded as attributes of the feature in the database, along with information on the type of amenity, and the source of the feature, whether a particular interpreter or one of the original files. If a previously digitized feature was modified in shape, size, or location by an interpreter, that information was noted as well. If interpreters were unable to determine the presence of an amenity (owing to the absence of photographs), a no-data value of –9 was recorded as that year's attribute. Finally, features that lay on the border between one interpretation area and another were flagged with a special attribute, so that duplication could be avoided. As a quality check on individual interpreters, border features were to be digitized by *both* interpreters, and the results compared.

The study team decided to quantify each amenity type in a way judged most likely to capture the relative recreational opportunities that each provided, with a few practical constraints. In the case of standardized playing areas, such as tennis courts and football fields, a count of amenities was deemed appropriate. In the case of scalable amenities, such as swimming pools and playgrounds, the area of the amenity was deemed the best measure. The opportunity available to each child would be taken as the sum of these measurements, as they fell within a given distance of the child's home address. For example, if 23 m^2 of a swimming pool fell within a half-mile radius around the child's address, this 23 m^2 was added to the value of the child's swimming pool opportunity.

Guidelines for Digitizing

- For baseball/softball, basketball, football, kickball, tennis, track and field, and volleyball, the playing area was to be digitized, as marked where possible.
- For baseball and softball, the boundaries of infield and outfield were to be digitized; where the outfield was unclear, an arc of radius about twice the size of the infield was to be digitized. For football, the field was to be digitized goal line to goal line. For kickball, the infield only was to be digitized. For volleyball, where markings are seldom present, an approximation of the playing area was sufficient.
- In the case of basketball, if no court were marked, a simple polygon around the hoop was to be digitized.
- Backyard amenities, specifically swimming pools and playground equipment, were to be ignored; the inclusion of all such amenities was deemed impractical. Beyond that, no distinction was made between public and private amenities, since the photography would not have informed us whether children could access the amenities or not. Private ownership, as might be determined from a plat overlay, would also not settle the question, as amenities owned by apartment complexes, homeowner groups, and private schools might well be accessible to the public.
- Tennis courts were to be digitized wherever found, to maintain consistency with the practice in creating the original file, and because these were relatively few and unambiguous.
- Equipment playgrounds with a mulched or sandy area surrounding the equipment were to be digitized to that area. In the absence of such an area, a convenient shape, a circle or rectangle, was to be placed around the equipment.
- Swimming pools were to be digitized to the water's area only; any previously added pools in which the deck area was also included were to be modified.
- Family centers were to be digitized to the building's footprint though these facilities were few and no additional ones were identified during the process.
- As soccer fields are not always permanently marked and goals moved frequently as needed, interpreters were instructed to digitize the entire area which, in their judgement, was set aside for playing soccer.
- In the case of fitness, the entire area in which fitness activities take place was to be digitized.
- Any areas where track or field events take place, including tracks, infields, or obviously designated external areas, were to be digitized.
- In cases where a particular area is clearly used for more than one of the chosen activities, overlapping polygons were to be created, according to the previous guidelines.

Limitations on the Final Product

- For amenity types that were to be quantified by count, interpreters were instructed not to correct minor inconsistencies in the original file, so long as general location and number were accurate. For instance, if a tennis court were digitized to its surrounding fence, rather than its playing surface, this was deemed sufficient. Thus, the inclusion or non-inclusion of marginal features within a buffer will be inconsistent by a few meters in the final data.
- While the quantification of playground equipment might be refined conceptually, none of these methods was practical for aerial photograph interpretation. The footprint area of a jungle gym, for instance, might best capture the opportunity represented by it, but trials showed this to be impractical, given the presence of shadows and inadequate resolution.
- Playgrounds were to be quantified by area, but the area of playgrounds is difficult to interpret consistently. Hard-surface playgrounds are often not demarcated clearly, as they coexist not only with basketball courts and kickball fields, but with parking lots. The presence of cars on a surface may be a temporary condition at the time the photograph was taken, which does not significantly alter the recreational opportunity in a longer time frame. Playground equipment is often located in a mulched area, but this mulched area is not always consistent from one year to the next. Such changes in area, therefore, were to be disregarded, so long as the playground equipment remained.
- Even in the presence of quality controls, the quality of interpretation must vary substantially with the individual, and nine individuals contributed to the final interpretation.

Each interpreter's completed work was selected from within his or her file; the areas covered by this work were assembled into a mosaic of recreational amenities. Border features were examined and redundancies removed, and any systematic errors discovered through the comparison were corrected; errors in naming were corrected, and any features marked as unknown were examined by a second interpreter, and either classified within one of the chosen types, or discarded. Finally, in those cases in 1996 and 1998 where no photographs were available, but where the preceding and following years matched in value, either both showing present or both showing absent, that value was substituted for the missing data. The four sets of Euclidean buffers used elsewhere in the larger study were intersected with the features in the recreational-amenities file.

We next performed a merger of all intersected vector features by original amenity, so that each resulting feature represented a single polygon resulting from the intersection of one buffer with one amenity. At this point, areas in square meters were calculated for all features. For those features that were to be quantified by area, this area was substituted as the value for each year in which the original amenity was present. Two copies of the file were created; in one file, every missing value was substituted with 0, and in the other file, every missing value was substituted with –9999999. A dissolve was then performed on the intersected features in each file, preserving buffer identification but grouping by amenity type, and summing the values for each year.

The resulting values in each feature were taken, in theory, as a measurement of recreational opportunity, as available to a child living at the center of each buffer, sorted by amenity type, with a value for each year. In the file in which 0 was substituted for missing data, the final measurement would represent a minimum. In the file in which –9999999 was substituted, every measurement in which *any* component value had been missing would be negative (as a single value of –9999999 would be greater than any possible value within the largest buffer used in the study), thereby allowing identification of the uncertain quantities. The file with the minimum values was used for the regressions in this study.

Appendix B
Land Use Variables

This appendix describes the data created for a set of social and physical environmental variables for use in the child obesity research. Data are provided for quarter-mile and half-mile buffers surrounding the children's residences. The variables for the quarter-mile buffers end in *25* and the variables for the half-mile buffers end in *5*.

Census Variables

Population density and the proportion of the population African American were created from the 2000 census block data from summary file 1. The education and income variables were created from the census block group data from summary file 3. Data from the surrounding counties were included, so there are no boundary issues near the border of Marion County.

Population Density—popden25 and popden5

This is the gross population density in persons per acre. Block population density was converted to a grid theme using fifty-foot grid cells (used in all of the data creation). The values are the means of the grid cell densities in the quarter-mile and half-mile buffers.

Proportion of the Population African American—prblk25 and prblk5

Block total population density and the population density African American were converted to the grid cells, the means for the buffers were calculated, and these were divided to obtain the proportion African American. Areas with zero population could not have a proportion calculated. This affected the variable *prblk25,* which has one missing value.

Proportion Graduated From High School—prhs25 and prhs5

This is the proportion of the population aged twenty-five and over who have graduated from high school. The densities of the population aged twenty-five and over and the numbers graduated from high school were converted to the grid cells, the means for the buffers were calculated, and these were divided to obtain the proportion graduated from high school. Areas with zero population aged twenty-five and over could not have a proportion calculated. This affected the variable *prhs25,* which has one missing value.

Proportion Graduate From College—prcoll25 and prcoll5

This is the proportion of the population aged twenty-five and over who have graduated from college. The densities of the population aged twenty-five and over and the numbers graduated from college were converted to the grid cells, the means for the buffers were calculated, and these were divided to obtain the proportion graduated from college. Areas with zero population aged twenty-five and over could not have a proportion calculated. This affected the variable *prcoll25,* which has one missing value.

Median Family Income—faminc25 and faminc5

This is an estimate of the median family income for the buffers. The block group median family income was converted to the grid cells, and the means for the buffers were calculated. Areas with no families and no median family income reported did not have values. This affected the variable *faminc25,* which has one missing value.

Road Network Variables

The planning literature suggests that greater density and interconnectedness of the road network (indicated by the density of intersections or nodes) should be associated with greater pedestrian use and physical activity. Data creation begins using the Etak road network for 2000. This was selected because it represented the network during the middle of the period for the obesity data, which seemed more reasonable than using the current road network. Limited-access highways and road segments associated with the interchanges were deleted from the network as these would not contribute to pedestrian activity. Data from the surrounding counties were included, so there are no boundary issues near the border of Marion County.

Road Network Density—rdlen25 and rdlen5

This is the sum of the length in miles of the road segments with their centroids within the buffers. The road segments were converted to a point layer with the line centroids, this was converted to the grid cells, and the results were summed for the buffers.

Number of Nodes—nodes25 and nodes5

The layer of road features was converted to a point layer of nodes. Dangling nodes and pseudonodes were deleted from this layer, leaving those nodes that represent intersections between roads. This layer was converted to the grid cells, and the count of the number of nodes in the buffers was obtained by summing those results.

Land Use Variables

The planning literature suggests that mixed land use, especially the presence of commercial land uses, should be associated with greater pedestrian use and physical activity. A parcel-based layer of land use in Marion County in 2002 from the Indianapolis Department of Metropolitan Development was used. Areas of streets and roads were not included in the delineation of land use. This data set covered only Marion County, so the proportions of land use near the boundaries reflect only land use within Marion County.

Proportion Land Use Commercial

This is the proportion of the classified areas of land use (not including areas of roads) that were classified in one of the commercial (retail and office) land use categories. The land use data were converted to the grid cells with values of 1 if commercial, 0 if other land use, and no data if road area. The means of these values were determined for the buffers to provide the proportion commercial.

Proportion Land Use Residential

This is the proportion of the classified areas of land use (not including areas of roads) that were classified in one of the residential categories. The land use data were converted to the grid cells with values of 1 if residential, 0 if other land use, and no data if road area. The means of these values were determined for the buffers to provide the proportion residential.

References

Anderson, M., and D. A. Matsa. 2007. Are restaurants really supersizing America? University of California Berkeley. Working Paper.

Booth, K. M., M. M. Pinkston, and W. S. Carlos Poston. 2005. Obesity and the built environment. *Journal of the American Dietetic Association* 105:S110–17.

Centers for Disease Control and Prevention. 2000. A SAS program for the CDC growth charts. Available at: www.cdc.gov/nccdphp/dnpa/growthcharts/resources/sas.htm.

Chou, S., M. Grossman, and H. Saffer. 2004. An economic analysis of adult obesity: Results from the behavioral risk factor surveillance system. *Journal of Health Economics* 23 (3): 565–87.

Chou, S.-Y., I. Rashad, and M. Grossman. 2008. Fast-food restaurant advertising on television and its influence on childhood obesity. *Journal of Law and Economics* 51 (4): 599–618.

Committee on Environmental Health. 2009. The built environment: Designing communities to promote physical activity in children. *Pediatrics* 123 (6): 1591–98.

Currie, J., S. DellaVigna, E. Moretti, and V. Pathania. 2009. The effect of fast food restaurants on obesity and weight gain. NBER Working Paper no. 14721. Cambridge, MA: National Bureau of Economic Research, February.

Estabrooks, P. A., and S. Shetterly. 2007. The prevalence and health care use of overweight children in an integrated health care system. *Archives of Pediatric Adolescent Medicine* 161:222–7.

Ewing, R., R. C. Brownson, and D. Berrigan. 2006. Relationship between urban sprawl and weight of United States youth. *American Journal of Preventative Medicine* 31:464–74.

Galvez, M. P., M. Pearl, and I. H. Yen. 2010. Childhood obesity and the built environment. *Current Opinion in Pediatrics* 22 (2): 202–7.

Gordon-Larsen, P., M. C. Nelson, P. Page, and B. M. Popkin. 2006. Inequality in the built environment underlies key health disparities in physical activity and obesity. *Pediatrics* 117 (2): 417–24.

Jeffery, R. W., A. Drewnowski, L. H. Epstein, A. J. Stunkard, G. T. Wilson, R. R. Wing, and D. R. Hill. Long-term maintenance of weight loss: Current status. *Health Psychology* 19 (1 suppl): 5–16.

King, A. C., R. W. Jeffery, F. Fridinger, L. Dusenbury, S. Provence, S. Hedlund, and K. Spangler. 1995. Environmental and policy approaches to cardiovascular disease prevention through physical activity: Issues and opportunities. *Health Education Quarterly* 22:499–511.

Los Angeles Times. 2008. Available at: www.latimes.com/news/local/politics/cal/la-me-fastfood30-2008jul30,0,7844906.

McDonald, N. C. 2007. Active transportation to school: Trends among U.S. schoolchildren, 1969–2001. *American Journal of Preventive Medicine* 32 (6): 509–16.

Margetts, B. 2004. WHO global strategy on diet, physical activity and health. Editorial. *Public Health and Nutrition* 7:361–3.

Merom, D., C. Tudor-Locke, A. Bauman, and C. Rissel. 2006. Active commuting to school among NSW primary school children: Implications for public health. *Health and Place* 12:678–87.

Papas, M. A., A. J. Alberg, R. Ewing, K. J. Helzlsover, T. L. Gary, and A. C. Klassen. 2007. The built environment and obesity. *Epidemiologic Reviews* 29 (1): 129–43.

Plantinga, A. J. and S. Bernell. 2007. The association between urban sprawl and obesity: Is it a two-way street? *Journal of Regional Science* 47 (5): 857–79.

Quigley, F. 2003. Indianapolis is missing the bus: IndyGo is worst-funded system in

Midwest. Available at: www.nuvo.net/archive/2003/12/24/indianapolis_is_missing _the_bus.html.

Sallis, J. F., A. Bauman, and M. Pratt. 1998. Environmental and policy interventions to promote physical activity. *American Journal of Preventive Medicine* 15:379–97.

Schlossberg, M., J. Greene, P. P. Phillips, B. Johnson, and B. Parker. 2006. School trips: Effects of urban form and distance on travel mode. *Journal of the American Planning Association* 72:337–46.

Singh, G. K., M. Siahpush, and M. D. Kogan. 2010. Neighborhood socioeconomic conditions, built environments, and childhood obesity. *Health Affairs* 29 (3): 508–15.

Tester, J., and R. Baker. 2009. Making the playing fields even: Evaluating the impact of an environmental intervention on park use and physical activity. *Preventative Medicine* 48 (4): 316–20.

Timperio, A., D. Crawford, A. Telford, and J. Salmon. 2004. Perceptions about local neighborhood and walking and cycling among children. *Preventive Medicine* 38:39–47.

Tobler, W. 1970. A computer movie simulating urban growth in the Detroit region. *Economic Geography* 46 (2): 234–40.

Wilfley, D. E., R. I. Stein, B. E. Saelens, D. S. Mockus, G. E. Matt, H. A. Hayden-Wade, R. R. Welch, K. B. Schechtman, P. A. Thompson, and L. H. Epstein. 2007. Efficacy of maintenance treatment approaches for childhood overweight: A randomized controlled trial. *Journal of the American Medical Association* 298 (14): 1661–73.

Food Stamp Program and Consumption Choices

Neeraj Kaushal and Qin Gao

8.1 Introduction

The growing prevalence of obesity among low-income families in the United States has created concerns amid health scientists and policymakers about the effect of the Food Stamp Program (FSP), the largest food and nutrition program in the country, on food consumption, obesity, and health.[1] When first designed over three decades ago, the primary objective of the FSP was to mitigate food insecurity and meet nutritional deficiencies in low-income families. Over the years, however, the nature of nutritional risk in low-income families has changed from food insufficiency to obesity, leading to a policy debate on whether the FSP has served its purpose and whether it needs to be redesigned to improve quality of food consumed in low-income families.

In a comprehensive review of literature on the effect of food and nutrition assistance programs on consumption, Fox, Hamilton, and Lin (2004, 84) conclude, "while the greater part of food stamp benefits given to households are used to free up resources to spend on things other than food, FSP benefits do cause households to spend more on food than they otherwise would." A

Neeraj Kaushal is associate professor of social work at Columbia University, and a research associate of the National Bureau of Economic Research. Qin Gao is an associate professor at Fordham University Graduate School of Social Service.

We would like to thank the IRP-USDA Small Grants Program for funding this research. We also thank Thomas Crossley, Michael Grossman, Robert Kaestner, Kerry Anne McGeary, and other participants at the NBER conference and preconference on Economic Aspects of Obesity for their suggestions and comments.

1. Recent research on examining the effect of the FSP on food security include: Borjas (2004) and Yen et al. (2008), and on the effect of the FSP on obesity and health include: Gibson (2003, 2004), Chen, Yen, and Eastwood (2005), Frongillo (2003), Kaushal (2007), Krueger (2004) and Ver Ploeg et al. (2007).

key challenge in many previous studies is to isolate the effect of individual circumstances, which influence food consumption, from the decision to participate in the FSP. Individuals who receive food stamps are poor, and due to their meager economic circumstances consume less expensive food (Drewnowski 2003). To isolate the effect of the FSP on food consumption, therefore, one needs a plausibly random change in FSP participation that is unrelated to individual circumstances, food prices, or societal changes in consumption patterns.

We use federal and state social policy changes in the United States since the mid-1990s that caused sharp fluctuations in food stamp participation to study the effect of food stamps on food consumption in low-income families. The 1996 federal welfare reform denied food stamps to legal immigrants, and imposed work requirements on able-bodied adults without dependents as a condition to participate in the FSP. More importantly, since state welfare agencies also administer the FSP, the decline in welfare caseload (number of participants) triggered by state and federal welfare reforms during the mid-1990s increased the transaction cost of obtaining food stamps for welfare leavers, in turn, reducing the food stamp caseload.[2]

Partly in response, several state governments took initiatives to ease access to the FSP such as the introduction of electronic benefit transfer cards (EBT) in place of paper food stamp cards and simplified certification (or recertification) procedures for food stamp eligibility. By June 2004, all states had introduced EBT and the proportion of Food Stamp participants with earnings who were required to certify eligibility every three months fell from more than 38 percent in 2000 to 10 percent in 2003 (Hanratty 2006). Between 1994 and 2001, the food stamp caseload declined by 37 percent, and has been rising since then. Researchers attribute 12 to 32 percent of the change in the food stamp caseload to state and federal policies and 20 to 35 percent to the business cycle (Currie and Grogger 2001; Danielson and Klerman 2006; Hanratty 2006; Wilde et al. 2000). We investigate whether these changes in the FSP caseload, resulting from social policy changes, had any influence on food expenditures in low-income families. We also examine how changes in policies that affected incentives for participation in the FSP—introduction of EBT cards, simplified certification, and welfare reform—affected food expenditures in low-income families. Note that measuring changes in food spending does not tell us anything directly about potential implications for obesity rates. However, any estimates about the effect of FSP on obesity prevalence should be interpreted in terms of the size of the policy's impact on food consumption. If the FSP has a modest effect on food spending, arguably its potential to influence obesity prevalence will also be modest. If, however, the FSP increases food expenditure substantially, it would be

---

2. Zedlewski and Brauner (1999) find that the decline in food stamps participation was higher among welfare leavers than others.

difficult to glean any insight into its impact on obesity since increased food spending could be on account of higher calorie intake or purchase of better quality food.

Our analysis suggests that changes in the food stamp caseload triggered by social policy changes during the mid-1990s (e.g., welfare reforms) did not have any statistically significant association with per capita expenditure on food in families headed by low-educated single mothers. We find that state and federal welfare reforms during the 1990s lowered the food stamp caseload by approximately 18 percent, and the introduction of the Electronic Benefit Transfer cards and simplified reporting procedures for recertification of food stamps increased participation by about 7 percent. However, we do not find any evidence that these policies had any effect on total food expenditure, nor do we find any consistent evidence that the policies affected expenditures on specific food items.

8.2   Social Policy Changes and the Food Stamp Caseload

Participation in the FSP in the United States has undergone dramatic changes since 1990. During the 1980s, the total food stamp caseload in the country hovered around 19 to 21 million recipients (figure 8.1). From 20 million in 1990, the caseload increased steadily to 27.5 million by 1994, and then fell sharply to around 17 million by 2000 to 2001, and rose again to 25.7 million by 2005. While the food stamp caseload has traditionally been countercyclical to economic trends[3]—when the economy is booming, food stamp caseload declines and vice versa—its recent trend has also been associated with dramatic changes in social welfare programs. Beginning in the early 1990s, states started moving from paper food stamps cards to electronic benefit transfer (EBT) cards, and a 1996 federal policy made it mandatory for states to move to EBT by 2002.[4] The EBT cards operate like automatic teller machine (ATM) cards and are designed to lower the stigma attached to food stamps usage, restrict misuse and illegal sale of benefits, and prevent theft or loss of benefits.

The second major change in the FSP came with the enactment of the federal welfare law in 1996 that denied food stamps to many immigrant groups and imposed work requirements on able-bodied adults without dependents. More significantly, state and federal restrictions on cash welfare implemented since the early 1990s that caused a sharp decline in welfare caseload were also instrumental in lowering the food stamp caseload. Since state welfare agencies also administer the FSP, the decline in the welfare caseload triggered by state Aid to Families with Dependent Children (AFDC) waivers

---

3. The FSP participation is restricted to families with a total gross income no more than 130 percent of the federal poverty line, with a net family income less than or equal to the federal poverty line, and household assets less than $2,000.

4. In June 2004, California was the last state to implement the EBT card system.

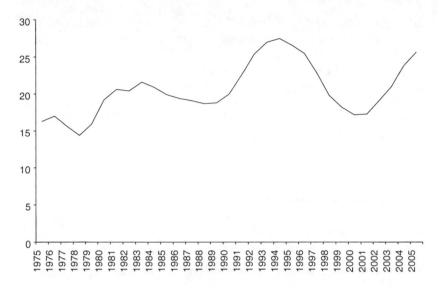

Fig. 8.1   Number of food stamp participants (in millions)
Source: Data from the U.S. Department of Agriculture, Food and Nutrition Service.

and the 1996 state and federal welfare reform increased the transaction cost of obtaining food stamps, and resulted in welfare leavers not seeking food stamps even when eligible (Zedlewski and Brauner 1999).

Finally, in 2002, the Farm Security and Rural Investment Act (FSRIA) allowed states to ease the burden of certification (or recertification) for eligibility to the FSP through a simplified reporting process.[5] Since 2000, forty-one states have implemented simplified reporting and increased the recertification period to six months. The FSRIA also restored food stamp eligibility to noncitizens who have lived in the United States for at least five years.

A number of researchers have studied the association between changes in the FSP and welfare reform and fluctuations in the food stamp caseload (Currie and Grogger 2001; Danielson and Klerman 2006; Wilde et al. 2000; Kabbani and Wilde 2003; Zedlewski and Brauner 1999; Ziliak, Gundersen, and Figlio 2003). This body of literature has concluded that welfare reform contributed to the decrease in the food stamp caseload, while policies aiming at lowering the stigma and burden of benefit receipt (e.g., EBT and simplified certification or recertification) helped increase FSP participa-

5. A household is certified to receive food stamps for a certain period depending on state policy and household structure. Prior to the 2002 FSRIA, the household was expected to report any changes in income and family structure that may affect eligibility and benefits, even during the certification period. Under the new simplified reporting system the household is expected to report changes during the certification period only if their incomes rise above 130 percent of the federal poverty line (Danielson and Klerman 2006; GAO 2004).

tion. Specifically, the most recent of these studies (Danielson and Klerman 2006) used administrative data from January 1989 to July 2004 to conduct policy simulations and found that welfare reform had a large negative impact on the food stamp caseload during 1994 to 2000, and EBT and simplified certification or recertification had a large positive impact on the caseload during 2001 to 2004. Danielson and Klerman (2006) attribute 32 percent of the decline in the caseload to state and federal social policy changes (waivers under the Aid to Families with Dependent Children [AFDC] and Temporary Aid to Need Families [TANF])[6] and 31 percent of the increase since 2000 to policies aimed at simplifying the FSP reporting system. Hanratty (2006) found that changes in recertification requirements from 2001 to 2003 increased participation rates of income eligible families by 2 to 9 percent.

8.3   Food Stamps and Consumption

Current regulations define eligible foods under the FSP as any food or food product intended for human consumption, except alcoholic beverages, tobacco, and hot meals and hot food products prepared for immediate consumption (GAO 2008). Beneficiaries can use food stamps to purchase eligible food items from a wide network of retail stores ranging from large supermarkets to convenience stores and farmers' markets. At the end of fiscal year 2007, approximately 165,000 retailers were authorized to participate in the FSP (GAO 2008).

Participation in the FSP can potentially affect food consumption in a number of ways. By making it mandatory that participants buy a minimum amount of food in order to use their stamps, the FSP is likely to increase food expenditure of a participant whose food expenditure is otherwise constrained due to low-income.[7] Such distortion is an intended aspect of the policy through which the government aims to ensure that participants consume at least a minimum amount of food.[8] A rational participant not constrained in spending on food on account of low income is likely to treat FSP benefits as cash income. Thus, participation in the FSP will increase the unconstrained participant's expenditure on food depending on his or her marginal propensity to spend on food.

Previous research, however, shows that the FSP distorts the monthly nutrition cycle of participants who tend to consume higher quantities of food

6. Their estimate is similar to that obtained by Currie and Grogger (2001), but higher than the computations by Wilde et al. (2000), who attribute 12 percent of the decline in the food stamp caseload to welfare reform.

7. An individual is constrained if her food stamp benefit is greater than what she would have spent on food in the absence of food stamps.

8. Since trading food stamps is illegal, benefits are typically sold for about 61 percent of their legal value (Whitmore 2002). In recent years, state governments have taken steps to reduce resale.

immediately after receipt of food stamps (Wilde and Ranney 2000; Shapiro 2005). Evidence from most previous studies also suggests that the marginal propensity to consume food is higher out of food stamp benefit than cash income. Devaney and Moffitt (1991) used the Survey of Food Consumption in Low-Income Households for 1979 to 1980, and found that the marginal propensity to consume food out of food stamp benefit was three to seven times the marginal propensity to consume food out of cash income. Using the Panel Survey of Income Dynamics for 1978 to 1979, Senauer and Young (1986) found that food stamps had a substantially greater impact in raising at-home food expenditure than an equal amount of cash income. Fraker, Martini, and Ohls (1995) conducted four demonstration projects and found that in three demonstrations cashout resulted in reductions in food expenditures ranging from 7 to 22 percent, but there was no effect at the fourth demonstration. Using Panel Survey of Income Dynamic from 1968 to 1978, Hoynes and Schanzenbach (2009) found that introduction of the FSP was associated with a statistically significant increase in expenditure on food, but that households were inframarginal and responded similarly to one dollar in cash income and one dollar in food stamps. Moffitt (1989), who used the experience of an actual conversion from stamps to cash in Puerto Rico, found no detectable influence of cashout of the stamps on food expenditure. Finally, Fox, Hamilton, and Lin (2004, 84), who reviewed a large body of literature on the effect of food stamps on dietary intake, conclude that there is "little evidence that the FSP consistently affects the dietary intakes of individuals."[9]

Most previous research is based on food expenditures data from the late seventies or the eighties. Changes in consumption patterns and living standards, however, may have influenced the association between food stamps and food expenditures. We use more recent data from the Consumer Expenditure Survey and build on previous research by investigating whether recent changes in the FSP and welfare reform have affected total food expenditure and expenditures on specific categories of food items.

8.4   Data

We use the Consumer Expenditure Survey (CES) for 1994 to 2004 to do the analysis. The CES has two components: a weekly Diary Survey (DS) and a quarterly Interview Survey (IS). Our analysis is based on the DS, which contains information on small, frequently purchased items such as food, beverages, food consumed away from home, gasoline, and housekeeping

---

9. Previous research provides weak to nil support for the hypothesis that food stamps cause obesity (Chen, Yen, and Eastwood 2005; Gibson 2003, 2004; Kaushal 2007; Krueger 2004; Frongillo 2003; Ver Ploeg et al. 2007).

supplies. About 7,500 consumer units[10] are sampled each year. Each consumer unit is asked to maintain expense records, or diaries, of all purchases made each day for two consecutive one-week periods, yielding approximately 15,000 weekly diaries a year. Relative to other surveys (e.g., the IS), DS is less susceptible to recall bias because of its diary nature (Battistin 2003).

The CES provides detailed information on each household unit including the respondent's (and spouse's) age, education (and spouse's education), marital status, race and ethnicity (and spouse's race and ethnicity), region of residence, family income and size, number of children and number of elderly persons (aged sixty-five or above) in the family. This information is used to construct demographic groups and control variables. The sample of analysis is restricted to families where the mother is aged eighteen to fifty-four years. We study only families with children since a majority (over 85 percent) of the food stamps recipients belong to such families.

We study nine main categories of food expenditures: food at home, food away from home, cereals and bakery products, meat, dairy products, fruits and vegetables, nonalcoholic beverages, alcoholic beverages, and miscellaneous expenses on food. All expenditures are expressed in per capita terms, except for expenditure on alcoholic beverages, which is expressed as per adult population in the family. Throughout the analysis, expenditures are expressed in 2004 dollars using the price index for food and beverages from the Bureau of Labor Statistics.

From 1994 onward CES has provided state identifiers for consumer units, a variable that is crucial to our analysis. For reasons relating to nondisclosure, each year codes for nine to ten states are either suppressed or recoded within CES, and in eighteen other states a tiny proportion of the consumer units are without state identifiers. Overall, consumer units without state identifiers constitute about 15 percent of the sample and are dropped from the analysis.[11] The food stamp caseload data, by state and year, are taken from various issues of the *Background Material and Data on the Programs within the Jurisdiction of the Committee on Ways and Means* of the U.S. House of Representatives (the Green book), and the Food and Nutrition Service of the U.S. Department of Agriculture.

The data on unemployment rate come from the U.S. Bureau of Labor Statistics, and real per capita income from the U.S. Bureau of Economic Analysis. The data on welfare policies are drawn from the State Documen-

10. A consumer unit is defined as: all members of a housing unit related by blood, marriage, adoption, or some other legal arrangement; or two or more persons living together who use their incomes to make joint expenditures; or a single person who is living with others but is financially independent (BLS 2005).

11. This study is based on CES data for the following thirty-five states: AL, AK, AZ, CA, CO, CT, DE, FL, HI, GA, ID, IL, IN, KS, KY, LA, MA, MI, MD, MO, NE, NJ, NY, NC, OH, OK, OR, PA, SC, TN, TX, UT, VA, WA, and WI.

tation Project of the Center on Budget and Policy Priorities (www.cbpp. org) and merged with the CES data, by state, month, and year. We code a state to have simplified reporting in year if it implemented simplified reporting with biannual certification. These data are taken from various years of Food Stamp Program State Options Reports, and the Food and Nutrition Service of the U.S. Department of Agriculture. Data on whether a state implemented the Electronic Benefit Transfer (EBT) card system are taken from Danielson and Klerman (2006). These data are merged with the CES data, by state, month, and year.

8.5   Research Design

We start with a regression model describing the association between the food stamp caseload and expenditure pattern:

$$Y_{ijt} = \beta_j + \beta_t + \beta_m + \lambda FS_{jt} + Z_{jt}\Phi + X_{ijt}\Gamma + u_{ijt}$$

(1) $i = 1, \ldots, N \text{ (persons)}$

$j = 1, \ldots, 35 \text{ (states)}$

$t = 1994, \ldots, 2004 \text{ (years)}.$

In equation (1), Y_{ijt} is per capita expenditure per week on food by family i living in state j in year t, and is defined as a function of the per capita food stamp caseload FS_{jt}; time-varying state characteristics (Z_{jt}), namely unemployment rate and log per capita income; individual characteristics (X_{ijt}) namely age (dummy variables for six age groups: eighteen to twenty-three, twenty-four to twenty-nine, thirty to thirty-five, thirty-six to forty-one, forty-two to forty-seven, and forty-eight to fifty-four), race and ethnicity (Hispanic, non-Hispanic white, non-Hispanic black, Asian, and others), family income,[12] whether the family lives in an urban area, family size, number of children under eighteen, and number of persons in the family aged sixty-five or above, state effects (β_j), month of the year effects (β_m) and year effects (β_t). The coefficient λ estimates the association between the food stamp caseload and food expenditure. All estimates compute Huber/White/sandwich standard errors. Since most consumer units appear twice in the data, the standard errors are estimated by clustering around the consumer unit.[13]

One problem with equation (1) is that it assumes that state-specific changes in the food stamp caseload (FS_{jt}) were entirely caused by changes in social policy. Previous research suggests that a substantial proportion of

---

12. Income is measured before taxes and transfers and does not include the value of food stamps benefits.
13. We also estimated all models by clustering the standard errors around state-year. Clustering on state-year lowered standard errors in a few cases. Those results are available from the authors upon request.

the change in food stamp caseload was on account of economic trends (Danielson and Klerman 2006; Ziliak, Gundersen, and Figlio 2002). Those who left the FSP during 1994 to 2001 because of government policy may have different experiences (e.g., increased food insecurity) than those who left for other reasons such as robust economic growth (e.g., decline in food insecurity). The effect of exiting the FSP on consumption of the two groups will vary depending on the cause of leaving. To some extent, inclusion of time-varying state effects (e.g., unemployment rate and state per capita income) and year effects allows us to control for state-specific business trends and national business trends.[14] In addition, we estimate equation (1) after including a state-specific cubic time trend to control for business cycle effects that may be correlated with the food stamp caseload.

Further, to control for unobserved time-varying state effects correlated with the food stamp caseload, we can employ a comparison group research design that involves selecting two groups (a target group and a comparison group), similar in all aspects, except for their dependence on the FSP. To implement this approach, an equation similar to (1) is estimated for both groups. The comparison group is assumed to be unaffected by policy and, therefore, the estimated value of (λ_c) for this group would capture the effect of factors correlated with the food stamp caseload on food consumption. To obtain the effect of changes in the food stamp caseload triggered by social policy on the target group, we can subtract the estimated value of the association between the food stamp caseload and food expenditure for the comparison group from the corresponding estimate for the target group ($\lambda_t - \lambda_c$). The identifying assumption of this research design is that time-varying state effects correlated with the food stamp caseload affected the target and comparison groups in the same manner. We return to this issue when we describe in detail the target and comparison groups chosen for the analysis.

Changes in the FSP and welfare policies may have affected food expenditure patterns in low-income families through channels other than participation in the FSP. For example, the primary aim of the EBT cards was to restrict misuse and illegal sale of benefits. If EBT reduced the illegal sale of food stamps, it should increase spending on food even if the food stamp caseload remained constant. Similarly, TANF and the AFDC waivers may have affected family expenditures not only by changing eligibility and incentives for FSP participation, but also by changing life opportunities for single-mother families. Previous research documents that welfare reform induced low-educated single mothers to exit welfare and increase their employment (Blank 2002). To investigate how these changes in the FSP and welfare poli-

---

14. Year fixed effects control for national level trends such as changes in lifestyles resulting in increased number of meals obtained away from home and increase in consumption of food from fast-food restaurants (Demory-Luce 2005; French et al. 2001; Nicklas et al. 2001).

cies affected expenditures on food items, next, we estimate equation (1) by replacing the food stamp caseload variable (FS_{jt}) with a number of policy variables denoted by vector Pol_{mjt} as specified in equation (2).

(2) $Y_{ijt} = \beta'_j + \beta'_t + \beta'_m + \lambda' \, Pol_{mjt} + Z_{jt}\Phi' + X_{ijt}\Gamma' + u'_{ijt}.$

We study the effect of four policy variables: TANF, AFDC waiver, EBT, and simplified reporting (SR). All four policies are introduced in the model as dummy variables, equal to 1 if a state had that policy in month m and year t, otherwise 0. Further, the variable on AFDC waiver is set to zero once TANF is implemented in a state.

8.5.1   Target and Comparison Groups

The target group of this analysis is families headed by single mothers with a high school or lower education. According to the March Current Population Survey, during 1979 to 1994, on an average this group had a 50 percent risk of receiving food stamps. The selection of the comparison group, although critical to the validity of our research design, is challenging. It is difficult to find a perfect comparison group because families that are similar to the target group are also likely to be affected by policies for low-income families (welfare policies and changes in the FSP). Conversely, families that are unaffected by welfare and FSP policies are also not likely to be similar to the target group in terms of their experience of the business cycle and other time-varying effects correlated with policy. We select two-parent families with children in which mothers have a high school degree or lower education as the group of comparison. This group is relatively similar to the target group in terms of the mother's economic opportunities, but during the previous period, only nine percent of its members received food stamps. While the mother's marital status is not a criterion for eligibility to the FSP, single-mother families are more likely to be dependent on the FSP due to their relatively lower incomes. Note that since only half of the treatment group (low-educated, single mother-headed families) receives food stamps, and a small proportion of the comparison group also receives food stamps, the difference-in-difference estimates would yield a downward biased estimate of the effect of policy on FSP participation.

The identifying assumption in our research design is that time-varying factors correlated with the food stamp caseload (or social policies) affected food expenditures of the target and comparison groups in the same manner. One way to test the validity of this assumption is to examine trends in food expenditures of the target and comparison groups during a period of relatively no change in social policies. For the identifying assumption to be valid, the estimated value of $(\lambda_t - \lambda_c)$ during a period of no change in the FSP and welfare policies should be zero. Unfortunately, CES do not provide data on state identifiers prior to 1994; therefore, we cannot test our identifying assumption in a period of relatively stable food stamp and welfare policies.

However, we can examine trends in FSP participation of the target and comparison groups using other data sets. If the two groups experienced similar trends in FSP participation during a period of relatively no major change in the FSP, that may provide some evidence that the comparison group is an appropriate counterfactual for the target group.

We use the March Current Population Surveys and examine trends in FSP participation of the two groups during 1979 to 1990, a period when there were no major changes in policies that would have affected FSP participation. Figure 8.2 shows that during 1979 to 1990, FSP participation among the two groups fluctuated marginally without any clear long-term trend. Thus, the pre-1991 trend in FSP participation among families headed by single mothers with a high school or lower education appears to be similar to the pre-1991 trend in participation among two-parent families in which mothers have a high school or lower education providing some validity to our comparison group research design.

The FSP participation among single-mother families started rising around 1990, reaching a peak in 1993, fell sharply during 1993 to 2002, and has registered a modest rise since then. The trend in FSP participation among the comparison group (two-parent families) is somewhat similar to that of the target group, with the decline during 1993 to 2002 being relatively modest for the former. Since two-parent families were mostly unaffected by welfare reform, the decline in their dependence on food stamps during 1993 to 2001

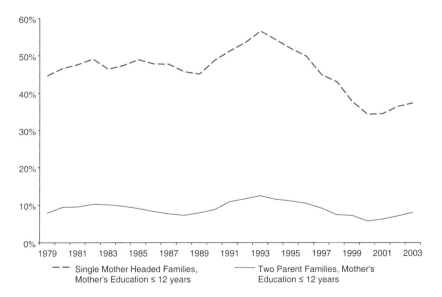

Fig. 8.2   Trends in FSP participation
Source: Authors' calculations based on the March Current Population Surveys, 1980 to 2004.

could be on account of the 1990s economic boom, while the decline experienced by single-mother families could be on account of both welfare reform as well as the 1990s economic boom. As mentioned, in the regression analysis we also include a rich set of variables to control for economic trends; for example, state unemployment rate and per capita income, year fixed effects, and a state-specific cubic trend.

The comparison group research design becomes more restrictive when we examine the effect of specific policies on expenditures. While the AFDC waivers and TANF primarily targeted low-educated, single-mother families, the other two policies relating to the FSP that we examine (EBT and Simplified Registration) targeted all low-income families, irrespective of mother's marital status. Hanratty (2006) found that Simplified Registration helped explain a much larger proportion of the increase in FSP participation since 2001 for two-parent families than it did for single-mother families. This finding questions the assumption that the experience of two-parent families is an appropriate counterfactual for testing the effect of EBT and SR on single-mother families.

We realize the limitations of the comparison group research methodology. Therefore, we believe it is most useful to simply present the estimates of the association between social policies (and food stamp caseload) on consumption patterns for the target and comparison groups, instead of explicitly estimating the difference-in-difference estimates. Doing so allows us to assess the credibility of the estimates, but also ensures that our estimates are not driven by trends in expenditures for the comparison group. It is most likely that the estimated effects based on equations (1) and (2) provide the effect of social policy changes and the food stamp caseload on the target group's food expenditure. If the estimates for the comparison group are large and statistically significant, that would suggest that there may be confounding factors affecting the target group estimates. At the very least, our approach identifies whether any observed effects of changes in the FSP and welfare reform on expenditure patterns are group-specific, and whether the effects are primarily found for the group of interest—the low-educated, single-mother target group.

8.6   Results

8.6.1   Descriptive Analysis

Table 8.1 provides average per capita weekly real (expressed in 2004 prices) expenditure on food items and patterns of expenditure among single-mother and two-parent families in which mothers have a high school or lower education. Each sample is further stratified by whether a family received food stamps in the previous year. During the period of our study, the per capita

Table 8.1   Per capita weekly food expenditure in low-educated families (mother's education ≤ HS) (Consumer Expenditure Survey, 1994 to 2004; expressed in 2004 prices)

	Single-mother families		Two-parent families	
	Received food stamp	Did not receive food stamp	Received food stamp	Did not receive food stamp
Total food expenditure	24.41	31.48	26.38	32.64
Food at home	19.69	21.04	19.12	21.80
Food away from home	4.72	10.44	7.26	10.85
Cereals and bakery products	3.02	3.33	2.82	3.33
Meat	5.69	5.95	5.25	5.81
Dairy products	2.37	2.42	2.25	2.66
Fruits and vegetables	2.80	3.24	2.91	3.34
Nonalcoholic beverages[a]	1.65	1.80	1.73	2.00
Alcoholic beverages	1.39	2.10	2.13	2.56
Other food at home	4.16	4.30	4.15	4.67
Food stamp amount	$12.14	—	$4.05	—
N	1,551	2,201	1,365	12,390

Note: Expenditure on cereals and bakery products, meat, dairy products, fruits and vegetables, nonalcoholic beverages, and other food at home sum to expenditure on food at home.
[a]Expenditure on alcoholic beverages is per adult population in the family, all other expenditures are expressed in per capita terms.

real weekly expenditure on food was $24 to $26 per week for families that received food stamps, and $31 to $33 for families that did not, depending on family structure. Overall, families on food stamps spent between 24 to 29 percent less on food. Finally, the average per capita weekly food stamp benefit was approximately 50 percent the expenditure on food in single-mother families who received any food stamps in a year. The corresponding number was 15 percent for two-parent families, suggesting relatively limited food stamps dependence among two-parent families.

Most of the difference in food expenditure between food stamp recipients and nonrecipients was on account of expenditure on food away from home. Among single-mother families, nonrecipients spent more than double of what recipients did on food away from home. In two-parent households the gap was relatively smaller, with food stamp recipients spending approximately 49 percent less on food away from home. This gap in expenditure on food away from home may be related to food stamps receipt as these cannot be used to buy restaurant food, or it may be due to differences in economic resources of recipients versus nonrecipients. Families on food stamps have lower incomes, and therefore, are less likely to spend on food away from home, which can be more expensive than homemade food. Expenditure on food away from home may also be related to the mother's employment status.

Mothers who work have higher earnings and are less likely to receive food stamps. They also have less time to prepare food at home, and thus spend more on food away from home.

Figures in table 8.1 also show that families receiving food stamps spent $19 to $20 per person per week on food at home, about 6 to 12 percent less than the corresponding expenditure in nonrecipient families, implying that food stamps do not entirely bridge the gap in food expenditure between the two groups. Single-mother families who received food stamps spent 16 percent less on average on fruits and vegetables as compared to those not on food stamps, 10 percent less on cereals, 5 percent less on meat, and 2 percent less on dairy products. Those on food stamps also spent a smaller proportion on beverages, alcoholic (one-third less) as well as nonalcoholic (8 percent less).[15] The story is more or less similar for two-parent families; those receiving food stamps spent less on food than those not on food stamps. These descriptive statistics on level and pattern of food expenditure suggest that food stamps do not bring complete parity in consumption levels of families receiving food stamps and those not receiving food stamps with relatively similar family structure and education levels. To investigate whether participation in the FSP affects consumption patterns in low-educated, single-mother households, we next study the association between the food stamp caseload (and social policies) and food expenditure using regression models presented in equations (1) and (2) that adjust for a rich set of control variables.

8.6.2   Multivariate Analysis

Table 8.2 presents the association between the food stamp caseload and food expenditure in families in which mothers have a high school or lower education. Columns (1) and (2) show results from a regression based on equation (1) in which the sample of analysis is restricted to families headed by single mothers and columns (3) and (4) present similar results for two-parent families. Each cell in this table is based on a separate regression. The dependent variable for each regression is listed in row headings. All models control for mother's age, race/ethnicity, family income,[16] whether she lives in an urban area, family size, number of children under eighteen, and number of persons in the family who are aged sixty-five or above, state monthly unemployment rate and per capita income, and state, year, and month fixed effects. Estimates in columns (2) and (4) also include an additional control

15. Food Stamps cannot be used to buy alcoholic beverages.
16. We used nine dummy variables as indicators for the following annual income (before tax and transfers) categories: < $5,000; $5,000 to $9,999; $10,000 to $14,999; $15,000 to $19,999; $20,000 to $29,999; $30,000 to $39,999; $40,000 to $49,999; $50,000 to $69,999 and $70,000 and over. We also repeated the analysis in table 8.2 in which we included controls for income net of transfers and taxes (continuous variable) but exclusive of food stamp benefits. The estimated effects were similar to those reported.

Table 8.2   **Estimated effects of per capita food stamp caseload on per capita weekly food expenditures in low-educated families (mother's education ≤ HS)**

Controls for state-specific cubic trend	Single-mother families		Two-parent families	
	No	Yes	No	Yes
Total food expenditure	0.941	2.655	–0.413	–2.341
	(0.722)	(3.584)	(0.362)	(2.570)
Food at home	0.415	–0.062	0.165	–2.813
	(0.563)	(2.898)	(0.242)	(1.747)
Food away from home	0.526	2.716*	–0.578**	0.473
	(0.355)	(1.616)	(0.246)	(1.999)
Cereals and bakery products	0.097	–1.180	0.043	–0.136
	(0.106)	(0.778)	(0.045)	(0.336)
Meat	0.202	0.981	0.074	–0.268
	(0.228)	(0.947)	(0.098)	(0.713)
Dairy products	0.046	0.256	0.005	–0.567**
	(0.065)	(0.361)	(0.033)	(0.229)
Fruits and vegetables	–0.045	–1.216**	0.008	–0.478
	(0.098)	(0.539)	(0.051)	(0.391)
Nonalcoholic beverages	0.058	0.269	–0.059*	–0.462*
	(0.064)	(0.342)	(0.035)	(0.261)
Alcoholic beverages	0.226	1.154	–0.251**	–0.179
	(0.194)	(1.154)	(0.099)	(0.790)
Other food at home	0.057	0.828	0.094	–0.903*
	(0.144)	(0.769)	(0.069)	(0.491)
N	3,249	3,249	11,471	11,471

Notes: Figures in each cell are based on a separate regression, using the Consumer Expenditure Survey, 1994 to 2004. Each regression controls for mothers' age, race/ethnicity, whether she lives in an urban area, family size, family income, number of children under eighteen, and number of persons in the family aged sixty-five or above, state monthly unemployment rate and per capita income, state, year, and month fixed effects. Regressions in columns (2) and (4) also include additional controls for a state-specific cubic trend. Expenditures are expressed in December 2004 dollars using the Bureau of Labor Statistics Food Price Index. Expenditure on alcoholic beverages is per adult in the family, all other expenditures are expressed in per capita terms. Heteroskodasticity adjusted standard errors clustered at consumer unit are in parentheses.

*** Significant at the 1 percent level.

** Significant at the 5 percent level.

* Significant at the 10 percent level.

for a state-specific cubic time trend.[17] Heteroskodasticity adjusted standard errors clustered at consumer unit are in parenthesis.

Figures in column (1) suggest that the food stamp caseload does not have any statistically significant effect on total food expenditure or on expenditures on major food items in single mother-headed families. All estimates

17. We also conducted analysis with state-specific quadratic trends. The estimated coefficients on the food stamp caseload variable were similar to those from models including state-specific cubic trends. We have opted to present a less restrictive trend here. The estimated coefficients using models with quadratic trends can be obtained upon request.

are small and statistically insignificant. The statistically insignificant point estimates indicate that a one percentage point increase in the per capita food stamp caseload raised total per capita weekly food expenditures in families headed by low-educated single mothers by a little less than a dollar, of which forty-two cents was spent on food at home, and fifty-three cents on food away from home.

During 1994 to 2004, the period covered by this study, the average per capita food stamp caseload was 8 percent, or 22.1 million participants. A one percentage point increase in per capita caseload is equivalent to expanding the program by adding 2.8 million more participants or a 12.5 percent increase in the food stamp caseload. Therefore, the previous estimates suggest that a 12.5 percent increase in the FSP would raise food expenditure in low-educated, single-mother families by 3.3 percent (based on the mean per capita weekly food expenditure of $28.56 incurred by families headed by low-educated single mothers during the period of this study).

One reason for these modest and statistically insignificant estimates could be that the expansions in food stamps we estimate have a relatively modest effect on the overall income of families headed by low-educated single mothers. In 2004, the maximum per capita weekly food stamp benefit was approximately $29 per person per week ($371 per month for a family of three). A 12.5 percent increase in the size of the program would mean a maximum increase in benefit amount of $3.6 per person per week, an increase too small to have much effect on an unconstrained consumer.[18] In addition, we may not have the power to detect such small-sized effect. Our statistically insignificant estimate implies a marginal propensity to consume (MPC) of around 0.26 (= 0.94 ÷ 3.6). Although crude, this estimate is not much different from the estimates from other studies; for example, Hoynes and Schanzenbach (2009) estimate a MPC for single mothers to be 0.296.

In regressions that include a state-specific cubic time trend (column [2]), the estimate of the association between the food stamp caseload and food expenditure in single-mother families remains statistically insignificant, but point estimate is larger. A 12.5 percent increase in exposure to the FSP increases total food expenditure in single-mother families by 9 percent, but all of the increase is on account of the rise in expenditure on food away from home. A 12.5 percent increase in the food stamp caseload is found to be associated with a $2.7 increase in per capita weekly expenditure on food away from home (or a 34 percent rise based on the mean expenditure of $8.08 on food away from home in single-mother families) and the coefficient

18. According to United States Department of Agriculture (USDA) estimates, income elasticity for food, beverages, and tobacco is 0.1; for clothing and footwear 0.9; for gross rent, fuel, and power 1.2; for house operations 1.2; for education 1.1, for medical care 1.2, for transportation and communication 1.2, and for recreation 1.3. These estimates are for the entire population and income elasticity for food is likely to be higher for low-income families (see: http://www.ers.usda.gov/Data/InternationalFoodDemand/).

is weakly significant ($p \leq 0.10$). Although food stamps cannot be used to buy restaurant food, families receiving food stamps may reallocate towards eating out the money they would otherwise have spent on food at home if they did not receive food stamps. Further, the analysis in column (2) suggests that a 12.5 percent increase in food stamp caseload is associated with a $1.22 reduction in expenditure on fruits and vegetables. This is a worrisome result as it suggests that the FSP adversely affects food quality. To further examine the association between food stamp participation and quality of food consumption, we estimated the association between the caseload and expenditure on fruits and vegetables, excluding potatoes. The estimated coefficient turned positive and weakly significant (coefficient = 1.12; s.e. = 0.51). This result suggests that the food stamp caseload is not associated with a decline in food quality (i.e., decline in consumption of fruits and vegetables). Since expenditure on potatoes is a tiny proportion (about 0.6 percent) of the total expenditure on food, we consider it prudent not to read too much into the positive and statistically significant association between the caseload and expenditure on fruits and vegetables (excluding potatoes).

Next, we investigate the association between the food stamp caseload and expenditure patterns in low-educated, two-parent families, who are much less likely to be at risk of food stamp receipt as compared to the single mother group. Therefore, any association between the food stamp caseload and expenditure on food for this group may be on account of omitted factors such as unobserved economic trends. Estimates suggest that the caseload has no statistically significant association with total expenditure on food or on food at home, using either of the two models (one that includes a state-specific cubic trend and one that does not).

In models that do not include state-specific time trends (column [3]), an increase in the food stamps caseload is associated with a decline in expenditure on food away from home and a fall in expenditure on alcoholic beverages in two-parent families, but the estimated coefficients turn statistically insignificant when state-specific trends are included as control variables. In models that include state-specific trends (column [4]), an increase in the food stamp caseload is associated with a decline in expenditure on dairy products, nonalcoholic beverages (weakly significant) and other food at home (weakly significant). Since two-parent, low-educated families face low-risk of receiving food stamps, these estimates may reflect that state-specific cubic trends perhaps do not fully control for the effect on expenditures relating to these food items of factors correlated with the food stamp caseload.

To sum up, our analysis so far suggests that expansions in the food stamp program, measured by increases in the food stamp caseload, do not appear to have any statistically significant effect on total expenditure on food and expenditure on most food items in low-educated, single mother-headed families. We also find some weak evidence that the caseload increase is associated with an increase in expenditure on food away from home in low-educated, single-mother families. It is possible that the expansions in the FSP that we measure have a rather small impact on family incomes and we don't have the power in our data to measure such small-sized effect.

Next, we investigate the association between welfare reform and changes in the FSP and the food stamp caseload. We regress the state per capita food stamp caseload on four policy variables[19] (EBT, SR, the AFDC waivers, and TANF) and state and year fixed effects. We first do the analysis on all states using the caseload data for 1994 to 2004, and then restrict the data to the thirty-five states for which we have state identifiers in the expenditure data. Estimates from this analysis are presented in table 8.3. These estimates suggest that EBT was associated with a 0.3 to 0.4 percentage points (or 4 to 5 percent, based on a per capita food stamp caseload of 8 percent) increase in the food stamp caseload; SR was associated with a statistically insignificant 0.2 percentage points (2.5 percent) increase in the food stamp caseload; the AFDC waivers were associated with a 0.3 to 0.5 percent (4 to 6 percent) decline in the caseload, and TANF was associated with a one percentage point (12.5 percent) decline in the food stamp caseload.

To evaluate these results against some of the other research in this area, we compare changes in the food stamp caseload during the period of our study. During 1994 to 2000, the per capita food stamp caseload fell from 10.5 to 6.1 percent. Our analysis suggests that 32 percent of this decline ($= 1.4 \div 4.4$) is associated with TANF and the AFDC waivers. Similarly, during 2001 to 2004, the per capita caseload increased from 6.1 to 8 percent, and our analysis suggests that 11 percent ($= 0.2 \div 1.9$) of the increase could be due to simplified reporting (although this estimate is statistically insignificant). Our analysis, although crude in comparison to the more sophisticated analysis in this field, confirms the general finding that social policy changes since the early 1990s help explain about a tenth to a third of the change in food stamp caseload.

Next, we examine how changes in the FSP and welfare policies affected expenditures on food using the model specified in equation (2). The results of this analysis are presented in tables 8.4 and 8.5. Models in table 8.4 include all the controls of the models in columns (1) and (3) in table 8.2, and models in table 8.5 also include additional controls for a state-specific cubic time trend.

In table 8.4, each row of a section is based on a single regression, and the dependent variable is listed in the row heading. Estimates of the effect of social policies on food expenditures—total as well as on various items—are small and statistically insignificant except for the effect on expenditure on meat. Our estimates suggest that the EBT cards increased weekly per capita

19. A policy variable is equal to 1 if a state had that policy throughout year t. In cases where a state implemented a policy during a year, the policy variable is equal to the fraction of the year that the policy was in place. If a state did not have a certain policy throughout the year the variable is equal to 0.

Table 8.3   **Effect of social policies on the per capita food stamp caseload**

	Per capita food stamp caseload			
Electronic Benefit Transfer	-0.335	0.378***	0.175	0.278*
	(0.330)	(0.144)	(0.348)	(0.159)
Simplified Reporting	1.483***	0.181	1.462***	0.165
	(0.369)	(0.170)	(0.371)	(0.189)
AFDC waiver	-0.613**	-0.487**	-0.880***	-0.316
	(0.250)	(0.193)	(0.256)	(0.204)
TANF	-2.353***	-0.972**	-2.595***	-1.050**
	(0.362)	(0.430)	(0.378)	(0.449)
State and year fixed effects	No	Yes	No	Yes
Sample restricted to 35 states in the CES sample	No	No	Yes	Yes

Note: Standard errors are in parentheses.
*** Significant at the 1 percent level.
** Significant at the 5 percent level.
* Significant at the 10 percent level.

expenditure on meat products by $1.2 (a 21 percent increase over the average weekly per capita expenditure of $5.84), and TANF increased weekly per capita expenditure on meat products by $2.14 (37 percent). All other estimated effects were small in size and statistically insignificant.

Section "Two-parent families" of table 8.4 presents regression results for two-parent, low-educated families. The EBT card system is associated with an increase in expenditure on food at home (weakly significant), meat (weakly significant), and expenditure on other food at home. Simplified reporting appears to have had no effect on expenditures on any of the food items or total food expenditure. The AFDC waivers raised expenditures on food at home, cereals and bakery products (weakly significant), fruits and vegetables; TANF raised expenditures on nonalcoholic beverages. Since the AFDC waivers and TANF did not have much effect on two-parent families, these statistically significant results suggest that our model does not fully capture the effect of time-varying factors that may be correlated with policy.

Next, we estimate models with additional controls for state-specific cubic time trends. The results from these regressions are presented in table 8.5, which has the same layout as table 8.4. Again, there appears to be no estimated effect of social policy changes on total food expenditures, expenditures on food at home and food away from home in low-educated, single-mother families. The estimated effect of policies on expenditures on specific items are also small and insignificant except for the effect of simplified reporting on alcoholic beverages, of AFDC waivers on expenditures on dairy products, and the effect of TANF on nonalcoholic beverages. These estimates suggest that simplified reporting was associated with a $2.32 reduction in per

Table 8.4   Estimated effects of Electronic Benefit Transfer, Simplified Reporting, TANF, and the AFDC waivers on per capita weekly food expenditures in low-educated families (mother's education ≤ HS)

	Single-mother families				Two-parent families			
Dependent variable	Electronic Benefit Transfer	Simplified reporting	AFDC waiver	TANF	Electronic Benefit Transfer	Simplified reporting	AFDC waiver	TANF
Total food expenditure	-0.060	-2.628	-0.300	5.073	1.269	-1.812	1.862	1.479
	(2.789)	(2.276)	(2.794)	(4.134)	(0.966)	(1.283)	(1.446)	(1.862)
Food at home	1.459	-1.731	-0.389	3.818	1.343*	-0.832	1.926**	1.292
	(1.619)	(1.719)	(2.345)	(3.091)	(0.691)	(0.791)	(0.978)	(1.438)
Food away from home	-1.518	-0.897	0.089	1.255	-0.074	-0.979	-0.064	0.187
	(2.034)	(1.362)	(1.100)	(2.072)	(0.557)	(0.895)	(0.982)	(1.012)
Cereals and bakery products	-0.002	-0.330	0.059	0.227	-0.046	0.046	0.335*	0.159
	(0.280)	(0.346)	(0.379)	(0.560)	(0.136)	(0.134)	(0.175)	(0.253)
Meat	1.180*	-0.839	0.268	2.143*	0.483*	-0.228	0.652	0.607
	(0.674)	(0.672)	(0.906)	(1.226)	(0.284)	(0.342)	(0.470)	(0.619)
Dairy products	0.062	-0.253	-0.312	0.355	0.109	-0.146	0.103	0.182
	(0.192)	(0.202)	(0.265)	(0.339)	(0.095)	(0.108)	(0.118)	(0.187)
Fruits and vegetables	0.224	-0.386	-0.236	0.455	0.142	-0.253	0.641***	0.416
	(0.287)	(0.337)	(0.412)	(0.581)	(0.142)	(0.162)	(0.214)	(0.267)
Nonalcoholic beverages	-0.245	0.226	-0.063	0.159	0.098	-0.105	0.099	0.396**
	(0.183)	(0.198)	(0.241)	(0.330)	(0.094)	(0.111)	(0.151)	(0.197)
Alcoholic beverages	-0.374	-0.079	-0.755	-0.231	-0.281	-0.193	0.533	0.179
	(0.564)	(0.643)	(0.587)	(1.103)	(0.319)	(0.377)	(0.478)	(0.546)
Other food at home	0.240	-0.149	-0.105	0.480	0.556***	-0.145	0.095	-0.468
	(0.410)	(0.477)	(0.572)	(0.744)	(0.192)	(0.229)	(0.274)	(0.394)

Notes: Figures in each row of a panel are based on a separate regression using the Consumer Expenditure Survey, 1994 to 2004. Panel heading describes the sample of analysis. Each regression controls for mothers' age, race/ethnicity, whether she lives in an urban area, family size, family income, and per capita income, number of children under eighteen, and number of persons in the family aged sixty-five or above, state monthly unemployment rate and per capita income, state, year, and month fixed effects. Expenditures are expressed in December 2004 dollars using the Bureau of Labor Statistics Food Price Index. Expenditure on alcoholic beverages is per adult in the family, all other expenditures are expressed in per capita terms. Heteroskodasticity adjusted standard errors clustered at consumer unit are in parentheses.

*** Significant at the 1 percent level.
** Significant at the 5 percent level.
* Significant at the 10 percent level.

Table 8.5 Estimated effects of Electronic Benefit Transfer, Simplified Reporting, TANF, and the AFDC waivers on per capita weekly food expenditures in low-educated families (mother's education ≤ HS) (Includes controls for a state-specific cubic trend)

Dependent variable	Single-mother families				Two-parent families			
	Electronic Benefit Transfer	Simplified reporting	AFDC waiver	TANF	Electronic Benefit Transfer	Simplified reporting	AFDC waiver	TANF
Total food expenditure	-2.880	0.651	-7.178	4.155	-0.738	-0.691	-0.089	-0.514
	(5.375)	(4.306)	(5.121)	(5.389)	(1.906)	(3.106)	(2.674)	(2.455)
Food at home	-0.006	1.850	-5.696	1.064	1.299	-0.883	0.411	-0.802
	(4.155)	(3.172)	(4.777)	(4.414)	(1.298)	(1.804)	(2.105)	(1.918)
Food away from home	-2.874	-1.199	-1.482	3.092	-2.037*	0.192	-0.500	0.288
	(2.754)	(2.628)	(2.200)	(2.514)	(1.161)	(2.316)	(1.409)	(1.319)
Cereals and bakery products	-0.698	0.255	-0.468	-0.480	-0.017	0.067	0.150	-0.212
	(0.608)	(0.622)	(0.772)	(0.927)	(0.235)	(0.306)	(0.390)	(0.355)
Meat	1.091	0.504	-1.376	1.329	0.506	-0.192	0.344	-0.438
	(1.606)	(1.188)	(1.744)	(1.588)	(0.487)	(0.736)	(0.836)	(0.762)
Dairy products	-0.082	-0.290	-1.123**	-0.149	-0.049	-0.085	0.063	0.047
	(0.439)	(0.341)	(0.551)	(0.547)	(0.186)	(0.217)	(0.265)	(0.267)
Fruits and vegetables	0.049	0.387	-0.519	0.935	0.256	-0.608*	-0.090	-0.090
	(0.817)	(0.574)	(1.031)	(1.004)	(0.287)	(0.346)	(0.448)	(0.347)
Nonalcoholic beverages	-0.092	0.058	-0.822	-0.884**	-0.091	-0.141	0.030	0.270
	(0.441)	(0.341)	(0.507)	(0.406)	(0.177)	(0.223)	(0.250)	(0.268)
Alcoholic beverages	-0.215	-2.315*	-1.239	1.612	-0.752	-0.289	-0.047	-0.598
	(1.495)	(1.181)	(1.304)	(2.180)	(0.576)	(0.602)	(0.944)	(0.668)
Other food at home	-0.275	0.935	-1.389	0.313	0.693*	0.076	-0.086	-0.378
	(0.965)	(0.860)	(1.172)	(1.168)	(0.382)	(0.488)	(0.583)	(0.520)

Notes: Figures in each row of a panel are based on a separate regression using the Consumer Expenditure Survey, 1994 to 2004. Panel heading describes the sample of analysis. Each regression controls for mothers' age, race/ethnicity, whether she lives in an urban area, family size, family income, number of children under eighteen, and number of persons in the family aged sixty-five or above, state monthly unemployment rate and per capita income, state, year, and month fixed effects and a state-specific cubic trend. Expenditures are expressed in December 2004 dollars using the Bureau of Labor Statistics Food Price Index. Expenditure on alcoholic beverages is per adult in the family, all other expenditures are expressed in per capita terms. Heteroskodasticity adjusted standard errors clustered at consumer unit are in parentheses.

*** Significant at the 1 percent level.

** Significant at the 5 percent level.

* Significant at the 10 percent level.

capita weekly expenditure on alcoholic beverages, the AFDC waivers were associated with a $1.12 decline in per capita weekly expenditure on dairy products, and TANF was associated with a $0.88 decline in expenditure on nonalcoholic beverages. All other estimates are small and statistically insignificant.

Estimated effects of changes in policies on food expenditures in two-parent families were also small and statistically insignificant, except for the effect of the EBT cards on expenditure on food away from home, which is negative (weakly significant), and the effect of simplified reporting on fruits and vegetables, which is also negative (weakly significant).

To sum up, our analysis confirms the findings from previous research that changes in the FSP and welfare reform help explain a tenth to a third of the change in the food stamp caseload. But we do not find any consistent association between these policies and food expenditures. Most models show that none of the four policies studied in this chapter had any statistically significant effect on total food expenditure. In some models, we found that TANF and EBT were associated with increased expenditure on meat products, but these effects disappeared when we used more rigorous models; that is, controlling for state-specific cubic trends. In some models we also found that TANF was associated with a decline in expenditure of nonalcoholic beverages, the AFDC waivers were associated with a decline in expenditures on dairy products, and simplified reporting discouraged expenditure of alcoholic beverages.

8.7   Conclusion

In this chapter, we investigate the effect of the Food Stamp Program in the United States on food expenditures in families headed by low-educated, single mothers during 1994 to 2004. We first study the association between the food stamp caseload and pattern and quantity of food expenditures. Our analysis suggests that the food stamp caseload does not have any statistically significant association with total expenditure on food. The point estimates were small and statistically insignificant. We also find some weak evidence that an increase in the caseload was associated with an increase in expenditure on food away from home, but the estimated associations between the caseload and expenditures on food items were small and statistically insignificant. It is possible that the expansions in the FSP that we measure have a rather small impact on family incomes and we do not have the power in our data to measure such small-sized effect. Our results, thus, support findings from some of the earlier analysis that the Food Stamp Program does not have any statistically significant effect on food consumption (Moffitt 1989).

We find that while the introduction of the EBT cards and simplified reporting were associated with an increase in food stamp participation (caseload), federal and state welfare reforms caused a decline in the caseload. Our analysis suggests that 32 percent of the decline in the food stamp caseload during 1994 and 2000 was associated with the implementation of TANF and the AFDC waivers, and 11 percent of the increase in the caseload during 2001 to 2004 could be due to simplified reporting. However, we do not find any evidence that these changes in the Food Stamp Program had any effect on total food expenditure, nor do we find any evidence that TANF or the AFDC waivers caused any statistically significant changes in spending on food.

Our analysis of the effect of social policy changes on expenditures on specific food items suggests that the AFDC waivers were associated with a decline in expenditure on dairy products and TANF was associated with a decline in expenditure of nonalcoholic beverages and some weak evidence that simplified reporting discouraged expenditure of alcoholic beverages.

References

Battistin, Erich. 2003. Errors in survey reports of consumer expenditures. The Institute for Fiscal Studies. Working Paper W03/07.

Blank, R. 2002. Evaluating welfare reform in the United States. *Journal of Economic Literature* 40 (4): 1–43.

Borjas, G. 2004. Food insecurity and public assistance. *Journal of Public Economics* 88:1421–43.

Bureau of Labor Statistics (BLS). 2005. 2003 consumer expenditure interview survey public use microdata documentation. Available at: http://www.bls.gov/cex/csxintvw .pdf.

Chen, Z., S. T. Yen, and D. B. Eastwood. 2005. Effects of food stamp participation on body weight and obesity. *American Journal of Agricultural Economics* 87 (5): 1167–73.

Currie, J., and J. Grogger. 2001. Explaining recent declines in food stamps program participation. In *Brookings-Wharton Papers on Urban Affairs,* ed. W. Gale and J. Rothenberg-Pack, 203–44. Washington, DC: Brookings Institution Press.

Danielson, C., and J. A. Klerman. 2006. Why did the food stamp caseload decline (and rise)? Effects of policies on the economy. Rand Corporation. Working paper WR 386.

Demory-Luce, D. 2005. Fast food and children and adolescents: Implications for practitioners. *Clinical Pediatrics* 44:279–88.

Devaney, B., and R. Moffitt. 1991. Dietary effects of the food stamp program. *American Journal of Agricultural Economics* 73 (1): 202–11.

Drewnowski, A. 2003. Fat and sugar: An economic analysis. Symposium: Sugar and fat-from genes to culture. *Journal of Nutrition* 133 (3): 838S–840S.

Fox, M. K., W. Hamilton, and B. H. Lin. 2004. *Effects of food assistance and nutrition programs on nutrition and health.* U.S. Department of Agriculture, Food Assistance and Nutrition Research Report no. 33871. Washington, DC: Food and Rural Economics Division, Economic Research Service.

Fraker, T. M., A. P. Martini, and J. C. Ohls. 1995. The effect of food stamp cashout on food expenditures: An assessment of the findings from four demonstrations. *The Journal of Human Resources* 30 (4): 633–49.

French, S. A., M. Story, D. Neumark-Sztainer, J. Fulkerson, and P. Hannah. 2001. Fast food restaurant use among adolescents: Associations with nutrient intake, food choices and behavioral and psychosocial variables. *International Journal of Obesity and Related Metabolic Disorders* 25 (12): 1823–33.

Frongillo, E. A. 2003. Understanding obesity and program participation in the context of poverty and food insecurity. *Journal of Nutrition* 133:2117–18.

Gibson, D. 2003. Food stamp program participation is positively related to obesity in low income women. *Journal of Nutrition* 133:2225–31.

———. 2004. Long-term food stamp program participation is differentially related to overweight in young girls and boys. *Journal of Nutrition* 134:372–9.

Hanratty, M. J. 2006. Has the food stamp program become more accessible? Impacts of recent changes in reporting requirements and asset eligibility limits. *Journal of Policy Analysis and Management* 25 (3): 603–21.

Hoynes, H. W., and D. Schanzenbach. 2009. Consumption responses to in-kind transfers: Evidence from the introduction of the food stamp program. *American Economic Journal: Applied Economics* 1 (4): 109–39.

Kabbani, N. S., and P. E. Wilde. 2003. Short recertification periods in the U.S. food stamp program. *Journal of Human Resources* 38 (S): 1112–38.

Kaushal, N. 2007. Do food stamps cause obesity? Evidence from immigrant experience. *Journal of Health Economics* 26 (5): 968–91.

Krueger, P. M. 2004. To help or to harm? Food stamp receipt and mortality risk prior to the 1996 welfare reform act. *Social Forces* 82 (4): 1573–99.

Moffitt, R. 1989. Estimating the value of an in-kind transfer: The case of food stamps. *Econometrica* 57 (2): 385–409.

Nicklas, T. A., T. Baranowski, K. W. Cullen, and G. Berenson. 2001. Eating patterns, dietary quality and obesity. *Journal of the American College of Nutrition* 20 (6): 599–608.

Senauer, B., and N. Young. 1986. The impact of food stamps on food expenditures: Rejection of the traditional model. *American Journal of Agricultural Economics* 68 (1): 37–43.

Shapiro, J. M. 2005. Is there a daily discount rate? Evidence from the food stamp nutrition cycle. *Journal of Public Economics* 89:303–25.

U.S. Government Accounting Office (GAO). 2004. Food stamp program: Farm bill options ease administrative burden, but opportunities exist to streamline participant reporting rules among programs. GAO-04-916, September. Washington, DC: GPO.

———. 2008. Food stamp program: Options for delivering financial incentives to participants for purchasing targeted foods. GAO-08-415, July. Washington, DC: GPO.

Ver Ploeg, M., L. Mancino, B.-H. Lin, and C.-Y. Wang. 2007. The vanishing weight gap: Trends in obesity among adult food stamp participants. *Economics & Human Biology* 5 (1): 20–36.

Whitmore, D. 2002. What are food stamps worth? Princeton University, Department of Economics, Industrial Relations. Working Paper 847.

Wilde, E. P., and C. K. Ranney. 2000. The monthly food stamp cycle: Shopping frequency and food intake decisions in an endogenous switching regression framework. *American Journal of Agricultural Economics* 82 (1): 200–13.

Wilde, P., P. Cook, C. Gundersen, M. Nord, and L. Tiehen. 2000. *The decline in food stamp program participation in the 1990's.* U.S. Department of Agriculture, Economic Research Service. Food Assistance and Nutrition Research Report no. 7.

Yen, S. T., M. Andrews, Z. Chen, and D. B. Eastwood. 2008. Food stamp program participation and food insecurity: An instrumental variables approach. *American Journal of Agricultural Economics* 90 (1): 117–32.

Zedlewski, S., and S. Brauner. 1999. *Are the steep declines in food stamp participation linked to falling welfare caseload?* Policy Brief no. B–3. Washington, DC: The Urban Institute.

Ziliak, J. P., C. Gundersen, and D. N. Figlio. 2003. Food stamp caseloads over the business cycle. *Southern Economic Journal* 69 (4): 903–19.

Physical Activity
Economic and Policy Factors

Melayne M. McInnes and Judith A. Shinogle

9.1 Introduction

While much research has focused on the costs of obesity and economic factors that drive obesity growth, little economic research has examined the factors that contribute to obesity—physical inactivity and poor nutrition. This chapter will examine correlates and predictors of physical activity over time with emphasis on economic factors. Using data for adults from the 2000 to 2005 Behavioral Risk Factor Surveillance System (BRFSS) survey, we examine the characteristics of individuals and their environments that determine their level of activity. Because BRFSS includes state and county codes for each individual, we are able to include additional information regarding economic variables such as price and supply variables.

9.2 Background

As more attention has been focused on the rising levels of obesity (defined as a Body Mass Index (BMI) of 30 or greater) in the United States, it is important to consider whether obesity trends are due to rising caloric intake, falling levels of activity, or both. Many studies have considered the economic factors that drive the obesity epidemic and caloric intake (Cutler et al. 2003; Anderson, Butcher, and Levine 2003; Rashad 2006; Smith, Bogin, and Bishai 2005; Bleich et al. 2007; Rashad and Markowitz 2007; Baum and

Melayne M. McInnes is associate professor of economics in the Moore School of Business at the University of South Carolina. Judith A. Shinogle is a senior economist at the Maryland Institute for Policy Analysis and Research.

We thank Jim Sallis and participants at the NBER Conference on Economic Aspects of Obesity for excellent comments and Chad Cotti for sharing data on sin taxes.

Ruhm 2007; Philipson 2001; Chou, Grossman, and Saffer 2004), but the physical activity side of the equation has received comparatively little attention. Even if changes in physical activity are not to blame for the dramatic changes in obesity, policies aimed at increasing physical activity may be a part of the solution. Understanding the determinants of physical activity is an important first step in determining whether policies aimed at increasing physical activity levels can be useful levers in reducing overall obesity levels.

9.3   Physical Activity and Health

Physical activity has unique health consequences. Murphy et al. (2007) find that activity as minimal as walking improves blood pressure control, lowers body fat percentages, and decreases BMI. Church et al. (2007) examines postmenopausal women with high blood pressure and finds that physical activity, even at low doses, improves cardiorespiratory fitness no matter the weight of the person. Other health research on the effects of obesity is starting to find that activity levels are important predictors of outcomes. Katzmarzyk, Church, and Blair (2004) find adding cardiorespiratory fitness to models comparing mortality (all cause and cardiovascular deaths) for men with metabolic syndrome to healthy men causes the association to be insignificant. They find that cardiorespiratory fitness provides a strong protective effect.

Besides examining health effects of physical activity, other researchers have estimated the impact of inactivity on medical expenditures. Keeler et al. (1989) find that those with sedentary lifestyles incur higher medical costs, but their life expectancy is less so they collect less public and private pensions. At a 5 percent rate of discount for future dollars, the lifetime subsidy from others to those with a sedentary lifestyle is estimated at $1,900. One more recent study examines the cost of inactivity to a health plan. Garret et al. (2004), utilizing a cost of illness methodology, finds that inactivity costs $86 million in one health plan. Another study utilizes the disease-by-disease epidemiological approach to examine the impact of inactivity in Canada. Katzmarzyk, Gledhil, and Shephard (2000) find that 2.5 percent of total direct health care costs in Canada in 1999 are attributable to physical inactivity. They further estimate that approximately 21,000 lives were lost prematurely in 1995 due to inactivity. Pratt, Macera, and Wang (2000) use the 1987 National Medical Expenditure Survey to perform a stratified analysis of medical expenditures and find that people who were physically active report an adjusted average annual medical expenditure of $1,019 compared to $1,349 for those who report being inactive. Shinogle (2008) uses linked National Health Interview Survey (NHIS) to Medical Expenditure Panel Survey (MEPS) to estimate the inactivity attributable fraction of medical expenditures range from 11 percent to 16 percent. In these models, inactivity did not significantly increase the probability of a medical expenditure but did increase the level of expenditures. This result may reflect that physically active people have an unobserved taste for preventive health measures. This taste for prevention services is also indicated in the following analysis of the 2000 to 2005 National Health Interview Survey. Examining office-based visits by physically active people (as defined by the Centers for Disease Control and Prevention [CDC]) we find that active people are more likely to have one to two visits but less likely to have a higher number of office visits based on visits in the past twelve months (see table 9.1). On the other hand, examining emergency room visits and the number of overnight hospital days, we find the opposite association: physically active people have fewer of these more expensive medical uses.

9.4   Trends in Physical Activity

In light of the obesity epidemic, it is perhaps surprising that Americans are spending more of their time and income on leisure, and at least some of that is going to physical activity (Sturm 2004). Between 1965 and 2000, industries catering to leisure activity are generally growing more quickly than the overall economy, but a disproportionate share of this growth is in sedentary activities (such as cable tv viewing) rather than more active pursuits (sports clubs, dance studios). Nonetheless, time spent in physical activity is increasing. Sturm's analysis shows that between 1990 and 2000, the median increase in reported physical activity is twenty minutes per week. While most Americans still do not meet federal recommendations for physical activity, the CDC (2004) reports that between 1988 and 2002, there has been a 9 percentage point drop in the prevalence of no leisure time physical activity. Estimates of physical activity trends vary depending on the survey and questions used. As shown in table 9.2, the National Health Interview Survey (NHIS) finds around 30 percent of the adult population is inactive. This can be compared to estimates from the BRFSS showing that approximately 77 percent of the adult population participates in any leisure time physical activity in the past thirty days. While it is encouraging that the majority of Americans report getting some physical activity, a much lower percent report regularly engaging in moderate or vigorous exercise. The BRFSS estimates that approximately 25 percent of the population is involved in vigorous physical activity while 46 percent are involved in moderate or vigorous physical activity.

9.5   Physical Activity and Economics

Perhaps the most intriguing evidence of a link between physical fitness, health, and economic factors comes from Chris Ruhm's studies of age-adjusted mortality over the business cycle (2005, 2000). Ruhm finds that

Table 9.1   **Health care utilization by activity status**

Number of occurrences in past 12 months	Not regularly active (%)	Regularly active (%)
Office visits for regularly active compared to not regularly active		
0	20.1	17.8
1	15.5	18.7
2 to 3	23.5	28.0
4 to 5	13.8	13.8
6 to 7	7.1	6.6
8 to 9	4.0	3.2
10 to 12	6.5	5.0
13 to 15	2.6	1.9
16 or more	6.9	5.0
	$p < 0.001$	
Visits to ER for regularly active compared to not regularly active		
0	78.11	81.81
1	13.52	12.81
2 to 3	5.92	4.23
4 to 5	1.35	0.65
6 to 7	0.48	0.21
8 to 9	0.17	0.09
10 to 12	0.22	0.10
13 to 15	0.06	0.03
16 or more	0.15	0.06
	$p < 0.001$	
Times in hospital overnight for regularly active compared to not regularly active		
0	88.4	92.8
1	8.4	5.9
2	1.9	0.9
3	0.7	0.2
>3	0.6	0.2
	$p < 0.001$	

Source: Shinogle (2008).

Table 9.2   **Estimates of physical activity (PA) from two surveys 2001–2005**

	Percent of adult population				
	2001	2002	2003	2004	2005
NHIS: "inactive"	29.9	30.1	29.5	30.4	29.3
BRFSS: "any exercise"	75.9	76.9	77.2	77.3	77.6
BRFSS: "vigorous PA"			25.0		24.5
BRFSS: "moderate or vigorous PA"			45.6		45.7

Source: Authors' tabulations from NHIS and BRFSS.

declines in mortality during temporary economic downturns are accompanied by increases in leisure time physical activity, declines in BMI, and smoking. These changes disproportionately occur among the least active, most severely obese, and heaviest smokers, respectively. Ruhm's findings point to the important role that economic levers can have in shaping physical activity levels and the need to better understand the relationships between lifestyle behaviors such as physical activity and smoking. If there are economies of scope in reducing unhealthy behaviors, then policymakers may be able to exploit this when designing a policy that ostensibly targets only one of these behaviors.

More recently, using the BRFSS 1996 to 2000, Rashad (2006) develops a model of cycling propensity and the health gains that result. Cycling rates are lower for those who are working, those with higher incomes, and females. She also finds that cycling rates respond negatively to urban sprawl and real gas prices, and that increased cycling is associated with significant health gains.

Another important aspect in the economics of physical activity is the time constraint. Mullahy and Rober (2008) examine the 2005 and 2006 American Time Use Study to explore factors associated with time spent in physical activity (PA). They find differences not only by gender but also by when the time is spent—during the week or on weekends. Education is associated with increased physical activity on weekends/holidays for both men and women. Males show a decline in physical activity as they age, and males with spouses have lower physical activity than those without. For females, physical activity is reduced on weekends and holidays. Further research is warranted on how shocks in time use (such as children, marriage, job change) affect physical activity.

9.6   Physical Activity and Policy

Policies directly aimed at promoting greater physical activity have almost exclusively focused on physical education in schools (Yancey et al. 2007). Increased physical education requirements generally do translate into more minutes of PE, but do not appear to alter obesity levels and do not clearly increase physical activity (Cawley, Meyerhoefer, and Newhouse 2005). Policy targeting the built environment may also promote physical activity, given studies that find the proximity and attractiveness of recreational facilities does appear to promote physical activity (Yancey et al. 2007). State and local spending on parks and recreation increases the likelihood and amount of participation in outdoor sports (Humphreys and Ruseki 2007). Outdoor sports, however, are a small component of physical activity (only 5 percent of BRFSS participants report participation in outdoor recreation such as backpacking, fishing, hiking, or waterskiing), and other more common forms of exercise, such as walking, were not affected by state spending levels.

The built environment is a key issue for policy aimed at increasing physical activity. Brownson, Boehmer, and Luke (2005) examine trends in activity for leisure, work, travel, and related behaviors and find that a combination of changes in the built environment and an increase in proportion of the population engaging in sedentary behaviors (such as television viewing) puts a significant part of the population at risk for physical inactivity. Another recent study finds that counties with a Walmart® are associated with lower physical activity, but the BMI in these counties is actually lower than those without a Walmart®. Adults in counties with Walmarts® have higher fruit and vegetable consumption and lower fat consumption than counties without a Walmart®. Having lower priced commodities close by increases the purchasing power of consumers, allowing for the purchase of higher cost, healthier foods (Courtemanche and Carden 2008).

Other government policies may have unintended spillover effects that indirectly promote or discourage physical activity levels. Rashad's study of cycling suggests that gas taxes may have an unintended benefit in terms of promoting physical activity. Other policies, such as those aimed at reducing smoking, may also have unintended consequences for physical activity. Clean indoor air policies and cigarette prices are both weakly associated with increased BMI (Chou, Grossman, and Saffer 2004, 2006). Given possible interactions between lifestyle behaviors, the spillover effects from policies aimed at reducing smoking are difficult to predict. Former smokers and less intense smokers may find leisure physical activity more enjoyable and more necessary to compensate for weight gain. On the other hand, when mandated to reduce risk along one margin, individuals may choose to offset this by increasing risk along another margin (Pelzman 1975). We discuss these effects in more detail later.

9.7   Basic Model of Economic Determinants of Physical Activity

In a model of household production, the price of physical activity includes the opportunity cost of time and the cost of inputs to physical activity. Thus, we consider later on factors that affect the individual's opportunity cost of time (such as education and income) as well as some input prices. We also consider whether environmental variables, such as availability of parks and crime rates, have an effect on physical activity levels. We also consider whether transportation costs and availability affect physical activity. An important question is whether other health behaviors are substitutes or complements with physical activity. For example, if one thinks of smoking as a weight reduction device, would the decrease in smoking cause individuals to find other weight reduction behavior such as physical activity? On the other hand, if smoking is an indicator for overall risky health behavior, a change in smoking would not affect physical activity. We make similar arguments for drinking.

Suppose that the individual receives utility from health H, physical activity A, and other goods Z as measured by the utility function $U(H, A, Z)$. Health depends on physical activity A and consumption of goods Z: $H(A, Z)$. Individuals produce physical activity by combining time and other exercise inputs (gym services, exercise equipment, natural amenities, physical trainer services, etc.): $A = A(x_A, t_A)$. Time inputs include the time spent in the activity as well as any travel time incurred to get to the bike path, gym, safe neighborhood for walking, or other exercise venue.

The vector Z includes goods that may be complements or substitutes for physical activity in two different pathways: (a) consumption, and (b) production of health. For a consumption example, a person might substitute an hour of drinking in a pub with friends for an hour of sailing, depending on which is cheaper. On the production side, a person who does not value exercise for it's own sake might increase activity levels if this were to enhance the productivity of other inputs to the health production. For example, reduced smoking may increase the productivity of exercise making the two complements in production. The consumer is assumed to maximize utility $U(H, A, Z)$ subject to the time constraint and income constraints yielding the Langrangian:

$$L = U(H(A, Z), A, Z)$$
$$- \lambda_m[\text{Income} = p_A X_A + p_Z X_Z + w X_A + w X_Z] - \lambda_t[24 = t_A + t_w + t_z].$$

Assuming that both constraints are binding, and treating A as the choice variable, we can write the Lagrangian in terms of the full income constraint as:

$$L = U(H(A, Z), A, Z) - \lambda[w24 = p_A X_A + p_Z X_Z + wt_A + wt_Z].$$

The first order condition for the level of physical activity is then:

$$U_H H_A + U_A = \lambda[p_A \partial X_A/\partial A + p_A \partial t_A/\partial A].$$

The left-hand side shows that the marginal benefit of physical activity includes the indirect effect through the health production as well as from the direct effect from enjoyment of the activity (or disutility, as individual tastes dictate.) The right-hand side measures the full price of physical activity and includes the opportunity cost of time, as well as the price of physical activity inputs. This first order condition applies to individuals who engage in some physical activity, but a substantial fraction of the population will be at a corner solution with:

$$U_H H_A + U_A - \lambda[p_A \partial X_A/\partial A + p_A \partial t_A/\partial A] < 0.$$

The first-order condition from this simple static model suggests several ways in which policy and price changes affect an individual's level of physical activity.

Own price. Policies that affect the full price of exercise include anything that reduces the cost of inputs to physical activity or the time cost of engaging in exercise. For example, the construction of new parks will reduce the travel time of individuals who live near the park. The built environment, which may affect the cost of exercise as well as the enjoyment of exercise, has been the subject of much study and the results are mixed. For example, Forsyth et al. (2007) find no relationship between residential density and overall physical activity. Decreases in physical activity on the job in combination with rising wages may both increase the opportunity cost of exercise (Philipson 2001). Our model includes measures of education, income, and employment status as factors that affect the opportunity cost of time. Because factors may also affect the cost of missed work due to poor health and the efficiency of health production, we do not have an unambiguous prediction of sign.

Prices of related goods. In looking at the effects of alcohol and tobacco prices on BMI and obesity, Cho, Grossman, and Saffer (2004, 2006) find that both weight measures increase with cigarette prices but decrease with alcohol prices. Thus, they suggest that calories and cigarettes are substitutes, while calories and alcohol are complements. The weight changes found by Cho, Grossman, and Saffer may also reflect changes in activity levels in addition to changes in caloric intake. For example, since the health benefits from exercise may ameliorate the damages from smoking and drinking, exercise may be a complement in the production of health to smoking or drinking. If that is the case, then policies that decrease smoking and drinking may decrease exercise as they no longer see the need for this offsetting health behavior. Alternatively, there may be complementarity in consumption. This may occur as one gets a pleasurable feeling from all three activities; thus, as the price increases for smoking, one may substitute with physical activity. Complementarities may also occur when individuals are trying to make behavioral changes. Changes in one health behavior may serve as a "gateway" for changes in other health behaviors (see Dutton et al. 2008, for an example). One may also have the "New Year's resolution effect" in that a person finds it easier to change a group of behaviors together, and thus simultaneously decreasing smoking and drinking while increasing physical activity.

The previous model is static and does not address the fact that some of the benefits and costs of physical activity are not immediately felt. The expression "no pain, no gain" illustrates the intertemporal tradeoffs that some people perceive in exercise. Other activities such as exercising, refraining from smoking, and controlling weight may share the characteristic of increasing short-term disutility and long health. Hence, we might find a high degree of correlation among health behaviors due to the unobserved taste parameter of time preference in a cross-sectional analysis.

9.7.1   Data and Methods

Data are from the Behavioral Risk Factor Surveillance System, a large nationally representative telephone survey of the noninstitutionalized adult population administered by the Centers for Disease Control and Prevention (Centers for Disease Control and Prevention 2004). All states participated between 2000 and 2005. We drop any pregnant women from the analysis, as physical activity recommendations are dependent on prior physical fitness. Annual sample sizes range from approximately 112,000 to over 258,000 leading to a combined sample size of over 1 million observations when all six years are used.

We utilize three different measures of physical activity as BRFSS obtains different information each year. Annually, BRFSS asks if the person participated in ANY leisure time physical activity in the past thirty days. This is a weak measure as it could be as simple as walking once in the past thirty days. The advantage of using this measure is that the question is asked every year and can be used to measure changes over time. The second and third measures follow the definitions created by the CDC. The first measure— physical activity that is vigorous or moderate—is defined as engaging in light to moderate leisure time physical activity for greater than or equal to thirty minutes at a frequency of greater than or equal to five times per week, or engaging in vigorous leisure time physical activity for greater than or equal to twenty minutes at a frequency greater than or equal to three times a week. Our last measure examines those that only have vigorous physical activity. These last two measures of physical activity are only asked on odd years and thus reduce our analysis to years 2001, 2003, and 2005.

Basic demographic data include age, age squared, race (black, white, Asian, with other race as the omitted category), Hispanic ethnicity, education (high school graduate, some college, college plus, with the omitted category less than high school graduate), eight household income categories (over $75,000 as omitted), married, and employment (unemployed, retired, student or homemaker with employed as omitted category). We test the effects of adding weight status that may be correlated with unobservables such as taste for health prevention or discount rates. We also add whether the individual got a flu shot. We include the flu shot as a measure of the person's tendency toward preventive care.

Data on area characteristics was obtained from a number of sources. Data on the number of establishments and employment in recreational industries and parks are obtained from the County Business Patterns Data Set from the Census. We created three measures: the number of fitness and recreation centers per 1,000 individuals in a county ("gyms per capita"; North American Industry Classification System [NAICS] code 713940), parks per 1,000 individuals in a county (NAICS code 712190), and the number of other recreation areas per 1,000 in a county (NAICS code for golf and country clubs 713190, ski venues 713920, marinas 713930, bowling facilities 713950, and all other 713990). Data on state tax policy for alcohol and tobacco are obtained from the Federation of Tax Administrators. We also added the American Chamber of Commerce Researchers' Association (ACCRA) data on pre-tax retail prices for tennis balls, bowling, bus fare, and gas. County level crime statistics for violent crime rate (murder, forcible rape, robbery, aggravated assault) and property crime rate (burglary, larceny-theft, motor vehicle theft, arson) from the FBI Uniform Crime Report System were added (U.S. Department of Justice, Federal Bureau of Investigation 2006).

We begin our analysis of the data by building a baseline model of participation in any leisure time physical activity in the past thirty days. Our strategy is to begin with a small set of demographic and socioeconomic variables and then proceed by adding additional variables in groups to examine the effects of the additional variables on existing variables' stability. The second group of variables includes area characteristics. Next, we add weight status (overweight and obese) to see whether the estimated effects of area characteristics are sensitive to the inclusion of a health status measure. Because weight measures are likely endogenous, we exclude them in the remaining specifications and consider instead a measure of risk attitude for health—did the person have a flu shot in the last twelve months? Finally, because exercise is measured for past thirty days and weather or climate for the time of year may affect the likelihood of exercise, we add month of interview fixed effects.

Because previous studies have found differences in women and men in their physical activity participation, we reanalyzed all models stratifying by gender. In addition, as access to amenities may vary by income, we again examined our results stratifying by income. All models include year, month, and state fixed effects and are run as simple linear probability models with robust standard errors. Therefore, we can interpret the estimates for state-level variables as measuring how physical activity changes due to changes in these independent variables.

Because more rigorous exercise habits are recommended in the health literature, we also consider two alternative measures of exercise: participation in vigorous exercise or participation in moderate or vigorous activity.

9.7.2   Results

Table 9.3 presents the means and standard deviations for our data set. These are means averaged over the six years of the data, and as such, the physical activity measure differs from those presented on an annual basis in the tables presented earlier. Over these six years, approximately 70 percent of our sample had any exercise. Yet, few met the CDC's definition of active with only 12 percent reporting moderate or vigorous activity, and only 7 percent reporting vigorous activity. Our sample is of adults, and the average age is

Table 9.3   **Descriptive statistics**

Variable	Mean	Std. dev.	Min.	Max.
Any leisure time activity in past 30 days	0.696	0.460	0	1
Moderate or vigorous PA	0.124	0.330	0	1
Vigorous PA	0.068	0.252	0	1
Age	47.874	16.594	18	99
Age squared	2567.315	1710.999	324	9,801
Male	0.420	0.494	0	1
Hispanic	0.068	0.252	0	1
White	0.833	0.373	0	1
Black	0.070	0.255	0	1
Asian	0.023	0.149	0	1
Married	0.574	0.494	0	1
High school diploma	0.284	0.451	0	1
Some college	0.285	0.451	0	1
College degree or more	0.351	0.477	0	1
Income < $10K	0.048	0.214	0	1
Income $15k < $20k	0.053	0.224	0	1
Income $20k < $25k	0.074	0.261	0	1
Income $25k < $30k	0.097	0.297	0	1
Income $30k < $35k	0.144	0.351	0	1
Income $35k < $50k	0.182	0.386	0	1
Income $50k < $75k	0.180	0.384	0	1
Income > $75k	0.221	0.415	0	1
Unemployed	0.043	0.203	0	1
Student or homemaker	0.097	0.295	0	1
Retired	0.175	0.380	0	1
Insured	0.882	0.323	0	1
Price of bowling	3.014	0.680	1	8.34
Price of tennis balls	2.427	0.387	1.51	4.99
Price of gas	1.553	0.258	0.98	2.54
Bus fare	1.125	0.498	0.25	3.35
Unemployment rate	5.233	1.597	1.6	15.9
Violent crime rate	4.473	3.329	0	48.31
Property crime rate	38.248	16.113	0	217.37
Number of gyms per capita	0.103	0.047	0	0.48
Number of parks per capita	0.002	0.007	0	0.14
Number of other rec areas per capita	0.141	0.114	0	2.72
Cigarette tax	0.690	0.474	0.025	2.05
Beer tax	0.214	0.154	0.02	0.92
Overweight	0.350	0.477	0	1
Obese	0.223	0.416	0	1
Flu shot	0.327	0.469	0	1

Number of observations = 383,950

close to forty-eight years old with the sample being predominantly white
(83 percent) and female (58 percent).

After briefly reviewing the results of all models, we discuss in more detail
the overall findings for key variables of interest across different specifications.

Baseline Model: Participation in Any Leisure Time Exercise

Results for models of participation in any leisure time physical activity in
the past thirty days are presented in table 9.4. Model 1 in table 9.4 includes
only demographic variables and shows that the likelihood of reporting participation in any leisure physical activity decreases for those who are older,
female, married, and uninsured. Those who are employed are less likely
to exercise during leisure time than students and homemakers, retirees,
or unemployed individuals. Greater education and income are associated
with an increase in the probability of engaging in some exercise. Comparing coefficient estimates for the demographic variables across the columns
in table 9.4 shows that the estimated effects are robust to the inclusion of
additional variables.

In model 2 of table 9.4, we include area variables to capture variation in
local availability of exercise venues, economic conditions, and crime. While
we would like to measure the causal impacts of changes in these area variables on physical activity, we interpret our coefficient estimates as correlation
measures due to concerns over reverse causality. Healthy, active individuals
may self-select areas with particular characteristics. While our analysis can
exploit intertemporal variation in these measures, and we include state and
year fixed effects in all models, our concern remains that there are unobservable factors correlated with both area characteristics and the decision to
engage in exercise.

The number of gyms per capita, parks per capita, and other exercise venues per capita are all positively associated with increased exercise participation. We find no relationship between participation in any exercise and the
property crime rate or violent crime rate for an individual's county. Given
the findings that obesity is related to cigarette prices and tax rates (Chou,
Grossman, and Saffer 2004, 2006; Gruber and Frakes 2006) we might expect
to find a relationship between sin taxes (cigarette and beer taxes) and physical activity. In particular, the puzzling finding of Gruber and Frakes (2006)
that obesity *declines* when cigarette taxes increase might make more sense if
we found higher taxes were associated with increased exercise. As individuals smoke less, they may decide to make overall health changes and exercise
more. Our results in table 9.4 do not support this conjecture. We find no
association between beer or cigarette taxes and participation in any leisure
time exercise.

We do, however, find a link between transportation costs and exercise.
Bus fare is positive and significant in all specifications while gas prices are

Table 9.4   Participation in any exercise

	Model 1: Basic demographics	Model 2: Add area variables to model 1	Model 3: Add weight to model 2	Model 4: Add flu shots to model 2	Model 5: Add months to model 4
Age	−0.0027*	−0.0025*	−0.0012*	−0.0024*	−0.0024*
	(0.0001)	(0.0002)	(0.0002)	(0.0002)	(0.0002)
Age squared	−3.03E-06*	−5.42E-06	−1.79E-05	−7.02E-06	−7.16E-06*
	(1.4E-06)	(2.3E-06)	(2.3E-06)	(2.3E-06)	(2.3E-06)
Male	0.0219*	0.0228*	0.0249*	0.0230*	0.0236*
	(0.0008)	(0.0013)	(0.0013)	(0.0013)	(0.0013)
Hispanic	−0.0389*	−0.0402*	−0.0407*	−0.0404*	−0.0405*
	(0.0018)	(0.0028)	(0.0028)	(0.0028)	(0.0028)
White	0.0188*	0.0141*	0.0115*	0.0141*	0.0146*
	(0.0016)	(0.0026)	(0.0025)	(0.0026)	(0.0025)
Black	−0.0289*	−0.0346*	−0.0294*	−0.0342*	−0.0341*
	(0.0021)	(0.0035)	(0.0034)	(0.0035)	(0.0034)
Asian	−0.0540*	−0.0702*	−0.0809*	−0.0704*	−0.0695*
	(0.0032)	(0.0049)	(0.0048)	(0.0048)	(0.0048)
Married	−0.0129*	−0.0148*	−0.0139*	−0.0149*	−0.0149*
	(0.0009)	(0.0014)	(0.0014)	(0.0014)	(0.0014)
High school diploma	0.0735*	0.0786*	0.0772*	0.0785*	0.0783*
	(0.0015)	(0.0025)	(0.0025)	(0.0025)	(0.0025)
Some college	0.1340*	0.1370*	0.1350*	0.1370*	0.1360*
	(0.0015)	(0.0026)	(0.0026)	(0.0026)	(0.0026)
College degree or more	0.1800*	0.1820*	0.1770*	0.1820*	0.1810*
	(0.0016)	(0.0026)	(0.0026)	(0.0026)	(0.0026)
Income < $10k	−0.1980*	−0.1920*	−0.1840*	−0.1920*	−0.1910*
	(0.0021)	(0.0034)	(0.0034)	(0.0034)	(0.0034)
Income $15k < $20k	−0.1780*	−0.1730*	−0.1660*	−0.1730*	−0.1730*
	(0.0020)	(0.0033)	(0.0033)	(0.0033)	(0.0033)
Income $20k < $25k	−0.1510*	−0.1480*	−0.1420*	−0.1480*	−0.1470*
	(0.0018)	(0.0029)	(0.0029)	(0.0029)	(0.0029)

(*continued*)

Table 9.4 (continued)

	Model 1: Basic demographics	Model 2: Add area variables to model 1	Model 3: Add weight to model 2	Model 4: Add flu shots to model 2	Model 5: Add months to model 4
Income $25k < $30k	-0.1240*	-0.1230*	-0.1170*	-0.1220*	-0.1220*
	(0.0016)	(0.0026)	(0.0026)	(0.0026)	(0.0026)
Income $30k < $35k	-0.0919*	-0.0896*	-0.0855*	-0.0894*	-0.0893*
	(0.0014)	(0.0023)	(0.0023)	(0.0023)	(0.0023)
Income $35k < $50k	-0.0623*	-0.0599*	-0.0563*	-0.0598*	-0.0597*
	(0.0013)	(0.0020)	(0.0020)	(0.0020)	(0.0020)
Income $50k < $75k	-0.0349*	-0.0348*	-0.0322*	-0.0347*	-0.0346*
	(0.0012)	(0.0020)	(0.0020)	(0.0020)	(0.0020)
Unemployed	0.0089*	0.0140*	0.0147*	0.0142*	0.0143*
	(0.0020)	(0.0031)	(0.0031)	(0.0031)	(0.0031)
Student or homemaker	0.0451*	0.0393*	0.0369*	0.0396*	0.0398*
	(0.0014)	(0.0022)	(0.0022)	(0.0022)	(0.0022)
Retired	0.0731*	0.0675*	0.0672*	0.0666*	0.0664*
	(0.0014)	(0.0023)	(0.0023)	(0.0023)	(0.0023)
Insured	0.0131*	0.0121*	0.0141*	0.0109*	0.0112*
	(0.0012)	(0.0020)	(0.0020)	(0.0021)	(0.0020)
Price of bowling		-0.0044	-0.0046	-0.0042	-0.0027
		(0.0028)	(0.0028)	(0.0028)	(0.0028)
Price of tennis balls		-0.0012	-0.0017	-0.0011	0.0001
		(0.0024)	(0.0024)	(0.0024)	(0.0024)
Price of gas		-0.0108*	-0.0103	-0.0104	-0.0102
		(0.0053)	(0.0053)	(0.0053)	(0.0053)
Bus fare		0.0118*	0.0123*	0.0113*	0.0073*
		(0.0035)	(0.0035)	(0.0035)	(0.0035)
Violent crime rate		-0.0008	-0.0009	-0.0008	-0.0008*
		(0.0003)	(0.0003)	(0.0003)	(0.0003)

Property crime rate	-2.54E-05	-2.20E-05	-2.86E-05	-3.73E-05
	(6.6E-06)	(6.6E-06)	(6.6E-06)	(6.6E-06)
Number of gyms per capita	0.1000*	0.0959*	0.1100*	0.1080*
	(0.0149)	(0.0149)	(0.0149)	(0.0149)
Number of parks per capita	0.2570*	0.2340*	0.2590*	0.2510*
	(0.0900)	(0.0897)	(0.0900)	(0.0898)
Number of other rec areas per capita	0.0239*	0.0217*	0.0244*	0.0250*
	(0.0065)	(0.0065)	(0.0065)	(0.0065)
Cigarette tax	0.0009	0.0008	0.0014	-0.0025
	(0.0042)	(0.0042)	(0.0042)	(0.0042)
Beer tax	0.0274	0.0257	0.0277	0.0175
	(0.0607)	(0.0605)	(0.0607)	(0.0606)
Overweight		-0.0065*		
		(0.0014)		
Obese		-0.0733*		
		(0.0016)		
Flu shot			0.0122*	0.0119*
			(0.0014)	(0.0014)
Observations	1,057,541	383,950	383,950	383,950
R^2	0.323	0.342	0.339	0.341

Notes: Standard errors in parentheses.
*Significant at the 10 percent level.

negative but generally insignificant. One interpretation of these results is that driving one's self is a complement to leisure time physical activity while activities available to bus riders are substitutes for leisure time exercise. As an example, high gas prices may decrease car trips to the gym while increased bus fares make playing basketball at a neighborhood park cheaper relative to taking the bus to see a movie. This explanation suggests we will see a stronger effect of bus fare at the low end of the income scale. Our stratifications by income, reported later, allow us to examine this conjecture more closely. The two exercise "prices" we include are probably poor proxies for an index of leisure time physical activity prices, and we find no significant effects for these variables in any model in table 9.4.

In the third and fourth columns of table 9.4, we find that the two measures of health status, maintaining a healthy weight and getting a flu shot, are both positively associated with leisure time physical activity. The estimated associations between availability of exercise amenities and the likelihood of engaging in exercise do not appear to be sensitive to inclusion of health status measures. In the final column, we show that adding fixed effects for month of interview reduces slightly the estimated association between most area variable and physical activity, but the significance is not changed.

Any Exercise: Stratified by Gender

Stratifying by gender reveals some interesting differences between the factors that affect men's and women's participation in any leisure time physical activity. We report these results for our preferred specification in table 9.5. The relationship between increasing income and the likelihood of exercise found in the pooled sample holds for both women and men. Similarly, the effects of employment (relative to unemployment or being out of the labor force) and marriage continue to hold in the stratified samples. The positive association between health insurance and exercise, however, holds only for men. The number of gyms per capita is significant for both men and women, but parks per capita and other exercise venues (e.g., ski areas and marinas) are positive and significant only for women. Because women's propensity to engage in exercise varies with the availability of outdoor exercise venues, we might expect greater sensitivity to crime rates. However, we do not find a significant association between exercise and crime rate in either stratified regression. Nor do we find any relationship between sin taxes and exercise. In examining price factors, we find that the positive association between bus fare and exercise participation found in the pooled regression holds only for women.

These results show that for both men and women, the greater the opportunity cost of physical activity because of work and higher earnings or because of reduced availability of exercise amenities, the lower the participation in physical activity. Nonpecuniary factors such as crime rates appear to have little effect. Perhaps the most interesting difference is the effect of overweight

Table 9.5   Participation in any exercise, stratified by gender

	Female	Male
Age	−0.0004	−0.0052*
	(0.0003)	(0.0003)
Age squared	−2.62E-05*	2.04E-05*
	(−3.02E-06)	(−3.51E-06)
Hispanic	−0.0464*	−0.0319*
	(0.0037)	(0.0040)
White	0.0192*	0.0097*
	(0.0035)	(0.0037)
Black	−0.0453*	−0.0104*
	(0.0046)	(0.0052)
Asian	−0.0778*	−0.0604*
	(0.0068)	(0.0068)
Married	−0.0204*	−0.0080*
	(0.0019)	(0.0020)
High school diploma	0.0805*	0.0756*
	(0.0034)	(0.0037)
Some college	0.1400*	0.1320*
	(0.0035)	(0.0038)
College degree or more	0.1880*	0.1730*
	(0.0036)	(0.0038)
Income < $10k	−0.1920*	−0.1860*
	(0.0045)	(0.0056)
Income $15k < $20k	−0.1720*	−0.1730*
	(0.0043)	(0.0053)
Income $20k < $25k	−0.1480*	−0.1470*
	(0.0039)	(0.0045)
Income $25k < $30k	−0.1210*	−0.1270*
	(0.0036)	(0.0039)
Income $30k < $35k	−0.0852*	−0.0968*
	(0.0031)	(0.0033)
Income $35k < $50k	−0.0572*	−0.0643*
	(0.0028)	(0.0029)
Income $50k < $75k	−0.0345*	−0.0353*
	(0.0028)	(0.0027)
Unemployed	0.0120*	0.0181*
	(0.0041)	(0.0046)
Student or homemaker	0.0398*	0.0526*
	(0.0025)	(0.0058)
Retired	0.0689*	0.0610*
	(0.0031)	(0.0035)
Insured	0.0053	0.0197*
	(0.0028)	(0.0030)
Price of bowling	−0.0055	0.0012
	(0.0037)	(0.0041)
Price of tennis balls	−0.0008	0.0015
	(0.0033)	(0.0036)
Price of gas	−0.0081	−0.0130
	(0.0072)	(0.0079)

(*continued*)

Table 9.5   (continued)

	Female	Male
Bus fare	0.0096*	0.0042
	(0.0047)	(0.0051)
Violent crime rate	–0.0006	–0.0010
	(0.0005)	(0.0005)
Property crime rate	–0.0001	6.02E-05
	(0.0001)	(0.0001)
Number of gyms per capita	0.0805*	0.142*
	(0.0202)	(0.0219)
Number of parks per capita	0.2660*	0.225
	(0.1220)	(0.1320)
Number of other rec areas per capita	0.0315*	0.0182
	(0.0089)	(0.0095)
Cigarette tax	–0.0023	–0.00253
	(0.0057)	(0.0062)
Beer tax	0.1110	–0.109
	(0.0828)	(0.0882)
Flu shot	0.0077*	0.0159*
	(0.0019)	(0.0021)
Observations	222,823	161,127
R^2	0.323	0.369

Notes: Standard errors in parentheses.
*Significant at the 10 percent level.

status. In the pooled regression, we found overweight to be negative and significant but it becomes positive and significant when we look at only men. Concern exists regarding the accuracy of BMI in diagnosing obesity. A study found that BMI had a better correlation with lean mass than body fat percentages (Romero-Corral et al. 2008); hence, active men with high muscle mass may be misclassified as overweight.

Results for Models of Vigorous Exercise

In the first column of table 9.6 we report the results for our preferred model for the pooled sample using participation in vigorous exercise as the dependent variable. The second two columns show the estimates for the models stratified by gender. The effects of age, gender, income, employment, and marital status are qualitatively similar to the findings for any exercise, but we find some changes in the estimated effects of race and insurance status. In comparing the correlations between area variables and physical activity, we find that none of the measures is significant for males, but gyms and other amenities are positive and significant for the pooled sample and for women. Sin taxes now have a negative and significant association with vigorous exercise (with the exception of cigarette taxes for women), indicating that higher taxes are associated with decreases in vigorous activity. We

Table 9.6   **Participation in vigorous exercise**

	Model 1: Females and males	Model 2: Female	Model 3: Male
Age	−0.0027*	−0.0022*	−0.0031*
	(0.0001)	(0.0002)	(0.0002)
Age squared	1.20E-05*	8.56E-06*	1.46E-05*
	(1.4e-06)	(1.7e-06)	(2.3e-06)
Male	0.0167*		
	(0.0008)		
Hispanic	−0.0067*	−0.0077*	−0.0045*
	(0.0016)	(0.0021)	(0.0026)
White	−0.0010	0.0003	−0.0032
	(0.0015)	(0.0020)	(0.0024)
Black	−0.0057*	−0.0096*	0.0020*
	(0.0021)	(0.0026)	(0.0034)
Asian	−0.0366*	−0.0351*	−0.0386*
	(0.0029)	(0.0038)	(0.0045)
Married	−0.0084*	−0.0075*	−0.0085*
	(0.0008)	(0.0011)	(0.0013)
High school diploma	0.0064*	0.0037*	0.0093*
	(0.0015)	(0.0019)	(0.0024)
Some college	0.0139*	0.0125*	0.0153*
	(0.0015)	(0.0019)	(0.0025)
College degree or more	0.0264*	0.0242*	0.0298*
	(0.0016)	(0.0020)	(0.0025)
Income < $10k	−0.0485*	−0.0469*	−0.0545*
	(0.0021)	(0.0025)	(0.0037)
Income $15k < $20k	−0.0419*	−0.0431*	−0.0410*
	(0.0020)	(0.0024)	(0.0035)
Income $20k < $25k	−0.0385*	−0.0398*	−0.0374*
	(0.0018)	(0.0022)	(0.0029)
Income $25k < $30k	−0.0346*	−0.0361*	−0.0326*
	(0.0016)	(0.0020)	(0.0026)
Income $30k < $35k	−0.0284*	−0.0312*	−0.0247*
	(0.0014)	(0.0017)	(0.0022)
Income $35k < $50k	−0.0234*	0.0241*	−0.0222*
	(0.0012)	(0.0016)	(0.0019)
Income $50k < $75k	−0.0155*	−0.0169*	−0.0137*
	(0.0012)	(0.0015)	(0.0018)
Unemployed	0.0044*	−0.0029	0.0143*
	(0.0018)	(0.0023)	(0.0030)
Student or homemaker	0.0126*	0.0107*	0.0275*
	(0.0013)	(0.0014)	(0.0038)
Retired	0.0103*	0.0128*	0.0067*
	(0.0014)	(0.0018)	(0.0023)
Insured	−0.0007	−0.0013	0.0007
	(0.0012)	(0.0016)	(0.0019)
Price of bowling	−0.0011	0.0009	−0.0036
	(0.0016)	(0.0021)	(0.0027)

(*continued*)

Table 9.6   (continued)

	Model 1: Females and males	Model 2: Female	Model 3: Male
Price of tennis balls	0.0061*	0.0074*	0.0050*
	(0.0015)	(0.0018)	(0.0024)
Price of gas	–0.0203*	–0.0239*	–0.0160*
	(0.0032)	(0.0040)	(0.0052)
Bus fare	0.0108*	0.0066*	0.0155*
	(0.0021)	(0.0026)	(0.0034)
Violent crime rate	8.30E-05	0.0001	5.33E-05
	(0.0002)	(0.0003)	(0.0003)
Property crime rate	–2.93E-05	–1.46E-05	–4.40E-05
	(3.9E-05)	(4.9E-05)	(0.0001)
Number of gyms per capita	0.0308*	0.0520*	0.0001
	(0.0089)	(0.0113)	(0.0143)
Number of parks per capita	0.0235	0.0009	0.0629
	(0.0536)	(0.0677)	(0.0864)
Number of other rec areas per capita	0.0124*	0.0136*	0.0109
	(0.0039)	(0.0049)	(0.0062)
Cigarette tax	–0.0094*	–0.0041	–0.0149*
	(0.0025)	(0.0032)	(0.0041)
Beer tax	–0.1410*	–0.0957*	–0.1570*
	(0.0362)	(0.0461)	(0.0576)
Flu shot	0.0018*	–0.0016*	0.0062*
	(0.0008)	(0.0011)	(0.0014)
Observations	383,950	222,823	161,127
R^2	0.22	0.193	0.256

Note: Standard errors in parentheses.
*Significant at the 10 percent level.

expect higher sin taxes will lead to reductions in smoking and drinking, but the resulting health gains may be offset by the concomitant reductions in vigorous exercise. Similar to the pattern observed earlier for any activity, we find that participation in vigorous activity is negatively and significantly associated with the price of gas, but positively associated with bus fare. One explanation is that people misreport walking to the bus as leisure time physical activity. If this is true, we would find the bus fare price to disappear when we examine vigorous physical activity, as walking would not fit this category. We expect tennis to be a larger component of vigorous exercise than any exercise, but we find an unexpected positive correlation between the price of tennis balls and participation in vigorous activity. This may be due to the fact that the price of tennis balls is a small component of the total price of tennis (court fees, time costs, racquet costs). In the pooled sample, and for men, we find a positive and significant association in our measure of the taste for preventative care (getting a flu shot) and engaging in vigorous exercise.

Results for Models of Vigorous and Moderate Exercise

Table 9.7 shows the results when the dependent variable is moderate or vigorous physical activity (PA). The results are generally consistent with the results for only vigorous exercise. For all measures of exercise we consider, we find gyms per capital are positively associated. The measures of recreation facilities per capita are generally positively and significantly associated with engaging in vigorous or moderate exercise. We continue to find that gas prices are associated with less exercise while bus fare has a positive association. Property crime rates are negatively associated with exercise for the pooled sample and men, but there is no significant association with violent crime rates. Cigarette and beer taxes are negative and significant factors (with the exception of the cigarette tax for women). Thus, we find no evidence that individuals change health behaviors together in response to a change in the price of smoking or drinking. Indeed, our results indicate that vigorous physical activity declines as either beer or cigarette taxes increase. The price of tennis balls and bowling have opposite effects on moderate or vigorous physical activity (positive and negative, respectively). The preventive health measure (flu shots) is positive for only for men.

Stratification by Income Category

We report the results stratified by income in tables 9.8, 9.9, and 9.10. While the coefficients of most demographic and socioeconomic variables in the model for participation in any leisure time exercise are stable across income categories, the effects of some variables do change. The effects of being married, retired, or a student or homemaker appear to have a larger impact at lower incomes than higher ones. The effect of being insured is generally positive with stronger effects as income increases. The effects of gender, race variables, and education variables do not appear to vary systematically with income. Based on our earlier findings that physical activity decreases when gas prices are high (or bus fares low), we expected to find stronger price effects at low incomes where prices presumably bite. Instead, we find neither is significant for any income group. The county crime rates generally have a negative effect where significant, but there is no apparent pattern by income. Similarly, exercise and recreation venues per capita are positive when significant, but the effects are nil for most income categories and no pattern emerges. Taxes have no effect for any income category. Flu shots have a robust positive effect across income categories.

9.8   Conclusions

In this chapter we examine factors associated with variation in leisure time physical activity. To explore these associations, we model three levels of leisure time physical activity—any exercise, physical activity that is moderate or vigorous, and vigorous physical activity in the past thirty days. Our

Table 9.7   **Participation in moderate or vigorous exercise**

	Model 1: Females and males	Model 2: Female	Model 3: Male
Age	−0.0011*	−0.0005*	−0.0018*
	(0.0002)	(0.0002)	(0.0002)
Age squared	−2.37E-06*	−7.04E-06*	4.14E-06*
	(1.6E-06)	(2.0E-06)	(2.0E-06)
Male	0.0072*		
	(0.0009)		
Hispanic	−0.0134*	−0.0134*	−0.0127*
	(0.0019)	(0.0025)	(0.0029)
White	0.0035*	0.0068*	−0.0006
	(0.0017)	(0.0023)	(0.0026)
Black	−0.0127*	−0.0151*	−0.0069
	(0.0024)	(0.0031)	(0.0037)
Asian	−0.0432*	−0.0395*	−0.0471*
	(0.0033)	(0.0045)	(0.0049)
Married	−0.0059*	−0.0042*	−0.0084*
	(0.0009)	(0.0013)	(0.0014)
High school diploma	0.0138*	0.0117*	0.0171*
	(0.0017)	(0.0022)	(0.0026)
Some college	0.0212*	0.0225*	0.0194*
	(0.0018)	(0.0023)	(0.0027)
College degree or more	0.0318*	0.0320*	0.0323*
	(0.0018)	(0.0024)	(0.0027)
Income < $10k	−0.0506*	−0.0495*	−0.0519*
	(0.0024)	(0.0030)	(0.0040)
Income $15k < $20k	−0.0431*	−0.0428*	−0.0430*
	(0.0023)	(0.0029)	(0.0038)
Income $20k < $25k	−0.0382*	−0.0386*	−0.0375*
	(0.0020)	(0.0026)	(0.0032)
Income $25k < $30k	−0.0322*	−0.0333*	−0.0308*
	(0.0018)	(0.0024)	(0.0028)
Income $30k < $35k	−0.0263*	−0.0286*	−0.0237*
	(0.0016)	(0.0021)	(0.0024)
Income $35k < $50k	−0.0198*	−0.0201*	−0.0202*
	(0.0014)	(0.0019)	(0.0021)
Income $50k < $75k	−0.0113*	−0.0123*	−0.0105*
	(0.0013)	(0.0018)	(0.0020)
Unemployed	0.0114*	0.0039	0.0212*
	(0.0021)	(0.0028)	(0.0033)
Student or homemaker	0.0246*	0.0227*	0.0311*
	(0.0015)	(0.0016)	(0.0041)
Retired	0.0273*	0.0263*	0.0271*
	(0.0016)	(0.0021)	(0.0025)
Insured	−0.0054*	−0.0075*	−0.0018
	(0.0014)	(0.0019)	(0.0021)
Price of bowling	−0.0097*	−0.0067*	−0.0137*
	−0.0019	−0.0025	−0.0029
Price of tennis balls	0.0092*	0.0106*	0.0074*
	(0.0017)	(0.0022)	(0.0026)

Table 9.7   (continued)

	Model 1: Females and males	Model 2: Female	Model 3: Male
Price of gas	–0.0386*	–0.0407*	–0.0363*
	(0.0037)	(0.0048)	(0.0056)
Bus fare	0.0165*	0.0101*	0.0247*
	(0.0024)	(0.0031)	(0.0037)
Violent crime rate	0.0004	0.0003	0.0006
	(0.0002)	(0.0003)	(0.0004)
Property crime rate	–0.0001*	–9.56E-05	–0.0002*
	(4.5E-05)	(5.9E-05)	(7.0E-05)
Number of gyms per capita	0.0392*	0.0683*	–0.0003
	(0.0102)	(0.0135)	(0.0156)
Number of parks per capita	0.2600*	0.2130*	0.3300*
	(0.0615)	(0.0809)	(0.0945)
Number of other rec areas per capita	0.0115*	0.0148*	0.0071
	(0.0045)	(0.0059)	(0.0068)
Cigarette tax	–0.0135*	–0.0082	–0.0199*
	(0.0029)	(0.0038)	(0.0045)
Beer tax	–0.1790*	–0.1550*	–0.1850*
	(0.0415)	(0.0551)	(0.0630)
Flu shot	0.0016	–0.0026	0.0071*
	(0.0010)	(0.0013)	(0.0015)
Observations	383,950	222,823	161,127
R^2	0.4	0.386	0.42

Notes: Standard errors in parentheses.
*Significant at the 10 percent level.

preferred specification includes state, year, and month fixed effects, as well as controls for area level recreation amenities, area crime rates, prices for related goods, and a preventive health measure (flu shots).

The estimated effects of socioeconomic factors are robust across model and exercise measure. We find that income has a strong and consistently positive association with physical activity across specifications. Education is also a positive and significant factor in all models, and the effects are fairly stable across gender and income. In almost every model, we find that individuals who report being married are generally associated with decreased participation in physical activity. For any exercise, the effect appears to be driven by those with lower income and women. For vigorous exercise, the effects of marriage are about the same for men and women. Holding marital status constant, men are more likely to exercise than women across all income levels. Individuals who work are less likely to engage in exercise by any measure than those who are unemployed, retired, or out of the labor force, and the effect for any exercise appears to be larger when income is low. To better understand these results, we would like to have better measures of the time constraints affecting men and women including family size, time

Table 9.8 Participation in any exercise, stratified by income

	< 10 K	10K–< 20K	20K–< 25K	25K–< 30K	30K–< 35K	35K–< 50K	50K–< 75K	> 75K
Age	-0.0081*	-0.0052*	-0.0031*	-0.0028*	-0.0029*	-0.0022*	-0.0006	0.0002
	(0.0010)	(0.0010)	(0.0008)	(0.0007)	(0.0006)	(0.0005)	(0.0006)	(0.0005)
Age squared	4.59E-05*	1.56E-05	7.62E-06	7.98E-06	5.77E-06	7.60E-06	2.34E-05	2.25E-05*
	(1.0e-05)	(9.3e-06)	(7.0e-06)	(7.0e-06)	(5.9e-06)	(5.7e-06)	(6.1e-06)	(5.2e-06)
Male	0.0371*	0.0300*	0.0342*	0.0259*	0.0166*	0.0170*	0.0225*	0.0218*
	(0.0075)	(0.0071)	(0.0057)	(0.0047)	(0.0036)	(0.0029)	(0.0027)	(0.0021)
Hispanic	-0.0614*	-0.0554*	-0.0644*	-0.0572*	-0.0410*	-0.0330*	-0.0183*	-0.0217*
	(0.0121)	(0.0116)	(0.0099)	(0.0086)	(0.0073)	(0.0067)	(0.0069)	(0.0059)
White	-0.0074	0.0209	0.0078	0.0136	0.0155*	0.0141*	0.0109	0.0190*
	(0.0107)	(0.0108)	(0.0092)	(0.0082)	(0.0069)	(0.0061)	(0.0062)	(0.0052)
Black	-0.0325*	-0.0215	-0.0381*	-0.0536*	-0.0351*	-0.0417*	-0.0272*	-0.0211*
	(0.0145)	(0.0151)	(0.0123)	(0.0112)	(0.0091)	(0.0082)	(0.0086)	(0.0073)
Asian	-0.0257	0.0058	-0.0789*	-0.0673*	-0.0663*	-0.0800*	-0.0800*	-0.0704*
	(0.0248)	(0.0268)	(0.0222)	(0.0189)	(0.0141)	(0.0105)	(0.0105)	(0.0078)
Married	-0.0220*	-0.0212*	-0.0336*	-0.0286*	-0.0204*	-0.0161*	-0.0131*	0.0009
	(0.0091)	(0.0079)	(0.0059)	(0.0047)	(0.0036)	(0.0030)	(0.0030)	(0.0028)
High school diploma	0.0549*	0.0657*	0.0624*	0.0762*	0.0947*	0.0788*	0.0691*	0.0576*
	(0.0087)	(0.0084)	(0.0074)	(0.0070)	(0.0066)	(0.0073)	(0.0089)	(0.0097)
Some college	0.1250*	0.1170*	0.1290*	0.1330*	0.1530*	0.1340*	0.1210*	0.1020*
	(0.0097)	(0.0094)	(0.0081)	(0.0074)	(0.0067)	(0.0072)	(0.0088)	(0.0096)
College degree or more	0.1840*	0.1750*	0.1850*	0.1850*	0.1980*	0.1780*	0.1640*	0.1440*
	(0.0122)	(0.0118)	(0.0098)	(0.0084)	(0.0071)	(0.0073)	(0.0087)	(0.0094)
Unemployed	0.0659*	0.0705*	0.0288*	0.0242*	0.0027	-0.0028	-0.0216*	-0.0090
	(0.0102)	(0.0118)	(0.0101)	(0.0093)	(0.0090)	(0.0082)	(0.0085)	(0.0074)
Student or homemaker	0.110*	0.0755*	0.0560*	0.0558*	0.0352*	0.0248*	0.0281*	0.0194*
	(0.0104)	(0.0106)	(0.0089)	(0.0078)	(0.0064)	(0.0053)	(0.0050)	(0.0036)
Retired	0.0973*	0.1050*	0.0913*	0.0758*	0.0788*	0.0648*	0.0619*	0.0286*
	(0.0115)	(0.0102)	(0.0090)	(0.0076)	(0.0062)	(0.0055)	(0.0057)	(0.0047)

Insured	−.0130	−0.0077	0.0071	0.0101	0.0119*	0.0180*	0.0236*	0.0363*
	(0.0082)	(0.0081)	(0.0066)	(0.0058)	(0.0051)	(0.0051)	(0.0061)	(0.0061)
Price of bowling	−0.0272	0.0117	−0.0211	0.0108	0.0056	0.0084	−0.0081	−0.0045
	(0.0161)	(0.0149)	(0.0125)	(0.0104)	(0.0079)	(0.0064)	(0.0057)	(0.0044)
Price of tennis balls	−0.0138	−0.0032	−0.0236*	0.0155	−0.0033	−0.0023	0.0063	−0.0053
	(0.0136)	(0.0129)	(0.0107)	(0.0089)	(0.0068)	(0.0056)	(0.0051)	(0.0041)
Price of gas	−0.0089	−0.0290	−0.0213	−0.0316	0.0025	−0.0168	−0.0138	−0.0011
	(0.0289)	(0.0275)	(0.0232)	(0.0194)	(0.0149)	(0.0123)	(0.0113)	(0.0090)
Bus fare	−0.0002	0.0277	0.0232	0.0236	0.0109	0.0136	0.0118	0.0084
	(0.0206)	(0.0194)	(0.0155)	(0.0134)	(0.0103)	(0.0083)	(0.0074)	(0.0053)
Violent crime rate	−0.0042*	−0.0021	−0.0021	0.0009	−0.0022*	0.0006	−0.0018*	−0.0013*
	(0.0017)	(0.0017)	(0.0014)	(0.0012)	(0.0009)	(0.0008)	(0.0008)	(0.0006)
Property crime rate	−0.0007	0.0003	0.0001	−0.0006	0.0001	−0.0001	0.0001	0.0002
	(0.0003)	(0.0003)	(0.0003)	(0.0002)	(0.0002)	(0.0001)	(0.0001)	(0.0001)
Number of gyms per capita	0.0219	0.0086	0.1060	0.1660*	0.0393	0.0944*	0.1290*	0.1210*
	(0.0790)	(0.0773)	(0.0639)	(0.0525)	(0.0414)	(0.0345)	(0.0322)	(0.0257)
Number of parks per capita	0.2910	0.1700	0.7310	0.3370	0.3250	0.1350	0.3150	0.0661
	(0.4790)	(0.4410)	(0.3880)	(0.3130)	(0.2370)	(0.1940)	(0.1990)	(0.1690)
Number of other rec areas per capita	0.0319	0.0070	−0.0017	0.0375	0.0431*	0.0443*	0.0205	0.0150
	(0.0371)	(0.0335)	(0.0275)	(0.0228)	(0.0176)	(0.0145)	(0.0137)	(0.0118)
Cigarette tax	−0.0031	0.0319	−0.0223	−0.0209	−0.0018	−0.0009	−0.0144	−0.0043
	(0.0240)	(0.0224)	(0.0183)	(0.0157)	(0.0120)	(0.0099)	(0.0090)	(0.0067)
Beer tax	0.1480	0.2540	−0.3370	−0.1280	0.2700	−0.0513	0.0346	−0.0433
	(0.3440)	(0.3200)	(0.2560)	(0.2190)	(0.1680)	(0.1360)	(0.1270)	(0.1050)
Flu shot	−0.0032	0.0130	0.0182*	0.0149*	0.0114*	0.0147*	0.0167*	0.0074*
	(0.0078)	(0.0074)	(0.0062)	(0.0052)	(0.0040)	(0.0033)	(0.0030)	(0.0023)
Observations	18,493	20,360	28,299	37,409	55,354	70,065	69,079	84,891
R^2	0.195	0.188	0.213	0.24	0.301	0.348	0.393	0.465

Notes: Standard errors in parentheses.
*Significant at the 10 percent level.

Table 9.9   Participation in vigorous exercise, stratified by income

	< 10 K	10K–20K	20K–<25K	25K–<30K	30K–<35K	35K–<50K	50K–<75K	> 75K
Age	−0.0045*	−0.0034*	−0.0031*	−0.0030*	−0.0025*	−0.0019*	−0.0018*	−0.0016*
	(0.0004)	(0.0004)	(0.0004)	(0.0003)	(0.0003)	(0.0003)	(0.0004)	(0.0004)
Age squared	3.32E-05*	2.08E-05*	1.82E-05*	1.60E-05*	1.03E-05*	1.90E-06	3.43E-06	−7.14E-07
	(4.1e-06)	(3.8e-06)	(3.5e-06)	(3.3e-06)	(3.1e-06)	(3.4e-06)	(4.2e-06)	(4.5e-06)
Male	0.0155*	0.0186*	0.0192*	0.0177*	0.0199*	0.0151*	0.0178*	0.0146*
	(0.0030)	(0.0029)	(0.0025)	(0.0023)	(0.0019)	(0.0018)	(0.0018)	(0.0018)
Hispanic	−0.0091	−0.0109*	−0.0162*	−0.0125*	−0.0113*	−0.0027	0.0038	0.0033
	(0.0049)	(0.0047)	(0.0043)	(0.0041)	(0.0039)	(0.0041)	(0.0048)	(0.0050)
White	0.0071	0.0050	0.0029	−0.0001	−0.0122*	−0.0064	−0.0036	−0.0024
	(0.0044)	(0.0044)	(0.0040)	(0.0039)	(0.0037)	(0.0037)	(0.0043)	(0.0045)
Black	0.0040	−0.0081	−0.0084	−0.0115*	−0.0185*	−0.0098*	−0.0023	−0.0083
	(0.0059)	(0.0061)	(0.0054)	(0.0053)	(0.0049)	(0.0050)	(0.0059)	(0.0063)
Asian	−0.0240*	−0.0225*	−0.0289*	−0.0439*	−0.0379*	−0.0408*	−0.0331*	−0.0465*
	(0.0101)	(0.0109)	(0.0097)	(0.0090)	(0.0075)	(0.0071)	(0.0073)	(0.0067)
Married	−0.0054	−4.74E-05	−0.0018	−0.0031	−0.0066*	−0.0119*	−0.0143*	−0.0088*
	(0.0037)	(0.0032)	(0.0026)	(0.0023)	(0.0019)	(0.0018)	(0.0021)	(0.0024)
High school diploma	0.0063	0.0033	0.0077*	0.0088*	0.0038	0.0066	0.0061	0.0158
	(0.0036)	(0.0034)	(0.0032)	(0.0033)	(0.0035)	(0.0044)	(0.0061)	(0.0083)
Some college	0.0170*	0.0126*	0.0168*	0.0172*	0.0091*	0.0133*	0.0149*	0.0258*
	(0.0040)	(0.0038)	(0.0036)	(0.0035)	(0.0036)	(0.0044)	(0.0061)	(0.0082)
College degree or more	0.0355*	0.0218*	0.0269*	0.0273*	0.0190*	0.0229*	0.0264*	0.0423*
	(0.0050)	(0.0048)	(0.0043)	(0.0040)	(0.0038)	(0.0044)	(0.0060)	(0.0081)
Unemployed	0.0055	0.0195*	−0.0001	0.0062	0.0031	0.0075	0.0097	0.0044
	(0.0042)	(0.0048)	(0.0044)	(0.0044)	(0.0048)	(0.0050)	(0.0059)	(0.0063)
Student or homemaker	0.0207*	0.0144*	0.0122*	0.0107*	0.0068*	0.0072*	0.0176*	0.0139*
	(0.0042)	(0.0043)	(0.0039)	(0.0037)	(0.0034)	(0.0032)	(0.0034)	(0.0031)

Retired	0.0079	0.0090*	0.0076	0.0090*	0.0073*	0.0164*	0.0109*	0.0135*
	(0.0047)	(0.0041)	(0.0039)	(0.0036)	(0.0033)	(0.0033)	(0.0039)	(0.0040)
Insured	-0.0052	-0.0049	-0.0059*	-0.0051	0.0027	-0.0036	0.0029	0.0023
	(0.0034)	(0.0033)	(0.0029)	(0.0028)	(0.0027)	(0.0031)	(0.0042)	(0.0052)
Price of bowling	0.0043	0.0004	-0.0162*	-0.0017	-0.0109*	-0.0027	-0.0038	-0.0013
	(0.0066)	(0.0061)	(0.0055)	(0.0050)	(0.0042)	(0.0039)	(0.0040)	(0.0037)
Price of tennis balls	-0.0002	-0.0006	0.0062	0.0000	0.0060	0.0059	0.0032	0.0067
	(0.0056)	(0.0052)	(0.0047)	(0.0043)	(0.0036)	(0.0034)	(0.0036)	(0.0035)
Price of gas	-0.0289*	-0.0224*	-0.0278*	-0.0156	-0.0331*	-0.0269*	-0.0184*	-0.0231*
	(0.0118)	(0.0112)	(0.0101)	(0.0093)	(0.0080)	(0.0075)	(0.0078)	(0.0077)
Bus fare	0.0152	0.0204*	0.0205*	0.0173*	0.0211*	0.0122*	0.0142*	0.0194*
	(0.0084)	(0.0079)	(0.0068)	(0.0064)	(0.0055)	(0.0050)	(0.0051)	(0.0045)
Violent crime rate	0.0002	-0.0010	0.0008	0.0007	0.0000	0.0005	-0.0006	-0.0001
	(0.0007)	(0.0007)	(0.0006)	(0.0006)	(0.0005)	(0.0005)	(0.0005)	(0.0005)
Property crime rate	-0.0001	0.0001	-0.0002	-0.0002*	0.0000	0.0000	0.0001	0.0000
	(0.0001)	(0.0001)	(0.0001)	(0.0001)	(0.0001)	(0.0001)	(0.0001)	(0.0001)
Number of gyms per capita	0.0249	-0.0238	0.0131	-0.0283	0.0300	-0.0016	0.0779*	0.0265
	(0.0322)	(0.0314)	(0.0280)	(0.0251)	(0.0221)	(0.0208)	(0.0222)	(0.0219)
Number of parks per capita	0.1150	0.2410	0.1380	0.0659	0.0731	0.1440	-0.1010	-0.1010
	(0.1950)	(0.1790)	(0.1700)	(0.1490)	(0.1260)	(0.1170)	(0.1370)	(0.1450)
Number of other rec areas per capita	0.0214	0.0168	0.0048	-0.0052	0.0043	0.0067	0.0257	0.0249*
	(0.0151)	(0.0136)	(0.0120)	(0.0109)	(0.0094)	(0.0088)	(0.0095)*	(0.0101)
Cigarette tax	0.0182	-0.0024	-0.0103	-0.0001	-0.0182*	-0.0101	-0.0118	-0.0128*
	(0.0098)	(0.0091)	(0.0080)	(0.0075)	(0.0064)	(0.0060)	(0.0062)	(0.0058)
Beer tax	-0.0954	-0.0429	-0.0875	-0.0438	-0.0481	-0.1450	-0.1130	-0.2600*
	(0.1400)	(0.1300)	(0.1120)	(0.1040)	(0.0897)	(0.0824)	(0.0876)	(0.0898)
Flu shot	-0.0010	0.0034	-0.0030	-0.0012	0.0023	0.0038	0.0009	0.0037
	(0.0032)	(0.0030)	(0.0027)	(0.0025)	(0.0022)	(0.0020)	(0.0021)	(0.0019)
Observations	18,493	20,360	28,299	37,409	55,354	70,065	69,079	84,891
R^2	0.143	0.137	0.152	0.169	0.194	0.216	0.246	0.296

Notes: Standard errors in parentheses.
*Significant at the 10 percent level.

Table 9.10 Participation in moderate or vigorous exercise, stratified by income

	< 10 K	10K–<20K	20K–<25K	25K–<30K	30K–<35K	35K–<50K	50K–<75K	> 75K
Age	-0.0034*	-0.0022*	-0.0018*	-0.0015*	-0.0009*	-0.0005	-0.0002	-0.0002
	(0.0006)	(0.0005)	(0.0005)	(0.0004)	(0.0004)	(0.0004)	(0.0004)	(0.0004)
Age squared	1.91E-05*	1.07E-05*	5.38E-06	7.21E-07	4.56E-06	-7.77E-06*	-8.39E-06	-9.47E-06*
	(5.6E-06)	(5.2E-06)	(4.6E-06)	(4.2E-06)	(3.7E-06)	(3.9E-06)	(4.7E-06)	(4.6E-06)
Male	0.0126*	0.0116*	0.0120*	0.0108*	0.0116*	0.0045*	0.0054*	0.0020
	(0.0041)	(0.0039)	(0.0033)	(0.0028)	(0.0023)	(0.0020)	(0.0020)	(0.0018)
Hispanic	-0.0191*	-0.0178*	-0.0248*	-0.0222*	-0.0163*	-0.0064	0.0055	-0.0103*
	(0.0067)	(0.0064)	(0.0056)	(0.0052)	(0.0047)	(0.0047)	(0.0052)	(0.0053)
White	0.0168*	0.0174*	0.0114*	0.0034	-0.0063	-0.0052	0.0042	-0.0075
	(0.0059)	(0.0060)	(0.0052)	(0.0049)	(0.0044)	(0.0047)	(0.0047)	(0.0047)
Black	0.0003	-0.0052	-0.0185*	-0.0170*	-0.0245*	-0.0170*	-0.0052	-0.0290*
	(0.0080)	(0.0083)	(0.0070)	(0.0067)	(0.0058)	(0.0057)	(0.0065)	(0.0065)
Asian	-0.0023	-0.0211	-0.0355*	-0.0567*	-0.0411*	-0.0489*	-0.0435*	-0.0606*
	(0.0137)	(0.0148)	(0.0126)	(0.0113)	(0.0090)	(0.0081)	(0.0080)	(0.0070)
Married	-0.0083	-0.0008	-0.0047	-0.0033	-0.0022	-0.0084*	-0.0100*	-0.0075*
	(0.0051)	(0.0043)	(0.0033)	(0.0028)	(0.0023)	(0.0021)	(0.0023)	(0.0025)
High school diploma	0.0177*	0.0102*	0.0090*	0.0138*	0.0136*	0.0111*	-0.0003	0.0206*
	(0.0048)	(0.0047)	(0.0042)	(0.0042)	(0.0042)	(0.0050)	(0.0067)	(0.0087)
Some college	0.0314*	0.0204*	0.0235*	0.0231*	0.0156*	0.0172*	0.0082	0.0267*
	(0.0054)	(0.0052)	(0.0046)	(0.0044)	(0.0043)	(0.0050)	(0.0066)	(0.0085)
College degree or more	0.0421*	0.0258*	0.0294*	0.0331*	0.0261*	0.0264*	0.0180*	0.0403*
	(0.0068)	(0.0065)	(0.0056)	(0.0050)	(0.0045)	(0.0051)	(0.0066)	(0.0084)
Unemployed	0.0190*	0.0285*	0.0059	-0.0003	0.0066	0.0150*	0.0113	0.0135*
	(0.0057)	(0.0065)	(0.0058)	(0.0055)	(0.0057)	(0.0057)	(0.0064)	(0.0066)
Student or homemaker	0.0273*	0.0245*	0.0159*	0.0162*	0.0209*	0.0219*	0.0275*	0.0268*
	(0.0058)	(0.0059)	(0.0051)	(0.0046)	(0.0041)	(0.0037)	(0.0038)	(0.0032)
Retired	0.0277*	0.0136*	0.0136*	0.0214*	0.0251*	0.0372*	0.0349*	0.0306*
	(0.0064)	(0.0056)	(0.0051)	(0.0046)	(0.0039)	(0.0038)	(0.0043)	(0.0041)

Insured	−0.0086	−0.0131*	−0.0068	−0.0060	−0.0008	−0.0071*	−0.0037	0.0040
	(0.0046)	(0.0045)	(0.0038)	(0.0035)	(0.0032)	(0.0035)	(0.0047)	(0.0054)
Price of bowling	−0.0124	−0.0081	−0.0386*	−0.0029	−0.0226*	−0.0089*	−0.0088*	−0.0103*
	(0.0089)	(0.0082)	(0.0071)	(0.0062)	(0.0051)	(0.0044)	(0.0043)	(0.0039)
Price of tennis balls	0.0022	0.0006	0.0010	0.0045	0.0100*	0.0123*	0.0074	0.0075*
	(0.0076)	(0.0071)	(0.0061)	(0.0053)	(0.0043)	(0.0039)	(0.0039)	(0.0036)
Price of gas	−0.0481*	−0.0299*	−0.0587*	−0.0469*	−0.0496*	−0.0477*	−0.0344*	−0.0322*
	(0.0160)	(0.0152)	(0.0132)	(0.0116)	(0.0095)	(0.0085)	(0.0086)	(0.0080)
Bus fare	0.0355*	0.0407*	0.0335*	0.0084	0.0287*	0.0166*	0.0198*	0.0211*
	(0.0114)	(0.0107)	(0.0088)	(0.0080)	(0.0066)	(0.0057)	(0.0056)	(0.0047)
Violent crime rate	0.0016	−0.0019*	0.0008	0.0005	0.0011	0.0004	−0.0004	0.0005
	(0.0010)	(0.0009)	(0.0008)	(0.0007)	(0.0006)	(0.0005)	(0.0006)	(0.0005)
Property crime rate	−0.0003	0.0001	−0.0002	−0.0002	−0.0003*	−0.0001	−5.66E-06	−0.0002
	(0.0002)	(0.0002)	(0.0002)	(0.0001)	(0.0001)	(0.0001)	(0.0001)	(0.0001)
Number of gyms per capita	0.0275	0.0171	0.0122	−0.0225	0.0710*	0.0139	0.0719*	0.0040
	(0.0438)	(0.0426)	(0.0364)	(0.0314)	(0.0264)	(0.0239)	(0.0244)	(0.0228)
Number of parks per capita	0.1050	0.0501	0.5080*	0.4150*	0.2640	0.1800	0.3930*	0.2080
	(0.2650)	(0.2430)	(0.2210)	(0.1870)	(0.1510)	(0.1350)	(0.1510)	(0.1500)
Number of other rec areas per capita	0.0114	0.0045	0.0073	−0.0090	0.0059	0.0119	0.0211*	0.0199
	(0.0206)	(0.0184)	(0.0155)	(0.0136)	(0.0112)	(0.0101)	(0.0104)	(0.0105)
Cigarette tax	−0.0128	−0.0129	−0.0157	0.0005	−0.0245*	−0.0130	−0.0127	−0.0144*
	(0.0133)	(0.0123)	(0.0104)	(0.0094)	(0.0077)	(0.0069)	(0.0068)	(0.0060)
Beer tax	−0.3780*	−0.1830	−0.2430	−0.0527	−0.0647	−0.2210*	−0.0993	−0.1990*
	(0.1910)	(0.1760)	(0.1460)	(0.1310)	(0.1070)	(0.0945)	(0.0962)	(0.0934)
Flu shot	−0.0010	0.0033	−0.0047	−0.0017	0.0056*	0.0013	0.0010	0.0019
	(0.0043)	(0.0041)	(0.0035)	(0.0031)	(0.0026)	(0.0023)	(0.0023)	(0.0020)
Observations	18,493	20,360	28,299	37,409	55,354	70,065	69,079	84,891
R^2	0.291	0.296	0.318	0.345	0.373	0.405	0.442	0.482

Notes: Standard errors in parentheses.

*Significant at the 10 percent level.

at work, commuting time, and time in other activities. Unfortunately, the BRFSS does not have a consistent measure of family size across the years of our data, nor does it contain any time use measures.

The effects of area-specific variables are also largely consistent across our specifications. These coefficients must be interpreted with caution because individuals who are likely to exercise may choose to live in areas with certain amenities and characteristics. We do not find that exercise levels vary with the two direct "own" price measures (price of tennis balls and price of bowling balls), but we do find a significant association between transportation costs and exercise. Gas prices are negatively and significantly related to leisure time exercise while bus fare is positive and significantly associated in most models of participation in any leisure time exercise or vigorous exercise. Contrary to what we might have expected, the effects of gas and bus fare do not differ by income. Individuals who are on the margin for exercising may be the ones who drive to an exercise venue and are deterred by the increased cost of transportation. The positive association with bus fare suggests that individuals do not take the bus to the gym or other exercise venue, but instead use the bus to access leisure time substitutes for physical activity. The results may also point to problems in the way physical activity is measured in the BRFSS. While the survey question specifies leisure time exercise, respondents may include transportation exercise (for example, walking to work) as part of this response. Another concern is the merging of the price data is at too gross of a level. Price and area measures may need to be at a census tract or lower area level, which is not available on this data set.

Sin taxes have no effect on the likelihood of any exercise, but generally have negative effects on vigorous exercise or moderate and vigorous exercise. These results suggest inactivity and smoking (or drinking) may be substitutes. People who are forced to become healthier in one dimension due to the higher taxes may be able to relax their health behaviors in another area and still keep health stock at the target level.

We find a weak association between violent crimes and participation in exercise and no effect from property crime rates. Physical activity is positively associated with areas where there are more parks per capita in a county, which is consistent with Humphrey and Ruseki's (2007) findings using state-level variation in total state, and local spending on parks is positively associated with outdoor activity.

Our earlier results are robust to the inclusion of use of flu shots. Individuals who get flu shots are generally more likely to report some exercise. While this measure is likely endogenous, we find that its inclusion does not affect the other results. If the area variables earlier were measuring the reverse causation that people who are active and have a higher taste for health preventions move to areas with low crime rates and high spending on parks, then we might expect that adding measures of taste for preventive medicine would reduce the effects of these variables. We consistently find that flu shots is positively associated with physical activity, indicating that people with higher tastes for prevention may bundle their preventive activities or treat them as complements.

Our results can be compared to Rashad's (2006) analysis of cycling rates using the 1996 to 2000 BRFSS data, and Humphrey and Ruseki's analysis of participation in five categories of leisure time physical activity (outdoor recreation, household activities, group sport, individual sport and walking) using the 1998 and 2000 BRFSS. While our demographic results are largely consistent with both studies, the Humphrey and Ruseki study shows that demographic effects can differ widely across physical activity categories.

The most important limitation in our study is due to the measures of physical activity. The BRFSS measure is based on self-report, and more precise physical activity measures are not consistently reported in every year of the survey. In addition, physical activity measures are not consistently reported in national health surveys, making it difficult to directly compare results. In addition, the most consistent physical activity variable (any exercise) does not conform to the CDC definitions for physical activity. The CDC measures of moderate or vigorous activity (which do conform to measures) are only captured in odd years, and thus, only in three years of our data. The results are also limited to analyzing only leisure time physical activity. Any physical activity is beneficial and future studies need to include measure of activity for transportation and work. Our future work will examine the effects of area variables on other data sets, such as the National Health Interview Survey, to examine more appropriate definitions of physical activity. In addition, measures of park access gym data are at the county level, which may be too large of a geographical dimension to capture the causal impact of increased access. Studies such as Sandy et al. (chapter 7, in this volume) that allow detailed description of the neighborhood may be more appropriate. We are also missing measures of home exercise such as purchasing of exercise equipment or videos that may influence leisure time activity. Finally, we do not have the ability to control for selection of individuals into areas. As people with preferences for exercise and health prevention may locate near amenities such as parks, gyms, or lower crime rates, future research should include the selection into neighborhood decision in their models relating physical activity and area characteristics.

9.9   Policy Implications

The strong relationship we find between education and exercise suggests that there may be positive spillovers from policies aimed at increasing educational attainment. Education aimed at increasing the awareness of the value of physical activity in the form of Public Service Announcements as advocated by Pratt et al. (2004) should be explored further. We also find income is positively associated with exercise. Our results also show that working individuals are less likely to exercise than those who are unemployed or out of the labor force, and that men are more likely to exercise than women. These reflect the importance of the time constraint in physical activity. Policies aimed to allow more time or flexibility in time may improve leisure time physical activity. Greater flexibility in working hours, increasing the use of telecommuting, providing job site exercise opportunities, and increasing access to childcare are all possible avenues for promoting physical activity through lowered time constraint. Designing appropriate policies will require a better understanding of how time constraints, income, education, and gender interact in determining physical activity. Two recent papers looking at time use (Mullahy and Rober 2008) and time constraints (Loh 2009) are important first steps in this analysis.

We find that certain area characteristics such as access to gyms, parks, and other recreational facilities are associated with an increase in exercise for adults. These effects remain consistent even when we include measures for unobservable tastes for prevention, such as flu shots. We do not find that these results are robust to income stratification, thus recreation stamps to subsidize the low income to attend gyms as advocated by Pratt et al. (2004) may not improve the amount of leisure time physical activity for low-income groups.

Finally, further investigation is warranted on the interaction between various health behaviors. While there are contradictory findings about the association between smoking and obesity (Chou, Grossman, and Saffer 2004, 2006; Gruber and Frakes 2006; Cawley et al. 2003), our findings suggest that smoking and physical activity may be substitutes, and would be consistent with increased obesity due to higher cigarette taxes/prices. Future research should examine the interaction between smoking, alcohol consumption, dietary behavior, and physical activity.

References

Anderson, P. M., K. F. Butcher, and P. B. Levine. 2003. Maternal employment and overweight children. *Journal of Health Economics* 22 (3): 477–504.
Baum, C. L., and C. J. Ruhm. 2007. Age, socioeconomic status, and obesity growth. NBER Working Paper no. 13289. Cambridge, MA: National Bureau of Economic Research, August.
Bleich, S., D. M. Cutler, C. J. Murray, and A. Adams. 2007. Why is the developed world obese? NBER Working Paper no. 12954. Cambridge, MA: National Bureau of Economic Research, March.
Brownson, R. C., T. K. Boehmer, and D. A. Luke. 2005. Declining rates of physical activity in the United States: What are the contributors? *Annual Review of Public Health* 26:421–43.

Cawley, J., S. Markowitz, and J. Tauras. 2003. Lighting up and slimming down: The effects of body weight and cigarette prices on adolescent smoking initiation. *Journal of Health Economics* 23 (2): 293–311.

Cawley, J., C. Meyerhoefer, and D. Newhouse. 2005. The impact of state physical education requirements on youth physical activity and overweight. *Health Economics* 16 (2): 1287–301.

Centers for Disease Control and Prevention. 2004. Prevalence of no leisure-time physical activity levels—35 states and the District of Columbia, 1988–2002. *MMWR Morbidity Mortality Weekly Report* 53, 83–6. Available at: http://www.cdc.gov/brfss.

Chou, S.-Y., M. Grossman, and H. Saffer. 2004. An economic analysis of adult obesity: Results from the behavioral risk factor surveillance system *Journal of Health Economics* 23 (3): 565–87.

———. 2006. Reply to Jonathan Gruber and Michael Frakes. *Journal of Health Economics* 25 (2): 389–93.

Church, T. S., C. P. Earnest, J. S. Skinner, and S. N. Blair. 2007. Effects of different doses of physical activity on cardiorespiratory fitness among sedentary, overweight or obese postmenopausal women with elevated blood pressure. *Journal of the American Medical Association* 297 (19): 2081–91.

Courtemanche, C., and A. Carden. 2008. The skinny on big-box retailing: Wal-Mart, warehouse clubs and obesity. Available at: http://ssrn.com/abstract=1263316.

Cutler, D. M., E. L. Glaeser, and J. M. Shapiro. 2003. Why have Americans become more obese? *Journal of Economics Perspectives* 17 (3): 93–118.

Dutton, G., M. A. Napolitano, J. A. Whiteley, and B. H. Marcus. 2008. Is physical activity a gateway behavior for diet? Findings from a physical activity trial. *Preventive Medicine* 46 (3): 21–221.

Forsyth, J. M. Oakes, K. H. Schmitz, and M. Hearst. 2007. Does residential density increase walking and other physical activity? *Urban Studies* 44 (4): 679–97.

Garret, N. A., M. Brasure, K. H. Schmitz, M. M. Schulz, and M. R. Huber. 2004. Physical inactivity: Direct cost to a health plan. *American Journal of Preventive Medicine* 27 (4): 304–9.

Gruber, J., and M. Frakes. 2006. Does falling smoking lead to rising obesity? *Journal of Health Economics* 25 (2): 183–97.

Humphreys, B. R., and J. E. Ruseki. 2007. Participation in physical activity and government spending on parks and recreation. *Contemporary Economic Policy* 25 (4): 538–52.

Katzmarzyk, P. T., T. S. Church, and S. N. Blair. 2004. Cardiorespiratory fitness attenuates the effects of metabolic syndrome on all cause and cardiovascular disease mortality in men. *Archives of Internal Medicine* 164 (10): 1092–97.

Katzmarzyk, P. T., N. Gledhil, and R. J. Shephard. 2000. The economic burden of physical inactivity in Canada. *Canadian Medical Association Journal* 163 (11): 1435–40.

Keeler, E. B., W. G. Manning, J. P. Newhouse, E. M. Sloss, and J. Wasserman. 1989. The external costs of a sedentary life-style. *American Journal of Public Health* 79 (8): 975–81.

Loh, C.-P. A. 2009. Physical inactivity and working hour inflexibility: Evidence from a U.S. sample of older men. *Review of Economics of the Household* 7 (3): 257–81.

Mullahy, J., and S. A. Rober. 2008. No time to lose? Time constraints and physical activity. NBER Working Paper no. 14513. Cambridge, MA: National Bureau of Economic Research, November.

Murphy, M. H., A. M. Nevill, E. M. Murtagh, and R. L. Holder. 2007. The effect of walking on fitness, fatness and resting blood pressure. *Preventive Medicine* 44 (5): 377–85.

Pelzman, S. 1975. The effects of automobile safety regulation. *Journal of Political Economy* 83:677–725.

Philipson, T. 2001. The world-wide growth in obesity: An economic research agenda. *Health Economics* 23 (1): 1–7.

Pratt, M., C. A. Macera, J. F. Sallis, M. O'Donnell, and L. D. Frank. 2004. Economic interventions to promote physical activity: Application of the SLOTH model. *American Journal of Preventive Medicine* 27 (3 Suppl): 136–45.

Pratt, M., C. A. Macera, and G. Wang. 2000. Higher direct medical costs associated with physical inactivity *The Physician and Sportsmedicine* 28 (10) (Available at: http://physsportsmed.com).

Rashad, I. 2006. Structural estimation of caloric intake, exercise, smoking, and obesity. *Quarterly Review of Economics and Finance* 46 (2): 268–83.

Rashad, I., and S. Markowitz. 2007. Incentives in obesity and health insurance. NBER Working Paper no. 13113. Cambridge, MA: National Bureau of Economic Research, May.

Romero-Corral, A., V. K. Somers, J. Sierra-Johnson, R. J. Thomas, M. L. Collazo-Clavell, J. Korinek, T. G. Allison, J. A. Batsis, F. H. Sert-Kuniyoshi, and F. Lopez-Jimenez. 2008. Accuracy of body mass index in diagnosing obesity in the general adult population *International Journal of Obesity* 32:959–66.

Ruhm, C. 2000. Are recessions good for your health? *Quarterly Journal of Economics* 115 (2): 617–50.

———. 2005. Healthy living in hard times. *Journal of Health Economics* 24 (2): 341–63.

Shinogle, J. A. 2008. Medical expenditures attributable to inactivity. Maryland Institute for Policy Analysis and Research. Working paper.

Smith, P. K., B. Bogin, and D. Bishai. 2005. Are time preference and body mass index associated?: Evidence from the National Longitudinal Survey of Youth. *Economics & Human Biology* 3 (2): 259–70.

Sturm, R. 2004. The economics of physical activity: Societal trends and rationales for interventions. *American Journal of Preventative Medicine* 27 (3S): 126–35.

U.S. Dept. of Justice, Federal Bureau of Investigation. 2006. *Uniform crime reporting program data [United States]: County-level detailed arrest and offense data, 2001–2005 [computer file]*. Available at: http://www.fbi.gov/ucr/ucr.htm.

Yancey, A. K., J. E. Fielding, G. R. Flores, J. F. Sallis, W. J. McCarthy, and L. Breslow. 2007. Creating a robust public health infrastructure for physical activity promotion. *American Journal of Preventive Medicine* 32 (1): 68–78.

10

Effects of Weight on Adolescent Educational Attainment

Robert Kaestner, Michael Grossman, and Benjamin Yarnoff

10.1   Introduction

The documented growth in obesity over the last thirty years has resulted in widespread public and private concern over the consequences associated with this significant change in the human body. Most of this concern is focused on health, as obesity has been linked to poor health, particularly diabetes and cardiovascular disease (National Heart, Lung and Blood Institute 1998). The perceived seriousness of the health consequences of obesity has resulted in an explosion of research seeking to identify the causes of obesity and policies that may reduce obesity.

While the health consequences of obesity are clearly important, researchers and others have recognized that obesity may adversely affect other determinants of well-being such as earnings and marriage.[1] Obesity may also affect educational attainment, which is arguably the most important determinant of well-being. Surprisingly, there is little research on this issue despite widespread belief that obesity has a negative impact on children's, and thus adult, educational achievement (National Education Association 1994).

Obesity may affect educational achievement in several ways. First, peers

Robert Kaestner is a professor in the department of economics and a member of the Institute of Government and Public Affairs at the University of Illinois at Chicago, and a research associate of the National Bureau of Economic Research. Michael Grossman is Distinguished Professor of Economics at the City University of New York Graduate Center, and a research associate and director of the Health Economics Program at the National Bureau of Economic Research. Benjamin Yarnoff is a graduate student in economics at the University of Illinois at Chicago.

1. See Averett and Korenman (1996), Cawley (2004), Cawley et al. (1996), Fu and Goldman (1996), Sobal, Rauschenbach, and Frongillo (1992), and Gortmaker et al. (1993).

and teachers may discriminate against overweight and obese children and this will adversely affect educational achievement (National Education Association 1994). Second, obesity may affect health in ways that lower achievement. Obesity is associated with sleeping disorders (e.g., sleep apnea) and depression and these illnesses may result in poor cognitive functioning and more missed days of school. Third, obesity may affect how children spend their time and, specifically, how much time they spend studying. Overweight and obese children may spend less time in physical activity and engaged in social activities, and as a result, spend more time studying, which suggests that obesity may positively affect educational achievement.

The possibility that obesity may affect education is more than a private issue of concern only to families. While it is true that families will make decisions about food consumption and children's education that incorporates any effects of obesity on education, these decisions will, in part, reflect government policy. For example, farm subsidies affect the price of food, and transportation policy and land regulation affect the price of physical activity (e.g., walking). These government interventions will partly determine obesity, and therefore possibly determine education. Thus, analyses of the effect of obesity on children's educational achievement are particularly relevant for public policy. Moreover, if obesity lowers educational attainment, this will worsen the already significant health problems of obese persons given the protective effects of education on health (Grossman 2006).

In this chapter, we investigate the effect of obesity on educational attainment of adolescents. We study a nationally representative sample of children aged fourteen to eighteen, drawn from the 1997 cohort of the National Longitudinal Survey of Youth. Our results indicate that weight status (under- and overweight) does not have large effects on educational attainment, as measured by grade progression and drop out status. While we cannot rule out the possibility that weight may have small effects on educational attainment, there is little evidence that being under- or overweight has large, systematically positive or negative effects on grade progression and the probability of dropping out.

10.2   Previous Literature

There are relatively few studies of the effects of obesity on educational achievement.[2] Studies of adolescents often find negative associations

2. This section draws heavily on Kaestner and Grossman (2008). There is a somewhat larger, although still relatively small, literature on the effects of child health on educational achievement, and some of these papers use weight as an indicator of child health (e.g., Edwards and Grossman 1979; Shakotko, Edwards, and Grossman 1981; Blau and Grossberg 1992; and Korenman, Miller, and Sjaastad 1995; Rosenzweig and Wolpin 1994; Kaestner and Corman 1995). However, all but Shakotko, Edwards, and Grossman (1981) and Edwards and Grossman (1979) focused on underweight as a measure of health.

between obesity and educational achievement. Shakotko, Edwards, and Grossman (1981) investigated the effect of being overweight in childhood (aged six to eleven) on scores from the Wechsler Intelligence Scale for Children (WISC) and the Wide Range Achievement Test (WRAT) in adolescence (aged twelve to seventeen) using children who were examined in two consecutive National Health Examination Surveys (II and III). Estimates were obtained in the context of a Granger-causality model. Coefficients of overweight were positive, but not significant. Falkner et al. (2001) studied grade progression among tenth, eleventh, and twelfth grade students in Connecticut. Results from multivariate regression analyses indicated that obese females were 1.51 times more likely to be held back a grade than normal weight females. A similar association was not found for males. Ding et al. (2006) studied the grade point average (GPA) of high school students in northern Virginia. They performed an instrumental variables estimation using a genetic obesity marker as an instrument for obesity and found that obese females had GPAs 0.45 points lower than normal weight females. This association was not found for males. Sabia (2007) studied a geographically broader sample of adolescents aged fourteen to seventeen drawn from the National Longitudinal Survey of Adolescent Health, and he used a variety of statistical methods (e.g., fixed effects and instrumental variables) to account for potential confounding from omitted variables. In general, he found that obesity was negatively correlated with grade point average (GPA), although the most robust and consistent evidence of this association was limited to white, female adolescents. For this group, the GPA of obese females was approximately 10 percent lower than that of normal weight females. However, Crosnoe and Muller (2004), who also used data from the National Longitudinal Survey of Adolescent Health, found no effect of obesity on GPA after controlling for prior achievement. Additionally, Fletcher and Lehrer (2009) use data from the National Longitudinal Survey of Adolescent Health and find no effect of obesity on Peabody Individual Achievement Test (PIAT) scores after controlling for confounding factors with fixed effects and instrumental variables. Finally, Sigfusdotir, Kristjansson, and Allegrante (2006) found that among Icelandic youth aged fourteen to fifteen, a high Body Mass Index (BMI) (1 or 2 standard deviations above mean) was associated with lower grades after adjusting for personal and family characteristics. While not an exhaustive review, these studies are the largest and most sophisticated, and their findings suggest that obesity is associated with lower educational achievement of adolescents.[3]

---

3. Canning and Mayer (1967) compared obese and nonobese high school students in suburban Boston and found no difference in test (SAT) scores or educational aspirations. Gortmaker et al. (1993) studied adolescents and young adults from the 1979 cohort of the National Longitudinal Survey of Youth and found that females between the ages of sixteen and twenty-three who were overweight had 0.3 years less education than normal weight females eight years later.

While the findings from previous studies suggest that obesity has an adverse effect on adolescent educational achievement, more study is warranted. First, there are relatively few studies, and only three that use nationally representative data from the United States (Sabia 2007; Crosnoe and Muller 2004; Fletcher and Lehrer 2008). These three studies use the same data (National Longitudinal Study of Adolescent Health) and surprisingly reached different conclusions. The paucity of research in this area is significant given the importance of education to lifetime well-being. Here we begin to address this shortfall by providing an analysis of the effect of weight on adolescent educational achievement using a large, national sample of children aged fourteen to eighteen that have not been previously used to study this question. Second, more research is needed that recognizes that current educational achievement is a function of a lifetime of influences (Todd and Wolpin 2003, 2007). Past research has not paid appropriate attention to this issue, and as a result, has proceeded in an ad hoc basis that may explain some of the inconsistent findings of past research. In this chapter, the cumulative nature of educational achievement is a central focus and we provide an arguably more theoretically consistent analysis than prior studies.

10.3   Empirical Framework

Our empirical analysis is based on the educational production function approach that is widely used to identify the effects of family and school resources on educational achievement (Hanushek 1986; Todd and Wolpin 2003, 2007). As Todd and Wolpin (2003, 2007) emphasize, an important aspect of these models is that current educational achievement is a function of all past family and school resources devoted to children's education.[4] Here, we incorporate this idea into our analysis using the following model:

$$\text{GRADE}_{it} = \alpha_i + \gamma_t + \sum_{k=0}^{t} (\tau_k \, \text{OWN}_{ik} + \beta_k \, \text{HEALTH}_{ik} + \delta_k \, \text{PAR}_{ik})$$

(1)
$$+ \sum_{k=0}^{t} (\lambda_k \, \text{TEACH}_{ik} + \pi_k \, \text{PEER}_{ik} + Z_{ik}\Gamma_k) + u_{it}$$

$$t = 14,15,16,17.$$

Equation (1) indicates that the grade level (GRADE) of child i at age t depends on a child-specific endowment (α_i), developmental age at time t (γ_t), the time the child spends in educational activities (OWN) at each age from birth to age t, child health (HEALTH) at each age from birth to age t, time spent by family members (e.g., mother) producing education (PAR) from birth to age t, the quantity and quality of school and teacher inputs (TEACH) from birth to age t, the quantity and quality of peer inputs (PEER) from birth to age

---

4. This section draws heavily on Kaestner and Grossman (2008).

t, and other market goods (Z) from birth to age t that are used to produce educational achievement.

Equation (1) allows determinants of educational achievement to have different effects depending on age; for example, the parental time input (PAR) may have a different effect at age fourteen than at age seventeen because at age fourteen children may spend more time at home with the parent studying. However, equation (1) assumes that effects of educational inputs do not depend on time since investments were made, which is equivalent to assuming that there is no depreciation of education capital. This specification was chosen to facilitate estimation, which we discuss in more detail later, including ways to test the restrictions embodied in equation (1).

Our interest is to obtain estimates of the effect of weight on educational achievement. As noted, there are several ways that weight (overweight) may affect educational achievement. One of the most cited potential causes is size (weight) discrimination. Overweight and obese children face a variety of discrimination from peers and teachers that may adversely affect educational achievement (Ritts, Patterson, and Tubbs 1992; NEA 1994; Neumark-Sztainer, Story, and Faibisch 1998; Jalongo 1999; Solovay 2000; Puhl and Brownell 2003; Schwartz and Puhl 2003; Eisenberg, Neumark-Sztainer, and Story 2003; Janssen et al. 2004). In terms of equation (1), size (weight) discrimination would affect the quantity and quality of school and teacher inputs and the quantity and quality of peer inputs. Weight may even affect the quantity and quality of parental inputs if households allocate resources in response to size discrimination (Crandall 1995; Puhl and Latner 2007).

Discrimination against overweight and obese children may also lead to depression ($HEALTH$ in equation [1]) that can adversely affect educational achievement (Wurtman 1993; Smith et al. 1998; Hoebel et al. 1999; Goodman and Whitaker 2002).[5] Childhood obesity is also associated with other aspects of health such as asthma, sleep apnea and sleeping disorders, which may adversely affect cognitive functioning and school attendance, and thus educational achievement (Gozal 1998; Dietz 1998; Must and Strauss 1999; Redline et al. 1999; von Mutius et al. 2001; Gilliland et al. 2003; Beuther, Weiss, and Sutherland 2006; Geier et al. 2007).[6]

Size (weight) discrimination could also affect the child's time use. Ostracism may lead a child to have fewer social relationships and engage in fewer social activities. This may result in greater time spent in educational activities and higher educational achievement (all else equal). A child's weight may also affect their physical fitness and prevent children from engaging in

---

5. However, the causal relationship between obesity and depression is unresolved and some have argued that depression causes obesity, for example, because of affective disorders such as binge eating. Others argue that there is a common genetic component linking depression and obesity (Mustillo et al. 2003; Bjorntorp and Rosmond 2000; Rosmond 2001).

6. In the case of sleeping disorders, the direction of causality is uncertain, as some have argued that inadequate sleep is a cause of obesity (Sekine et al. 2002).

recreational activities, which again may provide more time for educational activities.

In sum, past study from a variety of disciplines (e.g., psychology and medicine) suggests that overweight and obese children may have lower educational achievement than normal weight children, although the alternative, that obesity is associated with higher achievement, is plausible. One way to incorporate these causal pathways in the conceptual model is to replace the proximate causes of educational achievement (e.g., child health) with determinants of those causes, most notably child weight. Making these substitutions results in the following:

$$(2) \qquad E_{it} = \tilde{\alpha}_i + \tilde{\gamma}_t + \sum_{k=0}^{t} (\rho_k \, \text{WEIGHT}_{ik} + Z_{ik} \tilde{\Gamma}_k) + \tilde{u}_{it}.$$

Equation (2) is a quasi-reduced form model because we have substituted for the determinants of educational achievement, but weight (WEIGHT) remains endogenous. We discuss the source of this endogeneity below. We have used the symbol ~ to indicate a reduced form parameter. The coefficient on weight will measure the effect of weight that operates through changes in the quantity or quality of educational inputs (e.g., child's use of time, child health, and school resources).

The quasi-reduced form production function represented by equation (2) is the basis of our empirical model. The main problem associated with obtaining estimates of an empirical analog to equation (2) is that weight (WEIGHT) may be correlated with the error, which includes unmeasured exogenous determinants of the inputs in the production function (equation 1). Further, the data requirements necessary to obtain unbiased estimates of equation (2) are daunting, as the entire history of the exogenous determinants of production function inputs enter the model.

One way to reduce the data necessary to estimate equation (2) is to examine changes in educational achievement between two ages. Such a model is given by:

$$(3) \qquad \text{GRADE}_{it} - \text{GRADE}_{i(t-1)} = (\gamma_t - \gamma_{t-1}) + \rho_t \text{WEIGHT}_{it}$$
$$+ Z_{it}\Gamma_t + (u_{it} - u_{i(t-1)}).$$

As is made clear by equation (3), the difference in educational achievement between ages $t - 1$ and t depends on the difference in developmental age $(\gamma_t - \gamma_{t-1})$ and resources used between these ages. Notably, endowed intelligence (α_i) is eliminated from the model.[7] However, one consequence of this approach is that estimates of the effects of educational inputs are specific to age t (Todd and Wolpin 2003, 2007).

Three aspects of equation (3) merit discussion. The first point relates

---

7. This is not necessarily the case, as the endowment could have different age-specific effects. If so, there would be an age subscript on the endowment in equation (1) and differencing would not eliminate the endowment effect.

to the fact that the left-hand side of equation (3) is the change in educational achievement, but the right-hand side variables are the levels of inputs between ages $t - 1$ and t, or the change in stock (i.e., investment) of what may be referred to as educational capital. For example, it is the weight of the child between ages $t - 1$ and t that enters and not the change in weight between ages $t - 1$ and t. This specification results from the assumption of equation (1) that the effects of educational inputs are cumulative. Consider child weight and the hypothesis that there is size (weight) discrimination. The change in grade attainment between ages $t - 1$ and t depends on the child's weight at (during) age t. This is reasonable. It is not the change in weight that matters, but the weight itself that brings forth discrimination that adversely affects achievement. Analogously, it is not the change in family resources that matters, but the actual amount of time and money spent during the period producing child education. This point has not been well understood by previous researchers and, as a result, their models have been arguably misspecified (Todd and Wolpin 2003). For example, Sabia (2007) used fixed effects methods that regress differences in educational achievement (e.g., GPA) on differences in children's weight, which is incorrect given the specification of equation (1).[8]

Second, because most educational inputs are not measured, proxy variables (i.e., reduced form determinants) are often used. For example, mother's educational achievement is used as a measure of the quality of parental time input. This "quality" input enters the production function each period, and therefore is included in equation (3) even if it is time-invariant. Similarly, a time-invariant demographic characteristic such as race, which may be a proxy for unmeasured inputs, also enters the model because of the age-specific effects of inputs. The age-specific estimates of equation (3) merit further discussion. The coefficient on weight (e.g., obesity) measures the effect of obesity on the growth in educational attainment between time $t - 1$ and t. Obesity (and other inputs) may have a different effect at each age. For example, discrimination associated with obesity may be more important at older than younger ages.

While equation (3) reduces the data necessary to estimate the model considerably, it remains unlikely that all relevant variables will be measured and estimates of the effect of weight (obesity) may still be biased. Given the common set of underlying factors that affect resource allocation decisions, the quantities of measured inputs (weight) are likely to be correlated with the error, which includes time-varying, unmeasured exogenous (e.g., preferences) determinants of educational inputs. One solution is instrumental

8. There may be a measurement error problem given the nature of most available data. In our case, weight is measured at time $t - 1$ and t and may not be constant during the period. However, most interviews in the NLSY97 occurred between October and March and our dependent variable is grade progression. So, weight during the academic year is a reasonably good empirical measure. Using the difference in weight between periods, however, is not justified.

variables, and the structure of equation (3) suggests many potential instruments. Specifically, inputs in periods prior to $t - 1$ may be used as instruments because only time t inputs are included in equation (3) (Todd and Wolpin 2003). The assumption underlying this approach is that the future does not cause the past and so, for example, weight in period $t - 2$ will be uncorrelated with the error $(u_{it} - u_{i(t-1)})$ in equation (3). Therefore, weight (and all other inputs) in period $t - 2$ can be used as an instrument for weight in period t. Past weight is likely to be a particularly good instrument in that it is likely to be strongly correlated with current weight given the documented persistence of weight (Serdula et al. 1993; Lake, Power, and Cole 1997; McTigue, Garrett, and Popkin 2002; Whitaker et al. 1998).

The fact that past period inputs, or their determinants, do not enter equation (3) provides a basis for a specification test. If included, past period inputs should have no statistically significant effect on educational attainment. We implemented this test by including lagged values of respondent's weight, drinking and smoking behavior, and health. In all cases, we could not reject the null hypothesis that these lagged variables were jointly insignificant (at the 0.05 level of significance). These results provide some evidence to support the specification of equation (3).

10.4   Data

The data for the analysis are drawn from the National Longitudinal Survey of Youth 1997 Cohort (NLSY97). The NLSY97 is a national sample of individuals aged twelve to sixteen as of December 31, 1996, who were interviewed in 1997 and each subsequent year. The NLSY97 was designed to be representative of persons born in the United States between 1980 and 1984. Black and Hispanic persons are overrepresented in the data. We focused on children between the ages of fourteen and eighteen (grades eight through twelve) drawn from survey years 1997 to 2002.

Educational attainment was measured by grade progression and drop out status. As indicated by equation (3), we examined changes in grade, or grade progression, between two survey dates: when a person is age $t - 1$ and age t.[9] We define grade progression in two ways: as the change in highest grade attended, or the change in highest grade completed, from age $t - 1$ to age t.[10] In most cases, the interval between ages $t - 1$ and t is between ten and twenty-one months with a median of thirteen months, but the median time

9. The NLSY97 also collected data from school transcripts from which there is information on the number and types of credits taken in high school and grade point average. However, this information is missing for a large portion of the sample.

10. If grade progression, grade completion, or drop out was negative we dropped the observation. Similarly, if grade progression or grade completion appeared unreasonably large (e.g., > 3), we dropped the observation. Observations dropped for these reasons were 1.3 percent of the total.

between surveys was larger for younger age groups. For example, for those aged fourteen at time $t - 1$, the median time to the next interview (t) was eighteen months. We classified someone as a drop out if they were not enrolled in school and they did not have a high school degree. Someone who was not enrolled and had a General Equivalency Diploma (GED) was classified as a drop out. We grouped respondents by age (rounded to the nearest year) and conducted all analyses separately for persons aged fourteen, fifteen, sixteen, and seventeen at time $t - 1$.[11]

The weight and height of children was self-reported, and we used these self-reported measures to calculate body mass index (BMI).[12] We then categorize children's weight status according to where their BMI falls in the distribution of children's weight in the NLSY97 sample.[13] Separate weight distributions were calculated for males and females and by age. We use the following percentile categories: 0 to 10, 11 to 25, 26 to 75, 76 to 90, 91 to 100.[14] As described earlier, ideally we would be able to measure weight (and all educational inputs) during the interval between time $t - 1$ and t. Here we have opted to use values of weight and other inputs (determinants) at time $t - 1$. This is reasonable given that most interviews occurred during the academic year between October and March, and it is the performance during the academic year that determines whether a person will progress (drop out) in grade.

To control for other unmeasured determinants of educational attainment we used a variety of proxy variables. As is common in similar analyses, we are missing information on most inputs that are likely to enter the educational production function. Therefore, we use variables that proxy for these inputs such as mother's education and family structure (e.g., two biological parents), which are likely to be correlated with the quantity and quality of the inputs used to produce educational achievement. Specifically, we use the following variables: the number of months between surveys, dummy variables for respondent's age in months at baseline grade, dummy variables for month of interview at baseline grade, dummy variables for year of interview at baseline grade, dummy variables for highest grade attended at baseline, dummy variables for race/ethnicity (white, black, Hispanic, Asian, other), mother's age at birth of respondent (continuous), dummy variables

11. Some individuals will be the same age at two consecutive interviews, and in these cases we used the first interview we observed a person to be of a particular age.

12. We acknowledge that self-reported weight and height has considerable measurement error. In the best case, this will result in attenuation bias, but if measurement error is systematic, estimates may be upward or downward biased.

13. The distribution of weight in the NLSY97 is shifted to the right relative to a national sample from the National Health and Nutritional Survey. See appendix table 10A.1, which shows the distribution of the NLSY97 sample in terms of the National Health and Nutrition Examination Survey (NHANES) 2000 sample. For example, 15 percent of sixteen-year-old females in the NLSY97 are in the 91 to 100 percentiles of the NHANES distribution.

14. We performed the same analysis with the more traditional categories: 0 to 5, 6 to 15, 16 to 84, 85 to 94, 95 to 100. Results from this analysis was similar to those presented here.

for mother's educational attainment (less than high school [LTHS], high school [HS], some college, bachelor of arts [BA] plus), dummy variables for family structure (two biological parents, two parents, one biological parent, other, on own), dummy variables for respondent health (excellent, poor, other), number of days respondent smoked in last thirty days at baseline, number of cigarettes respondent smoked per day in last thirty days at baseline, number of days respondent drank in last thirty days at baseline, number of drinks respondent drank per day in last thirty days at baseline, dummy variables for residence in metropolitan statistical area (MSA) (MSA-central city, MSA-non-central city, non-MSA), continuous unemployment rate in local labor market, and county per capita income.

10.5 Results

10.5.1 Descriptive Analysis

Tables 10.1 and 10.2 present (unweighted) means for highest grade attended, highest grade completed, and drop out status by gender and weight status. Figures are presented separately by age. Figures in table 10.1 suggest that there is little difference in grade attainment and drop out status by weight for male adolescents. At younger ages (fourteen and fifteen), there is some evidence that underweight (0 to 10 percentiles) males have made less progress in school than average (26 to 75 percentiles) weight males. At older ages (sixteen and seventeen), drop out rates of overweight (91 to 100 percentiles) males tend to be higher. Overall, however, the figures in table 10.1 do not indicate large or systematic differences in grade progression and drop out status by weight among male adolescents. Table 10.2 provides sample means for females. For this group, we observe slower progress in school among overweight (91 to 100 percentiles) females ages sixteen and seventeen. Otherwise, there are few statistically significant, or large, differences in educational attainment among female adolescents.[15]

Table 10.3 presents (unweighted) sample means of other characteristics by weight for females.[16] The purpose of this table is to investigate whether there are significant differences in observed characteristics by weight that may confound the relationship between weight and educational attainment observed in tables 10.1 and 10.2. Figures in table 10.3 show some systematic differences. Children in the upper tail of the weight distribution are more likely to be black, be in poorer health, live in single-parent families, and live

15. In appendix table 10A.1, we show sample means for females by weight status when weight status is classified using NHANES distribution. Conclusions are similar as those stated in the text. Among older females, aged sixteen and seventeen, there is some evidence that overweight females have progressed in school more slowly than average weight females.
16. An analogous table for males provides similar evidence of some selection on observed characteristics.

Table 10.1   **Educational attainment of male adolescents by age and relative weight status**

	Relative weight status				
	0–10%	11–25%	26–75%	76–90%	91–100%
Age 14					
Highest grade attended	7.6*	7.8	7.8	7.9	7.9
Highest grade completed	6.8*	7.0	7.0	7.0	7.1
Dropout	0.00	0.02	0.01	0.03	0.04*
Number of observations	128	192	654	196	128
Age 15					
Highest grade attended	8.7*	8.8	8.9	8.9	9.0*
Highest grade completed	7.8*	7.9	8.0	8.0	8.1*
Dropout	0.00*	0.02	0.03	0.04	0.04
Number of observations	203	365	1122	341	223
Age 16					
Highest grade attended	9.8	9.8	9.8	9.9*	9.9
Highest grade completed	8.9	8.9	8.9	9.0	8.9
Dropout	0.03	0.03	0.05	0.05	0.08*
Number of observations	313	454	1513	421	288
Age 17					
Highest grade attended	10.7	10.7	10.7	10.8*	10.7
Highest grade completed	9.8	9.8	9.8	9.9*	9.8
Dropout	0.08	0.09	0.09	0.09	0.11
Number of observations	359	618	1,822	564	332

Notes: Data drawn from survey years 1997 to 2003.

*Indicates that the estimate is statistically different ($p < 0.05$) from the estimate for adolescents in 26 to 75 percentiles.

in central cities, and their mothers tend to be less educated and younger at the time of birth of the child. Figures in table 10.3 provide some evidence that children in the upper tails of the weight distribution may differ in measured and unmeasured ways, and that these differences may confound the relationship between weight and educational attainment.[17]

To further explore the extent of selection on observable variables, we present estimates of the association between weight and the respondent's score on the Peabody Individual Achievement Test (PIAT) in mathematics. The PIAT mathematics test is a widely used, validated assessment of a person's achievement in mathematics as taught in mainstream education. Estimates

17. In appendix table 10A.2, we present means of the Armed Services Vocational Aptitude Battery (ASVAB) test percentile score and other characteristics by weight status for children aged fourteen to seventeen. We do not present separate means by age because the ASVAB test was only administered in 1997. In appendix table 10A.2, we observe significantly lower test scores for males and females in the upper-right tail of the weight distribution. However, we also observe significant differences in other characteristics (females only presented) for those in the overweight (91 to 100 percentiles) category. These results are consistent with those presented in the text on grade progression.

Table 10.2   Educational attainment of female adolescents by age and relative
                  weight status

	Relative weight status				
	0–10%	11–25%	26–75%	76–90%	91–100%
Age 14					
Highest grade attended	7.9	8.0	8.0	7.9	8.0
Highest grade completed	7.1	7.2	7.2	7.1	7.1
Dropout	0.01	0.01	0.02	0.03	0.03
Number of observations	118	182	605	175	120
Age 15					
Highest grade attended	8.9	8.9*	9.0	9.0	9.0
Highest grade completed	8.0	8.1	8.1	8.1	8.1
Dropout	0.04	0.02	0.03	0.04	0.03
Number of observations	204	311	1011	296	211
Age 16					
Highest grade attended	9.9*	10.0	10.0	9.9	9.8*
Highest grade completed	9.0*	9.1	9.1	9.0	9.0*
Dropout	0.04	0.03	0.05	0.04	0.02
Number of observations	264	451	1391	419	284
Age 17					
Highest grade attended	10.9	10.9	10.9	10.8*	10.7*
Highest grade completed	10.0	10.1	10.0	9.9*	9.8*
Dropout	0.09	0.06	0.08	0.11*	0.11
Number of observations	340	488	1,780	495	322

Notes: Data drawn from survey years 1997 to 2003.
*Indicates that the estimate is statistically different ($p < 0.05$) from the estimate for adolescents in 26 to 27 percentiles.

of the association between weight and PIAT scores are obtained from a simple cross-sectional regression model because the PIAT test was administered most widely in 1997 (Round 1), and in a limited way in later interviews. Specifically, all respondents not yet enrolled in tenth grade were administered the test in 1997, and only those who were twelve as of December 1996 were administered the test in later rounds. Therefore, we are unable to exploit the longitudinal nature of the NLSY97 for this measure of achievement. Here, we limit the sample to those aged fourteen and fifteen in 1997 because this is part of the age range used in later analyses.

Table 10.4 presents the estimates. We obtain estimates for two regression model specifications: a basic specification that includes only a limited number of covariates and a model with additional controls for individual and family characteristics (see notes to table 10.4 for details). Estimates in table 10.4 suggest small differences in PIAT test scores by weight status, which is consistent with the small differences in educational attainment by weight observed in tables 10.1 through 10.2. Among males, the only statistically significant estimates are for those in the lowest weight category; those in the

| Table 10.3 | Individual and family characteristics of female adolescents by age and relative weight status |

	Relative weight status				
	0–10%	11–25%	26–75%	76–90%	91–100%
Age 14					
Black	0.14*	0.19	0.25	0.42*	0.48*
Hispanic	0.19	0.19	0.20	0.21	0.22
Excellent health	0.75	0.77	0.76	0.62*	0.53*
Smoke	0.25	0.29	0.34	0.37	0.27
Age in months	168.7	169.1	169.1	168.9	169.9*
Mom age at birth	26.1	25.7	26.0	24.2*	24.7*
Mom LTHS	0.18	0.19	0.20	0.24	0.23
Mom BA	0.22	0.21	0.19	0.07*	0.09*
Two biological parents	0.58*	0.55	0.48	0.44	0.38*
Central city resident	0.32	0.27	0.28	0.38*	0.47*
Age 16					
Black	0.20*	0.20*	0.24	0.33*	0.46*
Hispanic	0.13*	0.21	0.20	0.25	0.19
Excellent health	0.69	0.75	0.73	0.62*	0.50*
Smoke	0.47	0.42	0.46	0.42	0.44
Age in months	191.8*	192.5	192.5	192.8	192.5
Mom age at birth	25.5	25.8	25.9	25.0*	24.5*
Mom LTHS	0.19	0.21	0.20	0.25*	0.25*
Mom BA	0.14	0.21	0.17	0.11*	0.10*
Two biological parents	0.53	0.53	0.48	0.45	0.35*
Central city resident	0.26	0.29	0.32	0.34	0.40*

Notes: Data drawn from survey years 1997 to 2003. Sample sizes are same as in table 10.1.
*Indicates that the estimate is statistically different ($p < 0.05$) from the estimate for adolescents in 26 to 75 percentiles.

lowest weight category have test scores that are 3.24 points lower than those of average weight (reference group is 26 to 75 percentile). The magnitude of this estimate represents approximately 0.2 standard deviations, or 4 percent of the mean PIAT score. Other estimates for males are smaller. In the case of females, there are no statistically significant estimates once controls for observed characteristics are included. Moreover, among those in the overweight category (91 to 100 percentiles), controlling for observed characteristics greatly reduces the magnitude of the estimates. Finally, we reestimated the models in table 10.4 including controls for the highest grade attended and estimates from this model were quite similar to those presented in table 10.4. This is not surprising given the weak association between weight status and highest grade attended in tables 10.1 and 10.2. In sum, there are small differences in PIAT test scores by weight status that are similar to the small differences in grade attainment and drop out status by weight status. While these descriptive statistics and simple regression estimates are not definitive, they suggest that if there is a causal effect of weight status on educational

Table 10.4   **Estimates of the effect of relative weight status on PIAT math score: Adolescents ages 14 and 15 in round 1 (1997)**

	Males PIAT math score		Females PIAT math score	
	(1)	(2)	(1)	(2)
Weight 0–10%	–2.78*	–3.24**	2.09	0.70
	(1.62)	(1.46)	(1.60)	(1.48)
Weight 11–25%	–0.23	–0.69	0.71	–0.16
	(1.32)	(1.19)	(1.41)	(1.31)
Weight 76–90%	–2.01	–0.87	–2.43	0.48
	(1.37)	(1.23)	(1.36)	(1.29)
Weight 91–100%	–1.97	0.93	–4.68**	–1.46
	(1.63)	(1.49)	(1.67)	(1.58)
Basic model	Yes		Yes	
Extended model		Yes		Yes
Mean dep. var.	73		73	
Num. obs.	1,404		1,264	

Notes: The basic model includes the following: dummy variables for weight status (26 to 75 percentiles are reference category), dummy variables for respondent's age in months at time of survey, dummy variables for month of interview, and dummy variables for year of interview. Extended model includes all variables in basic model and the following: dummy variables for race/ethnicity (white, black, Hispanic, Asian, other), mother's age at birth of respondent (continuous), dummy variables for mother's educational attainment (LTHS, HS, some college, BA plus), dummy variables for family structure (two biological parents, two parents, one biological parent, other, on own), dummy variables for respondent health (excellent, poor, other), number of days respondent smoked in last 30 days at baseline, number of cigarettes respondent smoked per day in last 30 days at baseline, number of days respondent drank in last 30 days at baseline, number of drinks respondent drank per day in last 30 days at baseline, dummy variables for residence in MSA (MSA-central city, MSA-non-central city, non-MSA), continuous unemployment rate in local labor market, and county per capita income.
** Significant at the 5 percent level.
* Significant at the 10 percent level.

achievement, it is likely to be quite small. We now turn to analyses of grade progression, grade completion, and drop out status that exploit the longitudinal nature of the NLSY97 data.

10.5.2   Analyses of Grade Progression, Grade Completion, and Dropping Out

We begin the discussion with an analysis of the effect of weight status on the level of educational achievement. As we described previously, this model is inconsistent with a human capital production function in which current level of educational achievement is a function of all past inputs. Nevertheless, we present results of this specification in table 10.5, which is limited to those aged sixteen (other results are available from the authors). Estimates for the male sample are presented in the top panel and estimates for the female sample are presented in the bottom panel. For each dependent variable, two specifications of the model are estimated: a basic model (column [1]) and an

| Table 10.5 | Estimates of the effect of relative weight status on the level of educational attainment at age 16 |

Males	Highest grade attended		Highest grade completed		Dropped out	
	(1)	(2)	(1)	(2)	(1)	(2)
Weight 0–10%	–0.07	–0.04	–0.07	–0.08*	0.01	0.01
	(0.05)	(0.05)	(0.05)	(0.05)	(0.02)	(0.02)
Weight 11–25%	–0.06	0.07*	–0.04	–0.02	0.00	–0.01
	(0.05)	(0.04)	(0.04)	(0.04)	(0.02)	(0.02)
Weight 76–90%	0.09*	–0.03	0.09**	0.06	–0.02	–0.02
	(0.05)	(0.04)	(0.05)	(0.04)	(0.02)	(0.02)
Weight 91–100%	0.07	0.03	0.09*	0.10*	–0.03	–0.04*
	(0.06)	(0.05)	(0.05)	(0.05)	(0.02)	(0.02)
Basic model	Yes		Yes		Yes	
Extended model		Yes		Yes		Yes
Mean dep. var.	11.00	11.00	10.07	10.07	0.08	0.08
Num. obs.	2,612	2,176	2,612	2,258	2,608	2,254

Females	(1)	(2)	(1)	(2)	(1)	(2)
Weight 0–10%	–0.04	–0.04	–0.05	–0.04	0.03*	0.03*
	(0.05)	(0.05)	(0.05)	(0.05)	(0.02)	(0.02)
Weight 11–25%	0.07*	0.07*	0.05	0.06	–0.01	–0.00
	(0.04)	(0.04)	(0.04)	(0.04)	(0.01)	(0.01)
Weight 76–90%	–0.07	–0.03	–0.08**	0.01	0.03**	0.02
	(0.04)	(0.04)	(0.04)	(0.04)	(0.02)	(0.02)
Weight 91–100%	–0.10*	0.03	–0.10**	–0.00	0.00	0.00
	(0.05)	(0.05)	(0.05)	(0.05)	(0.02)	(0.02)
Basic model	Yes		Yes		Yes	
Extended model		Yes		Yes		Yes
Mean dep. var.	11.20	11.20	10.27	10.27	0.07	0.07
Num. obs.	2,461	2,176	2,461	2,176	2,452	2,168

Notes: See notes to table 10.4.

extended model that includes additional controls (column [2]). We will focus our discussion on estimates obtained from the extended model.

For males there are few statistically significant estimates. The exceptions are for those in the highest weight category; being in this category is associated with approximately a 10 percentage point increase in being in a higher grade, and 4 percentage point lower probability of being a drop out. For females, there are no statistically significant estimates. More importantly, the inclusion of an extended set of controls greatly reduces the magnitudes and significance of almost all estimates. The sensitivity of estimates to the addition of more control variables demonstrates that weight is correlated with observable characteristics. Much of this problem is addressed in the first-difference specification. We now turn to the presentation of these results.

Equation (3) is the basis of the estimates we now discuss. We obtain estimates for two specifications of this model. A basic specification that includes only a limited number of covariates: dummy variables for weight status (see table 10.1), dummy variables for number of months between surveys, dummy variables for respondent's age in months at baseline (t–1) grade, dummy variables for month of interview at baseline grade, and dummy variables for year of interview at baseline grade. We also estimated a model with additional controls for individual and family characteristics: dummy variables for race/ethnicity (white, black, Hispanic, Asian, other), mother's age at birth of respondent (continuous), dummy variables for mother's educational attainment (LTHS, HS, some college, BA plus), dummy variables for family structure (two biological parents, two parents, one biological parent, other, on own), dummy variables for respondent health (excellent, poor, other), number of days respondent smoked in last thirty days at baseline, number of cigarettes respondent smoked per day in last thirty days at baseline, number of days respondent drank in last thirty days at baseline, number of drinks respondent drank per day in last thirty days at baseline, dummy variables for residence in MSA (MSA-central city, MSA-non-central city, non-MSA), unemployment rate in local labor market, and county per capita income.

Table 10.6 presents estimates of the association between weight status and change in educational attainment between time t – 1 and t for children aged fourteen at time t – 1. Estimates for the male sample are presented in the top panel and estimates for the female sample are presented in the bottom panel. For each dependent variable, two specifications of the model are estimated: a basic model (column [1]) and an extended model that includes additional controls (column [2]). We will focus our discussion on estimates obtained from the extended model. The sample size and mean of the dependent variable are presented in the bottom rows of each panel. Note that the mean change in grade attended and grade completed is significantly greater than one because the interval between surveys, particularly for the younger age groups, is on average over a year and in some cases as much as two years.

The first point to note about table 10.6 is that there are few statistically significant estimates. For males, there are no statistically significant estimates. However, there is some consistent evidence that overweight (76 to 90 and 91 to 100 percentiles) males are less likely to progress in grade or complete an additional grade, and more likely to drop out. Effect sizes are relatively large. Consider estimates associated with dropping out. Males in the 91 to 100 percentiles have a probability of dropping out that is 1.6 percentage points higher than average (26 to 75 percentiles) weight males. Given a mean drop out rate of 4 percent, these are large estimates in relative terms.

These estimates illustrate that the power to detect small effects may be limited. According to the National Center for Education Statistics (2006), between 5 and 7 percent of students in grades six through twelve are retained

Table 10.6 Estimates of the effect of relative weight status on change in educational attainment from age 14

Males	Higher grade attended		Higher grade completed		Dropped out	
	(1)	(2)	(1)	(2)	(1)	(2)
Weight 0–10%	0.031	–0.045	0.041	–0.022	–0.023	–0.015
	(0.037)	(0.037)	(0.035)	(0.037)	(0.020)	(0.022)
Weight 11–25%	–0.011	–0.046	0.007	0.009	–0.014	–0.001
	(0.032)	(0.031)	(0.030)	(0.031)	(0.017)	(0.019)
Weight 76–90%	–0.010	–0.022	0.015	–0.004	0.010	0.015
	(0.031)	(0.031)	(0.029)	(0.030)	(0.017)	(0.018)
Weight 91–100%	–0.049	–0.026	–0.036	–0.038	0.033	0.016
	(0.038)	(0.038)	(0.036)	(0.037)	(0.021)	(0.022)
Basic model	Yes		Yes		Yes	
Extended model		Yes		Yes		Yes
Mean dep. var.	1.60	1.60	1.47	1.48	0.04	0.04
Num. obs.	1,182	1,040	1,180	1,040	1,184	1,042

Females	(1)	(2)	(1)	(2)	(1)	(2)
Weight 0–10%	0.087**	0.081**	0.040	0.034	–0.014	–0.010
	(0.038)	(0.037)	(0.038)	(0.038)	(0.021)	(0.022)
Weight 11–25%	–0.003	0.015	–0.010	0.003	–0.022	–0.027
	(0.031)	(0.031)	(0.031)	(0.032)	(0.017)	(0.018)
Weight 76–90%	–0.041	–0.025	–0.017	–0.006	–0.025	0.035*
	(0.033)	(0.033)	(0.033)	(0.034)	(0.018)	(0.019)
Weight 91–100%	–0.001	0.026	–0.005	0.044	–0.039*	–0.041*
	(0.039)	(0.039)	(0.039)	(0.041)	(0.021)	(0.023)
Basic model	Yes		Yes		Yes	
Extended model		Yes		Yes		Yes
Mean dep. var.	1.54	1.52	1.43	1.42	0.04	0.04
Num. obs.	1,079	968	1,080	969	1,079	968

Notes: The mean for "Higher Grade Attended (Completed)" is greater than 1 because some respondents may have skipped a grade or the interval between interviews was long enough to include more than one grade. The basic model includes the following: dummy variables for weight status (26 to 75 percentiles are reference category), dummy variables for each number of months between surveys, dummy variables for respondent's age in months at baseline grade, dummy variables for month of interview at baseline grade, and dummy variables for year of interview at baseline grade. Extended model includes all variables in basic model and the following: dummy variables for race/ethnicity (white, black, Hispanic, Asian, other), mother's age at birth of respondent (continuous), dummy variables for mother's educational attainment (LTHS, HS, some college, BA plus), dummy variables for family structure (two biological parents, two parents, one biological parent, other, on own), dummy variables for respondent health (excellent, poor, other), number of days respondent smoked in last 30 days at baseline, number of cigarettes respondent smoked per day in last 30 days at baseline, number of days respondent drank in last 30 days at baseline, number of drinks respondent drank per day in last 30 days at baseline, dummy variables for residence in MSA (MSA-central city, MSA-non-central city, non-MSA), continuous unemployment rate in local labor market, county per capita income, and dummy variables for highest grade attended at baseline survey.
** Significant at the 5 percent level.
* Significant at the 10 percent level.

in grade each year and between 5 and 6 percent of students in grade ten to twelve drop out. Data from the NLSY97 indicate somewhat higher retention rates. Among those interviewed during the school year (November to March) at time t and reinterviewed approximately one year later (ten to thirteen months), retention rates, specifically failing to attend a higher grade (which would encompass dropping out), are between 5 and 17 percent; retention rates increase with age and are somewhat larger for males than females.[18] Standard errors of estimates of the association between weight status and change in grade attended (completed) are in the 3 to 4 percentage point range indicating that we are unable to reject effect sizes smaller than 6 to 8 percentage points. These minimum effect sizes necessary to reject the null hypothesis of no effect are relatively large given an expected mean of the dependent variable of between 5 and 15 percent (on an annual basis, larger for longer intervals between interviews). So, only if weight status had particularly large effects—for example, 33 percent or more of the mean—would we be able to detect reliably such an effect.

Estimates in the bottom panel of table 10.6 pertain to adolescent females. Again, there are few statistically significant estimates, and standard errors are relatively large. For this group, estimates indicate that those in the lowest (0 to 10) and highest (91 to 100) weight categories are more likely to progress in grade and less likely to drop out than those in the average weight category. Again, effect sizes are relatively large; females in the 91 to 100 percentiles have a drop out probability that is 4.1 percentage points lower than average weight females. Other than these associations, there do not appear to be any further evidence of a systematic effect of weight status.

Estimates of the associations between weight status and educational attainment of fifteen-year-old persons are presented in table 10.7. For the male sample (top panel), there are few statistically significant estimates. Overweight (91 to 100 percentiles) males are more likely to progress in grade and more likely to drop out. These are inconsistent findings; faster grade progression should be associated with lower rates of dropping out. These results also contrast with the finding that among fourteen-year-olds, overweight males were less likely to progress in grade. For underweight (0 to 10 percentiles) males, there is consistent evidence of reduced achievement—slower grade progression and higher rate of dropping out—but these estimates are not statistically significant. Among fifteen-year-old females, estimates indicate that those in the lower weight classes (0 to 25 percentiles) have significantly higher rates of grade progression and grade completion and lower rates of dropping out than average weight females. Estimates indicate that low-weight females have approximately a 6 percent-

---

18. By age sixteen, 20 percent of males and 11 percent of females in the NLSY97 reported being held back a grade. However, approximately 20 percent of the sample is missing this information.

Table 10.7   **Estimates of the effect of relative weight status on change in educational attainment from age 15**

	Higher grade attended		Higher grade completed		Dropped out	
Males	(1)	(2)	(1)	(2)	(1)	(2)
Weight 0–10%	−0.011	−0.024	−0.003	−0.015	0.021	0.028
	(0.038)	(0.041)	(0.030)	(0.031)	(0.018)	(0.019)
Weight 11–25%	0.022	0.017	−0.020	−0.027	0.018	0.027
	(0.030)	(0.032)	(0.024)	(0.024)	(0.014)	(0.015)
Weight 76–90%	−0.028	0.008	−0.007	0.019	0.016	0.008
	(0.031)	(0.033)	(0.025)	(0.025)	(0.015)	(0.015)
Weight 91–100%	0.044	0.089**	−0.008	0.012	0.033*	0.033*
	(0.037)	(0.040)	(0.030)	(0.030)	(0.018)	(0.018)
Basic model	Yes		Yes		Yes	
Extended model		Yes		Yes		Yes
Mean dep. var.	1.33	1.32	1.28	1.27	0.05	0.05
Num. obs.	1,999	1,720	2,001	1,720	2,003	1,723
Females	(1)	(2)	(1)	(2)	(1)	(2)
Weight 0–10%	0.017	0.017	0.062**	0.059**	−0.037**	−0.030
	(0.034)	(0.034)	(0.027)	(0.028)	(0.018)	(0.018)
Weight 11–25%	0.067**	0.057**	0.047**	0.064**	−0.014	−0.009
	(0.028)	(0.029)	(0.023)	(0.023)	(0.015)	(0.015)
Weight 76–90%	0.007	0.028	0.020	0.026	0.013	0.008
	(0.029)	(0.029)	(0.024)	(0.024)	(0.015)	(0.016)
Weight 91–100%	−0.089**	−0.011	−0.061**	−0.007	0.016	0.009
	(0.035)	(0.036)	(0.028)	(0.029)	(0.018)	(0.019)
Basic model	Yes		Yes		Yes	
Extended model		Yes		Yes		Yes
Mean dep. var.	1.33	1.31	1.29	1.28	0.05	0.05
Num. obs.	1,778	1,584	1,782	1,586	1,784	1,587

Notes: See notes to table 10.6.

age point (5 percent) higher rate of grade completion than average weight females.

Table 10.8 presents estimates of the association between weight status and educational attainment for sixteen-year-old persons. Again, there are very few statistically significant estimates observed in table 10.8. The standard errors are somewhat smaller, too, for these moderately larger samples; standard errors associated with estimates of the effect of weight status on grade progression and grade completion are in the 2 to 3 percentage point range. Nevertheless, standard errors of this magnitude still result in relatively imprecisely estimated parameters.

For males aged sixteen, there is evidence that those in the lowest weight category (0 to 10 percentiles) have lower rates of grade progression and

Table 10.8   Estimates of the effect of relative weight status on change in educational attainment from age 16

Males	Higher grade attended		Higher grade completed		Dropped out	
	(1)	(2)	(1)	(2)	(1)	(2)
Weight 0–10%	−0.052*	−0.056*	−0.035	−0.041	0.003	0.007
	(0.029)	(0.031)	(0.027)	(0.028)	(0.018)	(0.018)
Weight 11–25%	−0.041	−0.025	−0.029	−0.0001	−0.002	−0.012
	(0.025)	(0.026)	(0.024)	(0.024)	(0.015)	(0.016)
Weight 76–90%	0.018	0.002	0.030	0.029	−0.012	−0.013
	(0.026)	(0.028)	(0.025)	(0.025)	(0.016)	(0.016)
Weight 91–100%	−0.007	0.035	0.010	0.039	−0.010	−0.031
	(0.031)	(0.033)	(0.029)	(0.030)	(0.019)	(0.019)
Basic model	Yes		Yes		Yes	
Extended model		Yes		Yes		Yes
Mean dep. var.	1.19	1.17	1.16	1.15	0.08	0.08
Num. obs.	2,597	2,245	2,601	2,249	2,606	2,252
Females	(1)	(2)	(1)	(2)	(1)	(2)
Weight 0–10%	0.025	−0.024	0.007	0.011	0.034*	0.029
	(0.034)	(0.033)	(0.027)	(0.028)	(0.018)	(0.018)
Weight 11–25%	0.024	0.020	0.028	0.004	−0.008	0.001
	(0.028)	(0.026)	(0.021)	(0.022)	(0.014)	(0.015)
Weight 76–90%	−0.010	−0.024	−0.021	−0.031	0.036**	0.022
	(0.029)	(0.028)	(0.022)	(0.023)	(0.015)	(0.015)
Weight 91–100%	−0.015	0.012	−0.058**	−0.060**	0.009	−0.0001
	(0.035)	(0.033)	(0.027)	(0.028)	(0.018)	(0.018)
Basic model	Yes		Yes		Yes	
Extended model		Yes		Yes		Yes
Mean dep. var.	1.23	1.21	1.20	1.18	0.07	0.07
Num. obs.	2,450	2,166	2,455	2,169	2,450	2,165

Notes: See notes to table 10.6.

grade completion than average weight males; estimates suggest that these low-weight males are 5.6 percentage points (4.8 percent) less likely to progress in grade and 4.1 percentage points (3.6 percent) less likely to complete an additional grade. The estimate pertaining to grade progression is significant at the 0.10 level. In contrast, overweight (91 to 100 percentiles) males have higher rates of grade progression and grade completion and lower rates of dropping out than average weight males. However, none of these estimates are statistically significant even though they are relatively large; for example, the estimate for dropping out is −0.031, which represents a 39 percent decrease from the mean drop out rate. Among sixteen-year-old females, there is little evidence that weight is systematically related to educational attainment. There are few statistically significant estimates and there are few consistent indications that weight status positively or negatively affects the three educational outcomes.

The final set of estimates is for persons seventeen years of age and these are presented in table 10.9. Similar to previous findings, there are few statistically significant estimates in table 10.8. Perhaps more importantly, there is little systematic evidence that weight status is associated with educational attainment.

We estimated several alternative specifications, all of which produced similar results to those presented here. We estimated a model using the four traditional relative weight categories (underweight, normal weight, overweight, and obese). Results from this specification were comparable to those from the models using five relative weight categories presented here. Additionally, we attempted to unpack the reduced form estimates and control for potential offsetting effects that would result in the reduced form estimate being zero. To this end, we estimated a model that included measures of physical health and depression. The results from this specification were similar to those from the models presented here, finding no evidence of a systematic relationship between weight status and educational attainment.

10.5.3   IV Estimates

The final set of estimates we present are instrumental variables (IV) estimates of equation (3) for both the basic and extended models. Theoretically, IV estimation will control for correlation between weight and the error term. Correlation is possible given that the error may include time-varying, unmeasured exogenous determinants of educational inputs such as preferences that are most likely determinants of weight as well. If we assume a myopic model of weight determination, unmeasured determinants of education and weight in the present do not cause weight in the past. This means that weight in period $t - 2$ will be uncorrelated with the error $(u_{it} - u_{i(t-1)})$ in equation (3), and we can thus use it as an instrument for weight between periods $t - 1$ and t. In order to increase efficiency, we also include two period lags of the other explanatory variables in the extended model as instruments.

Tables 10.10, 10.11, and 10.12 present the IV estimates. In general, IV estimates are imprecisely estimated and the pattern of estimates fails to indicate a consistent relationship between weight status and educational achievement. Because our data set is an unbalanced panel, IV estimates obtained using two period lags reduced the sample size that was used and further exacerbated the limited statistical power of the analysis. While some IV estimates are statistically significant, for example, estimates for fifteen-year-old females in table 10.10 (e.g., a 37 percent point reduction in the probability of attending a higher grade for those in the lowest weight category), the large standard errors and absence of a consistent pattern to the results makes us cautious about drawing inferences. Overall, IV estimates provide little new information.

Table 10.9   Estimates of the effect of relative weight status on change in educational attainment from age 17

Males	Higher grade attended		Higher grade completed		Dropped out	
	(1)	(2)	(1)	(2)	(1)	(2)
Weight 0–10%	0.016	−0.034	0.019	0.023	0.017	0.006
	(0.035)	(0.033)	(0.028)	(0.029)	(0.019)	(0.019)
Weight 11–25%	0.006	−0.005	−0.010	−0.010	−0.006	−0.011
	(0.028)	(0.026)	(0.022)	(0.023)	(0.016)	(0.015)
Weight 76–90%	−0.027	0.001	−0.008	0.009	0.004	−0.001
	(0.029)	(0.027)	(0.023)	(0.024)	(0.016)	(0.015)
Weight 91 100%	−0.018	0.046	−0.025	0.004	0.001	−0.009
	(0.036)	(0.034)	(0.028)	(0.030)	(0.020)	(0.019)
Basic model	Yes		Yes		Yes	
Extended model		Yes		Yes		Yes
Mean dep. var.	0.97	0.95	1.05	1.04	0.10	0.09
Num. obs.	2,937	2,577	2,939	2,580	2,931	2,570
Females	(1)	(2)	(1)	(2)	(1)	(2)
Weight 0–10%	0.018	0.014	0.018	0.023	0.002	0.006
	(0.035)	(0.032)	(0.028)	(0.029)	(0.017)	(0.016)
Weight 11–25%	0.057**	0.037	0.008	0.005	−0.001	0.003
	(0.029)	(0.027)	(0.023)	(0.025)	(0.014)	(0.013)
Weight 76–90%	−0.064**	−0.047*	−0.023	−0.002	0.044**	0.021
	(0.030)	(0.027)	(0.024)	(0.025)	(0.014)	(0.014)
Weight 91–100%	−0.051	−0.019	0.018	0.048	0.027	−0.009
	(0.036)	(0.033)	(0.029)	(0.031)	(0.017)	(0.017)
Basic model	Yes		Yes		Yes	
Extended model		Yes		Yes		Yes
Mean dep. var.	1.00	0.99	1.09	1.08	0.06	0.06
Num. obs.	2,773	2,505	2,779	2,508	2,771	2,499

Notes: See notes to table 10.6.

If individuals do not behave myopically, then past weight status will be a poor instrument for current weight status. Because of this potential problem, we also estimated an alternative IV specification, using county level weight category prevalence as an instrument for weight status. However, this alternative specification produces similar estimates, finding no evidence of a systematic relationship between weight status and educational attainment.

10.6   Conclusion

Obesity is an important health issue and the health consequences of obesity have received much attention because of the rapid growth in obesity over the last thirty years. But obesity may have other important consequences that have received less attention from policymakers and researchers. In

Table 10.10   **IV estimates of the effect of relative weight status on change in educational attainment from age 15**

Males	Higher grade attended		Higher grade completed		Dropped out	
	(1)	(2)	(1)	(2)	(1)	(2)
Weight 0–10%	0.03	0.07	0.03	0.02	–0.00	0.02
	(0.09)	(0.08)	(0.08)	(0.07)	(0.05)	(0.05)
Weight 11–25%	0.06	0.10	–0.11	–0.03	0.00	–0.00
	(0.13)	(0.12)	(0.11)	(0.09)	(0.07)	(0.07)
Weight 76–90%	0.03	0.10	–0.11	–0.05	0.03	0.02
	(0.09)	(0.09)	(0.08)	(0.07)	(0.05)	(0.05)
Weight 91–100%	–0.03	–0.03	–0.00	0.01	–0.01	0.00
	(0.07)	(0.07)	(0.06)	(0.05)	(0.04)	(0.04)
Basic model	Yes		Yes		Yes	
Extended model		Yes		Yes		Yes
Mean dep. var.	1.33	1.32	1.28	1.27	0.05	0.05
Num. obs.	1,027	933	1,032	936	1,030	935
Females	(1)	(2)	(1)	(2)	(1)	(2)
Weight 0–10%	–0.26**	–0.37**	0.03	–0.01	0.04	0.02
	(0.11)	(0.12)	(0.08)	(0.07)	(0.05)	(0.05)
Weight 11–25%	0.36*	0.69**	–0.05	0.01	–0.12	–0.07
	(0.20)	(0.24)	(0.13)	(0.14)	(0.09)	(0.09)
Weight 76–90%	0.04	0.16	–0.03	0.05	0.01	0.01
	(0.12)	(0.14)	(0.08)	(0.08)	(0.05)	(0.05)
Weight 91–100%	–0.04	0.01	–0.03	–0.04	–0.07**	–0.05
	(0.07)	(0.08)	(0.05)	(0.05)	(0.03)	(0.03)
Basic model	Yes		Yes		Yes	
Extended model		Yes		Yes		Yes
Mean dep. var.	1.33	1.31	1.29	1.28	0.05	0.05
Num. obs.	919	861	924	865	924	864

Notes: See notes to table 10.6.

this chapter we investigated whether obesity, and more generally weight status (over- or underweight), was associated with educational attainment of adolescents. This research was motivated by plausible causal mechanisms that link obesity to (lower) educational attainment and the potential importance of the issue in light of the central role that education plays in determining lifetime well-being. Moreover, the question of whether obesity affects educational attainment is interesting from a policy perspective because government intervention in several markets may significantly affect obesity, and possibly education, as a result. Therefore, policies that reduce obesity may have large long-term benefits if reductions in obesity increase educational attainment, as some prior research suggests. Finally, although we do not study the issue here, if obesity is associated with lower educational attainment and one of the causes of this is discrimination in

Table 10.11   **IV estimates of the effect of relative weight status on change in educational attainment from age 16**

Males	Higher grade attended		Higher grade completed		Dropped out	
	(1)	(2)	(1)	(2)	(1)	(2)
Weight 0–10%	–0.15*	–0.07	–0.15**	–0.04	0.08	0.03
	(0.08)	(0.07)	(0.07)	(0.06)	(0.06)	(0.05)
Weight 11–25%	0.07	0.10	0.09	–0.06	–0.14	–0.02
	(0.13)	(0.11)	(0.12)	(0.10)	(0.09)	(0.08)
Weight 76–90%	0.01	–0.04	–0.02	–0.10	–0.02	0.01
	(0.08)	(0.07)	(0.07)	(0.06)	(0.05)	(0.05)
Weight 91–100%	–0.04	0.03	0.02	0.05	–0.00	–0.02
	(0.05)	(0.05)	(0.05)	(0.04)	(0.04)	(0.03)
Basic model	Yes		Yes		Yes	
Extended model		Yes		Yes		Yes
Mean dep. var.	1.19	1.17	1.16	1.15	0.08	0.08
Num. obs.	1,589	1,442	1,593	1,447	1,597	1,449
Females	**(1)**	**(2)**	**(1)**	**(2)**	**(1)**	**(2)**
Weight 0–10%	0.02	–0.21**	0.01	–0.11*	0.01	0.02
	(0.08)	(0.07)	(0.07)	(0.06)	(0.05)	(0.04)
Weight 11–25%	0.10	0.24**	0.04	0.05	–0.03	–0.03
	(0.10)	(0.09)	(0.08)	(0.07)	(0.06)	(0.05)
Weight 76–90%	–0.02	–0.02	–0.04	–0.04	0.03	0.01
	(0.07)	(0.07)	(0.06)	(0.05)	(0.04)	(0.04)
Weight 91–100%	0.05	0.04	–0.09**	–0.12**	–0.03	–0.03
	(0.05)	(0.05)	(0.04)	(0.04)	(0.03)	(0.03)
Basic model	Yes		Yes		Yes	
Extended model		Yes		Yes		Yes
Mean dep. var.	1.23	1.21	1.20	1.18	0.07	0.07
Num. obs.	1,464	1,359	1,471	1,365	1,462	1,357

Notes: See notes to table 10.6.

the school context, government action to eliminate such discrimination may be justified.

To investigate the issue of whether weight status is associated with educational attainment, we used data from the NLSY97 cohort, which is a large, national sample of adolescents. We focused on adolescents fourteen to eighteen years of age. Educational attainment was measured by highest grade attended, highest grade completed, and whether a person had dropped out of school. We obtained age- and gender-specific estimates of the effect of weight status on changes in the educational attainment measures.

Our results suggest that the association between weight status and the measures of educational attainment we use are not large, and that there is little systematic evidence that weight status either adversely or positively

Table 10.12   **IV estimates of the effect of relative weight status on change in educational attainment from age 17**

Males	Higher grade attended		Higher grade completed		Dropped out	
	(1)	(2)	(1)	(2)	(1)	(2)
Weight 0–10%	–0.26**	–0.27**	–0.42**	–0.35**	0.18**	–0.06
	(0.13)	(0.12)	(0.12)	(0.11)	(0.08)	(0.07)
Weight 11–25%	0.35**	0.37**	0.54**	0.51**	–0.13	0.08
	(0.14)	(0.13)	(0.13)	(0.13)	(0.09)	(0.08)
Weight 76–90%	–0.05	–0.05	–0.01	–0.00	0.05	0.04
	(0.08)	(0.07)	(0.07)	(0.07)	(0.05)	(0.04)
Weight 91–100%	0.06	0.05	0.10*	0.10*	–0.01	0.04
	(0.06)	(0.05)	(0.05)	(0.05)	(0.04)	(0.03)
Basic model	Yes		Yes		Yes	
Extended model		Yes		Yes		Yes
Mean dep. var.	0.97	0.95	1.05	1.04	0.10	0.09
Num. obs.	2,119	1,919	2,125	1,922	2,122	1,920
Females	(1)	(2)	(1)	(2)	(1)	(2)
Weight 0–10%	0.04	0.08	0.02	0.02	0.02	0.03
	(0.06)	(0.06)	(0.04)	(0.04)	(0.03)	(0.03)
Weight 11–25%	0.07	–0.03	–0.01	–0.08	–0.07	–0.02
	(0.10)	(0.09)	(0.07)	(0.07)	(0.05)	(0.04)
Weight 76–90%	–0.01	0.01	–0.02	–0.04	–0.06	–0.05
	(0.09)	(0.08)	(0.07)	(0.06)	(0.05)	(0.04)
Weight 91–100%	–0.10*	–0.06	–0.03	0.04	0.02	0.01
	(0.06)	(0.06)	(0.05)	(0.05)	(0.03)	(0.03)
Basic model	Yes		Yes		Yes	
Extended model		Yes		Yes		Yes
Mean dep. var.	1.00	0.99	1.09	1.08	0.06	0.06
Num. obs.	1,979	1,842	1,983	1,844	1,975	1,836

Notes: See notes to table 10.6.

affects educational attainment. While there was some limited evidence of large associations between weight status and educational attainment for certain weight groups at certain ages for either males and females, over-all estimates were sufficiently mixed (sign and magnitude) to conclude that weight status does not seem to have a significant effect on grade progression and dropping out among teens aged fourteen to seventeen. However, a caveat of our analysis is that we lacked statistical power to detect reliably small effects. The explanation for this is that the outcomes we studied are relatively infrequent events with approximately 5 to 10 percent of the population likely to fail to progress in grade or drop out, and relatively small samples of teens that were in the upper or lower tails of the weight distribution.

The findings from our analysis raise questions as to whether obesity is associated with lower educational attainment, as suggested by some previous research and some professional groups such as the National Education Association (1994). In earlier research, we also found that obesity was not associated with young children's cognitive achievement as measured by scores on achievement tests (Kaestner and Grossman 2008). Indeed, simple descriptive statistics presented in this chapter, in the earlier paper by Kaestner and Grossman (2008) on younger children, and in Crosnoe and Muller (2004) suggest that the association between obesity and educational attainment is unlikely to be large, as there are relatively small differences in means between obese and average weight children. For example, tables 10.1 and 10.2 reported typical differences in highest grade attended between obese and average weight teens of 0.1, which is approximately 0.2 of a standard deviation. Appendix table 10A.2 presents differences in the Armed Services Vocational Aptitude Battery (ASVAB) percentile score by gender and weight status. Overweight females have an ASVAB score that is 11 percentage points lower than average weight females, but this 11 percentage point difference is 0.4 of a standard deviation. For males, the difference in ASVAB scores between overweight and average weight persons is only 0.17 of a standard deviation. Crosnoe and Muller (2004) reported that the difference in GPA between obese and nonobese teens was approximately 0.2 of a standard deviation. While not trivial, these simple differences in mean educational achievement suggest relatively small effects that are likely to be much smaller once the significant amount of selection on observed characteristics is eliminated.

In sum, we do not find much evidence that obesity, and more generally weight status, is significantly related to educational attainment. The potential importance of this issue and the limited amount of prior study make this a topic for further research. Additional research can also address several of the limitations of our study. Most importantly, we lacked statistical power to detect small effects. Second, we were unable to effectively address the likely endogeneity of weight status. While instrumental variables is a plausible solution in our context (i.e., first difference model), we did not have samples of sufficient size to draw reliable inference from this approach. Third, while our measures of educational attainment were of significant practical importance given the centrality to well-being of obtaining a high school degree, they are relatively limited in their ability to reflect differences in achievement by weight status. Finally, our measures of weight and height were self-reported and the measurement error associated with these variables may have biased estimates.

Appendix

Table 10A.1   **Educational attainment of female adolescents by age and NHANES 2000 weight status**

	NHANES 2000 relative weight status				
	0–10%	11–25%	26–75%	76–90%	91–100%
Age 14					
Highest grade attended	8.1	7.9	8.0	8.0	8.0
Highest grade completed	7.2	7.0	7.2	7.1	7.1
Dropout	0.00	0.01	0.02	0.02	0.03
Number of observations	35	83	642	231	209
Age 15					
Highest grade attended	8.9	9.0	9.0	9.0	9.0
Highest grade completed	8.0	8.1	8.1	8.1	8.1
Dropout	0.06*	0.02	0.02	0.03*	0.03
Number of observations	83	180	1037	414	319
Age 16					
Highest grade attended	9.9	9.9*	10.0	9.9*	9.9*
Highest grade completed	9.0	9.0	9.1	9.0*	9.0
Dropout	0.04	0.03	0.04	0.05	0.04
Number of observations	118	238	1487	538	428
Age 17					
Highest grade attended	10.9	10.9	10.9	10.8*	10.8*
Highest grade completed	10.0	10.0	10.1	9.9*	9.8*
Dropout	0.07	0.08	0.07	0.11*	0.11*
Number of observations	187	326	1,752	639	521

Notes: Data drawn from survey years 1997 to 2003.

*Indicates that the estimate is statistically different ($p < 0.05$) from the estimate for adolescents in 26 to 75 percentiles.

Table 10A.2   Educational achievement (ASVAB) of adolescents age 14 to 17 by gender and relative weight status

	Relative weight status				
	0–10%	11–25%	26–75%	76–90%	91–100%
Males age 14 to 17					
ASVAB percentile	42.5	46.1	45.5	44.2	40.3*
Number of observations	282	432	1441	397	244
Females age 14 to 17					
ASVAB percentile	46.9	51.5	49.2	41.9*	36.5*
Black	0.18*	0.20	0.24	0.33*	0.43*
Hispanic	0.17	0.15	0.18	0.22	0.22
Excellent health	0.72	0.78*	0.73	0.63*	0.55*
Smoke	0.43	0.37*	0.46	0.44	0.43
Age in months	182.1	183.3	182.8	181.6	181.8
Mom age at birth	25.9	25.9	25.6	24.5*	25.1
Mom LTHS	0.18	0.16	0.18	0.25*	0.24*
Mom BA	0.21	0.23	0.18	0.12*	0.07*
Two biological parents	0.54	0.51	0.50	0.47	0.34*
Central city resident	0.30	0.30	0.31	0.36	0.39*
Number of observations	247	398	1,359	399	251

Notes: Data drawn from 1997 survey year, as this is the year that ASVAB test was administered.

*Indicates that the estimate is statistically different from the estimate for adolescents in 26 to 75 percentiles.

References

Averett, S., and S. Korenman. 1996. The economic reality of the beauty myth. *The Journal of Human Resources* 31 (2): 304–30.

Beuther, D. A., S. T. Weiss, and E. R. Sutherland. 2006. Obesity and asthma. *American Journal of Respiratory and Critical Care Medicine* 174 (2): 112–9.

Bjorntorp, P., and R. Rosmond. 2000. Neuroendocrine abnormalities in visceral obesity. *International Journal of Obesity and Related Metabolic Disorders* 24: S80–5.

Blau, F., and A. J. Grossberg. 1992. Maternal labor supply and children's cognitive development. *Review of Economics and Statistics* 74 (3): 474–81.

Canning, H., and J. Mayer. 1967. Obesity: An influence on high school performance. *The American Journal of Clinical Nutrition* 20 (4): 352–54.

Cawley, J. 2004. The impact of obesity on wages. *Journal of Human Resources* 39 (2): 451–74.

Cawley, J., J. Heckman, L. Lochner, and E. Vytlacil. 1996. Ability, education and job training and earnings. University of Chicago. Working Paper.

Crandall, C. S. 1995. Do parents discriminate against their heavyweight daughters? *Personality and Social Psychology Bulletin* 21 (7): 724–35.

Crosnoe, R., and C. Muller. 2004. Body mass index, academic achievement, and school context: Examining the educational experiences of adolescents at risk of obesity. *Journal of Health and Social Behavior* 45 (4): 393–407.

Dietz, W. H. 1998. Health consequences of obesity in youth: Childhood predictors of adult disease. *Pediatrics* 101 (3): 518–25.

Ding, W., S. Lehrer, N. Rosenquist, and J. Audrain-McGovern. 2006. The impact of poor health on education: New evidence using genetic markers. NBER Working Paper no. 12304. Cambridge, MA: National Bureau of Economic Research, June.

Edwards, L. N., and M. Grossman. 1979. Adolescent health, family background, and preventive medical care. In *Health: What is it worth?* ed. S. J. Mushkin, and D. W. Dunlop, 273–314. Elmsford, New York: Pergamon Press.

Eisenberg, M. E., D. Neumark-Sztainer, and M. Story. 2003. Associations of weight-based teasing and emotional well-being among adolescents. *Archives of Pediatrics and Adolescent Medicine* 157:733–8.

Falkner, N. F., D. Neumark-Sztainer, M. Story, R. W. Jeffery, T. Beuhring, and M. D. Resnick. 2001. Social, educational, and psychological correlates of weight status in adolescents. *Obesity Research* 9 (1): 33–42.

Fletcher, J., and S. Lehrer. 2009. Using genetic lotteries within families to examine the causal impact of poor health on academic achievement. NBER Working Paper no. 15148. Cambridge, MA: National Bureau of Economic Research, July.

Fu, H., and N. Goldman. 1996. Incorporating health into models of marriage choice: Demographic and sociological perspectives. *Journal of Marriage and the Family* 58 (3): 740–58.

Geier, A., G. Foster, L. Womble, J. McLaughlin, K. Borradaile, J. Nachman, S. Sherman, S. Kumanyika, and J. Shults. 2007. The relationship between relative weight and school attendance among elementary schoolchildren. *Obesity* 15:2157–61.

Gilliland, F. D., K. Berhane, T. Islam, R. McConnell, W. J. Gauderman, S. S. Gilliland, E. Avol, and J. M. Peters. 2003. Obesity and the risk of newly diagnosed asthma in school-age children. *American Journal of Epidemiology* 158:406–15.

Goodman, E., and R. C. Whitaker. 2002. A prospective study of role of depression in the development and persistence of adolescent obesity. *Pediatrics* 109 (3): 497–504.

Gortmaker, S. L., A. Must, J. M. Perrin, A. M. Sobol, and W. H. Dietz. 1993. Social and economic consequences of overweight in adolescence and young adulthood. *The New England Journal of Medicine* 329:1008–12.

Gozal, D. 1998. Sleep-disordered breathing and school performance in children. *Pediatrics* 102 (3): 616–20.

Grossman, M. 2006. Education and nonmarket outcomes. In *Handbook of the economics of education* vol. 1, ed. E. Hanushek and F. Welch, 577–633. Amsterdam: North-Holland, Elsevier Science.

Hanushek, E. 1986. The economics of schooling: Production and efficiency in public schools. *Journal of Economic Literature* 24 (3): 1141–77.

Hoebel, B. G., P. V. Rada, G. P. Mark, and E. N. Pothos. 1999. Neural systems for reinforcement and inhibition of behavior: Relevance to eating, addiction, and depression. In *Well-being: The foundations of hedonic psychology,* ed. D. Kahneman, E. Diener, and N. Schwarz, 558–72. New York: Russell Sage Foundation.

Jalongo, M. R. 1999. Matters of size: Obesity as a diversity issue in the field of early childhood. *Early Childhood Education Journal* 27 (2): 95–103.

Janssen, I., W. Craig, W. Boyce, and W. Pickett. 2004. Association between overweight and obesity with bully behaviors in school-aged children. *Pediatrics* 113 (5): 1187–94.

Kaestner, R. and H. Corman. 1995. The impact of child health and family inputs on child cognitive development. NBER Working Paper no. 5257. Cambridge, MA: National Bureau of Economic Research, September.

Kaestner, R. and M. Grossman. 2008. Effects of weight on children's educational achievement. NBER Working Paper no. 13764. Cambridge, MA: National Bureau of Economic Research, January.

Korenman, S., J. Miller, and J. Sjaastad. 1995. Long-term poverty and child development in the United States: Results from the NLSY. *Children and Youth Services Review* 17:127–55.

Lake, J. K., C. Power, and T. J. Cole. 1997. Body mass index and height from childhood to adulthood in the 1958 British born cohort. *American Journal of Clinical Nutrition* 66 (5): 1094–101.

McTigue, K., J. Garrett, and B. Popkin. 2002. The natural history of the development of obesity in a cohort of young U.S. adults between 1981 and 1998. *Annals of Internal Medicine* 136 (12): 857–64.

Must, A., and R. S. Strauss. 1999. Risks and consequences of childhood and adolescent obesity. *International Journal of Obesity* 23 (s2): s2–s11.

Mustillo, S., C. Worthman, A. Erkanli, G. Keeler, A. Angold, and E. J. Costello. 2003. Obesity and psychiatric disorder: Developmental trajectories. *Pediatrics* 111 (4): 851–9.

National Center for Education Statistics. 2006. *The condition of education: Grade Retention.* Washington, DC: U.S. Department of Education.

National Education Association, 1994. *Report on size discrimination.* Washington, DC: National Education Association.

National Heart, Lung and Blood Institute (NHLBI). 1998. Clinical guidelines on the identification, evaluation, and treatment of overweight and obesity in adults. Available at: http://www.nhlbi.nih.gov/guidelines/obesity/ob_home.htm.

Neumark-Sztainer, D., M. Story, and L. Faibisch. 1998. Perceived stigmatization among overweight African American and Caucasian adolescent girls. *Journal of Adolescent Health* 23 (5): 264–70.

Puhl, R. M., and K. D. Brownell. 2003. Psychosocial origins of obesity stigma: Toward changing a powerful and pervasive bias. *Obesity Reviews* 4 (4): 213–27.

Puhl, R. M., and J. D. Latner. 2007. Stigma, obesity and the health of the nation's children. *Psychological Bulletin* 133 (4): 557–80.

Redline, S., P. V. Tishler, M. Schluchter, J. Aylor, K. Clark, and G. Graham. 1999. Risk factors for sleep-disordered breathing in children: Association with obesity, race and respiratory problems. *American Journal of Respiratory and Critical Care Medicine* 159 (5): 1527–32.

Ritts, V., M. L. Patterson, and M. Tubbs. 1992. Expectations, impressions and judgments of physically attractive students: A review. *Review of Educational Research* 62 (4): 413–26.

Rosenzweig, M. R., and K. I. Wolpin. 1994. Are there increasing returns to the intergenerational production of human capital? Maternal schooling and child intellectual achievement. *Journal of Human Resources* 29 (2): 670–93.

Rosmond, R. 2001. Visceral obesity and the metabolic syndrome. In *International textbook of obesity,* ed. P. Björntorp, 337–50. West Sussex, UK: John Wiley and Sons.

Sabia, J. 2007. The effect of body weight on adolescent academic performance. *Southern Economic Journal* 73 (4): 871–900.

Schwartz, M. B., and R. Puhl. 2003. Childhood obesity: A social problem to solve. *Obesity Reviews* 4:57–70.

Sekine, M., T. Yamagami, K. Handa, T. Saito, S. Nanri, K. Kawaminami, N. Tokui, K. Toshida, and S. Kagamimori. 2002. A dose-response relationship between short sleeping hours and childhood obesity: Results of Toyama birth cohort study. *Child: Care, Health and Development* 28 (2): 163–70.

Serdula, M. K., D. Ivery, R. J. Coates, D. S. Freedman, D. F. Williamson, and T. Byers. 1993. Do obese children become obese adults? A review of the literature. *Preventative Medicine* 22 (2): 167–77.

Shakotko, R. A., L. N. Edwards, and M. Grossman. 1981. An exploration of the dynamic relationship between health and cognitive development in adolescent. In *Contributions to economic analysis: Health, economics, and health economics,* ed. J. van der Gaag and M. Perlman, 305–25. Amsterdam: North Holland Publishing Company.

Sigfusdotir, I. D., A. L. Kristjansson, and J. P. Allegrante. 2006. Health behavior and academic achievement in Icelandic school children. *Health Education Research* 22 (1): 70–80.

Smith, D. E., M. D. Marcus, C. E. Lewis, M. Fitzgibbon, and P. Schreiner. 1998. Prevalence of binge eating disorder, obesity, and depression in a biracial cohort of young adults. *Annals of Behavioral Medicine* 20:227–332.

Sobal, J., B. S. Rauschenbach, and E. A. Frongillo. 1992. Marital status, fatness and obesity. *Social Science and Medicine* 35 (7): 915–23.

Solovay, S. 2000. *Tipping the scales of injustice: Fighting weight-based discrimination.* Amherst, NY: Prometheus Books.

Todd, P. E., and K. I. Wolpin. 2003. On the specification and estimation of the production function for cognitive achievement. *Economic Journal* 113 (485): F3–F33.

———. 2007. The production of cognitive achievement in children: Home, school, and racial test score gaps. *Journal of Human Capital* 1:91–136.

von Mutius, E., J. Schwartz, L. M. Neas, D. Dockery, and S. T. Weiss. 2001. Relation of body mass index to asthma and atopy in children: The National Health and Nutrition Examination Study III. *Thorax* 56:835–8.

Whitaker, R., M. Pepe, J. Wright, K. Seidel, and W. Dietz. 1998. Early adiposity rebound and the risk of adult obesity. *Pediatrics* 101 (3): e5.

Wurtman, J. J. 1993. Depression and weight gain: The serotonin connection. *Journal of Affective Disorders* 29 (2-3): 183–92.

Where Does the Wage Penalty Bite?

Christian A. Gregory and Christopher J. Ruhm

11.1 Introduction

How does BMI affect wages? At first blush, the answer seems obvious. Over the last fifteen years, a large literature has established the negative correlation between obesity—the condition of having a body mass index (BMI) greater than thirty—and wages, at least for women. On average, obese women make 2 to 8 percent less than their normal weight counterparts. Obese men do not make any less than men of normal weight, and heavy black men may earn slightly more.[1]

The question we ask is not about obesity, however, at least not obesity alone. We are interested in the more general relationship between BMI and wages. In particular, we examine two assumptions that characterize previous research. The first is that the BMI range above thirty is "where the action is." Although there are good reasons to focus on obese persons, the rest of BMI distribution has been treated as an afterthought in most of this literature. The second is that the conditional expectation of wages is linear in BMI, or characterized by some other relatively simple parametric relationship (such as a quadratic). While specifications based on these assumptions are valuable because they are tractable and easily interpretable, there are good reasons to assume they are not true *ex ante*. In the simplest case, if BMI really does reflect something meaningful about health, it could be that wages

Christian A. Gregory is a research economist at the Economic Research Service of the USDA. Christopher J. Ruhm is Professor of Public Policy and Economics at the University of Virginia and a research associate of the National Bureau of Economic Research.

1. Throughout, we use the conventional definitions of "underweight," "healthy" (or normal) weight, "overweight," and "obese" for persons in the BMI ranges of: < 18.5, $18.5 - < 25.0$, $25.0 - < 30.0$, and ≥ 30.0 (National Heart, Lung and Blood Institute 1998).

are negatively associated with both overweight and underweight. Linear models capture only the average effect—which, in this example, might well be zero—and therefore miss important ways that BMI affects earnings.

Only recently have economists begun examine the shape of the conditional wage function. Wada and Tekin (2007) is the first study we are aware of that allowed a measure of body weight to enter into a wage regression as a quadratic. Even more recent has been the adoption of semiparametric methods. Shimokawa (2008) used data from China to estimate semiparametric models and finds that wages are lower for men and women in the tails of the BMI distribution. Kline and Tobias (2008), using data from the 1970 British Cohort study, found that marginal increases in BMI are most harmful for men who are overweight or obese and for women in the "healthy" weight range.

In addition to examining the shape of the conditional wage function, we address potential biases resulting from endogeneity of BMI and possible reverse causation, whereby wages determine body weight. We deal with endogeneity using an instrumental variables (IV) approach, where the respondent's BMI is instrumented with sibling BMI. To address the potential problem of reverse causality, we follow previous research in using lagged body weight to rule out the effect of current wages on weight. However, our analysis employs longer lags (at least thirteen years) and BMI from relatively early in the typical worklife. Both general approaches have been used before, but ours is the first application on data for U.S. subjects using semiparametric (SPM) methods.

We also examine potential mechanisms by which BMI affects wages and, in particular, are interested in understanding gender differences in these effects. Researchers have pursued several possibilities in this regard. One is that body weight affects health expenditures for women in a way that it does not for men, and that overweight and obese women pay for these expected expenditures in the form of lower wages (Bhattacharya and Bundorf 2005). Another is that health differences due to obesity have disparate effects on marginal productivity (Baum and Ford 2004). Still another is that women working in professions requiring public interaction are more penalized for obesity than corresponding men (Baum and Ford 2004; Pagan and Davila, 1997; Han, Norton, and Stearns 2009). Or, finally, employers might discriminate against overweight or obese women, but not men. Although direct evidence is only provided on the first of these possibilities, we interpret our findings in context of the growing literature examining how beauty is related to earnings.

Our analysis produces three main results. First, women's wages peak at thresholds far below the obesity cutoff, usually at a BMI of twenty-three or lower. This finding is robust to specifications correcting for endogeneity or reverse causation and suggests that BMI does not serve as an index of underlying health or medical costs in a wage-setting context. We test and confirm this intuition through a nonparametric analysis of relationship between BMI and medical expenditures. An alternative, which we believe to be more consistent with our findings, is that BMI is a proxy for physical attractiveness (or beauty), which is known to affect earnings.

Second, the estimates for men are more dependent on the choice of preferred models. Our primary specifications suggest that the conditional wage function is increasing in BMI through the beginning of the range of overweight and remains constant or declines modestly thereafter. Conversely, models using long-lags of BMI or instrumental variables indicate that male wages peak at very low BMI levels, suggesting that, as for women, the observed patterns are more likely to indicate physical attractiveness than underlying health status or medical costs.

Third, there are often substantial differences for blacks and whites, with the main specifications suggesting that the conditional wage function peaks at a considerably higher BMI for minorities and declines more slowly thereafter. Such findings might be consistent with a role for attractiveness, if there are racial differences in perceptions of ideal body weight. However, the IV estimates reveal smaller racial disparities, so that these interpretations require caution.

11.2   Data

We use data on twenty-five to fifty-five-year-olds from the 1986, 1999, 2001, 2003, and 2005 waves of the Panel Study of Income Dynamics (PSID), a longitudinal survey that began in 1968 with 4,802 families.[2] An additional 581 immigrant families were added in 1997 and 1999, and new families were created from the existing ones due to the formation of new households (e.g., due to divorce or to grown children leaving home).[3] As of 2005, the PSID contained 8,041 families.

Previous related studies involving U.S. subjects have used data from the National Longitudinal Survey of Youth 1979 (NLSY). We chose instead to utilize the PSID, primarily because it has characteristics of both longitudinal and cross-sectional data. Since the NLSY provides information for a single, fairly narrow birth cohort covering a somewhat limited age range, previous analyses using it have been largely restricted to relatively young workers. By contrast, the PSID is a self-replenishing panel that began in 1968 and so is more suitable to addressing differences in the effects across age groups. As we argue later, such differences point to possible mechanisms by which BMI affects earnings. That said, we show that our results are not

2. The original sample includes a nationally representative group of 2,930 families, with the complement from a low-income sample.

3. An earlier attempt to include Latino immigrants dates to 1990, at which time 2,043 immigrant families from the three most prevalent Latino groups in the United States were included. This sample was dropped after 1995.

driven by use of the PSID sample: similar patterns are obtained using comparable age ranges in the PSID and NLSY.

The PSID gathers information through an interview with one primary adult—usually the male head of household, referred to as the "head." On occasion, the spouse or cohabiting partner, the wife/"wife," as she is called, is the family respondent. In the waves used for this study, the PSID collects data on height and weight of the head and wife/"wife" only. The survey respondent gives height and weight information about themselves as well as their spouse or cohabiting partner. In an effort to minimize reporting error, we include only observations for which the head or wife reports his or her own height and weight.

Self-reported height and weight contain errors. We adjust for these using the regression correction suggested by Lee and Sepanski (1995) and commonly employed in the literature (Cawley 2004; Chou, Grossman, and Saffer 2004; Lakdawalla and Philipson 2007). Specifically, using data from the National Health and Nutrition Examination Survey (NHANES) III (1986 to 1994), NHANES 1999, NHANES 2001, and NHANES 2003, we regress measured height (weight) on self-reported height (weight), its square and its cube. The results, for models stratified by gender and race, are used to predict actual BMI (in the PSID) as a function of self-reported BMI.[4]

Hourly wages are constructed by dividing total earnings for the calendar year previous to the interview by total hours worked in that year.[5] For all but a handful of persons, total earnings and hours refer to the main job: very few people report second jobs or overtime earnings. The PSID imputes wages for people who report earnings but not hours or vice versa. We retain these observations (less than 2 percent of our sample) although our results are not sensitive to doing so. Our sample includes twenty-five to fifty-five-year-olds who worked at least twenty hours per week in their main job. These restrictions limit the sample to prime-age workers. We normalize wages to 2005 dollars using the Consumer Price Index (CPI), drop observations reporting wages less than half of the federal minimum, and trim the top 1/2 percent of wage observations.[6] Our final analysis sample contains 7,251 person-years for women and 5,775 person-years for men. Among women, we observe 1,433, 1,095, 516, and 520 persons in 1, 2, 3, and 4 years, respectively. Among

4. We use multiple waves of NHANES so that we can restrict the age range of the prediction samples to those relevant to our earnings study: namely, persons twenty-five to fifty-five years old.

5. Validity of the PSID income and hours data has been repeatedly evaluated. In two of the most cited evaluations (Bound et al. 1994; Duncan and Hill 1985) earnings were found to be relatively free from reporting error, but work hours were subject to significant mistakes. This induces errors into hourly earnings unlikely to abide by textbook assumptions about correlations between these variables and key regressors. However, there is no reason to believe that work hours in the PSID are subject to more reporting mistakes than similar measures in other data sets such as the Current Population Survey or NLSY (Bound, Brown, and Mathiowetz 2001; Hill 1992).

6. This procedure drops women with a wage above $75.14 and men with a wage higher than $152.57.

men, we observe 1,007, 666, 424, and 541 persons in 1, 2, 3, and 4 years, respectively.

11.3   Methods

The estimates were obtained using a semiparametric (SPM) local linear regression framework that can be usefully distinguished from both ordinary least squares (OLS) and a univariate kernel regression model. As is well known, ordinary least squares assumes that the conditional mean of the dependent variable is a linear function of the independent variables. This makes it easy to make predictions and to gauge statistical significance of the coefficients. However, the assumption of linearity is restrictive in ways that can only partially be overcome through standard transformations, such as including higher order polynomials of the explanatory variables of key interest. Kernel regression drops the linearity assumption and instead models the expectation of the dependent variable as a weighted mean at every point in the distribution of the independent variable. While this model can produce accurate univariate estimates with relatively small samples, in multivariate settings, it is not possible to maintain a meaningful level of accuracy without the sample size increasing exponentially. In this context, we use the specification

$$(1) \qquad\qquad Y_i = z_i \cdot \beta + f(\text{BMI}_i) + \varepsilon_i,$$

where Y_i is hourly wages of individual i, z_i is a vector individual characteristics and year effects, and $f(\text{BMI})$ is the nonparametric function transforming BMI into wages, which we refer to as the "conditional wage function."[7] The resulting models are semiparametric because they assume that the covariates included in z are linearly related to wages, whereas flexibility is maintained in transforming BMI into earnings.

Our estimates use the stepwise double residual method outlined in Robinson (1988). In the first step, we estimate $\hat{Y}_i$ and $\hat{z}_i$, as predicted values from a nonparametric regression of each of the independent and dependent variables on BMI. From these we derive $e\hat{p}s_i^Y = Y_i - \hat{Y}_i$ and $e\hat{p}s_i^z = z_i - \hat{z}_i$, representing the portions of the dependent and explanatory variables that are unrelated to BMI. In the second step, we regress $e\hat{p}s^Y$ on $e\hat{p}s^z$ to get $\hat{\beta}_{eps}$. Finally, we estimate the conditional wage function, $f(\text{BMI}_i)$, by nonparametrically regressing the wage residual $Y_i - z_i \cdot \hat{\beta}_{eps}$ on BMI_i, using the techniques detailed in the appendix.[8] The intuition behind this procedure is to purge the dependent variable of the portion of the supplemental variables

---

7. We use levels instead of logarithms of wages to make our estimates easily interpretable in the figures and tables. Using log wages as the dependent variable yields quantitatively and qualitatively similar results.

8. We also estimated $f(\text{BMI})$ using the first differencing procedure outlined by Yatchew (2003), and obtained essentially the same results. However, we maintained the double residual method for our point estimates and confidence intervals to preserve efficiency.

that are unrelated to BMI and then provide a local linear regression estimate showing the relationship of this residual to BMI itself. We estimate confidence intervals using the "wild" bootstrap algorithm outlined by Yatchew (1998, 688) and Yatchew (2003, 160ff).[9]

For our instrumental variables estimates, we use the same stepwise procedure, but add to the first stage the residuals of a linear regression of BMI on the instruments. Just as with the other explanatory variables, we form a nonparametric prediction of the residual conditional on BMI ($iv\hat{e}ps$) and a residual ($e\hat{p}s^{iveps}$). We include that residual in the second stage residual regression and form our estimate of $\hat{f}$(BMI) as before. This procedure removes the variation in BMI *not* explained by the instruments from the second stage regression, so that what identifies $\hat{f}$(BMI) is what the instruments do explain (Shimokawa 2008; Yatchew 2003).

We employ two strategies to address the problems that hamper estimation of the causal effect of BMI on earnings. First, to deal with the issue of reverse causality, we estimate models in which the independent variable of interest is lagged BMI (see Seargent and Blanchflower 1994; Averett and Korenmann 1996; Baum and Ford 2004; Cawley 2004). The general argument subtending this strategy is that current wages might influence current BMI, but cannot affect BMI in previous years. However, a statistical association may exist if body weight or wages are correlated across time. We address this difficulty in two ways. First, where previous related studies have used BMI lags of up to seven years, we analyze wages in 1999 to 2005 as a function of BMI in 1986, or thirteen to nineteen years earlier. Second, we limit this portion of the analysis to individuals less than twenty-six years old in 1986, under the assumption that wages early in the person's work career are unlikely to determine BMI during middle adulthood.

To account for the potential endogeneity between BMI and wages, we follow an instrumental variables strategy similar to that developed by Behrman and Rosenzweig (2001), and more recently used by Cawley (2004), where sibling BMI is the instrument.[10] The validity of this strategy rests on the suppositions that sibling BMI is correlated with own BMI, and that it is uncorrelated with one's own earnings, except through BMI. The first assumption is uncontroversial and can be tested. The second is more problematic. In

---

9. This algorithm is often applied when heteroskedasticity is a concern. To form 95 percent confidence intervals, we resample 1,200 times from the residuals to form bootstrap data sets and perform the local linear regression procedure outlined in the appendix at between 200 and 300 points in the BMI distribution.

10. Kline and Tobias (2008) have similarly used parent BMI as an instrument; Shimokawa (2008) has used sibling BMI and lagged child weight as instruments. An alternative is to estimate fixed effects (FE) models (Baum and Ford 2004), which automatically account for all time-invariant sources of heterogeneity. However, FE methods may be problematic for this application because they assume that weight changes translate instantly (or very rapidly) into wage changes, whereas current earnings are likely to be affected by both contemporaneous and past body weight.

particular, sibling BMI could be independently related to wages if siblings share traits affecting both weight and wage outcomes due to environmental influences or genetics.

Until recently, much of the literature suggested that the environmental influences on body weight tend to be nonshared between siblings, and that their importance diminishes in adolescence (Maes, Neale, and Eaves 1997). However, recent developments suggest that environment may be more important than once thought.[11] Similarly, the emerging literature linking genetics to human behavior suggests caution. For example, certain polymorphisms of the D4 dopamine receptor gene are correlated with attention deficit hyperactivity disorder (ADHD) (Sunohara et al. 2000; El-Faddagh et al. 2004).[12] It is well known that the regulation of dopamine affects experiences of satiation and, therefore, eating behavior.[13] Research has also found that both childhood inattention and adult obesity are correlated with the dopamine D4 receptor gene in women with Seasonal Affective Disorder (SAD) (Levitan et al. 2004). These studies raise the possibility that child behaviors affecting learning and, subsequently, wages may be correlated with genetic factors also influencing body weight.[14] Therefore, care is needed in interpreting the results of IV models (like those following) identified by genetic variation in BMI.

11.4   Full Sample Results

We next summarize our semiparametric estimates of the relationship between BMI and wages. Throughout, we stratify by sex, since BMI could have quite different effects for men and women.[15] All models control for age, marital status, number of children, presence of a child less than two years old in the household, level of schooling, job tenure (in months), the survey

11. Most studies attribute the effect of genetics to the difference in the covariance between monozygotic (MZ) and dizygotic (DZ) twins' body weight, since DZ twins share only half their genetic material with the other twin. But in addition to having different genes, DZ twins may also have different dominant and recessive copies of shared genes. This "nonadditive" genotype variation might explain a significant amount of variation in traits such as body weight. One recent study (Segal and Allison 2002) identifying this variation through the use of "virtual twins"—same-aged siblings that don't share any genetic material—found that a 5 to 45 percent of the variation in BMI could be due to environmental influences.

12. Swanson et al. (2000) found no correlation between the presence of the genetic trait and neuropsychological abnormalities sometimes associated with ADHD; however, they did find a correlation between the genetic marker and extreme behavior.

13. However, at least one study failed to find a direct link between obesity and the D4 dopamine receptor gene (Poston et al. 1998).

14. Holtkamp et al. (2004) found that children with ADHD were also more likely to be obese, suggesting the plausibility of a genetic connection.

15. All estimates are unweighted, in part because the PSID assigns a zero weight to anyone entering the sample through cohabitation or marriage. To ensure that our results are not driven by this choice, we estimated models using only the nationally representative sample or limiting the analysis to observations with positive weights and using these weights in the second-stage regression (of $e\hat{p}s^Y$ on $e\hat{p}s^z$). In both cases, the results are essentially the same as those shown.

year, and region of residence.[16] Race/ethnicity are also held constant in the full sample estimates (but not when stratifying by race). Unless otherwise noted, the y-axis of the figures indicates the expected wage, calculated by adding $\hat{f}$(BMI) to the group-specific average predicted wage; results are displayed for BMI ranging from twenty to forty.[17]

11.4.1   Main Specifications

Figure 11.1 shows full sample estimates. The conditional wage function of women is characterized by a peak at a BMI of 22.8. Weight gains at lower BMI are associated with higher earnings, although the confidence intervals are sufficiently large that we can not generally reject the null hypothesis of no effect. By contrast, predicted wages decline rapidly at higher BMI levels, and monotonically, expect for a statistically insignificant upwards tick just below the obesity threshold.

These findings suggest that female wages begin to fall well before conventional cutoffs for obesity or overweight, and even well within the healthy weight range. Thus, there is little evidence of an obesity penalty per se. Instead, the data suggest that women whose weight rises above a relatively low threshold experience reduced earnings. Of course, BMI does not perfectly measure obesity and some women in the normal BMI range may actually be clinically obese.[18] However, even if there are classification errors, the very low BMI at which the wage function peaks makes it much more probable that we are observing the effects of appearance or beauty, rather than obesity or poor health. A growing literature suggests that attractive individuals earn more than their counterparts (Hamermesh and Biddle 1994; Biddle and Hamermesh 1998; Harper 2000; French 2002), although the mechanisms for this are not fully understood. A possible explanation for our results is that females are considered most attractive at low levels of BMI. Consistent with this, Maynard et al. (2006) provide evidence that the desired BMI of adult women is between 22 and 23, or almost exactly where the conditional wage function peaks.

The patterns for men differ substantially. Predicted wages are maximized at a BMI of 26.7—in the overweight range—with lower and higher body weight associated with substantial but imprecisely estimated decreases. Yet, these results also provide little evidence of a sizeable "obesity penalty," except perhaps at extremely high BMI. Instead, they raise

16. We excluded occupation from our primary estimates, since this is one mechanism through which BMI could affect earnings. Specifications adding controls for broad occupational categories resulted in similar estimates for women and flatter BMI-earnings profiles for men.

17. This range covers approximately the fifth through ninety-fifth percentiles of women and the first through ninety-eighth percentiles of men. We exclude from the analysis persons with BMI greater than forty-five, as these observations exert disproportionate influence on the semiparametric estimates. This trimming drops 34 men and 125 women.

18. Burkhauser and Cawley (2008) provide evidence that BMI is more likely to understate than to overstate obesity prevalence.

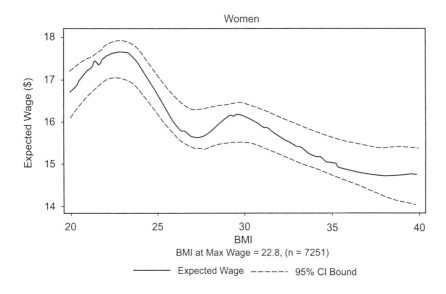

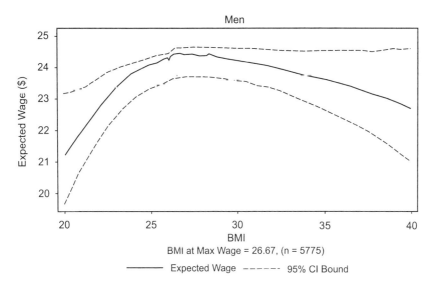

Fig. 11.1   BMI and expected wages, full sample

the possibility of wage reductions from being too light. For instance, the predicted hourly wage of a man with a BMI of thirty-five is just $0.81 per hour below that of his peer with a BMI of twenty-seven, while a BMI of twenty is associated with hourly earnings that are $3.19 less. Such results are consistent with the possibility, supported by previous evidence (DiGioachino, Sargent, and Topping 2001; Maynard et al. 2006), that males are held to a different appearance standard than females, with thin women viewed as attractive while corresponding men are considered scrawny. However, as discussed below, we obtain considerably different estimates for men (but not women) when using instrumental variables techniques, so these results should be interpreted with some caution.

11.4.2   Are Semiparametric Estimates Worth the Effort?

Are the benefits from using the semiparametric models worth the added complexity (and computational time) needed to estimate them? Our answer is a qualified yes. To illustrate the potential gains from these estimates, figure 11.2 plots the results from modeling wages as linear or quadratic in BMI, alongside the SPM estimates that are novel to this analysis. The conditional wage function of women is monotonically decreasing in BMI for the linear and quadratic specifications, which provide essentially identical estimates. While generally reasonable, the parametric models miss the increase in the wages occurring below a BMI of twenty-three (although the differences are small and often not significant), and understate the drop in earnings predicted immediately thereafter. At the very least, the SPM estimates suggest that the conditional wage function is flat until a BMI of twenty-three, and decreasing nearly monotonically thereafter.

For men, the gains to more flexible models are larger. In figure 11.2, it is clear that the linear specification fares the worst. The quadratic model does better in approximating the conditional wage function, and is sensible if we think that health effects or costs of obesity drive the BMI-wage relationship and begin to bind the wage function at *some* point in the BMI distribution. However, even the quadratic model is restrictive—overestimating wages at low BMI and in the overweight range, and indicating that the conditional wage function is maximized at a considerably higher BMI than the semiparametric model. These differences are nontrivial since the quadratic specification suggests an obesity penalty, while the more flexible estimates indicate that wages begin to decline much earlier, indicating that other factors may be at work.

Potentially useful, and computationally cheaper, alternatives to our SPM procedure might involve estimating models with higher order polynomials in BMI or linear splines.[19] Indeed, these could be time-efficient and relatively simple procedures for much future research. However, the preferred parametric specification may not be obvious a priori. The semiparametric procedures employed here may help to guide that choice and provide a more complete understanding of the conditional earnings function.

19. For example, Stata has a preprogrammed routine (the lpoly command) that will estimate local polynomial fits with usable, although not asymptotically correct, confidence intervals. This procedure does not address the issue of bandwidth selection, by which flexible models minimize mean squared error. For more on this procedure, see the appendix.

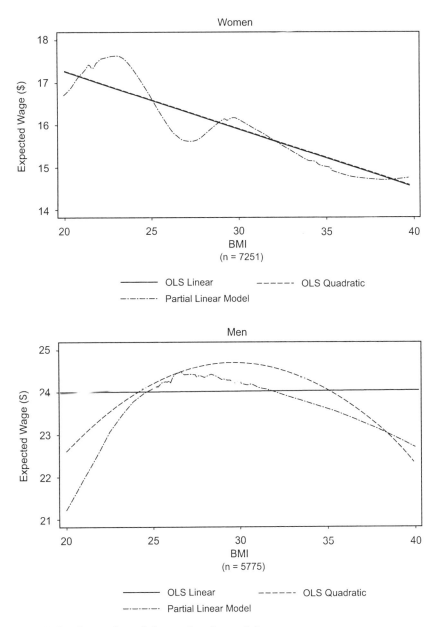

Fig. 11.2   Comparison of three estimation models

11.4.3   PSID versus NLSY

Previous related U.S. research has generally used data from the NLSY, rather than the PSID. Although the PSID is more comprehensive in several respects, most importantly because it is not limited to a single cohort or narrow age range, we checked whether the results were sensitive to its use. To do so, we obtained NSLY data for 1998 through 2004 (approximating the years of our main PSID analysis), during which time NLSY respondents were thirty-three to forty-seven years old. We constructed a sample of correspondingly aged individuals from the PSID and performed two analyses. First, we estimated simple OLS models for the two data sets.[20] For women, the estimates turned out to be quite similar. For instance, the coefficient (standard error) on BMI was –0.122 (0.017) in the PSID and –.168 (.024) in the NLSY.[21] For men, the results were somewhat different: using the PSID, we obtained a coefficient (standard error) of 0.017 (0.044), while the estimates were –.192 (.043) for the NLSY. The PSID findings are consistent with those shown in figure 11.2. Although the NLSY estimates for males run counter to some prior research (which does not uncover an obesity effect on wages), this is likely due to the young age range of the men previously examined. Gregory (2010) and Han, Norton, and Stearns (2009) have recently shown that the negative correlation between BMI and wages strengthens as men age, consistent with our results.

Second, we ran semiparametric models for the PSID and NLSY subsamples. These estimates, summarized in figure 11.3, reveal generally similar patterns.[22] However, there is evidence of greater nonlinearities for women in the PSID than the NLSY, while the male wage function reaches a maximum at a lower BMI in the NLSY. Overall, it seems likely that we would find even less evidence of a pure obesity effect in the NLSY, since the conditional wage function is maximized at a lower BMI. However, since the female wage function is approximately linear in the NLSY, there might be less gain from the flexible SPM estimates.

11.4.4   Reverse Causation

The preceeding findings could be biased due to reverse causation, where higher wages lead to lower BMI. For example, this could occur because high earners can more easily afford expensive foods, such as fruits and produce, that are healthy and low in calories. Alternatively, they may have greater flexibility in their jobs to find time to exercise and could more often join health

20. The NLSY data include only persons in the representative sample, and we use similar sample restrictions as in the PSID. The regressions are not weighted. Since we cannot easily identify pregnant women in the PSID, we run specifications for the NLSY data with pregnant women included. Separate NLSY models that exclude pregnant women yield similar results.
21. Our results are also similar to those obtained by Cawley (2004), when we estimate models using the log (rather than level) of earnings, as he did.
22. The smoothing estimates were normed to address some differences in scaling between the two data sets.

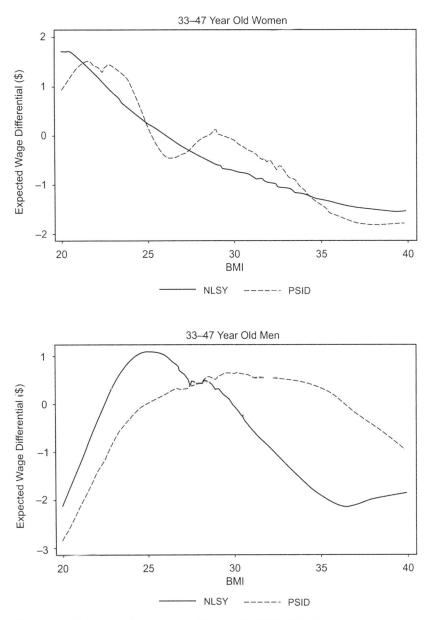

Fig. 11.3   BMI and estimated wage differentials, PSID-NLSY comparisons

clubs. We examine this issue in figure 11.4, which shows how lagged BMI is related to wages. Specifically, we measure BMI in 1986 and wages during 1999 to 2005. To reduce the possibility that lagged BMI itself is strongly influenced by (prior) earnings, we restrict this analysis to persons less than twenty-six years old in 1986, and so at the beginning of their work lives. Since

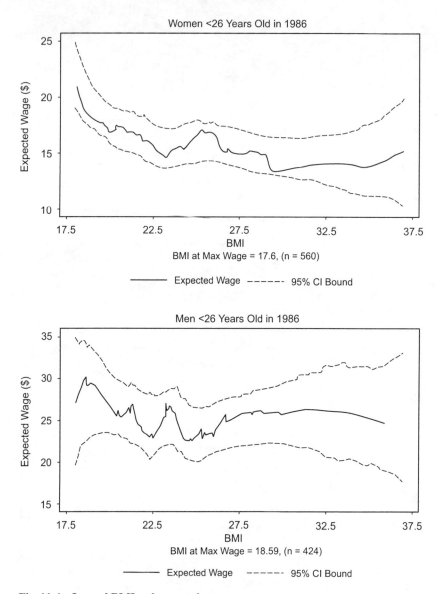

Fig. 11.4   Lagged BMI and expected wages

BMI typically rises with age, the distribution of lagged BMI is to the left of the contemporaneous distribution. Therefore, figure 11.4 displays BMI (in 1986) over the range eighteen to thirty-seven, rather than twenty to forty.[23]

The results for long-lags of BMI are fairly similar to those using con-

23. This corresponds to approximately the fifth to ninety-sixth percentile of the female BMI distribution in 1986.

temporaneous weight (and the full sample), once we account for the lower average BMI of young adults, and they again provide scant evidence of an obesity penalty. Specifically, the female wage function peaks at a very low BMI level (below eighteen) that is actually in the underweight category, although the earnings penalties thereafter are not always monotonic or statistically significant. For men, lagged BMI is essentially unrelated to contemporaneous wages, but with the peak predicted at a very low (18.6) BMI. These patterns are similar to those of women and suggest that being thinner is (almost always) better for males as well as females. We return to this result when examining our instrumental variables estimates.

11.4.5 Instrumental Variables

BMI could be correlated with unobserved factors also affecting wages. For example, persons earning high wages because they are motivated at work might similarly be motivated to exercise and consume healthy diets. The same might be true for individuals with low discount rates. In both of these cases, BMI will be correlated with the error term in our wage specification. We address this possibility by estimating instrumental variables estimates, using sibling BMI as the instrument.[24] These results are shown in figure 11.5.

For women, the IV estimates are similar to those obtained in the main models. Specifically, the conditional wage function is maximized at an even lower level of BMI (21.4), with a rapid decline in earnings predicted from the middle of the healthy weight range to just beyond the threshold for overweight. However, the wage function is flat after a BMI of twenty-six, further suggesting that we are not observing the effects of obesity.

The IV estimation makes a much larger difference for men. Where the main specifications indicated that the wage function increased into the overweight range, and then declined relatively slowly, the IV models suggest essentially no effect through a BMI of twenty-five or so, but with wages predicted to fall rapidly thereafter. Such results could indicate a role of poor health or medical costs but only if the effects begin to bind at the beginning of the overweight category. This seems unlikely, since most available research (Quesenberry, Caan, and Jacobson 1998; Andreyeva, Sturm, and Ringel 2004; Arterburn, Maciejewski, and Tsevat 2005) suggests that health costs are similar for healthy weight and overweight individuals but substantially higher for obese and, especially, severely obese persons.

11.5 Race

The wage functions of white and black females differ markedly (see figure 11.6). As in the full sample, the earnings of white women are predicted

---

24. In a standard linear model, first-stage F-statistics on the instruments are 29.5 for women and 16.2 for men, well in excess of the level of ten recommended by Staiger and Stock (1997) to avoid problems with weak instruments.

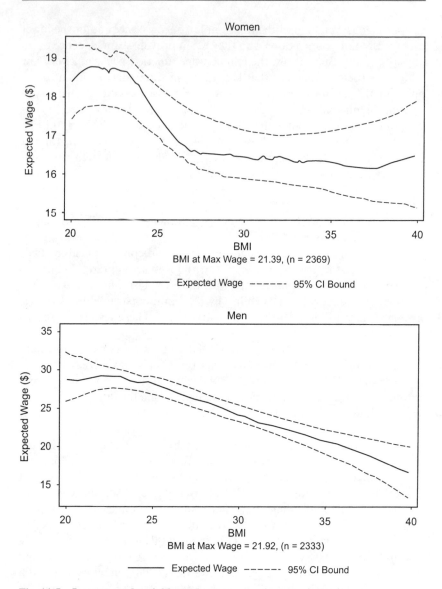

Fig. 11.5   Instrumental variables estimates

to peak well below the overweight threshold (at a BMI of 22.5), to decline markedly immediately thereafter, but then to be relatively flat beyond the middle of the overweight category. By contrast, the pattern for black women is consistent with a true obesity penalty, since the maximum predicted wage occurs at a BMI of 26.1, and nearly all of the economically or statistically significant reduction takes place at or beyond the obesity threshold. However, these results probably do not indicate that the obesity effect is due to

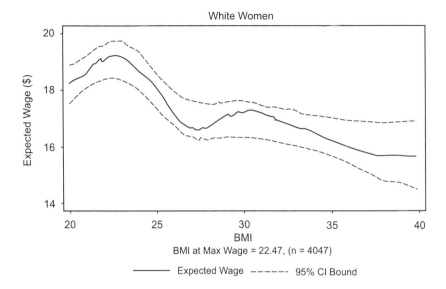

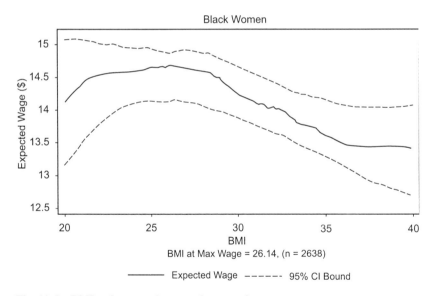

Fig. 11.6   BMI and expected wages of women, by race

higher medical costs or health problems. Were this the case, we would expect the wages of severely obese individuals to be substantially below those of their mildly obese counterparts (since severe obesity has by far the most deleterious health consequences). Instead, there is no evidence that the wage function continues to decline beyond a BMI of thirty-five.

The results for men are even more interesting. The wage function of white males reaches a maximum at a BMI of twenty-six, but remains relatively flat subsequently, with even severely obese men predicted to earn only modestly less. Conversely, the expected earnings of black males rise well past the obesity threshold (to a BMI of 32.1) and then remain flat or decline modestly.

These findings suggest substantial race differences in the BMI-wage profile, with greater and more binding weight penalties for whites than blacks that, except for black men, begin well before the obesity threshold.[25] Assuming that the relationship between BMI and health or medical costs is similar for blacks and whites, the racial disparities make it unlikely that the results in figures 11.6 and 11.7 reflect underlying effects of BMI on health conditions or medical costs. Instead, we think it more probable that these reflect appearance effects, combined with different standards of desired weight being applied to blacks and whites (and males and females).[26]

11.6   Simulations

Table 11.1 displays semiparametric estimates of the difference in predicted wages at specified BMI levels, relative to a reference group of females with a BMI of twenty-three or males with a BMI of twenty-seven.[27] The results are presented for subsamples, stratified by race and sex, for both our main SPM specifications (using actual BMI) as well as from semiparametric instrumental variables (SPM-IV) models. Standard errors are estimated from bootstrap replications, with p-values assigned using the percentile method. Coefficient estimates for the supplementary regressors are contained in appendix tables 11A.1 and 11A.2.

Table 11.1 highlights several points made previously, as well as some new ones. First, the wage function for females begins to decline at a relatively low body weight. Compared to women with a BMI of twenty-three, BMIs of twenty-five, thirty, and thirty-five predict statistically significant penalties of $0.96, $1.51, and $2.62 per hour. This pattern is driven by white females, where the conditional wage function indicates even larger (although less precisely estimated) gaps of $1.02, $1.93, and $3.51 per hour. The IV models reveal a similar pattern for white women, although with somewhat weaker predicted wage declines and standard errors that "blow up" at BMIs above thirty-five. Conversely, the findings for black females are more dependent on the choice of estimation techniques. Using actual BMI, predicted earn-

25. Instrumental variables suggest that this may also be the case for black males, as discussed below.
26. For example, college students report higher desired BMI for African American than white females, and for females than males (DiGioachino, Sargent, and Topping 2001).
27. The reference category is chosen to approximate the BMI level maximizing the conditional wage function in the main full sample specifications.

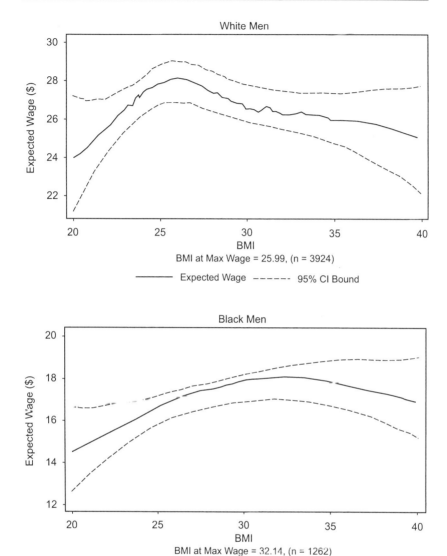

Fig. 11.7   **BMI and expected wages of men, by race**

ings reach a maximum at a BMI slightly above twenty-six and then decline relatively slowly. However, the IV estimates suggest a flatter conditional wage function prior to the peak, which occurs earlier (at a BMI of 21.6), and with a more rapid decline thereafter. Thus, the IV estimates for black females look relatively similar to the patterns seen for white women.

For men, the primary SPM estimates suggest that only a small wage pen-

Table 11.1   Wage difference ($) relative to predicted earnings at reference BMI

BMI	Women (reference BMI = 23)					Men (reference BMI = 27)				
	20	25	30	35	40	20	25	30	35	40
	Full Sample									
SPM	-.93*	-.96**	-1.51***	-2.62***	-2.89***	-3.19**	-.33	-.21	-.81	-1.72
	(.351)	(.277)	(.317)	(.311)	(.407)	(.928)	(.172)	(.195)	(.524)	(.993)
SPM-IV	-.24	-1.13*	-2.19***	-2.17**	-2.17**	2.28	1.84	-2.34***	-5.70***	-10.05***
	(.548)	(.319)	(.477)	(.658)	(.790)	(1.755)	(.574)	(.631)	(1.025)	(1.82)
	Whites									
SPM	-.90†	-1.02*	-1.93***	-3.51***	-3.50***	-3.87*	.01	-1.31*	-1.89*	-2.94†
	(.481)	(.419)	(.464)	(.717)	(.718)	(1.572)	(.668)	(.652)	(1.525)	(1.52)
SPM-IV	-.84	-1.45†	-1.79*	-1.17	.000	2.07	2.14**	-2.82***	-6.81***	-11.17**
	(.841)	(.686)	(.791)	(.852)	(1.274)	(2.101)	(.550)	(.565)	(1.29)	(2.660)
	Blacks									
SPM	-.49	.05	-.315	-1.16*	-1.17*	-2.82**	-.68**	.60*	.507	-.43
	(.355)	(.140)	(.316)	(.437)	(.437)	(1.02)	(.18)	(.210)	(.599)	(1.06)
SPM-IV	.02	-.27	-1.33**	-2.15**	-2.63**	3.61	-.18	-.25	-5.09**	-8.63**
	(.498)	(.223)	(.446)	(.619)	(.777)	(2.324)	(.559)	(.847)	(1.101)	(1.76)

Note: Results from Semiparametric (SPM) Models. Standard errors in parentheses.

***$p < .001$

**$p < .01$

*$p < .05$

†$p < .10$

alty is associated with high BMI, except perhaps for severe obesity. Thus, a BMI of thirty or thirty-five predicts hourly wages that are a statistically insignificant $0.21 and $0.81 lower than expected at a BMI of twenty-seven, with larger gaps for white males but positive predicted effects for blacks. On the other hand, hourly earnings are anticipated to be two to four dollars lower at a BMI of twenty than for the reference group.

The IV results for males are quite different: the wage function is monotonomically downward sloping beginning at low levels of BMI, with very large penalties associated with excess weight. Thus, men at the obesity threshold (BMI = 30) are anticipated to earn over four dollars per hour less than their counterparts with a BMI of twenty; those with a BMI of thirty-five are predicted to receive about eight dollars less. These differences are of similar size for white and black men, with the most important disparity being that the conditional wage function declines substantially between a BMI of twenty and twenty-five for blacks, and then flattens temporarily, whereas the pattern is reversed for whites.

11.7   BMI and Medical Expenses

Obese individuals might suffer a wage penalty because they have high medical costs that are partially paid by employers, through the health insurance system. Bhattacharya and Bundorf (2005) offer a version of this argument, providing evidence from the Medical Expenditure Panel Survey (MEPS) that the wage effects of obesity, for women, are borne entirely by those with employer-provided health insurance and, further, that the expected health costs of obesity are significantly higher for women than men.[28] Based on this, they claim that the effect of obesity on female wages is due to employers who offer insurance trading off wages against expected health expenditures, rather than because of any "beauty premium" or "appearance penalty."

We are doubtful of such a mechanism for the simple reason that the conditional wage function for women turns downwards so early—at a BMI of under twenty-three—far below either the obesity threshold or the level at which health costs might be expected to increase. Nevertheless, we directly test the possibility that health expenditures explain our results in two ways. First, we use MEPS data to produce a univariate nonparametric estimate of the log of total health expenditures (in 2005 dollars) as a function of BMI.[29] If our previous results are explained by employers using body weight to risk-rate employees, we would expect the pattern of medical expenditures to approximately track that for earnings. In particular, the medical costs of women should begin to rise at low BMI, starting at around twenty-three.

28. However, somewhat contradictory findings are obtained by Baum and Ford (2004).
29. We used data from the MEPS 1999, 2001, 2003, and 2005 samples and trimmed the top 1 percent of BMI observations. Using levels, rather than logs, of expenditures gives similar results.

The health expenditures for men should either not increase much prior to the obesity threshold (if we believe the results based on actual BMI), or show a similar pattern as for women, although starting to rise slightly later (if we place greater trust in the IV estimates).

Figure 11.8 displays the nonparametric relationship between BMI and log medical costs.[30] For women, predicted health expenditures change little prior to the obesity threshold but increase rapidly thereafter. This pattern is quite plausible, but almost certainly indicates that medical costs do *not* explain the observed conditional wage function, since earnings begin to fall much earlier—in a region where body weight is essentially unrelated to health costs. By contrast, we observe a monotonically increasing BMI-medical cost gradient for men, which has some potential for explaining the wage function obtained from the IV estimates (but less so when using actual BMI).

Second, we examine how the conditional wage function varies with BMI for subgroups stratified by age and gender. The medical costs of obesity are likely to increase with age (Finkelstein et al. 2007). If such expenditures are the source of the falloff in wages, we should therefore expect, ceteris paribus, a steeper BMI-wage gradient for older than younger persons. Instead, figure 11.9 shows that the conditional wage function declines from its peak much more rapidly for thirty-five to forty-four than for forty-five to fifty-five-year-old women. Similarly, wages are essentially unrelated to BMI for the oldest (forty-five to fifty-five-year-old) males, whereas the data suggest earnings penalties at high (and low) BMI for younger men (see figure 11.10). Finally, note that female wages are predicted to reach a maximum at a BMI of around twenty-two or twenty-three for all three age groups, well below the obesity or overweight thresholds. This seems inconsistent with the possibility that health expenditures are the primary determinant of the relationship between earnings and BMI.[31]

11.8   Discussion

The preceding analysis used semiparametric regression methods to examine how body weight is related to wages. Compared to previous research,

30. Our analysis does not account for two important characteristics of the expenditure data. First, there are a lot of zeros: in our sample, accounting for roughly 12 percent (29 percent) of women (men). Second, the distribution is extremely skewed. A more appropriate specification, in a semiparametric context, would be a partial general linear model using a gamma distribution and a log link (e.g., see Müller [2001]). However, such models are computationally expensive, even for parsimonious specifications, and we leave it to future research to explore the benefits of using them to examine the relationship between health expenditures and BMI.

31. It is less clear what age-pattern is expected if beauty play, a key role. If BMI becomes less closely tied to perceptions of beauty at higher ages, or if appearance itself becomes a less important determinant of wages, we would expect a steeper wage function for younger than older women. Conversely, appearance at young ages could have long-lasting consequences by directly influencing future productivity through, for example, its effects on self-esteem (Mobius and Rosenblat 2006; Mocan and Tekin 2006), or if initial labor market opportunities establish a path for future outcomes.

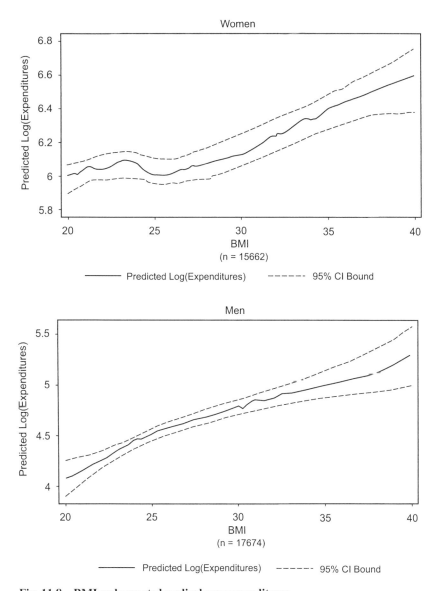

Fig. 11.8   BMI and expected medical care expenditures

these specifications allow great flexibility on the role of BMI, while imposing standard parametric restrictions on the other included controls.

A particularly striking finding is that increased BMI is associated with wage reductions for white females, beginning at low levels of weight—considerably below conventional thresholds for obesity or overweight. These results are robust to accounting for reverse causation or endogeneity and indicate that the conditional wage function is probably not being driven

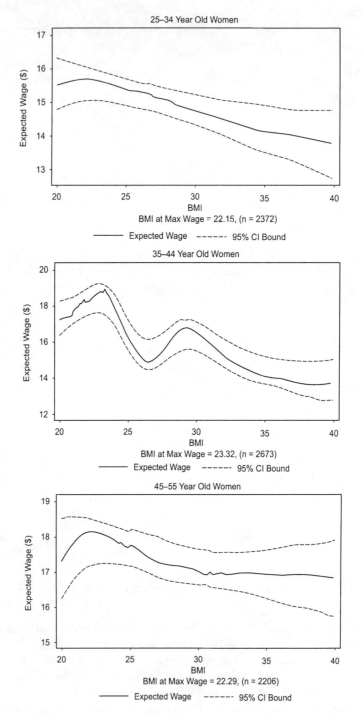

Fig. 11.9 BMI and expected wages, females by age

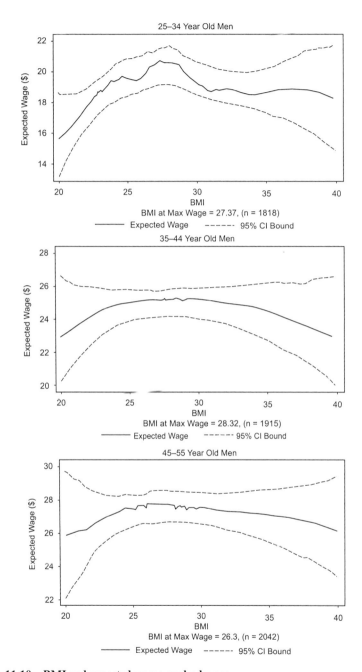

Fig. 11.10   BMI and expected wages, males by age

by the health effects of BMI or by obesity per se. Instead, they suggest that, over most of the BMI distribution, being "thinner is better" for white women, possibly due to social perceptions of beauty or desired appearance. The evidence for black females is more ambiguous. Our main specifications, conditioning on actual BMI, indicate that the earnings profile is flat prior to a BMI of around twenty-six, but then begins to decline fairly rapidly. This might reflect a different appearance standard for nonwhites, but also raises the possibility of an obesity penalty for this group.[32] However, instrumental variables estimates show a pattern more similar to that for white females, with earnings predicted to be maximized at a low BMI (21.8) and to decline rapidly thereafter.

The results for men are even more dependent on the estimation technique. In our main specifications, earnings increase through a BMI of around twenty-seven and then fall modestly. Conversely, the IV findings look similar to those for women, in predicting that wages decrease with BMI throughout virtually the entire range of the latter. Controlling for reverse causation (by including long-lags of BMI) also yields a conditional wage function that is maximized at a low BMI level and is fairly flat thereafter. The findings for black males differ from corresponding whites in that the main (noninstrumented) specifications show an increase in the conditional wage function until well into the obesity range, but with a more or less monotonic negative relationship between BMI and earnings predicted from the IV estimates.

Much can be done to clarify the interpretation of our results. Although health expenditures do not appear to drive the patterns, it is unclear whether the findings for women reflect labor market discrimination or some other cause. For example, females working in occupations requiring physical interaction might be subject to particular physical scrutiny. Adding controls for broad occupational categories slightly reduces the gradient of the wage function for females, consistent with occupational sorting; however, definitive answers to this question require controlling for occupational categories measuring the level of public interaction. Some results, particularly for males, are sensitive to the choice of specifications and we poorly understand why the results differ so starkly for whites and blacks. Modeling medical expenditures simultaneously with earnings, using data from a single source, could clarify the extent to which employers trade off wages for health expenditures.

These caveats notwithstanding, our analysis provides useful guidance for interpreting prior studies and conducting future research. First, when examining how BMI is related to earnings (and probably other outcomes),

---

32. For example, Stearns (1997) and Averett and Korenmann (1996) provide evidence that obesity has more deleterious effects on the self-esteem of white than black or Hispanic females.

it is important to allow for a variety of possible patterns rather than initially assuming that obesity is "where the action is." Indeed, we find little evidence of an obesity penalty per se, but instead often show that the conditional wage function is maximized at low levels of BMI, where excess weight is almost certainly not a key factor. Although we suspect that our results provide evidence of beauty or appearance effects, additional examination of these possibilities is needed. Second, the relationships are often highly nonlinear and benefit from models that permit considerable flexibility. We obtain this using our semiparametric specifications, but at the cost of considerable computational complexity. Simpler, although somewhat less flexible, modeling techniques might involve the use of higher order polynomials or linear splines. One possibility is to employ univariate nonparametric methods (without controls other than body weight) to establish the basic pattern, which then guide the choice of parametric models containing the full set of covariates.

Appendix

Nonparametric Smoothing Methods and Additional Econometric Estimates

Kernel regression drops the assumption of linearity and models the expectation of the dependent variable as a weighted mean at every point in the distribution of the independent variable. For example, the oft-used Nadarya-Watson kernel estimator can be defined as

(A1) $$\hat{r}_n(x) = \sum_{i=1}^{n} \ell_i(x) Y_i,$$

where $\hat{r}_n(x)$ is the predicted value of y at a given value x, and the weights are defined by the kernel function:

(A2) $$K(x) = \frac{70}{81}(1 - |x|^3)^3 I(x),$$

where

$$I = \begin{cases} 1 & \text{if } |x| \le 0 \\ 0 & \text{otherwise.} \end{cases}$$

The choice of the kernel function—Gaussian, uniform, Epanechnikov— generally does not affect the result. The weighting function, $\ell(x)$ is defined as

(A3) $$\ell_i(x) = \frac{K[(x - x_i) / h]}{\sum_{j=1}^{n} K[(x - x_i) / h]}$$

where h is the bandwidth or smoothing parameter. This kind of estimator has the advantage of allowing for highly nonlinear relationships that are frequently missed even with linear estimators that include quadratic, cubic, and higher order terms.

In our analysis, we use local linear regression, which is similar in spirit to kernel regression, but instead of modeling the data with a locally weighted average, it uses a locally weighted linear regression. Local linear regression relaxes the linearity assumption of OLS and minimizes both boundary bias and design bias introduced by the kernel framework.[33] In general, we define the estimator and kernel as in equation (A1), but define $\ell(x)$, X_x, and W_x as follows:

(A4)
$$\ell(x) = e_1^T (X_x^T W_x X_x)^{-1} X_x^T W_x,$$

$$e_1 = (1,0,0,\ldots)^T,$$

$$X_x = \begin{bmatrix} 1 & x_1 - x \\ 1 & x_2 - x \\ 1 & x_3 - x \\ \vdots & \vdots \\ 1 & x_n - x \end{bmatrix},$$

$$W_x = \begin{bmatrix} w_1(x) & 0 & \cdots & 0 \\ 0 & w_2(x) & & \vdots \\ \vdots & & \ddots & \\ 0 & \cdots & \cdots & w_n(x) \end{bmatrix},$$

$$w_i(x) = K\left(\frac{x - x_i}{h}\right).$$

This formulation implies that the predicted value for a given value of x is the inner product of the first row of $\ell(x)$ with Y.

The choice of smoothing parameter, h, involves the tradeoff between bias and variance, as h defines the window of observations that will be used in local regression. For nonlinear functions, small windows of observations give high variance and low bias, whereas large windows offer the converse. We choose the bandwidth by selecting the span, k, the fraction of the data to include in the linear estimate, to minimize mean squared error (*bias^2 + variance*) for the estimator. This implies that for each realization of x the bandwidth changes according to the distance to the observation $(k \cdot N) / 2$ observations away. In particular, we minimize the leave-one-out cross-validation score over the range of the span. The cross validation score is defined as

33. On this point, see Wasserman (2006, 73ff.), Fan and Gijbels, (17–18, 60ff).

$$(A5) \qquad CV(k) = \frac{1}{n} \sum_{i=1}^{n} (Y_i - \hat{r}_{(-i)}(x_i))^2$$

where $\hat{r}_{(-i)}$ is the estimator derived from leaving out the ith observation.[34]

Table 11A.1   Semiparametric regression results for women

	Full sample	Whites	Blacks	Age < 26 in 1986	IV
Black	–1.149***			–1.597	–1.986**
	(0.269)			(0.978)	(0.766)
Hispanic	–2.865***				3.532*
	(0.537)				(1.588)
Age	0.054***	0.106***	–0.005	–0.404*	0.032
	(0.014)	(0.020)	(0.021)	(0.190)	(0.031)
Year 2001	0.214	0.298	0.151	0.989	–0.059
	(0.340)	(0.474)	(0.498)	(1.168)	(0.696)
Year 2003	1.184***	1.323**	0.988*	3.173*	0.318
	(0.332)	(0.462)	(0.497)	(1.352)	(0.673)
Year 2005	0.585*	0.660	0.104	2.866*	0.518
	(0.271)	(0.409)	(0.352)	(1.414)	(0.527)
Number of kids	–0.055	0.317*	–0.269*	–0.540	–0.025
	(0.099)	(0.151)	(0.130)	(0.368)	(0.193)
Married	0.638*	0.174	0.708*	–0.156	0.534
	(0.261)	(0.397)	(0.349)	(0.905)	(0.489)
Child under 2	2.253***	3.472***	0.661	2.429	2.263**
	(0.381)	(0.570)	(0.502)	(1.389)	(0.734)
Northeast	3.284***	2.313***	4.768***	5.040***	3.506***
	(0.343)	(0.462)	(0.570)	(1.329)	(0.651)
Midwest	0.382	–0.108	0.795	–0.154	1.320*
	(0.283)	(0.391)	(0.411)	(1.089)	(0.552)
West	2.372***	1.817***	3.893***	1.246	3.361***
	(0.338)	(0.455)	(0.679)	(1.166)	(0.667)
HS dropout	–3.008***	–3.482***	–1.786***	–2.624*	–3.597***
	(0.364)	(0.621)	(0.447)	(1.158)	(0.784)
Some college	1.386***	1.367***	1.520***	3.430***	0.350
	(0.269)	(0.395)	(0.352)	(0.942)	(0.531)
College graduate	7.677***	7.235***	8.140***	11.803***	7.266***
	(0.297)	(0.396)	(0.477)	(1.517)	(0.594)
Job tenure (mos)	0.024***	0.025***	0.025***	0.034***	0.027***
	(0.001)	(0.002)	(0.002)	(0.006)	(0.003)
IV residual					–0.015
					(0.162)
Constant	0.010	0.069	0.043	–0.111	0.014
	(0.107)	(0.155)	(0.147)	(0.354)	(0.206)
N	7,251	4,047	2,638	544	2,369

Note: Regression coefficients for supplementary covariates. Standard errors in parentheses.
***$p < .001$
**$p < .01$
*$p < .05$

34. When smoothing the dependent variables, we execute least-squares cross validation at the roughly 500 points .2 percentile points apart in the middle 95 percent of the distribution of BMI.

Table 11A.2   Semiparametric regression results for men

	Full sample	Whites	Blacks	Age < 26 in 1986	IV
Black	−5.310***			−3.833*	−5.171***
	(0.580)			(1.824)	(1.143)
Hispanic	−7.346***				−1.536
	(0.968)				(3.082)
Age	0.240***	0.303***	0.085*	−0.102	0.375***
	(0.028)	(0.037)	(0.041)	(0.379)	(0.051)
Year 2001	0.570	0.756	−0.258	0.814	1.602
	(0.635)	(0.825)	(0.936)	(2.124)	(1.140)
Year 2003	0.662	0.846	−0.470	−1.708	1.320
	(0.625)	(0.822)	(0.902)	(2.538)	(1.141)
Year 2005	0.541	0.844	−0.896	0.559	0.618
	(0.550)	(0.745)	(0.718)	(2.919)	(0.919)
Number of kids	1.142***	1.945***	−0.317	−0.719	1.783***
	(0.206)	(0.289)	(0.282)	(0.691)	(0.368)
Married	2.641***	3.222***	2.613***	4.011*	3.501***
	(0.561)	(0.788)	(0.699)	(1.768)	(0.973)
Child under 2	0.482	0.330	−0.466	8.792***	−0.075
	(0.762)	(1.051)	(1.063)	(2.646)	(1.296)
Northeast	4.951***	5.772***	2.360*	5.169	5.590***
	(0.660)	(0.838)	(1.122)	(2.648)	(1.135)
Midwest	0.776	0.769	1.534	1.495	0.698
	(0.561)	(0.734)	(0.791)	(1.794)	(1.028)
West	1.335*	1.795*	2.325*	−1.126	1.254
	(0.614)	(0.820)	(1.045)	(2.216)	(1.120)
HS dropout	−3.942***	−4.056***	−2.050*	−6.972**	−5.171***
	(0.739)	(1.147)	(0.875)	(2.686)	(1.357)
Some college	3.286***	3.380***	3.498***	4.101*	3.371***
	(0.568)	(0.761)	(0.726)	(1.920)	(0.962)
College graduate	11.720***	12.349***	7.031***	26.354***	11.987***
	(0.549)	(0.703)	(0.872)	(2.325)	(1.132)
Job tenure (mos)	0.013***	0.009**	0.021***	0.020*	0.001
	(0.002)	(0.003)	(0.003)	(0.009)	(0.004)
IV residual					0.735
					(0.434)
Constant	0.322	0.037	0.341	−0.259	−0.004
	(0.212)	(0.282)	(0.291)	(0.676)	(0.360)
N	5,775	3,924	1,262	427	2,333

Note: Table shows regression coefficients for supplementary covariates. Standard errors in parentheses.
***p < .001
**p < .01
*p < .05

References

Andreyeva, T., R. Sturm, and J. S. Ringel. 2004. Moderate and severe obesity have large differences in health costs. *Obesity Research* 12:1936–43.

Arterburn, D., M. Maciejewski, and J. Tsevat. 2005. Impact of morbid obesity on medical expenditures in adults. *International Journal of Obesity* 29:324–39.

Averett, S. and S. Korenmann. 1996. The economic reality of the beauty myth. *The Journal of Human Resources* 31:304–30.

Baum, C. L., and W. F. Ford. 2004. The wage effects of obesity: A longitudinal study. *Health Economics* 13:885–99.

Behrman, J., and M. Rosenzweig. 2001. The returns to increasing body weight. PIER Working Paper 01-052. Available at: http://www.econ.upenn.edu/pier

Bhattacharya, J., and K. Bundorf. 2005. The incidence of the healthcare costs of obesity. *Journal of Health Economics* 28 (3): 649–58.

Biddle, J. E., and D. S. Hamermesh. 1998. Beauty, productivity and discrimination: Lawyers' looks and lucre. *Journal of Labor Economics* 16:172–201.

Bound, J., C. Brown, G. J. Duncan, and W. L. Rodgers. 1994. Evidence on the validity of cross-sectional and longitudinal labor market data. *Journal of Labor Economics* 12:345–68.

Bound, J., C. Brown, and N. Mathiowetz. 2001. Measurement error in survey data. In *The handbook of econometrics* (vol. 5), ed. J. Heckman and E. Leamer, 3707–3843. Amsterdam: Elsevier.

Burkhauser, R. V., and J. Cawley. 2008. Beyond BMI: The value of more accurate measures of fatness and obesity in social science research. *Journal of Health Economics* 27:519–29.

Cawley, J. 2004. The impact of obesity on wages. *Journal of Human Resources* 39:451–74.

Chou, S.-Y., M. Grossman, and H. Saffer. 2004. An economic analysis of adult obesity: Results from the behavioral risk factor surveillance system. *Journal of Health Economics* 23:565–87.

DiGioachino, R. F., R. Sargent, and M. Topping. 2001. Body dissatisfaction among white and African American male and female college students. *Eating Behaviors* 2:39–50.

Duncan, G. J., and D. H. Hill. 1985. An investigation of the extent and consequences of measurement error in labor-economic survey data. *Journal of Labor Economics* 3:508–32.

El-Faddagh, M., M. Laucht, A. Maras, L. Vohringer, and M. Schmidt. 2004. Association of dopamine D4 receptor gene with attention-deficit/hyperactivity disorder in a high risk community sample: A longitudinal study from birth to 11 years of age. *Journal of Neural Transmission* 111:883–9.

Fan, J., and I. Gijbels. 1996. Local polynomial modeling and its applications. CRC Press.

Finkelstein, E. A., D. S. Brown, J. G. Trogdon, J. E. Segel, and R. H. Ben-Joseph. 2007. Age-specific impact of obesity on prevalence and costs of diabetes and dyslipidemia. *Value in Health* 10:S45–S51.

French, M. T. 2002. Physical appearance and earnings: Further evidence. *Applied Economics* 34:569–72.

Gregory, C. A. 2010. Wages, age, and BMI. University of North Carolina at Greensboro. Unpublished Manuscript.

Hamermesh, D. S., and J. E. Biddle. 1994. Beauty and the labor market. *American Economic Review* 84:1174–94.

Han, E., E. C. Norton, and S. C. Stearns. 2009. Weight and wages: Fat versus lean paychecks. *Health Economics* 18 (5): 535–48.

Harper, B. 2000. Beauty, stature and the labour market: A british cohort study. *Oxford Bulletin of Economics and Statistics* 62:771–800.

Hill, M. S. 1992. *The panel study of income dynamics: A user's guide.* Newbury Park, NY: Sage Publications.

Holtkamp, K., K. Konrad, B. Muller, N. Heussen, S. Herpertz, B. Herpertz-Dahlmann, and J. Hebebrand. 2004. Overweight and obesity in children with attention-deficit/hyperactivity disorder. *International Journal of Obesity* 28: 685–89.

Kline, B., and J. L. Tobias. 2008. The wages of BMI: Bayesian analysis of a skewed treatment-response model with non-parametric endogeneity. *Journal of Applied Econometrics* 23:767–93.

Lakdawalla, D., and Philipson T. 2007. Labor supply and body weight. *Journal of Human Resources* 42:85–116.

Lee, L.-F., and J. H. Sepanski. 1995. Estimation of linear and non-linear errors-in-variables models using validation data. *Journal of the American Statistical Association* 429:130–40.

Levitan, R., M. Masells, R. Lam, V. Basile, U. Jain, A. S. Kaplan, S. Thramalingam, S. Kennedy, and J. Kennedy. 2004. Childhood inattention and dysphoria and adult obesity associated with the dopamine d4 receptor gene in overeating women with seasonal affective disorder. *Neuropsychopharmacology* 29:179–96.

Maes, H. H. M., M. C. Neale, and L. J. Eaves. 1997. Genetic and environmental factors in relative body weight and human adiposity. *Behavior Genetics* 27: 325–51.

Maynard, L., M. Serdula, D. Galuska, C. Gillespie, and A. Mokdad. 2006. Secular trends in desired weight of adults. *International Journal of Obesity* 30: 1375–81.

Mobius, M. M., and T. S. Rosenblat. 2006. Why beauty matters. *American Economic Review* 96:222–35.

Mocan, N., and E. Tekin. 2006. Ugly criminals. NBER Working Paper no. 12019. Cambridge, MA: National Bureau of Economic Research, February.

Müller, M. 2001. Estimation and testing in generalized linear models—A comparative study. *Statistics and Computing* 11:299–309.

National Heart, Lung and Blood Institute. 1998. *Clinical guidelines on the identification, evaluation, and treatment of overweight and obesity in adults: The evidence report.* Washington, DC: U.S. Government Printing Office.

Pagan, J. A., and A. Davila. 1997. Obesity, occupational attainment, and earnings. *Social Science Quarterly* 78:757–70.

Poston, W., M. Ericsson, J. Linder, C. Haddock, C. Hanis, T. Nilsson, M. Astrom, and J. Foreyt. 1998. D4 dopamine receptor gene exon III polymorphism and obesity risk. *Eating and Weight Disorders* 3:71–7.

Quesenberry, C. P., B. Caan, and A. Jacobson. 1998. Obesity, health services use, and health care costs among members of a health maintenance organization. *Archives of Internal Medicine* 158:466–72.

Robinson, P. 1988. Root-N-consistent semiparametric regression. *Econometrica* 56:931–54.

Seargent, J. D., and D. G. Blanchflower. 1994. Obesity and stature in adolescence and earnings in young adulthood. *Archives of Pediatric and Adolescent Medicine* 148:681–87.

Segal, N., and D. Allison. 2002. Twins and virtual twins: Bases of relative body weight revisited. *International Journal of Obesity* 26:437–41.

Shimokawa, S. 2008. The labor market impact of body weight in China: A semiparametric analysis. *Applied Economics* 40:949–68.

Staiger, D., and J. H. Stock. 1997. Instrumental variables regression with weak instruments. *Econometrica* 65:557–86.

Stearns, P. N. 1997. *Fat history: Bodies and beauties in the modern west.* New York: University Press.

Sunohara, G., W. Roberts, M. Malone, R. J. Schachar, and R. Tannock. 2000. Linkage of the dopamine d4 receptor gene and attention-deficit/hyperactivity disorder. *American Journal of Child and Adolescent Psychiatry* 39:1537–42.

Swanson, J., J. Oosterlaan, M. Murias, S. Schuck, P. Floodman, M. A. Spence, M. Wasdell, et al. 2000. Attention deficit/hyperactivity disorder children with 7-repeat allele of the dopamine receptor d4 gene have extreme behavior but normal performance on critical neuropsychological test of attention. *Proceedings of the National Academy of Science* 97:4754–9.

Wada, R., and E. Tekin. 2007. Body composition and wages. NBER Working Paper no. 13595. Cambridge, MA: National Bureau of Economic Research, November.

Yatchew, A. 1998. Non-parametric techniques in economics. *Journal of Economic Literature* 36:669–721.

———. 2003. *Semiparametric regression for the applied econometrician.* Cambridge, UK: Cambridge University Press.

Wasserman, L. 2006. All of nonparametric statistics. Springer.

Obesity, Self-Esteem, and Wages

Naci Mocan and Erdal Tekin

12.1 Introduction

Starting with the seminal work of Mincer (1974), economists have developed theoretical models and empirical procedures to investigate the determinants of wages. In addition to the analysis of the impact of schooling, job tenure, and experience, a huge literature investigated the impact on wages of market characteristics and establishment attributes, ranging from industry structure to firm size (Ferrer and Lluis 2008; Guadalupe 2007; Parent 2004; Troske 1999; Nickell, Vainiomaki, and Wadhwani 1994; Abowd and Lemieux 1993; Main and Reilly 1993; Evans and Leighton 1989; Krueger and Summers 1988). More recently, economists have identified the importance of noncognitive factors in wage determination. These studies are primarily motivated by the fact that a significant portion of the variation in wages across individuals remains unexplained even after controlling for human capital characteristics as well as job and industry attributes. For example, it has been shown that beauty has a positive impact on wages (Mocan and Tekin 2010; Harper 2000; Biddle and Hamermesh 1998; Hamermesh and Biddle 1994). Mocan and Tekin (2010) argue that the impact of beauty on criminal activity and wages works partly through human capital formation while in high school. They provide evidence indicating that less attractive

Naci Mocan holds the Ourso Distinguished Chair of Economics at Louisiana State University, and is a research associate of the National Bureau of Economic Research. Erdal Tekin is associate professor of economics at the Andrew Young School of Policy Studies, Georgia State University, and a research associate of the National Bureau of Economic Research.

We thank Duha Altindag and Tatsuya Hanabuchi for excellent research assistance. Sara Markowitz and the participants of the NBER seminar on the Economic Aspects of Obesity on Nov 10–11, 2008, provided valuable comments.

high school students accumulate less human capital in comparison to their attractive counterparts. This has an influence on wages and labor market activity later in life, and the impact is stronger for females. Persico, Postlewaite, and Silverman (2004) demonstrate that taller workers receive higher wages. This effect can be traced back to their height in high school, and it can be attributed to the impact of height on participation in high school sports and clubs. Similarly, Kuhn and Weinberger (2005) show that leadership skills in high school generate positive wage effects later in life.

The epidemic proportions of childhood and adolescent obesity in the United States pose serious social and health problems. For example, children who are obese are at greater risk for bone and joint problems, sleep apnea, and social and psychological problems such as stigmatization and poor self-esteem (Daniels et al. 2005; U.S. Department of Health and Human Services 2001). Obese young people are more likely than their normal weight counterparts to become overweight or obese in adulthood, and therefore, they are at greater risk for associated adult health problems, including heart disease, type 2 diabetes, stroke, several types of cancer, and osteoarthritis (U.S. Department of Health and Human Services 2001).

In addition to the health consequences, obesity and overweight are also associated with adverse economic outcomes, such as lower wages. Although research in this area has not reported uniformly robust results, the existing evidence indicates that obesity is usually associated with a wage penalty, especially for white females (Wada and Tekin 2007; Cawley 2004; Baum and Ford 2004, Averett and Korenman 1996). Obesity or overweight may impact wages through different channels. First, in some occupations obesity may have a direct detrimental impact on labor productivity because of reduced physical functionality. Second, obesity may cause discrimination by employers or by customers, which may generate a wage penalty even if there was no productivity difference between obese and normal weight individuals. Third, obesity may lower productivity through its impact on poor health. Furthermore, as obese individuals tend to be less healthy, the incremental health care costs associated with obese workers may be passed on to these workers by their firms in the form of lower wages (Bhattacharya and Bundorf 2005). Fourth, obesity may influence cognitive function, which in turn would impact productivity and wages. There is recent research that shows that obesity is associated with diminished cognitive function later in life.[1]

---

1. For example, Whitmer et al. (2005) used data on more than 10,000 members of the Kaiser Permanente medical care program of Northern California who underwent detailed health evaluations from 1964 to 1973 when they were aged forty to forty-five. The results showed that obesity is associated with increased risk of future dementia. Cournot et al. (2006) analyzed more than 2,000 healthy workers aged thirty-two to sixty-two years at baseline in 1995 who lived in three southern French regions. In 1996 and 2001 data were collected, among other items, on cognitive function. The results showed that higher BMI was associated with lower cognitive function at baseline, and that higher baseline BMI was related to a greater decline in word-list recall at follow-up, after adjusting for confounding factors.

Obesity can also impact wages through self-esteem. Mobius and Rosenblat (2006) find that physically attractive workers are more confident, and confidence impacts wages positively. Waddell (2006) finds that self-esteem in youth is associated with labor market outcomes later in life. If higher self-esteem increases wages, and if obesity impacts self-esteem, then obesity can have an indirect effect on wages through its impact on self-esteem.

As summarized by French, Story, and Perry (1995), the relationship between self-esteem and obesity has not been investigated using strong research methodologies. Much of the earlier work relied on associations identified from cross-sectional and small or nonrepresentative samples. For example, Sallade (1973) analyzed 120 obese and 120 nonobese children in grades three, five, eight and eleven. She found that there was no difference between obese and nonobese children in terms of social adjustment, but obese children had poorer self-concept. Wadden et al. (1984) studied 210 obese and normal weight children in grades three to eight, and did not find significant differences in self-concept between obese and normal weight children.

More recently, researchers utilized prospective longitudinal designs to determine the temporal sequence of obesity and self-esteem. Gortmaker et al. (1993) used a nationally representative sample of 10,039 individuals who were sixteen to twenty-four in 1981, and who were followed-up in 1988. They could not find a relationship between overweight and self-esteem. Strauss (2000) analyzed the National Longitudinal Survey of Youth, and found that the global self-esteem scores were not significantly different among nine-to-ten-year-old obese and nonobese children. However, over a four-year period obese Hispanic females and obese white females demonstrated lower levels of self-esteem in comparison to their nonobese counterparts; small decreases in self-esteem were observed for boys. Biro et al. (2006) used data on 2,379 girls aged nine and ten who were recruited into the National Health, Lung and Blood Institute Growth and Health Study, and who were followed to age twenty-two years. In that study, body mass index (BMI) was an important predictor of self-esteem. Similarly, Hesketh, Wake, and Waters (2004) reported that overweight/obesity precedes low self-esteem in a prospective cohort study of 1,157 elementary school children in Australia.

Although conceptually plausible, empirical evidence on the impact of low self-esteem on the development of obesity in children has not been established convincingly. As described by Hesketh, Wake, and Waters (2004), longitudinal research on the causal impact of self-esteem on obesity is extremely limited. For example, in a small sample of white children, who were observed for three years after the baseline assessment, Klesges et al. (1992) reported that self-esteem did not predict future body fat levels. Along the same lines, Hesketh, Wake, and Waters (2004) found that after accounting for baseline BMI, poorer parent-reported baseline self-esteem did not predict higher BMI scores at follow-up.

In this chapter we investigate whether obesity/overweight is associated with self-esteem of young adults. We also investigate the extent to which self-esteem and obesity influence wages. Section 12.2 describes the empirical specifications employed in the chapter. Section 12.3 provides information about the data. Section 12.4 presents the results, and section 12.5 is the conclusion.

12.2   Empirical Specification

The benchmark specification we estimate is of the following form:

$$(1) \qquad S_i = \alpha + \delta B_i + \mathbf{X}_i \beta + \varepsilon_i,$$

where S_i stands for a measure of self-esteem for person i, B_i is a measure of obesity, and $\mathbf{X}$ stands for a vector of personal characteristics that may impact self-esteem. As explained in the data section, we define self-esteem in a number of alternative ways. Similarly, we employ multiple measures of obesity. Versions of equation (1) will be estimated using data on young adults.

Although research could not identify an impact of self-esteem on body weight for children, we cannot rule out the possibility of reverse-causality from self-esteem to obesity. To address this potential confounding, models as depicted by equation (2) are estimated

$$(2) \qquad S_i = \alpha + \delta B_{i,t-5} + \mathbf{X}_i \beta + \varepsilon_i,$$

where $B_{i,t-5}$ stands for obesity measured five to six years earlier (baseline obesity). In this specification, past obesity impacts current self-esteem, but current self-esteem does not influence the extent of obesity five years earlier.

Equation (3A) conjectures that the level of self-esteem in year t (S_{it}) is determined by obesity in the past ($B_{i,t-5}$), and the extent of obesity in more distant years. If $\lambda < 1$, then the influence of past obesity is getting smaller in more distant past.

$$(3A) \quad S_{it} = \alpha + \pi B_{i,t-5} + \lambda \, \pi B_{i,t-6} + \lambda^2 \, \pi B_{i,t-7} + \lambda^3 \, \pi B_{i,t-8} + \ldots.$$

Multiplying (3A) by λ and lagging by one period gives

$$(3B) \qquad \lambda S_{i,t-1} = \lambda \alpha + \lambda \pi B_{i,t-6} + \lambda^2 \, \pi B_{i,t-7} + \lambda^3 \, \pi_{i,t-8} + \ldots.$$

Subtracting (3B) from (3A) and rearranging the terms yields a formulation where self-esteem depends on its lagged value and past BMI.

$$(4) \qquad S_{it} = \gamma + \lambda S_{it-1} + \pi B_{i,t-5} + \omega_i,$$

where $\gamma = \alpha(1 - \lambda)$, and ω captures the impact of very distant obesity. We augment equation (4) by individual-level control variables. As will be explained in the data section following, self-esteem is measured five years apart; thus, we estimate equation (5).

(5) $$S_{it} = \gamma + \lambda S_{i,t-5} + \pi B_{i,t-5} + \mathbf{X}_i \mathbf{\Omega} + \eta_i.$$

Finally, we estimate equation (6),

(6) $$W_i = \mu + \varphi S_i + \xi B_i + \mathbf{X}_i \mathbf{\Psi} + \nu_{i,}$$

where W stands for the wage rate of the young adult. This specification analyzes the extent to which self-esteem has an impact of wages, controlling for the impact of obesity. As mentioned earlier, models will be estimated using different measures of self-esteem and obesity.

Convincing causal inference on obesity-wages relationship could be obtained from analysis of experimental data. However, in this context such data do not exist because it is obviously unethical to design such an experiment where obesity and self-esteem are exogenously manipulated. In the absence of an experimental design, potential endogeneity issues can be addressed in different ways. An instrumental variable that is correlated with the explanatory variable, but uncorrelated with the outcome variable is one potential solution. However, it is difficult to find an instrument which is conceptually and empirically feasible. For example, it is plausible to think of a sibling's body mass index (BMI) as an instrument for the other sibling's BMI, as they are likely to be correlated. However, if BMI is influenced by unobserved family, school, and contextual factors that affect both siblings, then one sibling's BMI might proxy these factors and, therefore, would have a direct impact on the outcome (e.g., wages) of the other sibling, raising questions about the validity of the instrument.

Other potential instruments of BMI include school-based variables. For example, the existence of certain school programs and facilities, such as nutrition classes and athletic facilities, can be thought of as being correlated with the students' BMI, but uncorrelated with their future economic outcomes. But even in this case it can be hypothesized that children are not distributed randomly across schools and certain difficult-to-observe family attributes, which may be correlated with school characteristics, may also have a direct impact on children's future wages. Nevertheless, we tried school characteristics as instruments for obesity. Unsurprisingly, the first-stage regressions did not have power, indicating that school characteristics, are poor instruments for obesity in our data set.

An alternative procedure to control for unobserved heterogeneity that may be correlated with obesity is to include a large number of control variables in vector $\mathbf{X}$. Following this strategy, our regressions include variables such as age, gender, race and ethnicity, education, health status of the individual, whether the person was born in the United States, the number of siblings, family income, mother's age at birth, mother's education, and whether the respondent's father was ever jailed. Also included in some specifications are the scores obtained from the Add Health Peabody Picture

Vocabulary Test. We control for state fixed effects that would capture any differences across states in policies toward children that may be correlated with both obesity and self-esteem. Controlling for these characteristics and using lagged obesity as an explanatory variable should diminish the concerns for bias, although it is possible that some unobserved heterogeneity remains.

12.3 Data

The data are drawn from the National Longitudinal Study of Adolescent Health (Add Health). Add Health was specifically designed to study adolescents' health and risk behaviors, and it is considered to be the largest and most comprehensive nationally representative survey of adolescents ever undertaken in the United States.[2] An in-school questionnaire was administered to 90,118 students in grades seven through twelve between September 1994 and April 1995. All students who completed the in-school questionnaire and those who did not complete a questionnaire but were listed on a school roster were eligible for a more detailed in-home interview, which constituted the Wave I of Add Health. The Wave I in-home interviews were conducted with 20,745 adolescents and 17,700 parents between April 1995 and December 1995. Wave II was implemented with about 14,738 Wave I respondents between April 1996 and August 1996. Between July 2001 and April 2002, a third wave was conducted with the original Wave I respondents who could be located and reinterviewed, as well as a sample of the partners of the original respondents for a total of 15,197 young adults.[3] Our primary sample is drawn from Wave III respondents.

We construct multiple measures of self-esteem. Our first measure is based on replies to a series of questions that the respondents were asked about their self-image in Wave III. These include questions about how satisfied the respondent was with his/her life as a whole, whether the respondent agreed or disagreed that he/she had many good qualities, whether the respondent agreed or disagreed that he/she had a lot to be proud of, whether the respondent agreed or disagreed that he/she liked himself/herself just the way he/she was, and whether the respondent agreed or disagreed that he/she felt he/she was doing things just about right. The answers to the first question included the following values: (a) if very satisfied; (b) if satisfied; (c) if neither satisfied

2. The Add Health is a program project designed by J. Richard Udry, Peter S. Bearman, and Kathleen Mullan Harris, and funded by a grant P01-HD31921 from the National Institute of Child Health and Human Development, with cooperative funding from seventeen other agencies. Special acknowledgment is due Ronald R. Rindfuss and Barbara Entwisle for assistance in the original design. Persons interested in obtaining data files from Add Health should contact Add Health, Carolina Population Center, 123 W. Franklin Street, Chapel Hill, NC 27516-2524 (addhealth@unc.edu).

3. Finally, Wave IV is being conducted with the original Wave I respondents in 2007 to 2008. The data from Wave IV have not been released yet.

nor dissatisfied; (d) if dissatisfied; and (e) if very dissatisfied. The possible responses to the other four questions were (a) if strongly agree; (b) if agree; (c) if neither agree nor disagree; (d) if disagree; and (e) if strongly disagree. We created a single scale from these items after reverse coding each of them, with scores ranging from five to twenty-five. Higher scores indicate higher self-esteem. The items used in constructing this scale are either identical or very similar to the Rosenberg Self-Esteem Scale, which is a ten-item self-report measure of global self-esteem (Rosenberg 1965).[4] We constructed a binary indicator that takes on the value of one if the respondent falls into the top ninetieth percentile in the distribution of this scale; that is, the respondent is in the top 10 percent with the highest self-esteem. This variable is called *Very High Self-Esteem*. We also created a binary indicator, called *High Self-Esteem*, to represent whether the respondent falls into the top seventy-fifth percentile. We created one additional binary indicator to measure self-esteem. Each respondent was asked to assess his/her own confidence in a question, "How confident are you of yourself?" Possible responses to this question included, "very confident," "moderately confident," "slightly confident," and "not confident at all." We constructed a binary variable for being "very confident."

In some of our specifications, we use self-esteem measures from Wave II of the Add Health. Similar to Wave III, cut-off values for the ninetieth and seventy-fifth percentiles of the Rosenberg Self-Esteem Scale are constructed using responses to the relevant questions asked in Wave II. These include questions about the respondents' assessment of whether he/she has a lot of good qualities, feels socially accepted, feels like he/she is doing everything just about right, feels loved and wanted, likes himself/herself just the way he/she is, and has a lot to be proud of.[5]

Our obesity measure is based on Body Mass Index (BMI). The BMI is a universally accepted measure of obesity, defined as the ratio of weight in kilograms to height in meters squared. The main reason for the widespread use of BMI is its ease of calculation since most data sets used in socioeconomic research contain the necessary information on height and weight. The World Health Organization (WHO) sets the universally accepted cutoff points for classification of overweight and obesity. An individual with a BMI of less than 18.5 is considered underweight, a BMI between twenty-five and thirty classifies the person as being overweight, while an individual with a BMI of thirty or higher is considered obese. Both self-reported and measured values of height and weight of respondents are available in Wave III of Add Health. Although the BMI values derived from self-reported and

4. The Rosenberg Self-Esteem Scale is one of the most extensively used instruments to assess self-esteem (Swallen et al. 2005; Martin-Albo et al. 2007; Galliher, Rostosky, and Hughes 2004; Russell et al. 2008; Gabhainn and Mullan 2003).

5. We could not construct a variable for being "very confident" because this question was not asked in Wave II.

measured height and weight exhibit high correlation in our sample, we use the BMI derived from the measured height and weight. This allows us to avoid any spurious correlation that may result from respondents' misreporting their height and weight due to their self-esteem.

Note that for children and teens, the range of BMI that pertains to above normal weight is defined so that it takes into account normal differences in body fat between boys and girls and differences in body fat at various ages (Centers for Disease Control and Prevention 2008). Therefore, the criteria used to categorize individuals under age twenty are different from those used for adults. Specifically, for children and teens, BMI values are plotted on growth charts from the Centers for Disease Control (CDC) to determine the corresponding BMI-for-age percentile. Children and teens at or above the eighty-fifth percentile of the gender- and age-specific BMI distribution are coded as overweight, while those at or above the ninety-fifth percentile of the BMI distribution are coded as obese. These growth charts take into account the fact that the amount of fat changes with age and differs between girls and boys.[6] The Add Health respondents are between ages eighteen and twenty-six in Wave III. Therefore, we limited our sample to those who are older than twenty when we employed data from Wave III. To classify the respondents by their weight when they were younger (in Wave II), we used the CDC growth charts for each person.

Table 12.1 displays the descriptive statistics. Test Score 1 to Test Score 5 stand for dichotomous variables to indicate the quintile that the Peabody Vocabulary test score belongs. For example, if the test score of the person is at the bottom 20 percent of the Peabody Vocabulary test score distribution, *Test score 1* takes the value of one, and zero otherwise. *Healthy* takes the value of one if the respondent indicated that he/she is in good health or better. *Father jailed* is equal to one if the father was ever jailed, and zero otherwise. *U.S. born* is equal to one if the individual was born in the United States. *No Siblings, 1 Sibling,* and so forth, are a sequence of dummy variables indicating the number of siblings of the person. *Family income—1* is a dummy variable that takes the value of one if the individual's family's income was greater than or equal to 50 percent of the poverty threshold (adjusted for family size), but less than 100 percent of the poverty threshold. *Family Income—2* is equal to one if family income was greater than or equal

6. For additional information on the CDC growth charts, see http://www.cdc.gov/nccdphp/dnpa/growthcharts/resources/growthchart.pdf. Also, see http://www.cdc.gov/growthcharts/. Until recently, this nomenclature differed across children (aged two to nineteen) and adults. Children with BMIs above the ninety-fifth percentile of the gender- and age-specific distribution were considered "overweight," and those above the eighty-fifth percentile were considered "at-risk-for-overweight." However, an expert committee convened by the American Medical Association (AMA) in collaboration with the Department of Health and Human Services Health Resources and Services Administration (HRSA) and the CDC recently endorsed the use of "overweight" and "obese" for children. See this link for more information on the adjustment: http://www.ama-assn.org/ama1/pub/upload/mm/433/ped_obesity_recs.pdf.

Table 12.1   Descriptive statistics

	Whole sample (1)	Very high self-esteem = 1 (2)	Very high self-esteem = 0 (3)	High self-esteem = 1 (4)	High self-esteem = 0 (5)	Very confident = 1 (6)	Very confident = 0 (7)
High self-esteem	0.327	1.000***	0.241	1.000***	0.000	0.489***	0.179
	(0.469)	(0.000)	(0.428)	(0.000)	(0.000)	(0.500)	(0.383)
Very high self-esteem	0.113	1.000***	0.000	0.345***	0.000	0.191***	0.042
	(0.316)	(0.000)	(0.000)	(0.475)	(0.000)	(0.393)	(0.201)
Rosenberg Index	21.053	25.000***	20.552	24.032***	19.609	22.138***	20.081
	(2.767)	(0.000)	(2.529)	(0.810)	(2.158)	(2.361)	(2.737)
Very confident	0.475	0.804***	0.433	0.712***	0.360	1.000***	0.000
	(0.499)	(0.398)	(0.496)	(0.453)	(0.480)	(0.000)	(0.000)
Wage	11.200	11.780***	11.126	11.572***	11.013	11.317	11.126
	(5.500)	(6.057)	(5.422)	(5.745)	(5.364)	(5.621)	(5.420)
BMI	26.552	25.912***	26.633	26.280***	26.684	26.462	26.601
	(6.128)	(5.528)	(6.196)	(5.882)	(6.241)	(5.896)	(6.296)
Male	0.485	0.565***	0.475	0.521***	0.468	0.548***	0.428
	(0.500)	(0.496)	(0.499)	(0.500)	(0.499)	(0.498)	(0.495)
Age21	0.211	0.237**	0.207	0.212	0.210	0.219**	0.203
	(0.408)	(0.426)	(0.405)	(0.409)	(0.407)	(0.414)	(0.402)
Age22	0.250	0.236	0.252	0.253	0.249	0.253	0.246
	(0.433)	(0.425)	(0.434)	(0.435)	(0.433)	(0.435)	(0.431)
Age23	0.251	0.229*	0.254	0.244	0.254	0.241**	0.259
	(0.434)	(0.420)	(0.435)	(0.429)	(0.436)	(0.428)	(0.438)
Age24	0.210	0.214	0.210	0.212	0.209	0.203**	0.220
	(0.407)	(0.410)	(0.407)	(0.409)	(0.407)	(0.402)	(0.414)
Age25	0.067	0.073	0.067	0.069	0.066	0.072*	0.063
	(0.250)	(0.260)	(0.249)	(0.254)	(0.249)	(0.259)	(0.243)
Age26	0.009	0.010	0.009	0.008	0.009	0.009	0.009
	(0.095)	(0.099)	(0.094)	(0.092)	(0.096)	(0.095)	(0.093)
Hispanic	0.177	0.193	0.175	0.180	0.176	0.192***	0.165
	(0.382)	(0.395)	(0.380)	(0.385)	(0.381)	(0.394)	(0.371)
White	0.650	0.637	0.652	0.615***	0.667	0.595***	0.707
	(0.477)	(0.481)	(0.476)	(0.487)	(0.471)	(0.491)	(0.455)
Black	0.216	0.239**	0.213	0.262***	0.194	0.280***	0.150
	(0.411)	(0.427)	(0.409)	(0.440)	(0.395)	(0.449)	(0.357)

(continued)

Table 12.1 (continued)

	Whole sample (1)	Very high self-esteem = 1 (2)	Very high self-esteem = 0 (3)	High self-esteem = 1 (4)	High self-esteem = 0 (5)	Very confident = 1 (6)	Very confident = 0 (7)
Other race	0.117	0.108	0.118	0.106**	0.122	0.104***	0.129
	(0.321)	(0.311)	(0.322)	(0.308)	(0.327)	(0.305)	(0.335)
Test score 1	0.200	0.198	0.200	0.205	0.197	0.238***	0.162
	(0.400)	(0.399)	(0.400)	(0.404)	(0.398)	(0.426)	(0.368)
Test score 2	0.207	0.169***	0.212	0.197*	0.212	0.216**	0.196
	(0.405)	(0.375)	(0.409)	(0.398)	(0.409)	(0.412)	(0.397)
Test score 3	0.144	0.142	0.144	0.138	0.146	0.142	0.146
	(0.351)	(0.349)	(0.351)	(0.345)	(0.353)	(0.349)	(0.354)
Test score 4	0.214	0.235*	0.211	0.213	0.214	0.193***	0.234
	(0.410)	(0.424)	(0.408)	(0.409)	(0.410)	(0.394)	(0.424)
Test score 5	0.202	0.209	0.201	0.201	0.202	0.175***	0.230
	(0.401)	(0.407)	(0.401)	(0.401)	(0.402)	(0.380)	(0.421)
No degree	0.088	0.064***	0.091	0.070***	0.097	0.102***	0.074
	(0.284)	(0.245)	(0.288)	(0.255)	(0.296)	(0.302)	(0.262)
GED	0.073	0.064	0.074	0.062***	0.078	0.075	0.070
	(0.260)	(0.245)	(0.262)	(0.241)	(0.269)	(0.264)	(0.256)
High school degree	0.606	0.603	0.607	0.608	0.605	0.604	0.607
	(0.489)	(0.489)	(0.489)	(0.488)	(0.489)	(0.489)	(0.489)
Junior college degree	0.084	0.085	0.084	0.086	0.083	0.081	0.088
	(0.277)	(0.279)	(0.277)	(0.280)	(0.276)	(0.273)	(0.283)
Bachelor's degree	0.139	0.168***	0.136	0.163***	0.128	0.129***	0.151
	(0.346)	(0.374)	(0.342)	(0.369)	(0.334)	(0.335)	(0.358)
Master's degree	0.009	0.016***	0.008	0.010	0.008	0.009	0.010
	(0.094)	(0.124)	(0.089)	(0.100)	(0.090)	(0.092)	(0.097)
Healthy	0.956	0.983***	0.952	0.977***	0.946	0.967***	0.944
	(0.205)	(0.130)	(0.213)	(0.150)	(0.227)	(0.177)	(0.229)
Father jailed	0.134	0.114**	0.136	0.122**	0.139	0.142**	0.126
	(0.340)	(0.318)	(0.343)	(0.328)	(0.346)	(0.349)	(0.332)

	(1)	(2)	(3)	(4)	(5)	(6)	(7)
U.S. born	0.905	0.903	0.906	0.906	0.905	0.902	0.907
	(0.293)	(0.297)	(0.292)	(0.292)	(0.293)	(0.297)	(0.290)
No siblings	0.183	0.158**	0.187	0.175*	0.188	0.187	0.179
	(0.387)	(0.365)	(0.390)	(0.380)	(0.391)	(0.390)	(0.384)
1 sibling	0.343	0.349	0.343	0.350	0.340	0.326***	0.359
	(0.475)	(0.477)	(0.475)	(0.477)	(0.474)	(0.469)	(0.480)
2 siblings	0.247	0.259	0.245	0.250	0.245	0.249	0.247
	(0.431)	(0.438)	(0.430)	(0.433)	(0.430)	(0.432)	(0.431)
3 siblings	0.119	0.120	0.118	0.117	0.119	0.120	0.116
	(0.323)	(0.325)	(0.323)	(0.322)	(0.324)	(0.325)	(0.320)
4 or more siblings	0.050	0.091	0.090	0.091	0.089	0.099**	0.082
	(0.286)	(0.287)	(0.286)	(0.288)	(0.285)	(0.299)	(0.274)
Family income—1	0.060	0.054	0.061	0.061	0.060	0.071***	0.049
	(0.238)	(0.226)	(0.239)	(0.239)	(0.237)	(0.256)	(0.215)
Family income—2	0.140	0.127	0.142	0.135	0.142	0.147**	0.133
	(0.347)	(0.333)	(0.349)	(0.342)	(0.350)	(0.355)	(0.340)
Family income—3	0.754	0.774*	0.751	0.756	0.753	0.729***	0.779
	(0.431)	(0.418)	(0.432)	(0.429)	(0.431)	(0.445)	(0.415)
Mom's age at birth ≤ 19	0.077	0.079	0.077	0.075	0.078	0.082	0.073
	(0.267)	(0.270)	(0.266)	(0.263)	(0.269)	(0.274)	(0.261)
19 < Mom's age at birth ≤ 30	0.503	0.498	0.503	0.516*	0.496	0.503	0.500
	(0.500)	(0.500)	(0.500)	(0.500)	(0.500)	(0.500)	(0.500)
30 < Mom's age at birth ≤ 40	0.124	0.134	0.123	0.122	0.126	0.117**	0.133
	(0.330)	(0.341)	(0.329)	(0.327)	(0.332)	(0.322)	(0.339)
Mom's age at birth > 40	0.006	0.006	0.006	0.006	0.006	0.007	0.005
	(0.078)	(0.075)	(0.079)	(0.077)	(0.079)	(0.081)	(0.073)
Mom high school dropout	0.156	0.142	0.158	0.152	0.158	0.167***	0.147
	(0.363)	(0.349)	(0.365)	(0.359)	(0.365)	(0.373)	(0.354)
Mom finished high school	0.309	0.294	0.311	0.297*	0.314	0.306	0.309
	(0.462)	(0.456)	(0.463)	(0.457)	(0.464)	(0.461)	(0.462)
Observations	10,843	1,222	9,621	3,541	7,302	5,042	5,578

Notes: Standard deviations are in parentheses. The number of observations for the variable *Very confident* is 10,620; 1,196; 9,424; 3,467; and 7,153, respectively in columns (1) to (5). It is equal to "Observations" in columns (6) and (7). The number of observations for *Wage* is 7,089; 795; 6,294; 2,369; 4,720; 3,305; and 3,670 in (1) to (7), respectively. ***, **, and * indicate p-values less than 0.01, 0.05, and 0.1 for the test of the equality of means between groups in columns (2) and (3), (4) and (5), and (6) and (7).

to 100 percent of the poverty threshold but less than 200 percent, and zero otherwise. *Family Income—3* identifies the case where family income was greater than or equal to 200 percent of the poverty threshold. Other control variables include mother's education and mother's age at birth.

Table 12.1 also reports the means of the variables by self-esteem category. The stars next to the means indicate that the means are different between the groups. For example, the average hourly wage for those with very high self-esteem is $11.78, while the average wage for those who do not have very high self-esteem is $11.13, and the difference is statistically significant. The proportion of males with high self-esteem is greater than that of females.

12.4   Results

12.4.1   BMI and Self-Esteem

Table 12.2 displays the results obtained from the model depicted in equation (1), where self-esteem of young adults (aged twenty-one to twenty-six) is explained by BMI and other explanatory variables. Each specification reported in this table and in all other tables includes state fixed effects. Robust standard errors are reported in parentheses under the coefficients. Column (1) reports the results of the model where *Very high self-esteem* is the dependent variable. This is a dichotomous variable that takes the value of one if the person is ranked in the top 10 percent of the self-esteem distribution, and zero otherwise. Age and race have no statistically significant impact on self-esteem. Hispanic ethnicity is related to high self-esteem and confidence. Those with a high school degree or junior college degree are 3 and 4 percentage points more likely, respectively, to have very high self-esteem in comparison to those with a GED or with no high school diploma. The impact of bachelor's degree on very high self-esteem is twice as large as the impact of a high school diploma or a junior college degree, and the impact of a master's degree on very high self-esteem is twice as large as that of a bachelor's degree. Males and healthier individuals are more likely to have very high self-esteem. An increase in BMI is associated with a decrease in high self-esteem. One-standard deviation increase in BMI (6.13) lowers the probability of having very high self-esteem by about 1 percentage point, which represents a 9 percent decline from the baseline.

Column (3) displays the results of the model where *High self-esteem* is the dependent variable, which is a dichotomous variable that takes the value of one if the if the person is ranked in the top 25 percent of the self-esteem distribution, and zero otherwise. The results are very similar to those reported in column (1). In alternative specifications, displayed in columns (2) and (4), we estimate models by including both linear and quadratic BMI terms to investigate potential nonlinear impact of BMI on self-esteem. The coefficients are not significantly different from zero. However, the hypothesis

Table 12.2   **Determinants of self-esteem**

	A—BMI as a continuous variable					
	Very high self-esteem		High self-esteem		Very confident	
	(1)	(2)	(3)	(4)	(5)	(6)
BMI	-0.002***	-0.001	-0.002***	-0.001	-0.002**	0.008
	(0.0005)	(0.003)	(0.001)	(0.005)	(0.001)	(0.005)
BMI^2		-0.00001		-0.00001		-0.00016*
		(0.00004)		(0.00008)		(0.00009)
Male	0.040***	0.040***	0.057***	0.057***	0.124***	0.122***
	(0.006)	(0.006)	(0.009)	(0.009)	(0.010)	(0.010)
Age21	0.020	0.020	0.033	0.033	0.066	0.066
	(0.032)	(0.032)	(0.045)	(0.045)	(0.049)	(0.049)
Age22	-0.005	-0.004	0.028	0.028	0.049	0.050
	(0.031)	(0.031)	(0.045)	(0.045)	(0.049)	(0.049)
Age23	-0.010	-0.010	0.012	0.012	0.029	0.029
	(0.031)	(0.031)	(0.045)	(0.045)	(0.049)	(0.049)
Age24	-0.002	-0.002	0.018	0.018	0.024	0.025
	(0.031)	(0.031)	(0.045)	(0.045)	(0.049)	(0.049)
Age25	0.007	0.007	0.031	0.031	0.063	0.062
	(0.033)	(0.033)	(0.047)	(0.047)	(0.051)	(0.051)
Hispanic	0.030***	0.029***	0.036**	0.036**	0.045***	0.044***
	(0.010)	(0.010)	(0.015)	(0.015)	(0.015)	(0.015)
White	-0.006	-0.006	-0.011	-0.011	0.014	0.013
	(0.011)	(0.011)	(0.017)	(0.017)	(0.018)	(0.018)
Black	0.015	0.015	0.080***	0.079***	0.196***	0.196***
	(0.013)	(0.013)	(0.019)	(0.019)	(0.020)	(0.020)
GED	0.020	0.020	0.024	0.024	-0.036	-0.035
	(0.014)	(0.014)	(0.021)	(0.021)	(0.024)	(0.024)
High school degree	0.032***	0.032***	0.072***	0.072***	-0.048***	-0.048***
	(0.010)	(0.010)	(0.016)	(0.016)	(0.018)	(0.018)
Junior college degree	0.039***	0.039***	0.082***	0.082***	-0.045*	-0.044*
	(0.014)	(0.014)	(0.022)	(0.022)	(0.024)	(0.024)
Bachelor's degree	0.066***	0.066***	0.140***	0.140***	-0.034	-0.034
	(0.014)	(0.014)	(0.021)	(0.021)	(0.022)	(0.022)
Master's degree	0.125***	0.125***	0.127**	0.127**	-0.034	-0.033
	(0.042)	(0.042)	(0.051)	(0.051)	(0.052)	(0.052)
Healthy	0.054***	0.054***	0.134***	0.133***	0.133***	0.131***
	(0.010)	(0.010)	(0.018)	(0.018)	(0.022)	(0.022)
Father jailed	-0.011	-0.011	-0.022*	-0.022*	0.007	0.007
	(0.009)	(0.009)	(0.013)	(0.013)	(0.014)	(0.014)
U.S. born	0.005	0.005	0.010	0.010	-0.004	-0.004
	(0.012)	(0.012)	(0.017)	(0.017)	(0.018)	(0.018)
No siblings	-0.018	-0.018	-0.036*	-0.036*	-0.029	-0.029
	(0.013)	(0.013)	(0.019)	(0.019)	(0.020)	(0.020)
1 sibling	-0.002	-0.002	-0.009	-0.009	-0.040**	-0.041**
	(0.012)	(0.012)	(0.018)	(0.018)	(0.019)	(0.019)
2 siblings	-0.0002	-0.0003	-0.012	-0.012	-0.026	-0.027
	(0.012)	(0.012)	(0.018)	(0.018)	(0.019)	(0.019)
3 siblings	0.001	0.001	-0.009	-0.009	-0.014	-0.015
	(0.014)	(0.014)	(0.020)	(0.020)	(0.021)	(0.021)
Family Income—1	-0.010	-0.010	-0.007	-0.007	0.022	0.022
	(0.018)	(0.018)	(0.028)	(0.028)	(0.029)	(0.029)
Family Income—2	-0.008	-0.008	-0.011	-0.011	-0.010	-0.011
	(0.016)	(0.016)	(0.024)	(0.024)	(0.026)	(0.026)

(*continued*)

Table 12.2 (continued)

	Very high self-esteem		High self-esteem		Very confident	
	(1)	(2)	(3)	(4)	(5)	(6)
Family Income—3	0.005	0.005	0.005	0.005	−0.036	−0.036
	(0.016)	(0.016)	(0.023)	(0.023)	(0.024)	(0.024)
Mom's age at birth ≤ 19	0.012	0.012	0.021	0.021	0.025	0.025
	(0.015)	(0.015)	(0.021)	(0.021)	(0.022)	(0.022)
19 < Mom's age at birth ≤ 30	−0.004	−0.004	0.025*	0.025*	0.033**	0.033**
	(0.010)	(0.010)	(0.014)	(0.014)	(0.015)	(0.015)
Mom high school drop out	−0.009	−0.009	−0.001	−0.001	0.013	0.013
	(0.010)	(0.010)	(0.015)	(0.015)	(0.016)	(0.016)
Mom finished high school	−0.005	−0.005	−0.014	−0.014	0.001	0.000
	(0.007)	(0.007)	(0.011)	(0.011)	(0.012)	(0.012)
Observations	10,843	10,843	10,843	10,843	10,631	10,631

B—BMI as dichotomous variables

	Very high self-esteem (1)	High self-esteem (2)	Very confident (3)
Underweight	−0.004	0.015	−0.006
	(0.018)	(0.027)	(0.029)
Overweight	−0.004	0.003	0.017
	(0.007)	(0.011)	(0.011)
Obese	−0.024***	−0.023**	−0.022*
	(0.007)	(0.011)	(0.012)
Male	0.040***	0.056***	0.122***
	(0.006)	(0.009)	(0.010)
Age21	0.020	0.034	0.068
	(0.032)	(0.046)	(0.049)
Age22	−0.004	0.029	0.052
	(0.031)	(0.045)	(0.049)
Age23	−0.010	0.013	0.030
	(0.031)	(0.045)	(0.049)
Age24	−0.002	0.019	0.026
	(0.031)	(0.045)	(0.049)
Age25	0.007	0.032	0.065
	(0.033)	(0.047)	(0.051)
Hispanic	0.029***	0.035**	0.043***
	(0.010)	(0.015)	(0.015)
White	−0.006	−0.011	0.013
	(0.011)	(0.017)	(0.018)
Black	0.014	0.079***	0.196***
	(0.013)	(0.019)	(0.020)
GED	0.020	0.024	−0.036
	(0.014)	(0.021)	(0.024)
High school degree	0.032***	0.072***	−0.049***
	(0.010)	(0.016)	(0.018)
Junior college degree	0.038***	0.082***	−0.046**
	(0.014)	(0.022)	(0.024)
Bachelor's degree	0.066***	0.140***	−0.034
	(0.014)	(0.021)	(0.022)
Master's degree	0.125***	0.128**	−0.035
	(0.042)	(0.051)	(0.052)
Healthy	0.054***	0.134***	0.132***
	(0.010)	(0.018)	(0.022)

Table 12.2   (continued)

	Very high self-esteem (1)	High self-esteem (2)	Very confident (3)
Father jailed	−0.011	−0.022*	0.007
	(0.009)	(0.013)	(0.014)
U.S. born	0.005	0.009	−0.005
	(0.012)	(0.017)	(0.018)
No siblings	−0.018	−0.035*	−0.028
	(0.013)	(0.019)	(0.020)
1 sibling	−0.001	−0.008	−0.040**
	(0.012)	(0.018)	(0.019)
2 siblings	0.000	−0.012	−0.026
	(0.012)	(0.018)	(0.019)
3 siblings	0.001	−0.009	−0.014
	(0.014)	(0.020)	(0.021)
Family income—1	−0.010	−0.007	0.022
	(0.019)	(0.028)	(0.029)
Family income—2	−0.008	−0.011	−0.011
	(0.016)	(0.024)	(0.026)
Family income—3	0.005	0.005	−0.036
	(0.016)	(0.023)	(0.024)
Mom's age at birth ≤ 19	0.012	0.021	0.025
	(0.015)	(0.021)	(0.022)
19 < Mom's age at birth ≤ 30	−0.004	0.025*	0.033**
	(0.010)	(0.014)	(0.015)
Mom high school drop out	−0.009	−0.001	0.013
	(0.010)	(0.015)	(0.016)
Mom finished high school	−0.005	−0.014	0.000
	(0.007)	(0.011)	(0.012)
Observations	10,843	10,843	10,631

Notes: Regressions include state-fixed effects. Robust standard errors are reported in parentheses. ***, ** and * indicate p-values less than 0.01, 0.05 and 0.10, respectively.

that linear and quadratic BMI terms are jointly zero is strongly rejected in each case. Columns (5) and (6) present the results obtained from the models where the dependent variable is whether the person has very high confidence. As column (5) shows, an increase in BMI is negatively associated with confidence, and the magnitude of the association is the same as the ones reported in case of self-esteem.

To estimate a more flexible functional form, we classified BMI into four mutually exclusive categories, and used three of these indicators as explanatory variables. In table 12.2 we report estimation results obtained from these specifications. *Underweight* takes the value of one if the person's BMI is less than 18.5, and zero otherwise. *Overweight* is one if BMI is between twenty-five and thirty, inclusive; *Obese* takes the value of one if BMI is greater than thirty. The results demonstrate that the most significant impact on self-esteem is obtained from belonging to the *Obese* category. Specifically, being obese (BMI > 30) is associated with a decrease in the probability of having high or very high self-esteem by about 2.4 percentage points. Being obese is also associated with a reduction in the probability of being very confident by 2.2 percentage points.

To investigate the sensitivity of the results to the manner in which individuals are classified into high self-esteem and low self-esteem categories, we estimated two ordered-probit models. Each model contains the same set of explanatory variables as employed in table 12.2. The first model categorizes self-esteem into four groups: (a) if the person's self-esteem score is less than twenty, (b) if the self-esteem score is twenty or twenty-one, (c) if the self-esteem score is twenty-two or twenty-three, and (d) if the self-esteem score is twenty-four or twenty-five. Twenty-three percent of the observations belong to the first category, about 34 percent are in the second group, 21 percent are in the third group, and 23 percent are in the fourth group. In the second specification we categorized the young adults' self-esteem into three groups: (a) those with self-esteem score less than twenty (23 percent of the sample), (b) those with a score of twenty, twenty-one, or twenty-two (44 percent of the sample), and (c) those with a score twenty-three or greater (33 percent of the sample).

Table 12.3, panel A presents the marginal effects of the continuous measure of BMI (the top section) and the marginal effects of the dichotomous BMI indicators (the bottom section) that are calculated after estimating the ordered-probit models where self-esteem is classified into four categories. An increase in BMI increases the probability of belonging to the bottom two self-esteem categories, and it decreases the probability of being in the top two groups of self-esteem distribution. The same result is obtained when using the dichotomous BMI variables, and the statistically significant impact stems from being obese.

Table 12.3 panel B displays the same information with one difference: the dependent variable is based on a three-way categorization of self-esteem. As was the case in table 12.3 panel A, an increase in BMI is associated with a reduction in the probability of having high self-esteem (being in the top 33 percent of the self-esteem distribution), and it is associated with an increase in the probability of belonging to low-self-esteem groups.

In table 12.4 we display the results obtained from estimating versions of equation (2). Here, to minimize the concern of reverse causality from self-esteem to BMI, we explain the current self-esteem of the young adult (measured in the third wave of the survey) with his/her BMI measured five to six years ago (in the second wave of the survey). Columns (1), (2), and (3) reveal that past BMI has a statistically significant impact on current self-esteem. Furthermore, the magnitude of the BMI coefficient is the same as those reported in table 12.2.

Columns (4) and (5) of table 12.4 display the results of the models depicted in equation (5), where current self-esteem is expressed as a function of past self-esteem and past BMI. This specification cannot be estimated when *Very confident* is the dependent variable because the variable *Very confident* is not available in the second wave of the survey. Having high self-esteem (very high

Table 12.3   **Marginal effects on the probability of each category of self-esteem**

	4 Self-esteem categories			
	(1) (lowest)	(2)	(3)	(4) (highest)
BMI***	0.0021	0.0006	–0.0007	–0.0020
	(0.0005)	(0.0002)	(0.0002)	(0.0005)
Underweight	0.004	0.001	–0.001	–0.004
	(0.019)	(0.006)	(0.006)	(0.019)
Overweight	–0.008	–0.002	0.003	0.008
	(0.007)	(0.002)	(0.002)	(0.007)
Obese***	0.026	0.007	–0.008	–0.024
	(0.008)	(0.002)	(0.003)	(0.008)
Observations	10,863	10,863	10,863	10,863

	3 Self-esteem categories		
	(1) (low)	(2)	(3) (high)
BMI***	0.0019	0.0004	–0.0023
	(0.0005)	(0.0001)	(0.0007)
Underweight	0.0002	0.00003	–0.0002
	(0.0201)	(0.00413)	(0.0242)
Overweight	–0.007	–0.0014	0.008
	(0.008)	(0.0017)	(0.009)
Obese***	0.024	0.0042	–0.028
	(0.009)	(0.0013)	(0.010)
Observations	10,863	10,863	10,863

Notes: ***Indicates that the coefficient of the variable in the ordered probit regression is significant at less than 1 percent level.

self-esteem) in the past increases the likelihood of having high self-esteem (very high self-esteem) in the present. Keeping constant past self-esteem, an increase in BMI in the past is associated with a decrease in self-esteem today. The impact of past BMI on current self-esteem is smaller in specifications that control for past self-esteem (columns [4] and [5]) in comparison to the models that do not control for past self-esteem (columns [1], [2], and [3]).

The bottom panel of table 12.4 presents the results obtained from models where self-esteem and confidence indicators are explained by weight indicators in the past (five to six years earlier) as well as past self-esteem indicators. Past weight indicators are based on height and weight measured in Wave II, when the subjects were fifteen to twenty years of age. Thus, the classifications are based in CDC growth charts. Here, underweight indicates that the teenager belonged to the bottom 5 percent of the distribution for age in Wave II. He/she is considered overweight if the BMI was between the eighty-fifth

Table 12.4   **The determinants of self-esteem: Models with past BMI and past self-esteem**

	Very high self-esteem (1)	High self-esteem (2)	Very confident (3)	Very high self-esteem (4)	High self-esteem (5)
Past BMI	−0.002**	−0.003***	−0.002**	−0.001**	−0.002**
	(0.001)	(0.001)	(0.001)	(0.001)	(0.001)
Very high self-esteem in the past				0.164***	
				(0.014)	
High self-esteem in the past					0.225***
					(0.012)
Observations	8,106	8,106	7,919	8,090	8,090
Underweight in the past	−0.014	−0.020	−0.050*	−0.012	−0.010
	(0.016)	(0.024)	(0.026)	(0.016)	(0.024)
Overweight in the past	−0.018*	−0.021	−0.011	−0.018*	−0.019
	(0.010)	(0.015)	(0.017)	(0.010)	(0.015)
Obese in the past	−0.021**	−0.036**	−0.034*	−0.018*	−0.028*
	(0.010)	(0.016)	(0.017)	(0.010)	(0.016)
Very high self-esteem in the past				0.164***	
				(0.014)	
High self-esteem in the past					0.225***
					(0.012)
Observations	8,106	8,106	7,919	8,090	8,090

Notes: Regressions include state-fixed effects and variables used in table 12.2. Robust standard errors are in parentheses. ***, **, and * indicate *p*-values less than 0.01, 0.05, and 0.10, respectively. *Underweight in the past, Overweight in the past,* and *Obese in the past* are based on the BMI of the person in Wave 2, when he/she was aged 15–20. For these classifications, underweight indicates that the person belonged to the bottom 5 percent of the distribution for age. Overweight indicates that the BMI is between 85th and 95th percentiles; and obese indicates that BMI is equal to or greater than the 95th percentile. See the text for further details.

and ninety-fifth percentiles; the teenager is considered obese if the BMI was equal to or greater than the ninety-fifth percentile. The left-out category in the regressions is healthy weight (BMI between fifth and eighty-fifth percentiles). The results demonstrate that being obese in the past has a negative impact on current self-esteem. The impacts of being underweight and being overweight on self-esteem are also negative, although the significance of the coefficients is spotty.

12.4.2   BMI and Wages

Equation (6), which formulates the relationship between wages, obesity, and self-esteem is estimated using the logarithm of wages reported by young adults in Wave III.[7] Table 12.5 reports the benchmark specification where wages are explained by human capital attributes of the young adults as

7. It is not advisable to include in these regressions occupation dummies to control for the impact of individuals' occupations in their wages. This is because occupational choice may have been determined, in part, by BMI. Nevertheless, we also ran regressions that include twenty-two occupation dummies. The results did not change.

Table 12.5   **Determinants of wages: Models with self-esteem**

	(1)	(2)	(3)	(4)	(5)	(6)
Very high self-esteem	0.035***			0.035***		
	(0.013)			(0.013)		
High self-esteem		0.043***			0.042***	
		(0.009)			(0.009)	
Very confident			0.027***			0.028***
			(0.008)			(0.008)
Male	0.091***	0.090***	0.087***	0.090***	0.088***	0.085***
	(0.008)	(0.008)	(0.008)	(0.008)	(0.008)	(0.008)
Age21	−0.078*	−0.080*	−0.079*	−0.081*	−0.082*	−0.082*
	(0.045)	(0.045)	(0.045)	(0.045)	(0.045)	(0.045)
Age22	−0.023	−0.024	−0.026	−0.025	−0.027	−0.028
	(0.045)	(0.045)	(0.045)	(0.045)	(0.045)	(0.045)
Age23	0.038	0.036	0.037	0.035	0.034	0.035
	(0.045)	(0.045)	(0.045)	(0.045)	(0.045)	(0.045)
Age24	0.089*	0.087*	0.090**	0.087*	0.085*	0.088*
	(0.045)	(0.045)	(0.045)	(0.045)	(0.045)	(0.045)
Age25	0.088*	0.086*	0.091*	0.086*	0.085*	0.089*
	(0.048)	(0.047)	(0.047)	(0.047)	(0.047)	(0.047)
Hispanic	0.031**	0.031**	0.031**	0.036***	0.036***	0.036***
	(0.013)	(0.013)	(0.013)	(0.013)	(0.013)	(0.013)
White	−0.018	−0.018	−0.020	−0.020	−0.021	−0.023
	(0.016)	(0.016)	(0.016)	(0.016)	(0.016)	(0.016)
Black	−0.046***	−0.049***	−0.056***	−0.039**	−0.042**	−0.049***
	(0.018)	(0.018)	(0.018)	(0.018)	(0.018)	(0.018)
Test score 2				0.044***	0.043***	0.039***
				(0.013)	(0.013)	(0.013)
Test score 3				0.053***	0.053***	0.051***
				(0.015)	(0.015)	(0.015)
Test score 4				0.061***	0.061***	0.059***
				(0.014)	(0.014)	(0.014)
Test score 5				0.032**	0.032**	0.033**
				(0.014)	(0.014)	(0.015)
GED	0.085***	0.085***	0.083***	0.077***	0.077***	0.075***
	(0.021)	(0.021)	(0.021)	(0.021)	(0.021)	(0.021)
High school degree	0.095***	0.094***	0.094***	0.087***	0.086***	0.086***
	(0.016)	(0.016)	(0.016)	(0.016)	(0.016)	(0.016)
Junior college degree	0.183***	0.182***	0.181***	0.171***	0.170***	0.169***
	(0.021)	(0.021)	(0.021)	(0.021)	(0.021)	(0.021)
Bachelor's degree	0.327***	0.325***	0.328***	0.316***	0.314***	0.316***
	(0.020)	(0.020)	(0.020)	(0.021)	(0.021)	(0.021)
Master's degree	0.459***	0.462***	0.461***	0.450***	0.452***	0.451***
	(0.055)	(0.054)	(0.055)	(0.055)	(0.054)	(0.055)
Healthy	0.087***	0.084***	0.088***	0.085***	0.081***	0.085***
	(0.019)	(0.019)	(0.019)	(0.019)	(0.019)	(0.019)
Father jailed	−0.005	−0.005	−0.002	−0.006	−0.006	−0.003
	(0.012)	(0.012)	(0.013)	(0.012)	(0.012)	(0.013)
U.S. born	0.028*	0.028*	0.028*	0.023	0.023	0.023
	(0.014)	(0.014)	(0.015)	(0.015)	(0.015)	(0.015)
No siblings	0.001	0.001	0.000	−0.003	−0.003	−0.004
	(0.017)	(0.017)	(0.017)	(0.017)	(0.017)	(0.017)
1 sibling	−0.017	−0.017	−0.017	−0.019	−0.019	−0.019
	(0.016)	(0.016)	(0.016)	(0.016)	(0.016)	(0.016)
2 siblings	−0.012	−0.012	−0.011	−0.014	−0.014	−0.013
	(0.016)	(0.016)	(0.016)	(0.016)	(0.016)	(0.016)

(*continued*)

Table 12.5   (continued)

	(1)	(2)	(3)	(4)	(5)	(6)
3 siblings	−0.011	−0.011	−0.012	−0.013	−0.012	−0.013
	(0.018)	(0.018)	(0.018)	(0.018)	(0.018)	(0.018)
Family income—1	−0.020	−0.021	−0.021	−0.023	−0.023	−0.024
	(0.024)	(0.024)	(0.025)	(0.024)	(0.024)	(0.025)
Family income—2	−0.023	−0.023	−0.022	−0.026	−0.026	−0.025
	(0.022)	(0.022)	(0.022)	(0.022)	(0.022)	(0.022)
Family income—3	0.012	0.011	0.013	0.007	0.007	0.008
	(0.021)	(0.021)	(0.021)	(0.021)	(0.021)	(0.021)
Mom's age at birth ≤ 19	−0.005	−0.005	−0.006	−0.004	−0.004	−0.005
	(0.018)	(0.018)	(0.018)	(0.018)	(0.018)	(0.018)
19 < Mom's age at birth ≤ 30	−0.004	−0.004	−0.006	−0.004	−0.005	−0.007
	(0.013)	(0.013)	(0.013)	(0.013)	(0.013)	(0.013)
Mom high school drop out	−0.003	−0.003	−0.004	0.000	0.000	0.001
	(0.013)	(0.013)	(0.013)	(0.013)	(0.013)	(0.013)
Mom finished high school	0.000	0.001	0.001	0.002	0.003	0.003
	(0.010)	(0.010)	(0.010)	(0.010)	(0.010)	(0.010)
Observations	7,524	7,524	7,395	7,524	7,524	7,395

Notes: Regressions include state-fixed effects, and 22 occupation dummies. Robust standard errors are reported in parentheses. ***, **, and * indicate *p*-values less than 0.01, 0.05, and 0.10, respectively.

well as by their self-esteem. The results show that higher levels of education have bigger impacts on wages. A General Educational Development (GED) degree increases wages by 8.5 percent in comparison to having no high school diploma; and high school diploma has an 9.5 percent wage premium. The impact of a junior college degree on wages is an 18 percent increase in comparison to no high school diploma. Those with a bachelor's degree earn about 33 percent higher wages in comparison to those who have no high school degree and the premium associated with a master's degree is 46 percent. This result is not surprising, and it is consistent with the large literature in economics on the returns to education. However, these models do not control for potential endogeneity of education, therefore the magnitudes of the education variables should be interpreted with caution.[8] In fact, columns (4) through (6) show that, controlling for the vocabulary scores reduces the magnitude of the education coefficients. Holding constant education, higher vocabulary test scores have a positive impact on wages. This suggests that this dimension of ability, measured by Peabody Vocabulary test scores, is rewarded in the market in addition to the level of education acquired. In columns (1) through (3), we observe that having been born in the United States is associated with a 2.8 percent wage premium. However, controlling for the vocabulary test score in columns (4) through (6) eliminates the statistical significance of the coefficient of U.S. born, sug-

8. For example, individuals with higher ability are more likely to acquire more education, and they are also more likely to earn higher wages, regardless their level of education.

gesting English proficiency may be captured by the U.S. born variable. Being healthy generates an 8 percent wage premium, but other variables are not significantly associated with wages. Table 12.5 also shows that holding all else constant, having high self-esteem is associated with higher wages. This result is consistent with recent research that has demonstrated the importance of noncognitive skills in wage determination.

Table 12.6 panel A estimates the same models with one difference: in these models we include BMI as an additional explanatory variable. The results imply that a one-standard deviation increase in BMI is associated with a 1.2 percent reduction in wages. A comparison with table 12.5 shows that adding BMI does not impact the coefficients of most variables meaningfully. When the impact of BMI is controlled for, the coefficients of self-esteem decline slightly. Specifically, the impact of self-esteem is 11 to 15 percent smaller when the model includes BMI. Panel B in table 12.6 is similar to panel A, but instead of employing BMI as a continuous measure, we use three dichotomous variables that classify individuals into four weight categories, as was done before. This specification does not alter the estimated impact of self-esteem on wages, and the results show that the negative impact of BMI on wages is primarily due to being in the *Obese* category.

Table 12.7 displays the results that are obtained from the models where logarithm of wages are regressed on the same set of explanatory variables, including current self-esteem measures, but that also control for past BMI (BMI measured five to six years ago). Past BMI has a negative impact on current wages and the positive impact of self-esteem on wages remains robust.

12.4.3   Race and Gender-specific Analyses

To investigate how the relationship between BMI, self-esteem, and wages differ by race and gender, we estimated the models for the following four groups: black females, black males, white females, and white males. Each model contains the same set of explanatory variables as used in other models, including the indicator variable for Hispanic ethnicity. Such a breakdown is potentially important because previous research failed to find a consistent relationship between BMI and wages for groups other than white females, suggesting that the strength of the association between self-esteem, BMI, and wages may differ between race and gender groups.

Table 12.8 summarizes the results of the race and gender-specific self-esteem regressions. The models include full set of controls as in previous regressions, but they are not reported in the interest of space. In each panel we report the estimated coefficients of BMI and the corresponding standard error. The top panel demonstrates that BMI has a negative and statistically significant impact on self-esteem in the case of black females. The BMI has a negative impact of black men's self-esteem as well, although most of the estimates are not statistically significant at conventional levels. The bottom

Table 12.6 **Determinants of wages**

	(1)	(2)	(3)	(4)	(5)	(6)
A—Determinants of wages: Models with self-esteem and BMI as a continuous variable						
BMI	−0.002***	−0.002***	−0.002***	−0.002***	−0.002***	−0.002***
	(0.001)	(0.001)	(0.001)	(0.001)	(0.001)	(0.001)
Very high self-esteem	0.030**			0.030**		
	(0.014)			(0.014)		
High self-esteem		0.037***			0.037***	
		(0.009)			(0.009)	
Very confident			0.024***			0.025***
			(0.009)			(0.009)
Male	0.094***	0.093***	0.091***	0.093***	0.091***	0.089***
	(0.009)	(0.009)	(0.009)	(0.009)	(0.009)	(0.009)
Age21	−0.094*	−0.096**	−0.094*	−0.097**	−0.099**	−0.097**
	(0.049)	(0.049)	(0.049)	(0.049)	(0.049)	(0.049)
Age22	−0.037	−0.039	−0.039	−0.039	−0.041	−0.041
	(0.049)	(0.049)	(0.049)	(0.049)	(0.049)	(0.049)
Age23	0.025	0.023	0.024	0.023	0.021	0.021
	(0.049)	(0.049)	(0.049)	(0.049)	(0.049)	(0.049)
Age24	0.074	0.072	0.074	0.072	0.070	0.072
	(0.049)	(0.049)	(0.049)	(0.049)	(0.049)	(0.049)
Age25	0.076	0.074	0.079	0.075	0.072	0.078
	(0.051)	(0.051)	(0.051)	(0.051)	(0.051)	(0.051)
Hispanic	0.026**	0.026*	0.026**	0.030**	0.030**	0.031**
	(0.013)	(0.013)	(0.013)	(0.013)	(0.013)	(0.013)
White	−0.017	−0.017	−0.019	−0.019	−0.019	−0.021
	(0.016)	(0.016)	(0.016)	(0.016)	(0.016)	(0.016)
Black	−0.046**	−0.049***	−0.055***	−0.040**	−0.043**	−0.049***
	(0.018)	(0.018)	(0.018)	(0.018)	(0.018)	(0.019)
Test score 2				0.040***	0.040***	0.038***
				(0.013)	(0.013)	(0.013)
Test score 3				0.048***	0.048***	0.047***
				(0.015)	(0.015)	(0.015)
Test score 4				0.056***	0.056***	0.055***
				(0.014)	(0.014)	(0.014)
Test score 5				0.027*	0.027*	0.030**
				(0.015)	(0.015)	(0.015)
GED	0.090***	0.090***	0.087***	0.083***	0.083***	0.081***
	(0.022)	(0.022)	(0.022)	(0.022)	(0.022)	(0.022)
High school degree	0.097***	0.097***	0.097***	0.090***	0.089***	0.089***
	(0.016)	(0.016)	(0.016)	(0.016)	(0.016)	(0.016)
Junior college degree	0.184***	0.184***	0.183***	0.174***	0.174***	0.172***
	(0.021)	(0.021)	(0.021)	(0.021)	(0.021)	(0.021)
Bachelor's degree	0.329***	0.327***	0.330***	0.319***	0.317***	0.319***
	(0.021)	(0.021)	(0.021)	(0.021)	(0.021)	(0.021)
Master's degree	0.455***	0.458***	0.459***	0.447***	0.449***	0.450***
	(0.055)	(0.055)	(0.055)	(0.055)	(0.055)	(0.056)
Healthy	0.078***	0.074***	0.077***	0.075***	0.072***	0.075***
	(0.020)	(0.020)	(0.020)	(0.020)	(0.020)	(0.020)
Father jailed	−0.007	−0.006	−0.004	−0.008	−0.007	−0.005
	(0.013)	(0.013)	(0.013)	(0.013)	(0.013)	(0.013)
U.S. born	0.030**	0.030**	0.029*	0.026*	0.025*	0.024
	(0.015)	(0.015)	(0.015)	(0.015)	(0.015)	(0.015)
No siblings	−0.005	−0.005	−0.005	−0.008	−0.008	−0.009
	(0.018)	(0.018)	(0.018)	(0.018)	(0.018)	(0.018)
1 sibling	−0.022	−0.023	−0.022	−0.025	−0.025	−0.024
	(0.016)	(0.016)	(0.017)	(0.016)	(0.016)	(0.017)

Table 12.6   (continued)

	(1)	(2)	(3)	(4)	(5)	(6)
2 siblings	−0.015	−0.015	−0.013	−0.017	−0.017	−0.015
	(0.017)	(0.017)	(0.017)	(0.017)	(0.017)	(0.017)
3 siblings	−0.016	−0.015	−0.016	−0.017	−0.016	−0.017
	(0.019)	(0.018)	(0.019)	(0.019)	(0.018)	(0.019)
Family income—1	−0.034	−0.034	−0.031	−0.035	−0.035	−0.033
	(0.025)	(0.025)	(0.025)	(0.025)	(0.025)	(0.025)
Family income—2	−0.026	−0.027	−0.025	−0.029	−0.029	−0.027
	(0.022)	(0.022)	(0.022)	(0.022)	(0.022)	(0.022)
Family income—3	0.006	0.005	0.007	0.002	0.001	0.003
	(0.021)	(0.021)	(0.022)	(0.021)	(0.021)	(0.022)
Mom's age at birth ≤ 19	0.003	0.003	0.001	0.004	0.004	0.002
	(0.019)	(0.019)	(0.019)	(0.019)	(0.019)	(0.019)
19 < Mom's age at birth ≤ 30	0.004	0.003	0.002	0.003	0.002	0.001
	(0.013)	(0.013)	(0.013)	(0.013)	(0.013)	(0.013)
Mom high school drop out	−0.002	−0.002	−0.003	0.001	0.001	0.000
	(0.013)	(0.013)	(0.013)	(0.013)	(0.013)	(0.013)
Mom finished high school	0.000	0.001	0.001	0.002	0.003	0.003
	(0.010)	(0.010)	(0.010)	(0.010)	(0.010)	(0.010)
Observations	7,089	7,089	6,977	7,089	7,089	6,977

B—Determinants of wages: Models with self-esteem and BMI as dichotomous variables						
Underweight	0.016	0.016	0.007	0.017	0.017	0.008
	(0.026)	(0.026)	(0.026)	(0.026)	(0.026)	(0.026)
Overweight	0.010	0.010	0.010	0.010	0.010	0.010
	(0.010)	(0.010)	(0.010)	(0.010)	(0.010)	(0.010)
Obese	−0.035***	−0.035***	−0.035***	−0.035***	−0.036***	−0.036***
	(0.010)	(0.010)	(0.011)	(0.010)	(0.010)	(0.011)
Very high self-esteem	0.030**			0.030**		
	(0.014)			(0.014)		
High self-esteem		0.037***			0.037***	
		(0.009)			(0.009)	
Very confident			0.023***			0.025***
			(0.009)			(0.009)
Male	0.092***	0.091***	0.089***	0.091***	0.090***	0.087***
	(0.009)	(0.009)	(0.009)	(0.009)	(0.009)	(0.009)
Age21	−0.092*	−0.094*	−0.093*	−0.095*	−0.097**	−0.096*
	(0.049)	(0.049)	(0.049)	(0.049)	(0.049)	(0.049)
Age22	−0.035	−0.037	−0.037	−0.038	−0.040	−0.040
	(0.049)	(0.049)	(0.049)	(0.049)	(0.048)	(0.049)
Age23	0.026	0.024	0.024	0.023	0.022	0.022
	(0.049)	(0.049)	(0.049)	(0.049)	(0.048)	(0.049)
Age24	0.075	0.073	0.075	0.073	0.071	0.073
	(0.049)	(0.049)	(0.049)	(0.049)	(0.049)	(0.049)
Age25	0.078	0.075	0.081	0.076	0.073	0.079
	(0.051)	(0.051)	(0.051)	(0.051)	(0.051)	(0.051)
Hispanic	0.025*	0.024*	0.025*	0.029**	0.028**	0.029**
	(0.013)	(0.013)	(0.013)	(0.013)	(0.013)	(0.013)
White	−0.017	−0.017	−0.019	−0.019	−0.018	−0.021
	(0.016)	(0.016)	(0.016)	(0.016)	(0.016)	(0.016)
Black	−0.046**	−0.048***	−0.054***	−0.040**	−0.042**	−0.048***
	(0.018)	(0.018)	(0.018)	(0.018)	(0.018)	(0.019)
Test score 2				0.040***	0.040***	0.038***
				(0.013)	(0.013)	(0.013)
Test score 3				0.048***	0.048***	0.047***
				(0.015)	(0.015)	(0.015)

(*continued*)

Table 12.6 (continued)

	(1)	(2)	(3)	(4)	(5)	(6)
Test score 4				0.056***	0.057***	0.056***
				(0.014)	(0.014)	(0.014)
Test score 5				0.027*	0.027*	0.030**
				(0.015)	(0.015)	(0.015)
GED	0.090***	0.090***	0.087***	0.083***	0.083***	0.080***
	(0.022)	(0.022)	(0.022)	(0.022)	(0.022)	(0.022)
High school degree	0.096***	0.096***	0.096***	0.088***	0.088***	0.088***
	(0.016)	(0.016)	(0.016)	(0.016)	(0.016)	(0.016)
Junior college degree	0.182***	0.182***	0.181***	0.172***	0.172***	0.170***
	(0.021)	(0.021)	(0.021)	(0.021)	(0.021)	(0.021)
Bachelor's degree	0.328***	0.326***	0.329***	0.318***	0.316***	0.318***
	(0.021)	(0.021)	(0.021)	(0.021)	(0.021)	(0.021)
Master's degree	0.454***	0.457***	0.457***	0.446***	0.448***	0.449***
	(0.055)	(0.055)	(0.056)	(0.056)	(0.055)	(0.056)
Healthy	0.077***	0.074***	0.077***	0.075***	0.072***	0.074***
	(0.020)	(0.020)	(0.020)	(0.020)	(0.020)	(0.020)
Father jailed	−0.007	−0.006	−0.004	−0.008	−0.007	−0.005
	(0.013)	(0.013)	(0.013)	(0.013)	(0.013)	(0.013)
U.S. born	0.030**	0.029*	0.029*	0.025*	0.025	0.024
	(0.015)	(0.015)	(0.015)	(0.015)	(0.015)	(0.015)
No siblings	−0.004	−0.004	−0.004	−0.008	−0.007	−0.008
	(0.018)	(0.018)	(0.018)	(0.018)	(0.018)	(0.018)
1 sibling	−0.022	−0.022	−0.021	−0.024	−0.024	−0.023
	(0.016)	(0.016)	(0.017)	(0.016)	(0.016)	(0.017)
2 siblings	−0.014	−0.014	−0.012	−0.016	−0.016	−0.014
	(0.017)	(0.017)	(0.017)	(0.017)	(0.017)	(0.017)
3 siblings	−0.015	−0.015	−0.016	−0.017	−0.016	−0.017
	(0.019)	(0.019)	(0.019)	(0.019)	(0.018)	(0.019)
Family income—1	−0.033	−0.033	−0.031	−0.035	−0.035	−0.033
	(0.025)	(0.025)	(0.025)	(0.025)	(0.025)	(0.025)
Family income—2	−0.025	−0.025	−0.024	−0.027	−0.028	−0.026
	(0.022)	(0.022)	(0.022)	(0.022)	(0.022)	(0.022)
Family income—3	0.007	0.006	0.008	0.003	0.002	0.004
	(0.021)	(0.021)	(0.022)	(0.021)	(0.021)	(0.022)
Mom's age at birth ≤ 19	0.003	0.003	0.001	0.004	0.004	0.002
	(0.019)	(0.019)	(0.019)	(0.019)	(0.019)	(0.019)
19 < Mom's age at birth ≤ 30	0.003	0.003	0.001	0.003	0.002	0.001
	(0.013)	(0.013)	(0.013)	(0.013)	(0.013)	(0.013)
Mom high school drop out	−0.001	−0.001	−0.002	0.002	0.002	0.001
	(0.013)	(0.013)	(0.013)	(0.013)	(0.013)	(0.013)
Mom finished high school	0.000	0.001	0.001	0.002	0.003	0.003
	(0.010)	(0.010)	(0.010)	(0.010)	(0.010)	(0.010)
Observations	7,089	7,089	6,977	7,089	7,089	6,977

Notes: Regressions include state fixed-effects, and 22 occupation dummies. Robust standard errors are reported in parentheses. ***, **, and * indicate p-values less than 0.01, 0.05, and 0.10, respectively.

	(1)	(2)	(3)	(4)	(5)	(6)
Table 12.7	**Determinants of wages controlling for the baseline BMI**					
Past BMI	−0.002**	−0.002**	−0.002**	−0.002**	−0.002**	−0.002**
	(0.001)	(0.001)	(0.001)	(0.001)	(0.001)	(0.001)
Very high self-esteem	0.034**			0.033**		
	(0.015)			(0.015)		
High self-esteem		0.033***			0.032***	
		(0.010)			(0.010)	
Very confident			0.036***			0.038***
			(0.010)			(0.010)
Male	0.089***	0.089***	0.084***	0.089***	0.088***	0.082***
	(0.010)	(0.010)	(0.010)	(0.010)	(0.010)	(0.010)
Age21	−0.235***	−0.208***	−0.249***	−0.268***	−0.242***	−0.284***
	(0.024)	(0.024)	(0.024)	(0.026)	(0.027)	(0.027)
Age22	−0.180***	−0.155***	−0.197***	−0.213***	−0.188***	−0.232***
	(0.024)	(0.025)	(0.024)	(0.026)	(0.027)	(0.027)
Age23	−0.117***	−0.091***	−0.132***	−0.149***	−0.124***	−0.166***
	(0.024)	(0.025)	(0.024)	(0.027)	(0.028)	(0.027)
Age24	−0.081***	−0.055**	−0.093***	−0.112***	−0.087***	−0.127***
	(0.024)	(0.025)	(0.025)	(0.027)	(0.028)	(0.027)
Age25	−0.044	−0.018	−0.056	−0.076	−0.051	−0.089
	(0.052)	(0.053)	(0.053)	(0.054)	(0.055)	(0.055)
Hispanic	0.016	0.015	0.015	0.019	0.018	0.019
	(0.015)	(0.015)	(0.015)	(0.015)	(0.015)	(0.015)
White	−0.018	−0.018	−0.021	−0.019	−0.019	−0.023
	(0.019)	(0.019)	(0.019)	(0.019)	(0.019)	(0.019)
Black	−0.047**	−0.050**	−0.062***	−0.042**	−0.045**	−0.056***
	(0.020)	(0.020)	(0.021)	(0.021)	(0.021)	(0.021)
Test score 2				0.036**	0.036**	0.033**
				(0.015)	(0.015)	(0.015)
Test score 3				0.037**	0.037**	0.037**
				(0.017)	(0.017)	(0.017)
Test score 4				0.045***	0.045***	0.046***
				(0.016)	(0.016)	(0.016)
Test score 5				0.017	0.017	0.022
				(0.017)	(0.017)	(0.017)
GED	0.064***	0.065***	0.063***	0.059**	0.060**	0.057**
	(0.024)	(0.024)	(0.024)	(0.024)	(0.024)	(0.024)
High school degree	0.088***	0.088***	0.086***	0.082***	0.083***	0.080***
	(0.018)	(0.018)	(0.019)	(0.018)	(0.018)	(0.019)
Junior college degree	0.184***	0.184***	0.180***	0.176***	0.176***	0.171***
	(0.024)	(0.024)	(0.025)	(0.024)	(0.025)	(0.025)
Bachelor's degree	0.327***	0.327***	0.326***	0.321***	0.321***	0.319***
	(0.024)	(0.024)	(0.025)	(0.025)	(0.025)	(0.025)
Master's degree	0.404***	0.409***	0.406***	0.399***	0.404***	0.399***
	(0.076)	(0.076)	(0.076)	(0.076)	(0.076)	(0.076)
Healthy	0.070***	0.067***	0.070***	0.068***	0.066***	0.068***
	(0.022)	(0.022)	(0.022)	(0.022)	(0.022)	(0.022)
Father jailed	−0.020	−0.020	−0.017	−0.021	−0.020	−0.018
	(0.014)	(0.014)	(0.014)	(0.014)	(0.014)	(0.014)
U.S. born	0.009	0.009	0.010	0.005	0.005	0.006
	(0.018)	(0.018)	(0.018)	(0.018)	(0.018)	(0.018)
No siblings	0.006	0.006	0.005	0.003	0.003	0.002
	(0.021)	(0.021)	(0.021)	(0.021)	(0.021)	(0.021)
1 sibling	−0.021	−0.022	−0.021	−0.022	−0.023	−0.023
	(0.019)	(0.019)	(0.019)	(0.019)	(0.019)	(0.019)

(*continued*)

Table 12.7   (continued)

	(1)	(2)	(3)	(4)	(5)	(6)
2 siblings	–0.012	–0.012	–0.011	–0.014	–0.014	–0.013
	(0.019)	(0.019)	(0.020)	(0.019)	(0.019)	(0.020)
3 siblings	–0.011	–0.011	–0.013	–0.012	–0.012	–0.013
	(0.022)	(0.021)	(0.022)	(0.021)	(0.021)	(0.022)
Family income—1	–0.043	–0.043	–0.043	–0.045	–0.045	–0.045
	(0.029)	(0.029)	(0.030)	(0.029)	(0.029)	(0.030)
Family income—2	–0.051*	–0.051*	–0.048*	–0.053**	–0.053**	–0.051*
	(0.026)	(0.026)	(0.027)	(0.026)	(0.026)	(0.027)
Family income—3	–0.025	–0.025	–0.023	–0.028	–0.028	–0.026
	(0.026)	(0.026)	(0.026)	(0.026)	(0.026)	(0.026)
Mom's age at birth ≤ 19	–0.006	–0.007	–0.009	–0.006	–0.006	–0.008
	(0.021)	(0.021)	(0.021)	(0.021)	(0.021)	(0.021)
19 < Mom's age at birth ≤ 30	–0.003	–0.003	–0.005	0.004	–0.004	–0.006
	(0.015)	(0.015)	(0.015)	(0.015)	(0.015)	(0.015)
Mom high school drop out	0.006	0.006	0.006	0.008	0.008	0.009
	(0.015)	(0.015)	(0.015)	(0.015)	(0.015)	(0.015)
Mom finished high school	0.006	0.007	0.006	0.007	0.008	0.008
	(0.011)	(0.011)	(0.011)	(0.011)	(0.011)	(0.011)
Observations	5,212	5,212	5,113	5,212	5,212	5,113

Notes: Regressions include state fixed-effects, and 22 occupation dummies. Robust standard errors are reported in parentheses. ***, ** and * indicate p-values less than 0.01, 0.05, and 0.10, respectively.

panel displays the BMI effects for whites. In the case of while females, there is a negative association between BMI and self-esteem in every specification. For white males, BMI has no impact on self-esteem. When BMI is measured by a set of dichotomous indicators in the bottom panel, overweight has an unexpected positive coefficient in the regressions for white males.

Table 12.9 reports the BMI and self-esteem estimates obtained from the specifications as depicted by equation (5), where self-esteem is explained by past BMI and past self-esteem. The results of this specification are largely consistent with those reported in table 12.8. The impact of BMI is estimated with less precision for black females in comparison to the specifications reported in table 12.8. But, otherwise, the point estimates of BMI in the models for *High Self-Esteem* in table 12.9 are almost the same as those reported in table 12.8, and the coefficient of *Past BMI* is borderline significant ($p = 0.13$) in the first column. In the case of black males, the specifications reveal a negative impact of BMI on self-esteem and confidence that is significant in almost every specification. The same is true for white females. In the case of white males, on the other hand, the estimated coefficients of BMI are mostly positive, small in absolute value and never statistically significant. Thus, taken together, the results reported in tables 12.8 and 12.9 indicate that BMI has a negative impact on self-esteem in the case of females (both white and black), as well as black males. The BMI does not seem to influence the self-esteem of white males in a meaningful way.

Table 12.10 presents the results obtained from estimating wage regressions,

Table 12.8   **Determinants of self-esteem: Race and gender-specific regressions**

	Black females			Black males		
	Very high self-esteem	High self-esteem	Very confident	Very high self-esteem	High self-esteem	Very confident
BMI	−0.002†	−0.004*	−0.004*	−0.003*	−0.003	−0.002
	(0.001)	(0.002)	(0.002)	(0.002)	(0.003)	(0.003)
Observations	1,306	1,306	1,259	1,034	1,034	994
Underweight	−0.056	0.026	−0.024	−0.056	−0.016	−0.146
	(0.045)	(0.074)	(0.079)	(0.077)	(0.145)	(0.140)
Overweight	−0.059***	−0.036	−0.002	−0.022	0.001	0.030
	(0.021)	(0.036)	(0.035)	(0.028)	(0.039)	(0.036)
Obese	−0.024	−0.060*	−0.068**	−0.059**	−0.063	−0.012
	(0.022)	(0.033)	(0.034)	(0.027)	(0.040)	(0.040)
Observations	1,306	1,306	1,259	1,034	1,034	994
	White females			White males		
	Very high self-esteem	High self-esteem	Very confident	Very high self-esteem	High self-esteem	Very confident
BMI	−0.004***	−0.004***	−0.005***	0.001	0.002	−0.001
	(0.001)	(0.001)	(0.001)	(0.001)	(0.002)	(0.002)
Observations	3,568	3,568	3,518	3,483	3,483	3,430
Underweight	0.020	0.036	−0.018	0.003	−0.042	0.046
	(0.029)	(0.042)	(0.045)	(0.041)	(0.059)	(0.066)
Overweight	−0.017	−0.025	−0.032	0.030**	0.053***	0.054***
	(0.013)	(0.019)	(0.021)	(0.014)	(0.019)	(0.020)
Obese	−0.048***	−0.047**	−0.078***	0.004	0.018	0.013
	(0.011)	(0.019)	(0.020)	(0.015)	(0.022)	(0.023)
Observations	3,568	3,568	3,518	3,483	3,483	3,430

Notes: Regressions include state fixed-effects and all variables used in other regressions. Robust standard errors are reported in parentheses. ***, **, and * indicate *p*-values less than 0.01, 0.05, and 0.10, respectively.
†The coefficient of this variable is significant at the 12 percent level.

separately for race and gender groups. As before, each regression includes a complete set of control variables and state fixed effects; in the interest of space, we only report the BMI and self-esteem coefficients obtained from eight separate regressions. In each regression, the dependent variable is the logarithm of the wage rate of the young adult reported in Wave III of the survey. In the top two panels of the table, the BMI and self-esteem variables pertain to those reported in Wave III. The bottom two panels of the table report the specifications that employ past BMI or weight category dummies based on past BMI.

Columns (1) and (3) of table 12.10 indicate that there is evidence that deviations from normal body weight has a negative impact on wages of black females as well as white females. Similar to the coefficients of obese,

Table 12.9   **Determinants of self-esteem: Race and gender-specific regressions with baseline BMI and baseline self-esteem**

	High self-esteem	High self-esteem	Very high self-esteem	Very high self-esteem	Very confident
	Black females				
Past BMI	−0.004†	−0.003	−0.001	−0.0002	−0.001
	(0.003)	(0.003)	(0.002)	(0.0016)	(0.003)
High self-esteem in the past		0.239***			
		(0.034)			
Very high self-esteem in the past				0.148***	
				(0.036)	
Observations	1,006	1,003	1,006	1,003	957
	Black males				
Past BMI	−0.007*	−0.007*	−0.007***	−0.006***	−0.003
	(0.004)	(0.004)	(0.002)	(0.002)	(0.004)
High self-esteem in the past		0.200***			
		(0.039)			
Very high self-esteem in the past				0.175***	
				(0.045)	
Observations	760	758	760	758	724
	White females				
Past BMI	−0.003*	−0.002	−0.003***	−0.003**	−0.005**
	(0.002)	(0.002)	(0.001)	(0.001)	(0.002)
High self-esteem in the past		0.240***			
		(0.023)			
Very high self-esteem in the past				0.165***	
				(0.028)	
Observations	2,644	2,642	2,644	2,642	2,600
	White males				
Past BMI	0.0004	0.001	0.0004	0.0005	−0.002
	(0.0020)	(0.002)	(0.0014)	(0.0014)	(0.002)
High self-esteem in the past		0.219***			
		(0.021)			
Very high self-esteem in the past				0.169***	
				(0.024)	
Observations	2,625	2,619	2,625	2,619	2,585

Notes: Regressions include state fixed-effects and all variables used in other regressions. Robust standard errors are reported in parentheses. ***, ** and * indicate *p*-values less than 0.01, 0.05, and 0.10, respectively.

†The coefficient of this variable is significant at the 13 percent level.

the coefficients of underweight are negative for blacks in the regressions reported in table 12.10, indicating a wage penalty for being underweight, although the effect is statistically significant only for black males in the top panel. It should be noted that these race-and-gender specific samples are not large, and therefore most of the coefficient are borderline significant at the conventional levels.

Table 12.10   **Determinants of wages: Race and gender-specific regressions**

| | Black | | White | |
	Female (1)	Male (2)	Female (3)	Male (4)
BMI	−0.003**	0.0002	−0.004***	0.001
	(0.002)	(0.0025)	(0.001)	(0.001)
High self-esteem	−0.019	0.068**	0.043***	0.035**
	(0.024)	(0.032)	(0.016)	(0.015)
Observations	723	582	2,316	2,520
Underweight	−0.060	−0.229**	0.039	0.015
	(0.049)	(0.094)	(0.034)	(0.077)
Overweight	0.009	0.009	−0.016	0.040**
	(0.032)	(0.041)	(0.018)	(0.017)
Obese	−0.078***	0.025	−0.064***	0.002
	(0.027)	(0.041)	(0.018)	(0.020)
High self-esteem	−0.019	0.069**	0.044***	0.034**
	(0.024)	(0.032)	(0.016)	(0.015)
Observations	723	582	2316	2520
	Models with baseline BMI			
Past BMI	−0.005**	−0.00003	−0.003	−0.001
	(0.002)	(0.00339)	(0.002)	(0.002)
High self-esteem	−0.012	0.051	0.027[a]	0.031*
	(0.026)	(0.039)	(0 018)	(0.018)
Observations	557	410	1,696	1,876
Underweight in the past	−0.068†	−0.028	0.006	−0.018
	(0.043)	(0.129)	(0.035)	(0.039)
Overweight in the past	0.034	−0.054	−0.066***	−0.012
	(0.038)	(0.058)	(0.024)	(0.028)
Obese in the past	−0.084**	−0.05	0.016	−0.032
	(0.037)	(0.051)	(0.032)	(0.024)
High self-esteem	−0.013	0.048	0.027[b]	0.031*
	(0.026)	(0.039)	(0.018)	(0.018)
Observations	557	410	1,696	1,876

Notes: Regressions include state fixed-effects and variables used in other specifications. Robust standard errors are reported in parentheses. ***, **, and * indicate *p*-values less than 0.01, 0.05, and 0.10, respectively. a: significant at the 10.5 percent level; b: significant at the 14.7 percent level. *Underweight in the past, Overweight in the past, and Obese in the past* are based on the BMI of the person in Wave 2, when he/she was aged 15–20. For these classifications, underweight indicates that the person belonged to the bottom 5 percent of the distribution for age. Overweight indicates that the BMI is between 85th and 95th percentiles, and obese indicates that BMI is equal to or greater than the 95th percentile. See the text for further details.

†The coefficient is significant at the 11% level.

a. Significant at the 13 percent level.

b. Significant at the 12 percent level.

There is no strong evidence of an impact of obesity on wages in the case of black males, and there is no statistically significant relationship between body weight and wages for white males. Consistent with the results reported in tables 12.5 through 12.7, there is evidence of an impact of self-esteem on wages. This impact is weaker in the case of black males, and nonexistent in the case of black females.

12.5   Conclusion

In addition to being a serious health problem, obesity can have a variety of labor market implications. Obesity can impact wages by influencing worker productivity directly (through cognitive function or physical conditioning), indirectly through poor health, or because of employer or customer discrimination. Obesity can also influence self-esteem, which may impact wages.

We analyze a nationally representative sample of young American adults who were in the age range of twenty-one to twenty-six in 2001 to 2002. The results indicate that body weight has an independent impact on self-esteem controlling for a host of personal attributes, including education, health status, and family background characteristics. Specifically, being overweight or obese has a negative influence on self-esteem for females and black males. There is no strong evidence of an association of body weight with self-esteem in the case of white males.

Wages of women are influenced by their body weight. There is a wage penalty for being obese in the case of both white and black females. Men's wages are not impacted by their body weight, except for underweight black men. The results also indicate that self-esteem is associated with wages in the case of whites (both men and women). The results suggest that obesity has the most serious impact on white women's wages, because their wages are affected directly by obesity and indirectly through the impact of obesity on self-esteem, although the magnitude of the wage penalty that emerges through this second channel is small.

References

Abowd, J., and T. Lemieux. 1993. The effects of product market competition on collective bargaining agreements: The case of foreign competition in Canada. *Quarterly Journal of Economics* 108:983–1014.

Averett, S., and S. Korenman. 1996. The economic reality of the beauty myth. *Journal of Human Resources* 31 (2): 304–30.

Baum, C.-L., and W.-F. Ford. 2004. The wage effects of obesity: A longitudinal study. *Health Economics* 13 (9): 885–99.

Bhattacharya, J., and K. Bundorf. 2005. The incidence of healthcare costs of obesity.

NBER Working Paper no. 11303. Cambridge, MA: National Bureau of Economic Research, May.

Biddle, J. E., and D. S. Hamermesh. 1998. Beauty, productivity, and discrimination: Lawyers' looks and lucre. *Journal of Labor Economics* 16 (1): 172–201.

Biro, F., R. Striegel-Moore, D. Franko, J. Padget, and J. Bean. 2006. Self-esteem in adolescent females. *Journal of Adolescent Health* 39:501–7.

Cawley, J. 2004. The impact of obesity on wages. *Journal of Human Resources* 39 (2): 451–74.

Centers for Disease Control and Prevention. 2008. Defining overweight and obesity. Available at: http://www.cdc.gov/obesity/defining/html.

Cournot, M., J. C. Marquié, D. Ansiau, C. Martinaud, H. Fonds, J. Ferrières, and J. B. Ruidavets. 2006. Relation between body mass index and cognitive function in healthy middle-aged men and women. *Neurology* 67 (7): 1208–14.

Daniels, S. R., D. K. Arnett, R. H. Eckel, S. S. Gidding, L. L. Hayman, S. Kumanyika, T. N. Robinson, B. J. Scott, S. St. Jeor, and C. L. Williams. 2005. Overweight in children and adolescents: Pathophysiology, consequences, prevention, and treatment. *Circulation* 111:1999–2012.

Evans, D. S., and L. S. Leighton. 1989. Why do smaller firms pay less? *Journal of Human Resources* 24:299–318.

Ferrer, A., and S. Lluis. 2008. Should workers care about firm size? *Industrial and Labor Relations* 62:104–25.

French, S. A., M. Story, and C. L. Perry. 1995. Self-esteem and obesity in children and adolescents: A literature review. *Obesity Research* 3:479–90.

Gabhainn, S. N., and E. Mullan. 2003. Self-esteem norms for Irish young people. *Psychological Reports* 92:829–30.

Galliher, R. V., S. S. Rostosky, and H. K. Hughes. 2004. School belonging, self-esteem, and depressive symptoms in adolescents: An examination of sex, sexual attraction status, and urbanicity. *Journal of Youth and Adolescence* 33 (3): 235–45.

Gortmaker, S., A. Must, J. Perrin, A. Sobol, and W. Dietz. 1993. Social and economic consequences of overweight in adolescence and young adulthood. *The New England Journal of Medicine* 329:1008–12.

Guadalupe, Maria. 2007. Product market competition, returns to skills, and wage inequality. *Journal of Labor Economics* 25:439–74.

Hamermesh, D. S., and J. E. Biddle. 1994. Beauty and the labor market. *The American Economic Review* 84 (5): 1174–94.

Harper, B. 2000. Beauty, stature and the labour market: A British cohort study. *Oxford Bulletin of Economics and Statistics* 62 (1): 771–800.

Hesketh, K., M. Wake, and E. Waters. 2004. Body mass index and parent-reported self-esteem in elementary school children: Evidence for a causal relationship. *International Journal of Obesity* 28:1233–7.

Klesges, R., K. Haddock, R. Stein, L. Klesges, L. Eck and C. Hanson. 1992. Relationship between psychosocial functioning and body fat in preschool children: A longitudinal investigation. *Journal of Consulting and Clinical Psychology* 60 (5): 793–6.

Krueger, A. B., and L. H. Summers. 1988. Efficiency wages and the inter-industry wage structure. *Econometrica* 56:259–93.

Kuhn, P., and C. Weinberger. 2005. Leadership skills and wages. *Journal of Labor Economics* 23 (3): 395–436.

Main, B. G. M., and B. Reilly. 1993. The employer size-wage gap: Evidence for Britain. *Economica* 60:125–42.

Martin-Albo, J., J. L. Nunez, J. G. Navarro, and F. Grijalvo. 2007. The Rosenberg self-esteem scale: Translation and validation in university students. *The Spanish Journal of Psychology* 10 (2): 458–67.

Mincer, J. 1974. *Schooling, experience and earnings.* New York: National Bureau of Economic Research.

Mobius, M., and T. Rosenblat. 2006. Why beauty matters? *American Economic Review* 96:222–35.

Mocan, N., and E. Tekin. 2010. Ugly Criminals. *Review of Economics and Statistics* 92:15–30.

Nickell, S., J. Vainiomaki, and S. Wadhwani. 1994. Wages and product market power. *Economica* 61:457–73.

Parent, D. 2004. Incentives? The effect of profit sharing plans offered by previous employers on current wages. *Economics Letters* 83:37–42.

Persico, N., A. Postlewaite, and D. Silverman. 2004. The effect of adolescent experience on labor market outcomes: The case of height. *Journal of Political Economy* 112 (5): 1019–53.

Rosenberg, M. 1965. *Society and the adolescent self-image.* Princeton, NJ: Princeton University Press.

Russell, S. T., L. Crockett, Y.-L. Shen, and S.-A. Lee. 2008. Cross-ethnic invariance or self-esteem and depression measures for Chinese, Filipino, and European American adolescents. *Journal of Youth and Adolescence* 37 (1): 50–61.

Sallade, J. 1973. A comparison of the psychological adjustment of obese and non-obese children. *Journal of Psychosomatic Research* 17:89–96.

Strauss, R. 2000. Childhood obesity and self-esteem. *Pediatrics* 105:e15. Available at: http://www.pediatrics.org.

Swallen, K. C., E. N. Reither, S. A. Haas, and A. Meier. 2005. Overweight, obesity, and health-related quality of life among adolescents: The national longitudinal study of adolescent health. *Pediatrics* 115:340–7.

Troske, K. 1999. Evidence on the employer size-wage premium from worker-establishment matched data. *The Review of Economics and Statistics* 81:15–26.

U.S. Department of Health and Human Services. 2001. The surgeon general's call to action to prevent and decrease overweight and obesity. Rockville, MD: U.S. Department of Health and Human Services, Public Health Service, Office of the Surgeon General.

Wada, R., and E. Tekin. 2007. Body composition and wages. NBER Working Paper no. 13595. Cambridge, MA: National Bureau of Economic Research, November.

Waddell, G. 2006. Labor-market consequence of poor attitude and low self-esteem in youth. *Economic Inquiry* 44:69–97.

Wadden, T., G. Foster, K. Brownell, and E. Finley. 1984. Self-concept in obese and normal-weighted children. *Journal of Consulting and Clinical Psychology* 52 (6): 1104–5.

Whitmer, R. A., E. P. Gunderson, E. Barrett-Connor, C. P. Quesenberry, Jr., and K. Yaffe. 2005. Obesity in middle age and future risk of dementia: A 27 year longitudinal population based study. *British Medical Journal* 330:1360.

Contributors

Jay Bhattacharya
117 Encina Commons
Center for Primary Care
and Outcomes Research
Stanford University
Stanford, CA 94305-6019

M. Kate Bundorf
Health Research and Policy
Stanford University
HRP T108
Stanford, CA 94305-5405

John Cawley
124 MVR Hall
Department of Policy Analysis and
Management
Cornell University
Ithaca, NY 14853

Frank J. Chaloupka
Department of Economics
University of Illinois
College of Business Administration
601 S. Morgan Street, Room 2103
Chicago, IL 60607-7121

Zhuo Chen
Centers for Disease Control and
Prevention (CDC)
1600 Clifton Road, MS-33
Atlanta, GA 30333

O. T. Ford
Department of Geography
University of California, Los Angeles
1255 Bunche Hall Box 951524
Los Angeles, CA 90095

Qin Gao
Graduate School of Social Service
Fordham University
113 West 60th Street
New York, NY 10023

Lisa C. Gary
Department of Healthcare
Organization and Policy
University of Alabama at Birmingham
1665 University Boulevard
Birmingham, AL 35294

Dana Goldman
Schaeffer Center for Health Policy and
Economics
University of Southern California
650 Childs Way
Los Angeles, CA 90089-0626

Christian A. Gregory
Economic Research Service, USDA
1800 M St. NW
Washington, DC 20036

Michael Grossman
PhD Program in Economics
City University of New York Graduate
    Center
365 Fifth Avenue, 5th Floor
New York, NY 10016-4309

Robert Kaestner
Institute of Government and Public
    Affairs
University of Illinois
815 West Van Buren Street, Suite 525
Chicago, IL 60607

Neeraj Kaushal
School of Social Work
Columbia University
1255 Amsterdam Avenue
New York, NY 10027

Darius Lakdawalla
Schaeffer Center for Health Policy and
    Economics
University of Southern California
650 Childs Way
Los Angeles, CA 90089-0626

Gilbert Liu
Children's Health Services Research
Indiana University
HITS 1020
410 W. 10th Street
Indianapolis, IN 46202

Melayne M. McInnes
Department of Economics
Moore School of Business
University of South Carolina
Columbia, SC 29208

David O. Meltzer
Section of General Internal Medicine
University of Chicago
5841 S. Maryland Avenue, MC 2007
Chicago, IL 60637

Stephen Mennemeyer
Department of Healthcare
    Organization and Policy
University of Alabama at Birmingham
1665 University Boulevard
Birmingham, AL 35294

Naci Mocan
Department of Economics
Louisiana State University
2119 Patrick F. Taylor Hall
Baton Rouge, LA 70803-6306

John Ottensmann
Center for Urban Policy and the
    Environment
Indiana University-Purdue University
    Indianapolis
342 N. Senate Avenue
Indianapolis, IN 46204

Noemi Pace
Department of Economics
"Ca.Foscari" University of Venice
Cannareggio, 873
30121 Venice, Italy

Lisa M. Powell
Institute for Health Research and
    Policy
University of Illinois at Chicago (MC
    275)
448 Westside Research Office Bldg.
1747 West Roosevelt Road
Chicago, IL 60608

Joshua A. Price
Department of Economics
University of Texas at Arlington
COB 326
Arlington, TX 76019

Christopher J. Ruhm
Frank Batten School of Leadership
    and Public Policy
University of Virginia
Varsity Hall
136 Hospital Drive
P.O. Box 400893
Charlottesville, VA 22904-4893

Robert Sandy
Department of Economics
Indiana University-Purdue University
    Indianapolis (IUPUI)
425 University Boulevard
Indianapolis, IN 46202

Bisakha Sen
Department of Healthcare
 Organization and Policy
University of Alabama at Birmingham
RPHB 330, 1665 University Boulevard
Birmingham, AL 35294-0022

Judith A. Shinogle
Maryland Institute for Policy Analysis
 and Research
University of Maryland, Baltimore
 County
1000 Hilltop Circle
Baltimore, MD 21250

Neeraj Sood
Department of Clinical Pharmacy
University of Southern California
 School of Pharmacy
1985 Zonal Avenue
Los Angeles, CA 90033

Erdal Tekin
Department of Economics
Andrew Young School of Policy
 Studies
Georgia State University
P.O. Box 3992
Atlanta, GA 30302-3992

Rusty Tchernis
Department of Economics
Andrew Young School of Policy
 Studies
Georgia State University
P.O. Box 3992
Atlanta, GA 30302-3992

Jeff Wilson
Department of Geography
Cavanaugh Hall
Indiana University-Purdue University
 Indianapolis (IUPUI)
Indianapolis, IN 46202

Benjamin Yarnoff
Department of Economics
University of Illinois at Chicago
601 South Morgan Street
Chicago, IL 60607

Yuhui Zheng
RAND Corporation
1776 Main Street
Santa Monica, CA 90401-3208

Author Index

Subject Index

Health club memberships, consumer behavior and, 6
Health insurance coverage: BMI and, 12; body weight and, 5; conclusions about body weight and, 54–57; effect of increasing generosity of, on body weight, 45–48; external costs of obesity associated with, 38–39
Health insurance elasticities, 36–37
Health insurance pools, obesity and, 36
Health insurance premiums, obesity rates and, 5
High-socioeconomic status (SES) children, BMI gap between low-socioeconomic status (SES) children and, 7

Incentives. *See* Financial rewards
Indiana University Regenstrief Medical Records System (RMRS), 186
Instrumental variable (IV) estimates, for educational attainment, 303–4
Insurance coverage. *See* Health insurance coverage
Insured, vs. uninsured, body weight and, 48–54

Long-term consequences of food prices and body weight, 5
Low-socioeconomic status (SES) children, BMI gap between high-socioeconomic status (SES) children and, 7

Maternal perceptions of neighborhood quality, child body weight and, 156–68
Medical expenses, BMI and, 335–36, 337f
Minimum wage. *See* Real minimum wage

Neighborhood characteristics: background literature on, 146–48; BMI and, 7–8; data for, 153–56; descriptive statistics, 157–58t; endogeneity of amenity location and, 207–10; maternal perceptions of, and child body weight, 156–68; Oaxaca-Blinder decomposition, 168–73; police protection and, 164–68, 172; theoretical framework for, 149–53

Oaxaca-Blinder decomposition, 168–73; correlates of perceived, 173–76
Obesity: aggregate U.S. medical spending on, 2–3; availability of convenience stores and, 11–12; conclusions about

health insurance coverage and, 54–57; deaths and, 2; determinants of, 3; economic factors and, 128; education and, 12–13; external costs of, 36, 38–39; fast-food restaurants and, 6–7, 18; generosity of health insurance coverage and, 45–48; health care costs of, 36; health care expenditures and, 37; health insurance pools and, 36; impact on wages and, 10; insured vs. uninsured and, 48–54; measuring, 1; model of social costs of, 39–44; nonhealth consequences of, 10; policy implications of, 13–14; positive externality of, 14; primary economic causes of, 35; public health consequences of, 1; real minimum wage and, 25–29; recent evidence on causes of rising, 127–28; socioeconomic status and, 3; trends, and physical activity, 249–50. *See also* Adult obesity; Body weight; Child obesity
Obesity rates, 1–2, 2t, 17; health insurance premiums and, 5
Obesogenic environments, 146

Panel Study of Income Dynamics (PSID), 317–19
Peabody Individual Achievement Test (PIAT), 293–95
Physical activity, 9–10; basic model of economic determinants of, 254–56; data for, 257–59; determinants of, 9–10; economics and, 251–53; by gender, 264–66, 265–66t; health and, 250–51; by income category, 269, 272–77t; methodology for, 259; obesity trends and, 249–50; participation in any, 260–64, 261–63t; policies and, 253–54; policy implications between education and, 279–80; results for models of vigorous, 266–68, 267–68t; results for models of vigorous and moderate, 269, 270–71; results of study of, 259–69; sin goods and, 12; trends in, 251
Police protection, child body weight and, 164–68, 172
Price elasticities, child obesity and, 142

Race: child obesity and, 148–49; wages and, 329–32
Real food prices, body weight and, 66